"Nolo's home page is worth bookmarking."
—WALL STREET JOURNAL

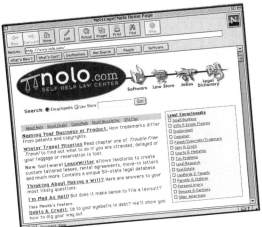

LEGAL INFORMATION ONLINE ANYTIME

24 hours a day

www.nolo.com

AT THE NOLO.COM SELF-HELP LAW CENTER ON THE WEB, YOU'LL FIND

- Nolo's comprehensive Legal Encyclopedia, with links to other online resources
- SharkTalk: Everybody's Legal Dictionary
- Auntie Nolo—if you've got questions, Auntie's got answers
- Update information on Nolo books and software
- The Law Store—over 250 self-help legal products including:
  Downloadable Software, Books, Form Kits and E-Guides
- Discounts and other good deals, plus our hilarious Shark Talk game
- Our ever-popular lawyer jokes
- NoloBriefs.com, our monthly email newsletter

Quality LAW BOOKS & SOFTWARE FOR NON-LAWYERS

Nolo.com legal books and software are consistently first-rate because:

- A dozen in-house Nolo legal editors, working with highly skilled authors, ensure that our products are accurate, up-to-date and easy to use.

- We know our books get better when we listen to what our customers tell us. (Yes, we really do want to hear from you—please fill out and return the card at the back of this book.)

- We are maniacal about updating every book and software program to keep up with changes in the law.

- Our commitment to a more democratic legal system informs all of our work.

OUR "NO-HASSLE" GUARANTEE

Return anything you buy directly from Nolo for any reason and we'll cheerfully refund your purchase price. No ifs, ands or buts.

An Important Message to Our Readers

FIRST EDITION

Getting Permission

HOW TO LICENSE & CLEAR COPYRIGHTED MATERIALS ONLINE & OFF

BY ATTORNEY RICHARD STIM

Keeping Up to Date

To keep its books up-to-date, Nolo issues new printings and new editions periodically. New printings reflect minor legal changes and technical corrections. New editions contain major legal changes, major text additions or major reorganizations. To find out if a later printing or edition of any Nolo book is available, call Nolo at 510-549-1976 or check our website at www.nolo.com.

To stay current, follow the "Update" service at our website at www.nolo.com. In another effort to help you use Nolo's latest materials, we offer a 35% discount off the purchase of the new edition of your Nolo book when you turn in the cover of an earlier edition. (See the "Special Upgrade Offer" in the back of the book.)

FIRST Edition	JANUARY 2000
Editors	PERI PAKROO
	STEPHEN FISHMAN
Illustrations	MARI STEIN
Cover Design	TONI IHARA
Book Design	TERRI HEARSH
Production	LORI PACHECO
Proofreading	ROBERT WELLS
Index	JANET PERLMAN
Printing	CONSOLIDATED PRINTERS, INC.

Stim, Richard
   Getting permission : how to license & clear copyrighted materials online & off / by Richard Stim.
     p.   cm.
   Includes index.
   ISBN 0-87337-536-X
   1. Copyright--Computer programs--United States. 2. Copyright licenses--United States. 3.Online information services--Law and legislation--United States. I. Title.
KF3024.C6S75 1999
346.7304'82--dc21   99-28701
                                 CIP

Acknowledgments

Thanks to:

Peri Pakroo, Steve Fishman and the Nolo production, sales and marketing departments. Thanks to those who provided me with helpful information in various chapters, including: Bobby Neel Adams, Paula Berinstein, Bruce Blank, Denise D'Ambrosia, Mary Goljenboom, Phillip Greenspun, Bill Hammons, Joan Menschefreund, Robert Panzer, Cheryl Pickerell and Richard Vittenson. Thanks to acc for editing and tray services.

This book is dedicated to A.C. Settel, a master of permissions.

About the Author

Richard Stim is an attorney and adjunct professor at San Francisco State University. He is the author of five other books: *Music Law: How to Run Your Band's Business* (Nolo), *License Your Invention* (Nolo), *Intellectual Property: Patents, Trademarks and Copyrights* (West/ITP), *Copyright Law* (West/ITP) and *Trademark Law* (West/ITP).

Table of Contents

4 Getting Permission to Use Artwork

5 Getting Permission to Use Music

Appendices

A How to Use the Forms Disk

B Forms

Text Permission Worksheet

Text Permission Letter Agreement

Text Permission Agreement

Photo Permission Worksheet

Photo Permission Agreement

Artwork Permission Agreement

Agreement to Use Artwork in Motion Picture

Lyric Permission Letter Agreement

Notice of Intention to Obtain Compulsory License for Making and Distributing
Sound Recordings

Music Synchronization and Videogram License Agreement

Master Use and Videogram License

Linking Agreement

APS/CCC Coursepack Agreement

Coursepack Permission Request Form

Coursepack Permission Agreement

Basic Permission to Use a Trademark in a Book or Magazine

Basic Permission to Use a Trademark in a Movie

Basic Permission to Use a Trademark in a Photograph or Artwork

Trademark License Agreement

Merchandise License Agreement

Merchandise License Worksheet

Short-Form Merchandise License Agreement

Unlimited Personal Release Agreement

Index

Introduction to the Permissions Process

*F*rom the Indies to the Andes, what a mission.
Stopping only now and then to do some fishing
And he went without a copyright permission
What a very daring thing to do.

"From the Indies to the Andies in His Undies" by
Lawrence Royal, Ernie Burnett and William E. Faber
© Rialto Music Publishing.

These whimsical song lyrics, written more than 50
years ago, express a basic truth about copyright
law: using someone's creative work without permission can be a very daring thing to do. An unhappy
copyright owner may sue you, seeking monetary
damages, preventing you from publishing your
work or both.

This book is intended to lower your risks by
guiding you through the permissions process and
explaining how to obtain the appropriate rights
when using other people's creative work. Information is provided about locating copyright owners,
asking for permission, assessing the conditions of
the permission agreement and avoiding potential
disputes.

This chapter offers an overview of the whole
process, explaining the purpose and legal basis for
permission, as well as the potential risks of operating without permission. It also serves as a guide to
how to use this book.

A. Permission: What Is It and Why Do I Need It?

Obtaining copyright permission is the process of
getting consent from a copyright owner to use the
owner's creative material. Obtaining permission is
often called "licensing"; when you have permission,
you have a license to use the work. Permission is
often (but not always) required because of intellectual property laws that protect creative works such
as text, artwork or music. (These laws are explained
in more detail in the next section.) If you use a
copyrighted work without the appropriate permission, you may be violating (usually called "infring-

ing") the owner's rights to that work. Infringing
someone else's copyright may subject you to legal
action, including being forced to stop using the
work or paying financial damages.

As noted above, permission is not always required. In some situations you can reproduce a
photograph, a song or text without a license. Generally, this will be true if the work has fallen into
the public domain, or if your use qualifies as what's
called a "fair use." Both these legal concepts involve
quite specific rules and are discussed more fully in
subsequent chapters. In most cases, however, permission is required, so it's important never to assume that it's okay to use a work without permission.

Many people operate illegally, either intentionally or through ignorance. They use other people's
work and never seek consent. The problem with
this approach—besides its questionable ethics—is
that the more successful the project becomes, the
more likely that a copyright owner will learn of the
use. Therefore, if you want your project to become
successful, unauthorized uses become an obstacle.

Some people avoid permissions because they
don't understand the permissions process or consider it too expensive. However, the process is not
foreboding and the fee for common text, photo or
artwork uses is commonly under $150 per use—and
in some cases, it is free. On the other hand, the legal fees for dealing with an unauthorized use lawsuit can easily cost ten to 50 times the average permission expense…or more!

B. The Basics of Getting Permission

This section outlines the basic steps for obtaining
permission. Subsequent chapters provide more detailed information about this process for each type
of permission you may be seeking (for text, music,
artwork, etc.).

In general, the permissions process involves a
simple five-step procedure:

1. Determine if permission is needed.
2. Identify the owner.

3. Identify the rights needed.

4. Contact the owner and negotiate whether payment is required.

5. Get your permission agreement in writing.

Let's look at each step in more detail.

1. Determine If Permission Is Needed

The first step in every permission situation is to determine whether you need to ask for permission. In other words, do you need an agreement or can you use the work without permission? Determining whether to ask for permission is based upon two questions:

- Is the material protected under law?
- Would your use of the material violate the law?

Unfortunately, it is not always possible to answer these questions with a definitive "yes" or "no." Sometimes, you may have to analyze the risk involved in operating without permission. Below are some basic legal principles you'll need to know. In subsequent chapters, we'll explore these principles in more depth.

a. Is the Material Protected Under Intellectual Property Law?

As a practical rule, you should always start with the presumption that, if the creative work you want to use was first published after 1922, copyright law protects it. There are only two ways that a work published after 1922 is not protected: the owner of the work made a mistake (such as failing to renew the copyright); or the work does not meet the minimum standards for copyright protection. In later chapters that discuss specific permission rules for particular types of creative works, we'll provide guidelines to determine if the work you intend to use is protected.

A work that isn't protected by intellectual property laws is in the public domain and can be used without asking for permission. Most works fall into the public domain because of old age. Public domain status may also be due to other reasons discussed in more detail in Chapter 8.

EXAMPLE: Bill wants to include his recording of the song "Give My Regards to Broadway" on his website. Because the song was first published in 1904, it is in the public domain and Bill can use it without obtaining permission.

b. Would Your Use of the Material Constitute a Violation of Law?

If a creative work is protected under intellectual property laws, your unauthorized use may still be legal. This is because there are exceptions to each of the laws protecting creative work—situations where authorization is not required. For example, under copyright law, a principle known as fair use permits you to copy small portions of a work for certain purposes such as scholarship or commentary. Under the fair use doctrine, you could reproduce a few lines of a song lyric in a music review without getting permission from the songwriter (or whoever owns the copyright in the song). Chapter 9 discusses fair use in greater depth and detail.

c. What is the Risk of Not Asking for Permission?

Our goal in this book is to minimize the risks of lawsuits. As we'll explain in each chapter, the risk of a lawsuit depends not just upon your particular use, but also upon other factors such as the likelihood that the use will be spotted, whether you are a "worthy" target for litigation or whether the other side is inclined to sue.

Generally, we recommend a conservative approach. Unless you are certain that the material is in the public domain or that your use is legally excusable, we advise you to seek permission. If you are not sure, you'll have to either make your own risk assessment analysis or obtain the advice of an attorney knowledgeable in copyright or media law. As explained throughout this book, an informed decision will lower your risks of proceeding without permission.

> EXAMPLE: We wanted to use the lyrics from the song "From the Indies to the Andies in His Undies," featured at the beginning of this chapter. We located information about the writers of the song from a compilation recording of country music. Then we located the name of the publisher, Rialto Music, Inc., from the American Society of Composers, Authors and Publishers (ASCAP), who informed us that the owner had ended its affiliation with the organization in 1975. We searched for the songwriters and for Rialto Music on the Web using a search engine to no avail. We also checked the online Library of Congress records but there was no reference, either because the song was never registered or the song was written before the date of their online computer records. We contacted the Harry Fox Agency, another agency that controls rights and they had a reference for Rialto in Providence, Rhode Island. We tried using operator assistance, but could find no listing. We decided to proceed without permission because our limited use of the lyrics (four lines) for purposes of commentary, combined with our good faith attempt to find the owner, probably qualifies as a fair use.

2. Identify the Owner

Identifying the owner of the work you want to use is crucial to obtaining permission. Sometimes, this task is simple. Often, you may be able to locate the rights owner just by looking at the copyright notice on the work. For example, if the notice reads "Copyright 1998, Jones Publishing," you would start by finding the Jones Publishing company. Sometimes, more detailed research is required. Copyright ownership may have passed through several hands since your copy of the work was published.

In addition, some kinds of art, such as film and recorded music, can involve multiple owners—each with a separate right to different underlying works. For example, in order to use a Johnny Cash recording, you would have to obtain permission from the record company, the music publisher (the owner of the song) and in some cases from Mr. Cash himself.

You'll find that the method of identifying owners differs from industry to industry. For example, photographic reproduction rights are often owned by stock photo organizations; music performance rights are owned by collectives known as performing rights societies. In subsequent chapters that discuss specific permission rules for particular types of creative works, we will advise you on the particulars for locating owners. In addition, Chapter 13 discusses the process of searching for owners in Copyright Office records.

3. Identify the Rights You Need

The next step in getting permission is to identify the rights you need. Each copyright owner controls a bundle of rights related to the work, including the right to reproduce, distribute and modify the work. Because so many rights are associated with copyrighted works, you need to specify the rights you need. This can be as simple as stating your intended use—for example, you want to reproduce a photograph in your magazine.

Asking for the proper rights can be a balancing act. You don't want to pay for more than you need, but you don't want to have to return for a second round of permissions. Sometimes this requires negotiating with the rights owner to find a middle ground for fees.

Besides identifying the type of intended use, you'll need to figure out some details of your use of the material. Specifically, your permissions agreement will need to deal with three common variables: exclusivity, term and territory.

a. Exclusive or Nonexclusive

All permissions agreements are either exclusive or nonexclusive. A permissions agreement is exclusive if you are the only person who has the right to use the work as described in the agreement. For example, if you entered into an agreement with the owner of a photograph for the exclusive use of a photograph in a cookbook, the photograph could not be used in anyone else's cookbook. Exclusivity can be as narrow or as broad as you choose. For example, you could expand the exclusivity by obtaining the exclusive right to print the photo in any book, not just cookbooks.

Most permission requests are nonexclusive and others can use the material in the same way as you. For example, if you have a nonexclusive agreement to use a photo in your cookbook, the same photo could be used in someone else's cookbook (provided permission was granted). The permission agreements throughout this book offer you the option to choose exclusive or nonexclusive rights.

b. Term of Use

The length of time that the use is allowed is often referred to as the "term." Your rights under a permission agreement will often be limited in duration. For example, if you are licensing the right to display a photograph at a website, the copyright owner may limit the length of your use to one year. Alternatively, you might obtain what's called a "one-time use," meaning that you can only use the material in one edition of a magazine, not in subsequent editions. If there is no express limitation on the use, you are allowed to use the material for as long as you want or until the copyright owner revokes the permission. Some agreements prohibit the copyright owner from revoking rights by granting permission "irrevocably." Sometimes an agreement states that it is "in perpetuity," which means that rights are granted without time limits. In reality, the copyright owner can only grant permission for as long as copyright protection lasts. After that, anyone can use the material without permission.

c. Territory

Your rights under a permission agreement may be limited to a geographic region referred to as the "territory." For example, the copyright owner of a book may grant you permission to reprint a chapter only in the U.S. and Canada.

As we proceed through the various chapters, we'll advise you how to shape your permission agreement so that you obtain the necessary rights.

4. Plan Ahead for Permissions

Expect permissions to take anywhere from one to three months. Permission should be obtained before you complete your work. It is sometimes more difficult and more expensive to obtain permission after a book, film or recording is completed. If the copyright owner becomes aware that you have a vested interest in obtaining permission (for example, your book is already in production), the price may rise. In addition, if you can't obtain permission, you'll have to re-do the work, which is expensive and time consuming. The best policy is to start seeking all required permissions as soon as possible.

5. Negotiate Whether Payment Is Required

The primary issue that arises when seeking permission is whether payment is necessary. Sometimes, the owner of the work will not require payment if the amount being used is quite small or the owner wishes to contribute to an educational or nonprofit effort. In some cases, an artist or musician eager for exposure may agree to suspend payment unless the work becomes profitable, or may condition payment on other factors.

EXAMPLE: Sam is making a low-budget documentary film and wants to include photographs of vintage accordions. He contacts the copyright owner of the photographs, and in return for a credit at the end of the film, the owner signs an agreement allowing use of the photographs in the film. However, the agreement also provides that if the photographs are used in the film's poster or an advertisement for the film, an additional one-time payment of $1,500 must be made.

Although many uses are free, expect to pay at least $50 or more for each copyright permission. Some types of permission almost always require payment. For example, using a photo owned by a stock photo agency usually requires a payment of $100 or more. Using a song in a commercial usually requires a payment of several thousand dollars.

Generally, fees are linked to the popularity of your work. A large metropolitan newspaper will pay more to use a photograph than a small town newspaper. Commercial uses, such advertisements, cost more than nonprofit or educational uses. The fees for website uses may depend upon on the number of visitors to the site. In each chapter, we will discuss the likelihood of payment and the current rates for common uses. However, these figures can vary widely, as the copyright owner has discretion when quoting a fee.

6. Get It in Writing

Relying on an oral or implied agreement is almost always a mistake. You and the rights owner may have misunderstood each other or remembered the terms of your agreement differently. This can lead to disputes. If you have to go to court to enforce your unwritten agreement, you'll have difficulty proving exactly what the terms are. We strongly recommend getting written permission agreements and we advise against relying on oral agreements.

That said, an oral permission may be legally enforceable if it qualifies as a contract under general contract law principles. Moreover, even if you have no explicit oral agreement you still may have a right to use a work if permission can be inferred from the conduct of the parties.

EXAMPLE: Sam is writing a book and asks for permission to reproduce Tom's photo. Tom quotes Sam a fee of $50, which Sam sends to Tom. After receiving the payment, Tom sends the photograph to Sam. A permission agreement may be inferred from Tom's conduct.

What If You Hire Someone to Create a Work?

Most of the situations described in this book deal with obtaining permission to use an existing work. However, it's possible that you may hire an artist or other creative person to create the work for you. If the creative person qualifies as your employee, you will automatically own all rights to the work he or she creates on your behalf and no permission is required. The Supreme Court has established standards for determining whether a creative person is an employee. These standards include factors such as whether the person is given weekly or monthly payments (instead of being paid by the job), whether employee taxes are withheld and whether the creator receives employee benefits.

If the person creating the work is not an employee, he or she is an independent contractor. In this event, your ownership of the contractor's work is not automatic. To guarantee your ownership of an independent contractor's work, you should use either a work-for-hire agreement (if your commission meets the requirements) or an assignment. We'll address these agreements in Chapter 15. For a thorough analysis of acquiring rights from independent contractors, see *The Copyright Handbook,* by Stephen Fishman (Nolo).

C. Overview of Intellectual Property Laws

A wide body of federal and state laws protect creative property such as writing, music, drawings, paintings, photography and films. Collectively, these laws are called intellectual property law, which includes (among others) copyright, trademark and patent laws, each applicable in various situations, and each with its own set of technical rules. When obtaining permission to use creative works, we're concerned primarily with copyright law. However, trademarks, trade secrets and the rights of publicity and privacy sometimes come into play when permission to use certain types of works is sought. Below we've summarized the various types of intellectual property laws that are relevant to the permissions process. We'll provide more details as needed in later chapters.

- **Copyright.** Original creative works such as paintings, writing, architecture, movies, software, photos, dance and music are protected under federal copyright law. A work must meet certain minimum requirements to qualify for copyright protection (discussed in Chapters 8, 9 and 13. The length of protection also varies depending upon when the work was created or first published. (See Chapter 8 for an explanation of copyright duration.)
- **Trademark.** Brand names such as Nike and Avis, as well as logos, slogans and other devices that identify and distinguish products and services are protected under federal and state trademark laws. Unlike copyrighted works, trademarks receive different degrees of protection depending on numerous variables including the consumer awareness of the trademark, the type of service and product it identifies, and the geographic area in which the trademark is used. (See Chapter 10.)
- **Right of Publicity.** The image and name of a person are protected under a patchwork of state laws known as the right of publicity. These laws protect against the unauthorized use of a person's name or image for commercial purposes—for example, the use of your picture on a box of cereal. The extent of this protection varies from state to state. (See Chapter 12.)
- **Trade Secrets.** State and federal trade secret laws protect some business information. An example of a trade secret would be a confidential marketing plan for the introduction of a new software product or the secret recipe for a brand of salsa. The extent of trade secret protection depends on whether the information gives the business an advantage over competitors, is kept secret and is not known by competitors. (See Chapter 10.)
- **Right of Privacy.** Although not part of intellectual property laws, state privacy laws preserve the right of all people to be left alone. Invasion of privacy occurs when someone publishes or publicly exploits information about another person's private affairs. Invasion of privacy laws prevent you from intruding on people, exposing private facts or falsely portraying someone. The extent of this protection may vary if the subject is a public figure—for example, a celebrity or politician. (See Chapter 12.)

D. Permission Tools: Licenses and Releases

Obtaining permission to use a protected work requires entering into an agreement with the owner of that work. Your agreement may give you the right to use the work (a "license") or it may be a promise that the owner will not sue you for an unauthorized use (a "release").

1. Licenses, Permissions and Clearances

A license is the legal right to do something that you otherwise would not be permitted to do—such as a driver's license that gives you the right to drive a car. The owner of a copyrighted work such as a photograph can authorize someone else to use the photograph—for example, to reproduce it in a website or on a greeting card—by granting a license to the user. If no license has been given, the copyright owner can sue for the unauthorized use of the work, referred to as "infringement."

The terms "license" and "permission agreement" are often used interchangeably. You may also find that in some situations a license or permission agreement is referred to as a "clearance agreement." "Clearance" is a general term used to describe the process by which permission is granted.

> **EXAMPLE:** Don is writing a book on British horror films and wants to reproduce a photograph from a 1950s film. Don must obtain a license to reproduce the photograph from the owner of rights in the film.

2. Releases

A release is an agreement by which someone releases you from legal liability for a certain activity. In essence, the person is agreeing ahead of time to give up (or release) any rights to sue you that may arise from a particular situation. Releases are often used to avoid lawsuits involving someone's right of privacy (which is the right to be left alone) or their right of publicity (the right to control how their image, voice or persona is used to sell things). A release may also protect against claims of defamation (a false statement that injures the reputation of a person). Releases are discussed in more detail in Chapter 12.

> **EXAMPLE:** "Makeover" is a TV show in which audience members are selected for beauty and fashion makeovers. The audience members must sign a release before appearing on the show. This way the TV show can avert any potential lawsuits from disgruntled participants who are unhappy with the final results and seek damages for legal claims such as infliction of emotional distress or defamation.

Don't rely on the title of an agreement. In many cases, licenses and releases overlap. For example, a release agreement may contain license language and vice versa. You may find that either type of agreement is used to grant rights or to prevent lawsuits. Because of this overlap, the title of an agreement is always less important than the content. Always review the agreement and compare it to the model agreements in this book.

E. How to Use This Book

The information in this book deals with three basic issues involved in the permissions process:

- Whether permission is necessary. If it isn't needed, you can save time and money.
- What types of work you are using. The permissions process often varies according to what type of work you want to use—such as photographs, text, artwork, music, trademark or a person's image.
- How you plan to use the work. Obtaining permission also depends on how you use the work—such as in an article, on T-shirts, posted at a website, shown in a video or film or included in an academic publication.

Depending on which issue you're dealing with, you may want to focus on different chapters of the book. Below we outline the chapters that deal with each of these specific issues.

1. Whether Permission Is Necessary

Permission is not always necessary to use creative materials. The following chapters discuss how to evaluate whether permission is necessary.

- **Academic permissions.** Chapter 7 explains that permission is not required for certain academic and library uses.
- **The public domain.** Chapter 8 deals with materials that are not protected by copyright law.

- **Fair use.** Chapter 9 provides information about fair use, the copyright principle that enables limited uses of materials without permission.
- **Releases.** Chapter 12 discusses when permission is needed to use a real person's image.
- **Copyright research.** Chapter 13 explains how to research whether copyright protection exists, and if so, who owns the copyright.
- **Acquiring ownership.** Chapter 15 provides information on acquiring ownership of copyrighted material, not merely permission to use it.

2. What Types of Work You Are Using

This book deals with the following types of materials: text, photographs, artwork, music, trademarks, characters and images of real people. The type of material used affects the type of permission, the fee and the permissions process. For example, the rules for locating photographers, musicians and writers are different, as are the permission agreements for using trademarked versus copyrighted material. If you know what material you are using, you can proceed directly to the relevant chapter.

- **Text.** Chapter 2 discusses most textual uses such as quoting from books, magazines or other written material.
- **Photographs.** Chapter 3 details photographic permissions and focuses on the wide variety of stock photography.
- **Artwork.** Chapter 4 provides background on using fine art, graphic art, stock art and cartoons.
- **Music.** Chapter 5 is devoted to uses of music and song lyrics.
- **Trademarks and characters.** Chapter 10 explains the rules regarding the use of trademarks and trademarked characters (for example, Mickey Mouse).
- **Images of people.** If you are using an image of a real person, whether for a news article or in an advertisement review, read Chapter 12.

3. How You Plan to Use the Work

Creative materials can be used in books, journals, movies, recordings, video, websites, software programs, in artwork and on merchandise. The medium in which you use the material and the rights that you need affect the permissions process. The rights you obtain may include certain limitations: how long you may use the material, where you may distribute your project and whether you have exclusive use of the material. The following chapters discuss the rules for specific uses.

- **Website uses.** Chapter 6 includes some special rules for use of materials in websites.
- **Academic uses.** Chapter 7 explains the unique rules for academic permissions.
- **Merchandise.** Chapter 11 discusses rules for using copyrighted works on merchandise.

A website has been created as a companion to this text. The address is members.aol.com/rwstim/permissions/update.htm. This page will list any changes that have occurred since publication. Comments and suggestions for improving the text are appreciated.

Getting Permission to Use Text

This chapter is about getting permission to use text, whether from a book, magazine, newspaper, newsletter, website or journal. We'll help you identify the company or person who owns the rights to the text (the "rights holder") and offer some suggestions for making your permissions request. We'll also discuss some special situations that occur when using text from interviews, speeches or from print publications. At the end of the chapter you'll find two sample text permission agreements: a short one-page agreement and a more detailed text permission agreement.

This chapter does not cover song lyrics, literary characters or academic coursepacks. For information on:

- song lyrics, refer to Chapter 5.
- literary characters, refer to Chapter 10.
- academic coursepacks, refer to Chapter 7.

 Before seeking out the copyright owner, confirm whether permission is necessary. No permission is required if the text you want to use is in the public domain. And, many uses of text are permitted without permission under a principle of copyright law known as fair use. The public domain is discussed in Chapter 8, and fair use in Chapter 9.

A. Start With the Publisher

If you want permission to use text, start your search with the publisher, which is the company that produced and distributed the work. For example, Nolo.com is the publisher of the book you're reading now. In the case of a quote from a magazine or journal article, the publisher is the company that produces and distributes the magazine or journal. For example, Time-Life Inc. is the publisher of *Time* magazine.

1. Permissions Departments

Many publishers have permissions departments or a person who handles reprints, permissions and clearances. Information about the permissions department is usually found on or near the copyright page of a book, or in a magazine or journal's masthead page. Online magazines and book publishers' websites generally include copyright and permissions information on the introductory Web page (the index or home page).

If the book, magazine or journal contains no specific information about permissions, direct your inquiries to the "Permissions Department" at the publisher's main business address, usually listed somewhere in the publication.

2. Locating Publishers

Contact information for book publishers can be located through publications such as *Books in Print, Literary Market Place* and *International Literary Market Place,* all published by R.R. Bowker (www.bowker.com/main/home/index.html). *Books in Print* includes information about books currently available for sale and is searchable online for a fee. *Writer's Market* (Writer's Digest Books) provides a listing of U.S book publishers as well as publishers of magazines, journals, and greeting cards. You'll find Writer's Digest online at www.writersdigest.com.

For information on locating periodical publishers, consult *The National Directory of Magazines* and the *Standard Periodical Directory,* both published by Oxbridge Communications (www.mediafinder.com/home.cfm), or review *Ulrich's International Periodicals Directory* (R.R. Bowker) or *The Directory of Small Press and Magazine Editors and Publishers,* published by Dustbooks (www.dustbooks.com). For information on academic publishers, check out *The Association of American University Presses Directory* published by the University of Chicago Press (www.press.uchicago.edu). Additional publisher resources are provided in Chapter 16, "Help Beyond This Book."

Are You Under Contract to Write a Book?

Have you signed a contract to write an article or book? Publishing contracts usually indicate who has responsibility for obtaining permissions, either the author or the publisher. Your publishing contract may also specify the language to be used in the permission agreement. Inquire whether your publisher has its own permissions forms.

3. When There Is More Than One Publisher

Different publishers reprint some books in different versions. For example, a book may be published the first time in hard cover, and later published as a soft cover or paperback book by a different publisher, and then published outside the United States in a foreign language by yet another publisher. Articles may be printed in magazines and then reprinted in digests or books by different publishers.

In cases of multiple publishers, you must find out who controls the right to reprint the work in another publication (known as "reprint rights"). The person or company who controls reprint rights is known as the "primary rights holder." Often, the first publisher is the primary rights holder. In the case of a book, that's usually the hard cover publisher. If you don't already know it, the name of the hard cover publisher can be determined by searching online bookstores such as Amazon (www.amazon.com) and Barnes & Noble (www.barnesandnoble.com) using the title and/or author of the book.

If the hardcover publisher tells you it doesn't have the right to reprint the work, ask them if they know whom you should contact. If they don't know, your next step is to contact the author. We discuss contacting and negotiating with authors below in Section B.

Changing Rules for Rights

Before the 1980s, the author of an article was usually the primary rights holder because periodicals only acquired first "North American serial rights"—the right to publish the article once in the U.S. and Canada. However, in the past two decades, magazines, journals and other periodicals have increasingly obtained reprint, syndication and other primary rights from writers. Therefore, in the case of multiple publishers of an article published in the past 20 years, start by contacting the original publisher of the article. For older articles, contact the author first. (See Section B.)

Also keep in mind that the primary rights holder may only control rights in one country. If you intend to reproduce a work outside that territory, you may have to seek additional permission. For example, one rights holder may have the right to publish a work in the U.S., another in Great Britain and yet another in Canada. If the work for which you're seeking permission will be distributed in the U.S., Britain and Canada, you will need permission from all three rights holders. The primary rights holder can often lead you to foreign rights holders. If not, information about foreign publishers can be located in the *International Literary Market Place* (see Section A2).

Regional Rights v. Foreign Language Rights

The territory in which a publication is distributed and the language in which it is published involve two separate rights. In other words, reprint rights are sold language by language and territory by territory. When dealing with U.S. publishers, unless you specifically ask for reprint rights in a foreign language, you will only be given the right to reprint the work in English in the territory specified. This means, for example, that acquiring "world" rights is not the same as acquiring rights in all languages. Rather, it means you have the right to publish the work in English throughout the world.

Be specific in your requests and permission agreements and keep your fees down by asking only for rights you need. If your work will only be published in English, don't ask for foreign language rights. For example, if your magazine is distributed primarily in the U.S. and Canada, you probably only need one-time North American rights—the right to publish the work one time in the U.S. and Canada in English. However, if you print a French language edition for Canadian readers, you would need one-time North American rights and French language rights.

Check the Copyright Notice

Information about the publisher or other rights holder is often located in the publication's copyright notice. The notice has three elements: the word "Copyright," or a "C" in a circle (©), the name of the copyright owner, and the year of first publication of that version of the work.

EXAMPLE: © 1995 by the Bathroom Reader's Institute

While the name in the copyright notice will indicate the rights holder as of the date of publication, remember that ownership may have been transferred since the notice was published. For example, the original publisher may have been acquired by another, or the copyright owner may have designated someone else to handle permissions. In either case, the name in the notice provides a starting point.

Note: Text first published before March 1, 1989, without a copyright notice may be in the public domain. For more information see Chapter 8.

B. Contacting the Author

If the publisher doesn't own the rights you need, it may be able to put you in contact with the author by forwarding your request to the author or, if the author is dead, to the author's estate. For privacy purposes, it's unlikely that the publisher will give you the author's address or phone number. You may be able to locate an author using the Author's Registry (www.Webcom.com/registry) which maintains a directory of authors and will search for one or two names, usually free of charge. Information about over 1,000 nonfiction writers may be found through the American Society of Journalists and Authors (www.asja.org).

The University of Texas (www.lib.utexas.edu/ Libs/HRC/WATCH/) maintains a searchable database entitled WATCH (Writers, Artists, and Their Copyright Holders). This database contains the names and addresses of copyright holders or contact persons for authors and artists whose works are housed in libraries and archives in North America and the United Kingdom. The WATCH database also contains limited information as to whether an author's or artist's copyrighted work has entered the public domain.

If the rights for the text are owned by two or more authors, you will need to obtain permission from only one of them—provided that your use is non-exclusive and for U.S. or North American rights. Non-exclusive means that other people can use the text for the same purpose as you. If you obtain permission from one of several co-authors, your permission agreement should include a statement that the rights holder has the authority to grant the rights in the agreement. For example, "Licensor warrants that it has the right to grant permission." (This language is included in the sample licenses included in this chapter; see Section G4.) This provision places you in a better legal position if a dispute arises over the right to use the material.

You will need permission from all the co-authors if:

- you want to use the text on an exclusive basis—for example, you are the only person who can use the text for a specific purpose; or
- you want to use the text on a worldwide nonexclusive basis—some countries require consent of all co-owners even for nonexclusive uses; or
- you want to use the text for a commercial purpose, to sell a service or product. For example, you wish to include a quotation from a book in an advertisement. Keep in mind, however, that simply using the text in a book or article you're writing for money is not considered to be a commercial purpose.

C. Photocopying Text: Copyright Clearance Center

Businesses often make multiple photocopies of articles that appear in journals, periodicals and books. The photocopies may only be used internally by the business's employees, or they may be distributed outside the company to clients. For example, an insurance company that subscribes to a legal newsletter may make 200 photocopies and distribute them to employees and customers. A business must obtain permission for this type of photocopying. This rule was established in a 1995 case in which an oil company was found liable for unauthorized photocopying of academic and scientific journals. *(American Geophysical Union v. Texaco, Inc., 60 F.3d 913 (2d Cir. 1995).)*

Illegal photocopying of articles can be expensive. In 1999, a national law firm paid over $100,000 when confronted with a charge of illegal photocopying. How do publishers learn about this type of in-house photocopying? Generally, the information comes from disgruntled employees or from publications that offer payments (sometimes as high as $10,000) for information about illicit copying.

Permission to photocopy and distribute materials can be acquired directly from the publisher or from the Copyright Clearance Center (CCC) (www.copyright.com). The CCC provides individual-permission services (as well as "repertory" or "blanket" licensing services) including its basic Transactional Reporting Service (TRS).

The CCC clears millions of works and represents more than 9,600 publishers and hundreds of thousands of authors and other creators, directly or through their representatives. Most periodicals, journals and books that participate in the CCC licensing program include a notice to this effect on the same page as the copyright notice.

The CCC is so firmly established that many publishers do not grant photocopy rights directly and instead direct requests to the CCC. The CCC also benefits from its classification as an international Reproductive Rights Organization (RRO) and has access to hundreds of thousands of international works licensed by 30 international RROs.

CCC services do not come cheap. There is an annual fee of approximately $120, with additional charges per clearance and use. The CCC may, on occasion, waive the annual fee for one-time users. In some cases, a business can obtain an annual blanket license that permits unlimited photocopying from the CCC's collection of 1.75 million works. These blanket licenses are based on the industry and number of employees. For example, law firms pay a blanket license of $156 per year for each professional employee.

Educational Copying and Coursepacks

Some types of photocopying for educational purposes are permitted without permission. However, this does not extend to the wholesale copying of articles for classroom use in coursepacks. The CCC has a special program that assists educators in obtaining permission for coursepacks. The rules for using copyrighted material in academic coursepacks are discussed in detail in Chapter 7.

D. Special Situations: Ann Landers and Beyond

Finding rights holders for certain types of text, such as syndicated columns, speeches, interviews and letters may prove a little tricky. Below are suggestions for these types of works as well as for unpublished and out-of-print texts.

1. Syndicated Text

Rights for works by newspaper columnists such as Dave Barry and Ann Landers are usually controlled by national syndicates. A list of the syndicates and contact information is in Chapter 4 where we list syndicates for comic strips. Many of these same syndicates also handle text.

For example, to acquire permission to reprint a "Dear Abby" column in a book with an initial printing of 5,000 copies, you would first examine the column in a daily newspaper to determine the syndicate's name—Universal Press Syndicate. Then, you would contact the syndicate and request permission to reprint the column. At the time of our request, the syndicate fees for using "Dear Abby" in our book were $175 for North American rights and $100 more for world rights. In addition, use of the column required a specific credit line supplied by Universal.

2. Interviews

If you want to use an interview from a magazine or book, contact the publisher of the book or magazine. To use a written transcript of an interview from a radio or television show, contact the network or station that originally aired the show. For interviews first published on a website, contact the owner of the site, usually indicated on the bottom of the home or index page.

If seeking permission for a transcript of a television or radio interview, most stations have permissions departments that will furnish you a printed version. Sometimes you can download interview transcripts from the station's website. If you want to use the actual audio or audio-visual recording of an interview, you will need to obtain the consent of the person or company who recorded the material, often the radio or television station that initially broadcast it. If you are interviewing someone yourself and want to make sure you have the necessary rights, read Chapter 12, "Releases."

If the publisher, website owner or television or radio station is not the rights holder and cannot lead you to the rights holder, try to locate the interviewer through one of the author resources listed in Section B.

There are occasions when determining the rights holders for an interview can get messy. In some cases, such as celebrity interviews, the interview subject may have placed restrictions on the use of interview material. In other situations, the interview subject may seek to prevent republication of the interview, claiming copyright ownership of his or her responses. A publication may write to you, "We are unable to grant your request because our publication holds no rights to the re-use of this material. Quotations that appear within text remain proprietary to the speaker."

Unfortunately, sometimes a publication will provide you the interview text even if they don't own the rights to it. The result may be a lawsuit filed by the interview subject against you for unauthorized reproduction of their remarks. To deal with this possible scenario, when seeking permission to reprint an interview, ask if there is a written consent by the interview subject on file and ask for a copy. If there is no release, ask if the rights holder is willing to sign a written assurance that it has authority to grant the rights you need. Such a document should state that "Licensor warrants that it has the right to grant permission." This will not shield you from liability as effectively as a signed release from the interview subject, but it does provide some legal recourse. If the interview subject later files a lawsuit, you will have a stronger case against the licensor for breach of the warranty. If you are still worried about whether you have the right to reproduce the interview, your only option is to seek a release from the interview subject. We have provided a sample interview release in Chapter 12.

3. Letters

The writer of a letter is usually the owner of the copyright in the letter. However, there are two exceptions to this rule: Letters written by employees within the course of employment are owned by the employer; and letters written by federal employees within the course of employment are in the public domain.

Don't assume that the recipient of the letter is the owner of the rights you need. The recipient only owns the physical letter itself. For example, the owner of a letter written by Elvis Presley could sell the letter, but only the Estate of Elvis Presley could grant rights to reproduce the letter. And don't assume you can use an unpublished letter, no matter how old, without permission. Review Section D6 which discusses unpublished works.

4. Speeches

Not all speeches are protected by copyright. Copyright law will only protect a speech if it is written down or recorded and the writing or recording was done with the speechwriter's permission. If a speaker improvises and her words are not written down or recorded under her authority, there is no copyright protection. Both criteria, fixation and authorization, are necessary. If the text of a speech is not fixed with the authorization of the speaker, you are free to use it without violating the copyright law.

The Right to Use Monica's Words

Monica Lewinsky's infamous telephone conversations with confidante Linda Tripp about President Clinton are not protected under copyright law because they were recorded by Tripp without Lewinsky's authorization. On that basis, Ms. Lewinsky has no claim against Tripp or any of the companies who have published the conversations. It's possible that her statements may be protected under principles known as state common law copyright, but as a practical matter it's difficult to enforce such claims.

This is not to imply that you can lure interview subjects into a phone interview, tape it and use it without their authorization. Some states, such as California, have laws prohibiting the recording of telephone conversations without the consent of both parties. In addition, publication of such conversations may trigger claims of invasion of privacy.

a. Determining Whether a Speech Has Been Published

If a speech is protected by copyright, it is important to determine whether it has been published, because unpublished works enjoy longer periods of copyright protection (see Section D6). Giving a speech or lecture in public is not a publication. Only when copies of the speech or lecture are distributed to the public has publication occurred.

b. Who Owns the Copyright?

If a speech is written down before it's given, the copyright owner is usually the author (assuming the author also delivered the speech—see below for rules on ghostwriters). However, if the speech was written as part of an employment obligation—for example, a speech written by the president of General Motors for a shareholders' meeting—the speech would be owned by the author's employer. If the speech was written by a federal government employee as part of his employment—for example, a speech by the Secretary of the Treasury to Wall Street investors—it is in the public domain. If the speech was ghostwritten—written by someone other than the speaker—the ghostwriter owns rights unless the ghostwriter was the speaker's employee or transferred rights under a written agreement.

If the speech was given extemporaneously (not written down in advance) and recorded with the speaker's permission, copyright ownership of the speech itself is usually the author/speaker, just the same as if it was written down as described above. However, in this case the only copy of the speech may be in the hands of the people who recorded it—for example, a TV station news crew or a newspaper reporter. A video, film or sound recording of a speech is a copyrighted work in its own right, owned by the person who made the work. (However, a verbatim written transcription of a speech—made, for example, by a newspaper reporter at the scene—is not separately copyrightable).

In this event, to use the recorded copy of the speech, you'll need to obtain permission from both the speaker and the people who recorded the speech. The same rule holds true whenever you want to use a sound recording or film or video of a speech, instead of the written text.

If you cannot locate the speaker, contact the organization that sponsored the event. It is quite common, nowadays, for the full text of a speech to be reprinted on the World Wide Web, so Internet search engines may help you locate the rights holder.

Titles and Short Phrases May Be Protected Under Trademark Law

In Chapter 8 we explain that titles and short phrases are not protected under copyright law. However, despite their public domain status, names, titles and short phrases may be protected under trademark laws. Take, for example, the slogan "Just Do It." It does not qualify for copyright protection. You can use it in a song lyric, movie or in your book, but you cannot use it in a manner that is likely to confuse consumers into thinking that you are associated with Nike, or in a manner that tarnishes Nike's reputation. For more information on customer confusion and tarnishment see Chapter 10.

5. Out-of-Print Works

Just because a book or magazine is out of print does not mean that it is out of copyright. Your use, without permission, may amount to an infringement. Therefore, if you intend to use text from an out-of-print publication, start by contacting the publisher as described in Section A. A good way to find the name of the publisher is through online bookstores such as Amazon and Barnes & Noble, who have extensive listings of out-of-print books and publishers.

Locating the copyright owner of out-of-print works becomes more complicated if the publisher is no longer in existence. Authors often own the rights to their out-of-print works because publishing contracts often contain provisions giving rights to the author if the publisher stops selling the book. You should research the author's whereabouts using the resources in Section B. If your search for the publisher and author lead to dead ends, you will have to perform more extensive copyright research or hire a copyright search firm to determine the current owner. See Chapter 13.

If you're not sure whether a book is out of print, try consulting *Books Out of Print,* published by R.R. Bowker, which contains a listing of out-of-print books. Dating back to 1979, *Books Out of Print* is searchable at the R.R. Bowker website (www.bowker.com/main/home/index.html). Sometimes, it is easier to check if the book is not listed as being "in print," in which case it's probably out of print. Another R.R. Bowker title, *Books in Print,* lists all books currently in print, though it's not searchable for free like *Books Out of Print.* You can, however, search *Books in Print* at your local library. Other ways finding out if a book is in print include searching online bookstores or calling a local bookstore and asking if the book is available for sale. The ISBN number (see Sidebar) located on or near the title page may help locate the book.

ISBNs and ISSNs

ISBNs (International Standard Book Numbers) and ISSNs (International Standard Serial Numbers) identify books and magazines, and are sometimes required when seeking permission. ISBNs are used for books; ISSNs are for magazines, journals, newsletters and other serialized publications. These numbers can be found on or near the title or copyright page or near the publication's UPC bar code. Since several numbers may be printed on the bar code, make sure the number is preceded either by ISSN or ISBN.

6. Unpublished Text

Don't ever assume that an unpublished work is free to use. The rules regarding copyright protection for unpublished works depend upon when the author died, and, in the event the work was finally published, the date of publication. Below are some general rules regarding unpublished works such as letters, diaries and manuscripts.

Unpublished works created after January 1, 1978, are protected for the life of the author plus 70 years. Unpublished work created after January 1, 1978, that are works made for hire, pseudonymous or anonymous are protected 120 years from creation or, in the event the work is finally published, 95 years from first publication, whichever comes first.

If an unpublished work was created before January 1, 1978:

- Copyright expires 70 years after the death of the author—unless the author has already been dead more than 70 years. In that case, protection expires on January 1, 2003. In other words, any unpublished work of any author will be protected until at least until January 1, 2003, no matter when written or when the author died.
- Regardless of when the author died, the copyright in an unpublished work created before 1978 but published before January 1, 2003, will not expire before December 31, 2047.

EXAMPLE: Jane Austen died in 1817, but an unpublished Austen manuscript was located in the 1990s. If the book remained unpublished, it would be protected until 2003. However, the book was published in the 1990s and will be protected in the United States through December 31, 2047—230 years after her death.

For more information copyright protection for unpublished works, see Chapter 13.

As you can imagine, it can be quite difficult to locate copyright owners for unpublished works—obviously you can't contact the publisher. Copyright

Office records may help, as some unpublished works are registered. Determining ownership for unpublished works is especially difficult if the author is dead and the estate or heirs are hard to track down. The WATCH database described in Section B may assist in tracking down the author of an unpublished work. Review the research techniques suggested in Chapter 13.

What Does "Published" Mean?

A "publication" occurs for copyright purposes when the copyright owner, or someone acting with the copyright owner's authority, distributes one or more copies of the work to the general public or offers the work for distribution, public display or public performance. Copies don't necessarily have to be sold for a publication to occur—they can be leased or rented, loaned or even given away, so long as the work has been made available to the general public.

Publication does *not* occur where:

- copies of the work are made but not distributed
- the text is publicly performed (e.g., a speech is presented), or
- the text is displayed.

A "limited publication" is also not considered a publication. A limited publication occurs if copies are distributed only to:

1. a selected group of people
2. for a limited purpose, and
3. without the right of further reproduction, distribution or sale.

For example, it is not a publication when an author solicits several publishers by sending copies of a manuscript to each.

7. Using Text From Advertisements

Text in advertisements is usually owned by the corporate sponsor of the ad. However, in some cases it may be owned by the advertising agency or publication that prepared the ad. To locate a business such as an ad agency or corporate advertiser, try using an online search engine, a Web "Yellow Pages" directory or *The Standard Directory of Advertising Agencies* (Reed Reference Publishing), an advertising agency directory.

Keep in mind that using advertising text will trigger many of the same issues raised by using a corporate trademark. For detailed guidance on trade related uses, see Chapter 10, "Getting Permission to Use Trademarks."

If the Text Contains Trademarks

A trademark is any word, photograph or symbol that is used to identify products and services. Permission is not required to use a trademark if:

- your use is for informational or editorial purposes—for instance, if you use the trademark as part of an article or story, or
- your use is part of accurate comparative product statements.

You do need to obtain permission if:

- your use is commercial and likely to create confusion among consumers of the trademarked product or service
- your use is commercial and reflects poorly or "tarnishes" the trademark, or
- you modify the trademark.

See Chapter 10, "Getting Permission to Use Trademarks," for an explanation of trademark rights and rules.

E. When You Can't Find the Rights Holder

If you've used the techniques discussed in this chapter and cannot find the person or business whose permission you need, you have a few options. One is to try delving deeper into copyright records at the Copyright Office. These records may assist you in determining who currently owns the work, since many copyright transfers are recorded with the Copyright Office. Copyright Office renewal records will reveal if the publisher has failed to renew the copyright in the work, placing it in the public domain if it was published between 1923 and 1964. Chapter 13 offers guidance on the three most common methods of searching Copyright Office records: hiring a search firm, paying the Copyright Office to do the search or searching the Copyright Office records using the Internet (in conjunction with a system known as Telnet).

If you still cannot locate the rights holder, it may be time to consider using the material without permission. As you might imagine, this poses risks. If the rights holder finds out about your use, you (or your publisher) may receive a letter from the rights holder or an attorney demanding that you stop using the material (known as a "cease and desist letter").

Before you use any material without permission, you should answer two questions:

- How likely is it that the rights holder will see your work?
- What is your potential legal liability in the event of a claim of copyright infringement?

1. Likelihood of Discovery

The likelihood that your unauthorized use will be discovered by the author or other rights holder depends on the extent of the distribution of your work and the popularity of the rights holder's work. For example, if you use an excerpt from an obscure writer's work in a book that sells under 2,000 copies, the odds are in your favor that the writer will

not learn of your use. On the other hand, if you use a well-known quote from a famous play in an article that will appear in a major magazine that sells millions of copies, your use has a much greater chance of being discovered. The more likely that the rights holder will see your use of the copyrighted work, the more caution you should use in proceeding without the owner's permission.

2. Potential Liability

There is always a risk and a potential liability when using material without authorization. The amount of risk depends on several factors, listed below. As a general rule, if you can show that you made a good faith effort to search for the copyright owner, you will probably only have to pay the rights holder the standard fee within the trade for a similar use. This is the general rule, but there may be exceptions. A disgruntled copyright owner may refuse to grant permission and insist that you halt distribution of your work. Alternatively, a copyright owner may demand an exorbitant payment and drag you into court.

Consider the following risk factors when proceeding without authorization:

- the investment in the project using the copyrighted work—the more money spent on your project, the greater the risk in the event that you must halt publication. It may not be worth risking a hundred thousand dollar project for the sake of one unauthorized illustration.
- the diligence of the search—the more diligent the search, the less risk. A thorough search demonstrates that you acted in good faith and also may demonstrate that it's not possible to locate the copyright owner.
- the nature of your work and how easy it would be to remove the offending portion—there is less risk involved if it is easy for you to remove the unauthorized material. For example, a photo posted at a website can be easily removed, while one printed in a book

is essentially there to stay, making it necessary to waste any remaining inventory and reprint the whole thing.

- the nature of the copyrighted portion and how easy it is to replace—although this is not as important as the other factors, your risk analysis should incorporate how hard it will be to replace the material in the event that you must remove it.

EXAMPLE: Jim publishes a newsletter for seafood restaurants and wants to use material from a cookbook entitled *Steamed Eels,* published in 1977. Jim was unable to locate the publisher; his letters to the publisher were returned with a notice that the company had moved with no forwarding address. Jim later learned from a distributor that the publisher had gone bankrupt in 1983. Jim paid the Copyright Office to perform research, but that research only turned up an address for the author who died in 1986. Jim wrote to the author's last known address, but his letter was returned as undeliverable. Jim searched on the Internet for people with the same last name as the author and posted requests for information at several cooking websites. Jim documented this search and then researched what the standard fee is for a similar text license. Based on this, Jim proceeded to use the material without permission, citing *Steamed Eels* and its author in his work. In the event that the copyright owner turns up, Jim is prepared to pay a reasonable fee for using the work. Jim's risk is relatively low because his search was very diligent and, given the obscurity and relatively low value of the work he's copying, the financial risk for infringement is low.

When weighing the risk factors, consider the expenses and aggravation in the two types of worst-case scenarios—litigation and halting distribution of your work.

- **Litigation.** Any "wronged" party can file a lawsuit regardless of the merits of their claim.

A frivolous lawsuit can drag on for months, and the attorney fees can amount to several thousand dollars. Even worse, a lawsuit based on a nonfrivolous claim (one in which there is a reasonable basis for the claim) may proceed for years and your attorney fee costs can soar into the tens of thousands of dollars.

- **Halting distribution.** If a copyright owner forces you to halt distribution, you face losing the money spent on the printing or distribution of the work, as well as the additional expenses to reprint and redistribute it. In addition, your costs may include recovery of unsold copies from distributors, notification to purchasers and loss of revenue from advertisers.

F. Paraphrasing, Omissions and Facts

If you use someone's copyrighted work but don't copy it exactly, do you need permission? This can be a tricky question. When you paraphrase a work or omit text or facts taken from the text, there are no fixed rules regarding whether permission is necessary. Instead, you'll have to work with general guidelines that have been fashioned from language in the Copyright Act and court decisions.

For more detailed information on paraphrasing and other issues covered in this section, refer to *The Copyright Handbook,* by Stephen Fishman (Nolo).

1. Paraphrasing

Paraphrasing consists of using different wording to summarize or restate preexisting text. There are two general rules about paraphrasing you need to understand:

- paraphrasing will not always prevent a claim of infringement, and
- paraphrasing may be prohibited by a permissions agreement.

a. Paraphrasing May Not Avoid Infringement

Some writers believe they can avoid a claim of infringement if they alter a text's wording instead of copying the words verbatim. This can work if the wording is changed so much that it is not recognizable as having been copied from the prior work. In the words of one court, "Copying so disguised as to be unrecognizable is not copying." *(See v. Durang, 711 F.2d 141 (9th Cir. 1983).)* Therefore, if you radically paraphrase a work and disguise any copying, you won't need to ask for permission.

However, don't assume that paraphrasing is always an infringement cure-all. The problem is that there is no bright-line test that clearly tells when paraphrasing is or is not an infringement. In one case, for example, an author of a biography of novelist J.D. Salinger paraphrased many copyrighted letters. The biographer identified Salinger as the author, but, in an attempt to skirt copyright law, paraphrased the original letters. In one letter, Salinger had written, "She's a beautiful girl, except for her face." The author paraphrased this as: "How would a girl feel if you told her she was stunning to look at but that facially there was something not quite right about her?" The court held that the author's paraphrase infringed upon Salinger's original letter—and the court took offense at how inadequately the paraphrasing had been performed. The court further determined that many readers would have had the impression they had read Salinger's words. (*Salinger v. Random House*, 811 F.2d 90 (2d Cir. 1987).) In other words, even though the paraphrasing was dissimilar, it was considered infringing by the court because it was so poorly accomplished that it reflected negatively on the author.

b. Permissions Agreements May Prohibit Paraphrasing

Many publishers prohibit paraphrasing. A permission agreement may include a statement such as "You may not alter or adapt this material." This is included to preserve the author's work as written and to guarantee that the text is not misconstrued.

Why would you paraphrase a work if you had permission to use it? Sometimes an editor wants to shorten the text or to create an abridgment because of space limitations. It is possible that some paraphrasing may be excused as a fair use. However, if you paraphrase in violation of a permissions agreement, you may be subject to a claim of breach of contract. If possible, always clear any major paraphrasing with the rights holder.

2. Omitting Text

As with paraphrasing, consult your permissions agreement to determine your right to omit part of the text that you have licensed. For example, one permission agreement we analyzed included a statement, "You may not alter the material. You may omit up to 5% of a story by marking the omission with ellipses." A simple solution is to ask permission for only the material you want to use. Otherwise, your omissions may violate the permissions agreement and subject you to a claim of breach of contract.

3. Using Facts

If you wish to use text that is primarily factual, you may or may not have to obtain permission, depending upon your use. In general, you don't need to ask for permission if you are only using facts or fact-based theories themselves.

EXAMPLE: The author of a book on the gangster John Dillinger uncovered certain facts and concluded that Dillinger did not die in 1934, but was alive in California as of 1979. A television series incorporated this theory and the supporting facts into one of its episodes. The writer sued and a federal court ruled that the television show was free to use the writer's facts and theories. (*Nash v. CBS, Inc.*, 691 F.Supp. 140 (N.D. Ill. 1988).)

a. Copying Facts and Expression

Although you can copy facts themselves, you cannot copy the unique words by which a writer expresses those facts. For example, anyone is free to use facts about the life of Abraham Lincoln. However, you cannot copy the exact language Carl Sandburg used to express those facts in his biography of Lincoln.

> EXAMPLE: A company translated and summarized financial business and news articles from a Japanese newspaper. These summaries were offered to the public as abstracts. The Japanese newspaper sued the abstract company and the court ruled that the creation of the abstracts was an infringement. The court found that 20 of the abstracts were literal translations of portions of the articles. The abstract company had copied more than the facts—they had copied the protectible expression of them. *(Nihon Keizai Shimbun, Inc. v. Comline Business Data, Inc.,* 166 F.3d 65 (2d Cir. 1999).)

A major exception to this rule occurs when there are a limited number of ways to express the facts. For example, you are probably permitted to copy the expression, "The U.S.S. *Spiritualized* sank June 12, 1944, as a result of an explosion in the galley." because there are only so many ways of expressing these facts. This is referred to as the "merger doctrine" because the fact and the expression are merged or inseparable.

b. Copying Compilations of Facts

Although individual facts are not protectible, a creatively organized collection of facts such as the "Harper's Index" are protectible. That's because the editors of the "Harper's Index" organize their facts in a unique manner that creates connections in the reader's mind. You may be infringing if you copy a collection of facts from such compilations.

There is no clear line as to how many facts you can use from a fact compilation without permission. In some cases, courts have held that people were free to copy an entire factual database such as a phone book or a compilation of codes used on dental bills. In other cases, courts have prevented copying any facts from compilations. For example, a compilation of used car values was held protectible by a court because the values were arranged by locales, equipment and mileage, which was considered to be sufficiently original to be protected by copyright. *(CCC Info. Servs. v MacLean Hunter Mkt. Reports,* 44 F.3d 61 (2d Cir. 1994).)

The owners of factual compilations have sought, but never obtained, legislation that would effectively protect the data in databases and facts in factual compilations. As of the writing of this book, legislation has again been proposed in Congress to protect databases.

c. Copying "Fictional" Facts

You cannot freely copy "fictional facts" such as the plot elements and characters of a television show. If, for example, you are writing a book that summarizes the plots and characters of the 1970s show "Charlie's Angels," you will need to acquire permission from the production company that owns rights in the show.

For example, in 1997, a publisher was sued after releasing a book of trivia questions about the events and characters of the television series "Seinfeld." The book included questions about 84 "Seinfeld" episodes and actual dialogue from the show was quoted in 41 of the book's questions. The defendant argued that all that was taken were facts; however, the court ruled that the events and characters in the television show were fiction, not fact, and therefore copying was an infringement. *(Castle Rock Entertainment v. Carol Publishing Group Inc.,* 955 F. Supp. 260 (S.D. N.Y. 1997).)

Unfortunately, the "Seinfeld" case is indicative of a trend among the owners of television and motion pictures to sue the creators of works that summarize or celebrate popular shows. This can be an intimidating tactic, especially when the rights holder is a well-funded motion picture studio. It is possible that a trivia book may be permitted if a court judges it to be a fair use (see Chapter 9 for an explanation of fair use principles), but as a general rule, if a book or website is primarily trading off the popularity of a movie or television show, the copyright owner is likely to send a letter requesting the publisher to cease and desist (stop) making any further references to the show.

G. Negotiating Text Permission and Fees

Obtaining permission to use text involves a four-step process:

- First, you must clearly and specifically identify what material you want to use and how you want to use it (see Section G1).
- Next, you need to send a permission request letter to the publisher or rights holder (see Section G2).
- Then you and the publisher or rights holder must negotiate a permission fee, if any (see Section G3).
- Finally, in some cases you may need to draft a separate permission agreement (see Section G4), or your permission request letter may serve as a license (see Section G2).

The View From the Permissions Desk: Be Specific

From the point of view of people who grant permissions, the biggest problem with permission inquiries is vagueness. "The biggest tip [for obtaining permission] is simply that people should provide as much specific information as possible," says Richard Vittenson, Director of *Copyrights & Contracts,* American Bar Association Publishing. "It's surprising how often people request permission without giving their name, an address or fax number to which we can respond, the organization that will be publishing our information, or the title or issue number of the publication from which they wish to reprint."

Bill Hammons, manager of rights and permissions for *Newsweek* magazine, agrees. "Definitely, one suggestion I would give is to provide concrete details. A lot of times we get people who don't have issue dates or page numbers. We also need to know how many copies there will be or how many uses." If requesting permission for use on a website, be prepared to provide information about the site and its use. "We may ask for a report on the number of hits per month or the commercial uses of the site," says Hammons. "It's not just the number of hits [we're interested in] but how the site is being used."

1. Identifying the Material and Rights You Need

Your first task is to identify the text and the rights you need. You can do this by completing the following worksheet. This information will then be summarized in your permission request letter, described in Section G2. A tear-out form for this worksheet is provided in the Appendix and a digital copy is included on the forms disk that comes with this book.

The Text Permission Worksheet is on the forms disk in the back of this book under the file name TXTWKSHT.

Text Permission Worksheet

MATERIAL YOU ARE USING: THE SELECTION	
Title of text you want to use:	
Name of author:	
The source publication or product from which it came:	
If from a periodical, indicate the ISSN, volume, issue and date:	
If from a book, indicate the ISBN:	
If from the Internet, the entire URL address (the website address that starts with "http") as it appears when viewing the document:	
Number of pages or segments to be used (actual page numbers are helpful). If you can, provide a word count, since some permission fees are based upon word use:	

INTENDED USE: YOUR WORK	
Title of your publication, program, product or website:	
Name of publisher or sponsor:	
Type of publication in which the selection will appear (book, periodical, handout, diskette, electronic program, website):	
If it is a website use, the average number of visitors to the site per month:	
Estimated number of copies to be printed or produced. If a book, include the estimated first print run:	
If copies are to be sold, indicate the price. If copies are free to attendees of an event, indicate cost of event:	
The date the material will be distributed (for example, the estimated publication date of your book):	
Rights needed (for example, right to translate or modify the agreement):	

What Is an "Edition"?

An edition is a new version of a book, distinguished from a reprinting, which is simply a new press run to produce more copies of the book. A new edition signifies a publication in which substantial changes are made to the text.

2. Making a Request to the Rights Holder

After you identify the text and rights you need, you should send a letter to the rights holder requesting permission to use the material. Your permission request letter should provide all of the details about the source text, your expected use and the rights you want.

There are two different types of request letters you can use:

- One type of letter simply informs the rights holder of your needs and anticipates that you and the rights holder will later complete and sign a separate permission agreement.
- The other type of permission request serves as both a request and a simple permission agreement for the text—the copyright owner reviews the request and gives permission by signing and returning the letter. This approach is recommended for simple requests to reproduce text.

We'll look at the second type of letter—one that serves both as a request and an agreement—later in this chapter when we discuss permission agreements. For now, let's look at a basic permission request letter that contemplates that a separate license will be negotiated and signed later.

Permission Request Letter

Dear Ms. Hitchcock:

I am writing to you about your article, "Why I Hate Surround Sound." *New Audio Magazine* informed me that you were the owner of rights in the article. I'm writing a book entitled *DDA: Death to Digital Audio,* and I'd like to use an abridged version of your article in the book. The details are as follows:

Title of Your Article (the "Selection"): "Why I Hate Surround Sound"

Author: Michelle Hitchcock

Source of Article: *New Audio Magazine*

Volume, Issue, ISSN: Vol 23, No. 6, ISSN 1099-8722

Number of Pages: 4

My intended use of the Selection is as follows:

Title (the "Work"): *DDA: Death to Digital Audio* (trade paperback book)

Publisher: Cumberland Books

Type of Publication: book

Rights Needed: 1) the right to shorten or modify the Selection (I'll send you a copy of the abridged version for your approval); and 2) the nonexclusive right to reproduce the Selection in all editions of the trade paperback *DDA: Death to Digital Audio.*

Estimated First Print Run: 6,000

Expected Price $12.95

Projected Published Date: September, 2000

I'm seeking these rights for myself and my publisher, Cumberland Books, and for any company who might acquire my rights to the book in the future. Please review this request and let me know the terms for licensing rights as well as the required credit. Once you let me know, I can prepare a permission agreement.

Sincerely,

Roberta Weston

Whichever type of request letter you use, it is often helpful to furnish a copy of the text that you wish to reproduce.

Keep Your Rights Request Simple

Most text requests are for the right to reproduce all or part of a work. For example, say you want to reproduce text in your magazine or website. If that's all you need, keep your rights request short and simple.

EXAMPLE: Chris wants to reprint a newspaper column on his website. The request he sends is basically as follows: "I am creating a website for the Association of Barking Dog Observers (ABDO) and would like to post the Jan. 20, 1999, Dave Barry column at our site for one month. I would like to know how much it would cost to post this column. Also, I would appreciate it if you could fax or email me a sample permission agreement."

---

3. Negotiating Permission Fees

Next you'll need to work out how much you'll have to pay for the rights you've requested. The publishing industry does not have standard rates for using text. Some magazine and newspaper publishers use fixed rates for common permission situations and can furnish you with what is known as a rate card listing such fees. In other instances, the owner won't be able to assess the fee until after reviewing your request. Below, we've summarized some fee information.

a. Using Text in a Book

The fees for using text in a book are commonly affected by:

- the number of copies to be printed. Pricing is often calculated at print runs of 5,000, 10,000 and 100,000 copies.
- the price of the book
- territorial and language rights. World rights may cost double or triple the cost of U.S. rights alone. A rights holder may charge 25% more for permission to reprint in a second language
- whether the use is for a nonprofit purpose
- placement of the text within the book. For example, a half-column quote placed at the beginning of a chapter or book may result in a higher fee.

Generally you should expect to pay anywhere from $50 to $300 for use of text in a book, depending upon the size of the print run and your rights request. By way of example, one national magazine charges $100 per column of text (there are three full columns to a standard page) for use in a book with a print run over 5,000 copies and $125 for print runs over 100,000. Sometimes, the fees may seem outrageously high. For example, a professor who sought to use four lines from a poem by Emily Dickinson was quoted a fee of $200 by a university press. (Note, because of copyright rules regarding unpublished works, not all of Dickinson's work is in the public domain.)

b. Using Text on Your Website

The fees for website uses are evolving, which is another way of saying that nobody is quite sure how much to charge. The fees are affected by:

- the extent of advertising at the website
- whether the site is intended primarily to provide information to the public (sometimes referred to as an "editorial" purpose). The rights holder may want to know whether the purpose of the site is to provide information or sell products or services.
- whether the organization sponsoring the site is nonprofit
- number of visitors to the site per day
- whether the text will be used in a print publication as well as a related website—for example, whether you will use the text in a magazine and the magazine's website.

A national magazine may charge between $100 to $500 for posting an article at a website, with the higher fees being charged for popular commercial sites—for example, posting a review of a movie at a high-traffic Hollywood studio website. Because website uses are in their infancy, many publishers limit the length of time for these permissions to one year or less.

c. Minimizing Fees

It's possible to get fees lowered or avoid them entirely by doing any combination of the following:

- seeking a one-time nonexclusive use, as long you are not planning to write future editions or different versions of your work.
- narrowing your permission request. The narrower your request, the less you may have to pay. For example, don't ask for "worldwide rights, all languages" if you only need "United States, English."
- acquiring multiple items from one publisher. Often, you can reduce your per-item fees by licensing more than one work from the publisher.
- paying up front. You may be able to lower the fees by offering to pay up front instead of waiting 30 or 60 days.

Giving Credit Where It Is Due

Your permission agreement will detail your obligation to include credits for the author or publisher. Make sure the credit is correct. This is a serious subject between you and the rights holder. Unless otherwise required under your permission agreement, you can group credits together on the copyright page. For example:

"Elvis's Toothbrush" originally appeared in *Meet the Stars* © 1985, by Missy Laws. Reprinted by permission of Ross Books.

"You Can Collect Toilet Paper" originally appeared in Antique and Collecting Magazine © 1990, by Harriet L. Rinker. Reprinted by permission of the author.

---

4. Executing a Permission Agreement

Once the rights holder has agreed to grant permission and you've agreed on a fee, you need to complete and sign a written text permission agreement. There are two ways you can go with your permission agreement:

- you can use a permission request letter that has been converted into a permission agreement, or
- you can draft and execute a detailed permission agreement that should suffice for most text-licensing situations.

We'll call the first type a permissions letter agreement, and the second type a plain-old permissions agreement. This section provides samples of each type.

Does the Agreement Have to Be in Writing?

Unless you have an "exclusive" agreement, (see Chapter 1, Section B3), your license or permission agreement doesn't have to be written to be valid. A nonexclusive oral permission may be enforceable as long as it qualifies as a contract under general contract law principles. However, there are limits on oral agreements. For example, in most states, an oral agreement is only valid for one year. And it can be very difficult to prove that an oral agreement exists, not to mention what its terms are. Because of these limitations, we strongly recommend against relying on an oral licensing or permission agreement. As the old saying goes, get it in writing.

a. Sample Permission Letter Agreement

This short-form agreement is similar to those used by many magazines. A variation on the permission request letter in Section G2 above, it is intended for authors and publishers who want only to reprint text, whether in printed form or on a website. This approach—turning the request letter into an agreement—is recommended if your request is simple and you have agreed upon all terms. For example, if you wanted to include several paragraphs from an essay on your website, newsletter or book, this form will suffice. A tear-out form is included in the Appendix, and a digital copy is included on the forms disk that comes with this book.

The Text Permission Letter Agreement is included on the forms disk in the back of this book under the file name TXTPRMLT.

What If the Copyright Owner Furnishes the Permission Agreement?

Many publisher permissions departments and other copyright owners furnish their own agreements. If it is a short permission agreement, it's probably not too difficult to sort out and comprehend its terms. If this is not the case, review Chapter 11, Section C, which explains how to review an agreement.

Text Permission Letter Agreement

To _____ ("Licensor"):

I am writing to you to request permission to use the following material.

Licensor Information

Title of Text (the "Selection"): _____

Author: _____

Source publication (or product from which it came): _____

If from a periodical, the ISSN, volume, issue and date. If from a book, the ISBN: _____

If from the Internet, the entire URL: _____

Number of pages (or actual page numbers) to be used: _____

If you are not the copyright holder or if worldwide rights must be obtained elsewhere, please indicate

that information: _____

Licensee Publication Information

The Selection will appear in the following publication(s) (the "Work"): _____

Title: _____

Name of publisher or sponsor ("Licensee"): _____

Author(s): _____

Type of publication: _____

If print publication, estimated print run: _____

If print publication, projected publishing date: _____

If print publication, expected price: $ _____

If website, the URL: _____

If website, estimated monthly hits: _____

If website, the posting date: _____

Rights needed: _____

Fee

Licensee shall pay a fee of $ _____ to Licensor at the following address:

_____ upon publication of the

Work or within 6 months of executing this agreement, whichever is earlier.

Credit

A standard credit line including your company name will appear where the Selection is used. If you have a special credit line you would prefer, indicate it below:

_____

Samples

Upon publication, Licensee shall furnish _____ copies of the Work to Licensor.

Signed by Licensee: _____

Name: _____

Title: _____

Address: _____

Date: _____

Licensor's Approval of Request

I warrant that I am the owner of rights for the Selection and have the right to grant the permission to republish the materials as specified above. I grant to Licensee and Licensee's successors, licensees and assigns, the nonexclusive worldwide right to republish the Selection in all editions of the Work.

Permission Granted By: _____

Signed by Licensor: _____

Name: _____

Title: _____

Address: _____

Date: _____

b. Explanation for Permission Letter Agreement

If you use this form, you don't need a separate request letter such as the one discussed in the previous section. This permission letter agreement is similar to the worksheet in Section G1. Complete the agreement as if you were preparing the worksheet or a request letter. Here are some explanations for various sections.

- At the end of the Licensor Information section is a section the licensor should fill in if he or she does not own the rights you need. If this section is filled in, that means the "licensor" cannot grant you the necessary permission, so you will need to obtain permission from whoever is indicated in the blank.
- The Licensor's Approval of Request section is a combination of the warranty and grant of rights, both discussed in Chapter 11, Section C11.
- It is possible that the licensor will only want to grant rights for a specific print run or for a specific time period. Or, the licensor may not want to grant you permission to transfer the rights to someone else, and may ask you to strike the language regarding "successors, licensees and assigns." In this event, modify the grant to reflect these requests.
- It's possible that you will want more rights than are granted in this letter agreement. For example, you may need rights for all foreign translations and derivative rights and you may want these rights in all media. If you want a broader grant of rights, you can use the Licensor's Approval of Request language below to replace the language in the agreement above. Be aware that the licensor may object to such a broad grant, causing a delay in the permissions process.

Licensor's Approval of Request. I warrant that I am the owner of rights for the Selection and have the right to grant permission to republish the materials as specified above. I grant to Licensee and Licensee's successors, licensees and assigns, the nonexclusive worldwide right to adapt and republish the Selection in all languages, in all editions of the Work and in all versions derived from the Work in all media now known or hereafter devised.

Make the process convenient for the copyright owner. When sending your permission letter agreement, always enclose a stamped self-addressed envelope for the licensor's convenience.

c. Sample Permission Agreement

The permission agreement below is intended for authors and publishers who are negotiating for more than basic reproduction rights—for example, assembling an anthology of short stories, assembling contributions for a CD-ROM encyclopedia or acquiring multiple or foreign rights to reproduce a work. A tear-out form of this agreement is included in the Appendix, and a digital copy is included on the forms disk that comes with this book.

The Text Permission Agreement is included on the forms disk in the back of this book under the file name TXTPRM.

Text Permission Agreement

_____ ("Licensor") is the owner of rights for certain textual material defined below (the "Selection"). _____ ("Licensee") wants to acquire the right to use the Selection as specified in this agreement (the "Agreement").

Licensor Information

Title of Text (the "Selection"): _____

Author: _____

Source publication (or product from which it came): _____

If from a periodical, the ISSN, volume, issue and date. If from a book, the ISBN: _____

If from the Internet, the entire URL: _____

Number of pages or actual page numbers to be used: _____

Licensee Publication Information

The Selection will appear in the following publication(s) (the "Work"): _____

(check if applicable and fill in blanks)

- [ ] book—title: _____
- [ ] periodical—title: _____
- [ ] event handout—title of event: _____
- [ ] website—URL: _____
- [ ] diskette—title: _____

Name of publisher or sponsor: _____

Author(s): _____

Estimated date(s) of publication or posting: _____

Estimated number of copies to be printed or produced (if a book, the estimated first print run): _____

If for sale, the price: $ _____

If copies are free to attendees of a program, cost of program: _____

If a website, indicate the average number of visitors per month: _____

Grant of Rights

Licensor grants to Licensee and Licensee's successors and assigns, the:

(select one)

☐ nonexclusive

☐ exclusive

right to reproduce and distribute the Selection in:

(select all that apply)

☐ the current edition of the Work.

☐ all editions of the Work.

☐ all foreign language versions of the Work.

☐ all derivative versions of the Work.

☐ in all media now known or later devised.

☐ in promotional materials published and distributed in conjunction with the Work.

☐ other rights _____

Territory

The rights granted under this Agreement shall be for _____ (the "Territory").

Fees

Licensee shall pay Licensor as follows:

(select one and fill in appropriate blanks)

☐ **Flat Fee.** Licensee shall pay Licensor a flat fee of $_____ as full payment for all rights granted. Payment shall be made:

　　☐ upon execution of this Agreement

　　☐ upon publication

☐ **Royalties and Advance.** Licensee agrees to pay Licensor a royalty of _____ % of Net Sales. Net Sales are defined as gross sales (the gross invoice amount billed customers) less quantity discounts and returns actually credited. Licensee agrees to pay Licensor an advance against royalties of $_____ upon execution of this Agreement. Licensee shall pay Licensor within 30 days after the end of each quarter. Licensee shall furnish an accurate statement of sales during that quarter. Licensor shall have the right to inspect Licensee's books upon reasonable notice.

Credit & Samples

(check if applicable and fill in blanks)

☐   **Credit.** All versions of the Work that include the Selection shall contain the following statement: _____

☐   **Samples.** Upon publication, Licensee shall furnish _____ copies of the Work to Licensor.

Warranty

Licensor warrants that it has the right to grant permission for the uses of the Selection as specified above and that the Selection does not infringe the rights of any third parties.

Miscellaneous

This Agreement may not be amended except in a written document signed by both parties. If a court finds any provision of this Agreement invalid or unenforceable, the remainder of this Agreement shall be interpreted so as best to effect the intent of the parties. This Agreement shall be governed by and interpreted in accordance with the laws of the State of _____.This Agreement expresses the complete understanding of the parties with respect to the subject matter and supersedes all prior representations and understandings.

Licensor	Licensee
By: _____	By: _____
Name: _____	Name: _____
Title: _____	Title: _____
Address: _____	Address: _____
Date: _____	Date: _____
	Tax ID # _____

d. Instructions for Permission Agreement

- In the introductory paragraph, insert the names of the licensor (the party who owns the material) and the licensee (you or the person who is seeking permission).
- In the Licensor Information and Licensee Publication Information section, complete the blank spaces as if you were filling out the worksheet in Section G.
- In the Grant of Rights section, complete the grant to reflect the rights that you have negotiated. More information on the rights associated with grants is provided in Chapter 11, "Art & Merchandise Licenses."
- Complete the Territory section to reflect the regions in which you have acquired rights—the World, United States, or Canada or whatever region you have agreed upon. For more help, review Chapter 11, Section C7.
- In the Fees section, indicate what type of fee has been negotiated, check the appropriate boxes and complete the information. For more information on fees, particularly as to the nuances of royalty payments, review Chapter 11, Section C9.
- Complete the Credit and Samples section per your agreement with the licensor. For more information, review Chapter 11, Section C16.
- As we explain in Chapter 11, Section C11, a warranty is a contractual promise made by the licensor. Some licensors do not want to make promises, particularly a promise that the work does not infringe any third parties' copyright or other rights. You may have to modify the Warranty section or strike it entirely if the licensor objects.
- If you have the bargaining power, you may want to include an indemnity provision in the agreement. Indemnity is a financial punishment if the licensor breaks its promises. We have not included any indemnity provisions here. If you wish to add such a provision, samples and explanations are provided in Chapter 11, Section C11.
- Explanations for the Miscellaneous section (also called "boilerplate" provisions) are provided in Chapter 11, Section C22. If you have the bargaining power, you may want to include an attorney fees or an arbitration provision.

Uses for commercial endorsements can be more complex. If you are seeking permission to use text on behalf of an advertising agency or a company selling a product or service (for example, Nike or American Airlines), your use is more likely to be categorized as a commercial endorsement, which will trigger additional legal issues. Review Chapter 12 regarding the releases that may be required.

Getting Permission to Use Photographs

If you're planning on using a photograph in your book, film, website or other media, you have essentially two options:

- you can hire a photographer to prepare a photograph for a specific purpose, or
- you can obtain the rights to an existing photograph.

This chapter explains the second option: how to obtain permission to use existing photographs. This includes photos you may see in magazines or on the Web, and photos available through image banks (described below). The first option—hiring a photographer to create a specific photograph—is known as assignment photography. Chapter 15 provides sample agreements you can use to acquire ownership of a photograph. Assignment photography is typically used when a unique photo is needed: for example, a photo of a particular automobile for a magazine advertisement. It's common for a photographer to sell all rights in assignment photography so that the person who pays the photographer is free to use the photograph for any purpose.

Using existing photos—often called stock photos—is generally a cheaper and easier route than hiring a photographer for a specific job. A common way to obtain rights to an existing image is to go through a company known as an image bank. Millions of existing photographs are available for license from image banks, which generally specialize in different subjects, such as images of nature, food, or historical eras. The agreement (license) you'll enter into with an image bank depends on the type of image you want to use—either a rights-protected or royalty-free image (explained in Section E below). Or, rather than seeking out an image bank to provide the photo you need, you may already have found a specific photograph—say, one you've clipped from a magazine—that you want to use. In this case, you'll need to find the owner of the photograph to obtain permission to use it.

This chapter explains how image banks work, how to find the photos you need, how to find photo owners and negotiate rights with them, and how to work with photo researchers—people who

make a living hunting down photographs and obtaining permission to use them. At the end of the chapter you'll find pricing information and a sample photograph permission agreement for use when licensing stock photographs.

Merchandising involves different rules. If you want to use a photo on a poster, cup, T-shirt or other merchandise, refer to Chapter 11, "Art & Merchandise Licenses."

Review public domain rules. Any photograph first published in the U.S. before 1923 is in the public domain and you can use it without asking for permission. Photos published after 1923 and before March 1, 1989, are in the public domain only if: 1) the owner failed to renew copyright or 2) the owner forgot to include copyright notice.

Don't assume that photographs published without copyright notices are in the public domain. And don't assume that public domain works are free. You may have to pay a fee to obtain a copy of the photograph as explained in Section E.

For more information on public domain issues, refer to Chapter 8.

What's in the photo may trigger other rights. If the photo you want contains trademarks, copyrighted artwork or people, you may need additional permission. Review Section G below.

A. The World of Stock Photos

A stock photograph is any photo available for license. Stock photos encompass every conceivable subject—celebrities, science, entertainment, sports, travel and history—and conjure up every imaginable occasion and emotion. Stock photos are typically handled by agencies known as image banks (also known as stock photo agencies), who control the right to license the stock photos in their databases. Image banks typically specialize in certain types or themes of photos, such as nature, vintage Hollywood or race car images. Later in this chapter we explain how to find the right image bank, and provide a list of image bank resources.

In addition to the general selection of stock photographs, the entertainment industry has a vast selection of promotional photos and movie stills. If you're looking for an image of a celebrity figure, chances are that there's a promotional photo available for license. Celebrity photos are discussed in Section C.

1. Royalty-Free vs. Rights-Protected Photos

In addition to the different subject matter categories of available photos, there are different ways that you can obtain rights to a photo. There are two basic categories of stock photos: rights-protected and royalty-free.

A rights-protected photo can only be used once you've negotiated for the rights to use that particular image. Generally, you'll be restricted to using it according to specific guidelines outlined in your license. With royalty-free photos, on the other hand, you'll typically be allowed to reproduce the images in a much broader range of uses. You'll usually have to buy a CD-ROM or pay for access to a website that contains a certain number of royalty-free photos. Once you've paid for the CD-ROM or subscribed to the website, you'll be able to use all the royalty-free photos that are included. There may be some restrictions as to how you may use the images—use on merchandise, for example, is typically excluded—but you'll have much more leeway than with a rights-protected photo. Sometimes, the term "copyright-free" is used instead of royalty-free, though the term is a misnomer because such photos are not in the public domain.

Which type of photo is better for you? That depends on your photo needs. As a general rule, the quality and variety of choice is better with rights-protected photos. Most historic, news, celebrity and entertainment photos are only available as rights-protected. On the other hand, royalty-free stock is generally much less expensive, and works well for certain standard corporate and advertising imagery. For example, there are a wide variety of lifestyle, business and scenic travel photos available in royalty-free format.

There are some significant drawbacks to using royalty-free images that may make them unacceptable for some projects. For example, with many royalty-free CD-ROMs, the photographs come in low resolution formats (72 DPI)—suitable only for websites or limited graphic uses. In addition, you cannot obtain exclusive rights to use royalty-free photos. This means, for example, if you are using a royalty-free photo in a national ad campaign, your competitors are free to use the same image by buying the same CD-ROM. This problem can be avoided by choosing a rights-protected photo instead. With a rights-protected photo, the image bank can tell you whether the photo has been used in advertisements and may be able to grant you exclusive rights, thus preventing competitors from using it.

Listings of rights-protected and royalty-free image banks are provided at the end of this chapter.

2. Not All Image Banks Are Alike

All image banks are not created equal. Large corporations run some image banks; individual photographers manage others. Some license rights-protected photos; some sell royalty-free photos; some offer both. Many image banks specialize in particular genres (for example, travel photos or American history) and some are more general and cover a broad range of imagery. To give you an idea of how image banks work, below we highlight two of the largest: Corbis and Time, Inc.

a. Corbis

Corbis (www.corbisview.com) has a reputation for a wide photo selection, fast service and reasonable professional rates. Corbis has acquired several stock agencies, including the Bettmann Archive, which contains 16 million images documenting 20th Century civilization.

EXAMPLE: Our goal was to find a photo of 1960s jazz musician Rahsaan Roland Kirk. We posed a request to several image banks, and within hours a photo researcher at Corbis informed us they had three images of Mr. Kirk. The cost to use a black-and-white image in our book was reasonably priced at $100. We were unable to locate any images of Kirk at any other image banks.

b. Time, Inc.

In 1999, Time, Inc., made hundreds of thousands of images available online (at www.thepicturecollection.com) from its stable of magazines, including *Time, Life, People* and *Sports Illustrated*. Like Corbis, the Time, Inc., collection is available for license to a broad range of publishers and consumers. At the Time, Inc., site, free searches can be performed based on keywords, or you can pay for a Time, Inc., researcher to locate images. The $85-per-hour research fee can be reduced or waived if one or more pictures are licensed. Fees for licensing use are posted at the site.

EXAMPLE: Our goal was to find a 1970s photo of rock musician Jimi Hendrix. We searched the Time, Inc., site and located two color photos of Hendrix. The cost to use a photo in our book (with a press run of over 4,000 copies) was $225.

Looking for Historic Photos?

In addition to Time, Inc., and Corbis, Archive Photos has 20 million photographs, engravings and drawings spanning over 3,000 years of world history. You can find Archive Photos online at www.archivephotos.com.

3. Finding and Working With Image Banks

Finding the right photo is often a matter of finding the right image bank. That's because each image bank's subject matter, pricing, ease of use and quality of image affect the choice of photo. The main difficulty is that with so many photographs available and such a wide variety of quality and pricing choices, searching for the right image bank may prove daunting.

Fortunately, there are many search tools, including the World Wide Web and print resources. Keep in mind that most image banks are listed in the New York, Los Angeles or Washington, D.C., phone books. In most cases, a researcher at the image bank will be able to tell you by phone if the image you want is available and what the cost is.

The World Wide Web contains a number of helpful resources for sorting through image banks. For example, the Stock Photo Deskbook's site (www.stockphotodeskbook.com) has an extensive searchable database. AG Editions' website (www.agpix.com) also provides listings for image banks and photographers. Email your request to these directories (you'll find their email addresses at their websites) and they will lead you to the proper agency or photographer to contact for permission. Paula Berinstein's site (www.berinsteinresearch.com), an online extension of her book, *Finding Images Online,* provides a category directory with links to various online photo resources.

You can also locate image banks by using an Internet search engine. If you want to find a particular image bank online, enter its name as a keyword for the search engine which will find the company's website (if it has one). If you aren't looking for a particular company, try using keywords like "stock photo" or "image bank" to find photo-related websites.

In addition to the common method of using search engines to find what you want online, a new type of image bank searching has developed in recent years—specialized search engines that scan various image banks. For example, 1StopStock (www.1stopstock.com) searches nine massive image banks including PhotoDisc, Corbis, WestStock and Tony Stone Images. 1StopStock identifies royalty-free and rights-protected sources and displays the images. Another image search engine, Arriba Vista (www.arribavista.com), searches for images throughout the complete Web, not simply at professional image banks. Yahoo! also has an image search engine (ipix.yahoo.com).

Here are some suggestions for researching image banks.

- **Categorize your needs.** To determine which image bank to use, you must define a general category (current events, American history, landscapes, celebrities, motion pictures, etc.). There are no established standards for keyword searching. One agency might categorize a bald eagle under "wildlife" while another categorizes it under "birds," so be prepared to try alternative categories. For example, search for John Travolta under both "celebrity" and "movie actor."

- **Locate appropriate image banks and search them.** Find image banks that contain your categories. Call or fax the image bank to describe your needs or search the image bank website. Website searches are based upon keywords, photo titles or category searching. For example, you might search an American history database for photos of bank robbers Bonnie and Clyde by typing in keywords such as "Clyde Barrow," "Bonnie Parker," "bank robbers" or "criminals."

EXAMPLE: Our goal was to find an image bank that had a stock photo of a pelican. We started with the Stock Photo Deskbook website and searched by category, first selecting "animals" and then "birds." Both terms led us to image banks, and we emailed requests to them. Only one image bank, Comstock, responded, and a photo researcher allowed us to see the pelican photos by establishing a website for our private viewing. The cost to reproduce a black-and-white image of a pelican on a quarter of a page in our book would be $230.

Next we used the AG Editions' website and searched in the "animals" category and located numerous banks that offered pelicans, including Arthur "Birds As Art" Morris, who has over 70,000 high-quality stock photos of birds. Mr. Morris's fee for a quarter-page use of his pelican pictures was reasonably priced at $100. Next, we searched using 1StopStock.com and that led us to various image banks including PhotoDisc, where there were a variety of inexpensive royalty-free choices (pelican in flight, pelicans in a tree, pelican close-up).

Finally, we searched using the Arriba Vista image search engine and located pelican images at photo.net. We contacted the photographer, Philip Greenspun, who permitted reproduction of his image in this book at no charge.

Photo credit: © Philip Greenspun (photo.net/ philg/). Reprinted with permission of the photographer.

If website searching on your own proves unsuccessful, most image banks will research your photo requirements and provide alternatives when the particular photo you want is unavailable. An image bank may charge a research fee to determine if a photo is available. Often, this fee is waived if you subsequently license the photo.

For a list of resources for locating image banks, see the end of this chapter.

⚠️ **Always confirm that the image bank possesses all rights for the stock photo.** It may seem odd, but there are occasions when an image bank possess a stock photo, but not licensing rights for it. This is sometimes the case for rare photos or movie stills. In such cases, you need to contact the rights holder to obtain permission to reproduce the photo. (See Section B.)

If You Can't Budge the Budget

Your choice of image bank probably depends on your budget if you—not your publisher—are paying the fees for acquiring photo rights. Review stock photo prices and prepare a budget before beginning your photo search. Stock photo pricing guides are available (see Section H6).

Digital Watermarks

Some image banks allow you to view stock photos online, but attempt to prevent piracy by encoding the photos with a digital watermark. This may take two forms: a visible watermark (usually the name of the stock agency imprinted across a portion of the photo) or an invisible digital mark that is buried in the software code of your digital photo. Sometimes, the watermark appears only when you print the photo. In 1998, Congress passed legislation making it a violation of copyright law to remove digital watermarks.

Public and Private Institutions

Photographs of historical interest, whether of people or events, and photos of works of art can be obtained from museums, foundations, art galleries, libraries and historical societies. These institutions function much like image banks, licensing works in their collection, and may have unusual, very old or obscure photos not obtainable from image banks. Locating these institutions requires the same phone and Internet research techniques used to locate image banks. You can also obtain information on obtaining photos of artworks at many art museums from the *Guide to Rights and Reproductions at American Art Museums* available from the Visual Resources Association. Contact The Visual Resources Association, c/o The Department of the History of Art, Slide and Photograph Collection, The University of Michigan, Ann Arbor, MI 48109.

B. Obtaining Rights to a Photo You've Found

Instead of searching for an image at a stock photo company, you may have already found an image you want to use. If, for example, you've come across a photo in a magazine or a website and want to use it, your task is to find who owns copyright in the photo and obtain permission from that owner.

This procedure is usually simple. First, find the photo credit—the listing of who owns the copyright in the photo. If the photo appeared in a book or magazine, the credit is usually on the same page as the photograph, although in some cases photo credits are listed on one page near the beginning or end of the publication. If the photo credit is for a publication, contact the publisher's rights and permissions department. If the credit indicates an image bank (for example "Photo: Reuters"), locate the image bank using the information and resources described in this chapter. If there is no photo credit, contact the publication in which the photograph was reproduced. See Chapter 2 for detailed guidance on locating a publisher.

If the credit is for a photographer, contact the photographer, his estate (if the photographer is dead) or the photographer's representative. You can locate a photographer three ways:

- contact the publication in which the photograph appeared
- search the Internet using the photographer's name as a keyword, or
- contact photographer trade organizations.

You'll find a list of photographer trade organizations at the end of this chapter.

EXAMPLE: We sought to locate photographer Bobby Neel Adams, whose work has been featured on the cover of *Life* magazine, to obtain permission to print one of his photographs in this book. We first contacted *Life* magazine by calling the editorial phone number listed in the magazine's masthead. We learned that *Life* doesn't handle the rights for Adams's photos; they suggested we contact Time-Life Syndication services. We did, and they suggested we contact the Time Picture Collection. After several unreturned phone calls, we switched to the Internet—using a search engine to search for the keywords "Bobby Neel Adams" and found an agency called Focal Point F8 that represents Adams. This company was able to provide contact information for him.

Photo credit: Self-Portrait (Age-Map Series) © 1989, Bobby Neel Adams. Reprinted with permission of the photographer.

C. Celebrity Photos and Movie Stills

In addition to the vast libraries of photos at image banks, the entertainment industry is a rich source for thousands of promotional photographs of entertainers and stills from motion pictures and television programs. Whether you are looking for a photo of Bob Dylan, Jakob Dylan or Dylan McDermott, you can bet there's a promotional photo available.

Actually, there are two types of celebrity/entertainment photographs available. One type is created by freelance photographers (paparazzi) and sold to the media, such as a photo of Jack Nicholson walking into the Cannes film festival. Stock photo houses and magazines usually own these photos. The other type of photo is prepared by the entertainment industry as a promotion for a specific project such as a film, musical recording or television show, such as a picture from the film *Groundhog Day* or a portrait of the Rolling Stones. The entertainment production companies generally own these photos. There are a few unique twists to locating and using these types of photos as outlined below. The process of finding the copyright owner and obtaining permission varies depending upon whether you already have a copy of the photo you want to use.

If you already have a copy of the photograph you want to use, examine it for a legend or copyright warning such as:

> *"Permission to reproduce this photograph is limited to editorial uses in regular issues of newspapers and other regularly published periodicals and television news programming."*

If your use is not permitted or if there is no legend on the photograph, you will need to contact the rights holder—either the photographer, the stock house or the entertainment production company that owns the rights. If the photo includes a photographer credit—particularly if it indicates the photographer retained copyright (for example, the notice "Copyright 1982, Roberta Bayley")—contact the photographer using the methods in Section B.

If there's no credit on the photo, you still may be able to track down either an image bank or production company that either owns copyright or who can lead you to who does. Certain image banks specialize in entertainment-related stock photos. You might try contacting them and asking if they represent the photo you have. You'll find a list of image banks, including those that specialize in entertainment photos, at the end of this chapter. Keep in mind that in some cases, particularly for rare motion picture and television stills, image banks may not control the rights and will direct you to the production company or photographer for permission.

If the photo is from a television show or movie, you can locate the name of the production company by using the Internet Movie Database (www.imdb.com), a searchable database of thousands of films and television shows. You can also find entertainment production companies in the New York, Nashville or Los Angeles telephone listings, through Internet search engines and in directories such as Yahoo!, the Internet Yellow Pages, Infoseek and Alta Vista. When you contact the production company, ask for the publicity, media relations or public relations department.

If you don't have a copy of the photo you want to use, but you know that you need a photo of say, Bette Midler in *The Rose,* you must either contact an image bank that has the photo you need or find the production company that owns the rights. Search image banks that specialize in that type of entertainment or use the resources described in this chapter (such as the Internet Movie Database) to find the company that produced the show in question.

EXAMPLE: We sought to locate stills from the 1974 film *The Conversation.* We started our search with the Stock Photo Deskbook website (www.stockphotodeskbook.com), searching by category to locate image banks that specialize in entertainment, motion pictures or movie stills. Several sites came up, including Star File Photo and the Motion Picture & Television Photo and Archive. We contacted these sites, but they didn't have stills for this film.

Next, we tried the Internet Movie Database (www.imdb.com) and located the production company for the film—Paramount Pictures. We located a phone and fax address for Paramount from the Internet Yellow Pages. Paramount directed us to the Paramount Pictures Stock Footage & Stills Library, which licenses stills and footage from Paramount movies, including *The Conversation.*

Commercial uses can get tricky. The permissions situation may become more complex if you are using the photograph as part of an advertisement or to sell a product. We discuss these uses in Chapter 12.

D. Using Photo Researchers

Think of a photo researcher as an art detective who can track down an elusive image. If you perform photo licensing regularly—for example, you are a website designer or a photo acquisitions editor—you may want to consider using a photo researcher as a matter of course. Many photo researchers have specialties—for example, Chicago-based photo researcher Mary Goljenboom has an expertise in science, business and historical images, particularly women's history. New York-based researcher Joan Menschefreund specializes in images of fine arts, current events and personalities.

Photo researchers are usually paid day rates (approximately $250) although some charge by the hour. A researcher will prepare a budget for your needs and she (most picture researchers happen to be women) may also be able to arrange photo shoots for materials located in archives. The American Society of Picture Professionals (www.aspp.com) publishes a directory with membership specialties and can assist you in finding the proper researcher for your purposes. Additional resources for locating photo resources are listed at the end of this chapter.

E. Photo Fees

A picture may be worth a thousand words, but is it worth a thousand dollars? How about $450 or $225? As soon as you start pricing photographs, you'll discover that stock photo prices vary widely. The minimum fee for using a stock photo from a high-end agency is usually $150 and may rise to several thousand dollars, especially if the agency charges re-use fees—additional payments that you must make when you re-print the book or article in which the photo first appeared. Some image banks such as Muse charge lower rates ($10–$100) and may not seek re-use fees. At the bottom of the pricing tier are sources that often advertise as being royalty-free or copyright-free.

Below we describe some of the factors that affect pricing. If you perform photo clearances on a regular basis, you may want to consult one of several books that focus exclusively on photo pricing guidelines. They are listed at the end of this chapter.

As explained above in Section A, there are two categories of stock photos: rights-protected and royalty-free. Each type has its own rules regarding fees.

1. Fees for Rights-Protected Photos

Fees for rights-protected photos vary widely and are closely tied to your intended use of the photo, which must be clearly disclosed to the licensor upfront. As a general rule, the more intended uses you have for the photo, the more you'll have to pay. For example, you may be charged according to the length of time a photo is used at your website or according to the size of a print run for a book in which a licensed photo will appear. If you want to use the photo for a different purpose in the future, you ordinarily pay an additional re-use fee.

For the most part, the image bank or photographer is concerned with how many people will be seeing the image. The larger the viewing audience, the higher the fee. The worksheet below lists the information an image bank will typically require from you, including information necessary for it to calculate its fee. A tear-out form of this worksheet is included in the Appendix, and a digital copy is included with the forms disk that comes with this book.

The Photo Permission Worksheet is included on the forms disk in the back of this book under the file name PICWKSHT.

Photo Permission Worksheet

PHOTOGRAPHIC USE	
Title of Publication, program, product, or website in which the photograph will appear:	
Name of publisher or sponsor:	
Type of publication (book, periodical, annual report, handout, diskette, electronic program):	
Estimated number of copies to be printed or produced. If a book, include the estimated first print run:	
If copies are to be sold, indicate the price. If copies are free to attendees of an event, indicate cost of event:	
The date the material will be distributed (for example, the estimated publication date of a book, or the posting date of a website):	
Will the publication be in any language other than English?	yes no
If yes, identify which language:	
Website uses:	
Does the site include advertising?	yes no
Is the site commercial or editorial?	commercial editorial
Will the photo be used on a home or on an internal page?	home page internal page
The number of visitors or hits per day:	
Will the photograph be used in both a print publication and a related website (for example, in a magazine, and in the magazine's website)?	
If using in a presentation, the sponsor of the presentation, the number of attendees, and the cost of attendance:	

Rights needed:
 	
    (1) reproduction of the photograph
 	
    (2) display of the photograph
 	
    (3) modification of the photograph	

PHOTOGRAPHIC USE (cont.)	
Territory (for example, North American or world rights):	
The format in which you will need the photograph: scan, print, transparency, digital (if digital, what DPI and file format):	
The date you need the photo:	
If for a film or TV show, the context of the use (supply a synopsis of the plot):	

Fee Multipliers

Some image banks use a multiplier system to determine the fee. Here's how it works: The image bank starts with a minimum fee, usually the lowest amount that the image bank accepts for a use. For most image banks, the minimum fee is usually between $150 to $200 (the amount charged for reproducing the photo on a quarter of the page in a 5,000-edition book). Every other use of the fee is based upon a multiplier. For example, the multiplier for using a photo on a magazine cover is 4. If the minimum fee is $150, the cover use would be $600. The highest multipliers are for national advertising uses. For example a full-page photo use on the back cover of a national magazine could be 20, raising the $150 minimum fee to $3,000.

a. Advertising Fees

If you intend to use a rights-protected photo in an advertisement, the fee you will be charged by an image bank will be based on the circulation of your advertisement and its placement. Expect to pay $1,000 to $3,000 to use a photo in a full-page ad in a national magazine; at least $500 for a quarter-page ad on an inside page. Rates may be based on the number of insertions (an insertion occurs when an ad is placed in each edition of a magazine). An image bank may charge re-use fees for subsequent insertions (see Section E). Rates for advertising for nonprofit organizations or for or advertorials may be lower. (Advertorials are advertisements dressed up to look like a news article.)

Color and Black-and-White Fees

Don't expect to pay less for black-and-white photos. Some image banks claim it costs as much, or more, to reproduce quality black-and-white prints.

b. Corporate Use Fees

Image banks charge more for corporate uses—including photos used in corporate brochures, annual reports and in-house publications—than for editorial uses. For example, an image bank may charge

$500 for a quarter-page photo in an annual report with a distribution of 50,000, versus $250 for a similar use in a magazine with similar circulation.

c. Digital Photograph Quality

Fees may be affected by the resolution of the photo. Resolution refers to the dots per inch (DPI) that make up the photo. The denser the dots, the better the resolution, the higher the DPI and the more expensive the photo. A low-resolution photo (72 DPI) is usually only suitable for use on websites or for non-professional uses. Graphics professionals prefer high-resolution photos (300 to 600 DPI). Some stock houses will furnish bundles of low-resolution images sometimes referred to as royalty-free or copyright-free. (See Section A.) Other image banks may charge a sliding scale—for example, $50 for low resolution (72 DPI) to $250 for high resolution (300 DPI or higher).

Keep in mind that resolution also affects the file size. A 72 DPI photo may only take up 500K in disk space, enough to fit on a floppy disk. The same photo at 300 DPI may have a file size of 10-20 megabytes, requiring a hard disk or large storage device such as a Zip or Jaz drive.

Drum Scans vs. Flatbed Scans

Scanned photograph quality can vary widely. If you need high quality scans, say for reproduction in a coffee-table book, you should ask for drum scanning—a higher quality scanning process than used by flatbed scanners. If the image bank doesn't indicate the type of scan, ask.

Know your computer. Before downloading a digital image, make sure that your computer and graphics software can accommodate or convert that type of image file (for example, JPG or GIF).

d. Website Use Fees

Web fees can vary widely. Jim and Cheryl Pickerell, authors of *Selling Stock Online,* report that the fee for using a 4x4-inch stock photo on one major corporate home page cost $1,000 for six months. Time, Inc. (www.thepicturecollection.com), on the other hand charges $200 for use of one of its photos for the same time period. At the low end of the spectrum, Muse offers images for Web publishers for as low as $30. Chances are you'll be able to find a photo for your website that will fit your budget.

Most image banks base fees for website uses on the following factors:

- the sponsor of the site (who is paying for it)
- whether the photo will reside on the home page or a secondary one
- the prominence or size of the photo
- how long the photo will be displayed, and
- whether the photo will be used on any additional sites.

Image banks may want to know how long the image will be stored on the site, even if it is a relatively short period of time. Some image banks determine fees based on the number of visitors to the site (also known as "hits"). Sometimes, fees may be waived if the website use is ancillary to use in a printed work. For example, a Web fee may be waived if a magazine has licensed the photograph for print publication and also wants to use the photo in its online edition.

e. Additional Fee Factors

In addition to standard fees, the following factors may increase the fees you're required to pay for a rights-protected photo.

- **Exclusive or nonexclusive rights.** Obtaining an exclusive right to use a photo means that no one else can use that photo in the same manner as you're using it. Exclusive rights are always more expensive than nonexclusive rights. An exclusive rights arrangement often means getting exclusive rights for a specific use—for example, the exclusive right to reproduce the photo in Canada or the exclusive right to use the photo in automobile advertising.

- **Re-use fees.** It is possible that the image bank will only want to grant you rights for a specific print run or for a specific time period. If you are planning subsequent uses, you may be charged a re-use fee, usually a reduced version of your original fee. Some image banks charge re-use fees for new editions, not re-printings. (A new edition is a significant revision of a book, as opposed to a simple reprint when inventory has been depleted.) There may be an additional fee (similar to a re-use fee, though not titled as such) when a work is converted to a new medium—for example, when a documentary film is reproduced for sale in videocassette format. Find out the cost for a one-time fee for all potential uses and compare that to the cost of a series of re-use fees.

- **North American or world rights.** Worldwide rights are more expensive than U.S. rights. For example, if you had to pay $100 for North American rights for a quarter-page photograph inside a textbook with a print run of 5,000 copies, you might have to pay $150–$200 for world rights. Note, there is a difference between world rights in all languages versus world rights in only one language, such as English (see Chapter 1, Section A).

2. Fees for Royalty-Free Photos

In contrast to rights-protected fees, fees for royalty-free photos are not based on use. Overall, the fees are less expensive. You generally pay a flat fee from $25 to $300 for a CD-ROM or a website subscription and get a wide range of rights to use all the photos on the CD-ROM or website. While the rights granted are broad for royalty-free photos, there usually are some limitations, such as not using the images on merchandise. (Merchandise uses are discussed in Chapter 11.) As long as your use falls within the rights granted, you do not have to pay anything extra for your use of the photo. This means, for example, that you may use the photo several different times in various ways.

Since the scope of royalty-free rights may vary, you must review the written documentation that accompanies your purchase of the images. If you purchased a CD-ROM product, the limitations on use should be listed in the shrink-wrap agreement (typically a written agreement printed on the envelope containing the software) or in a "Read Me" file on the disk. If you obtain the images from a website, the legal limitations on your use may be presented in a click-wrap agreement, which is a screen that appears when you prepare to download the images. For more information on the enforceability of shrink-wrap and click-wrap agreements, see Chapter 4, Section E. We have listed some suppliers of royalty-free CD-ROM products in Section H.

F. Photo Permission Agreements

Permission agreements to use photographs vary quite a bit depending on whether you're using a rights-protected or royalty-free image. Agreements to use royalty-free photographs are generally much less specific than agreements for rights-protected photos. Typically, once you purchase a CD-ROM or pay an access fee for a website containing royalty-free photos for your use, you can go ahead and use the images within the general limitations outlined on the CD or at the website.

If you're using a rights-protected photo, you'll generally need to enter into a more specific agreement that outlines the terms of your use. This section outlines the terms commonly found in licenses for rights-protected photos, and offers a sample basic photo permission agreement with explanations for its terms. While using royalty-free photos doesn't ordinarily involve entering into the specific type of agreement discussed in this section, you may want to read Section 2, which explains some of the general terms that may apply to all agreements, including those for royalty-free photos.

⚠ Check the print or slide for more conditions. When an image bank furnishes you with photos, always review the back of the photos or the mounts for the slides for additional limitations on the license—for example, a requirement to provide a specific photographer credit. These limitations become a condition of your photo license agreement.

1. Agreement Terms

After agreeing upon a fee for a rights-protected photo, the image bank will usually furnish you with the images (usually transparencies, prints, scans or digital images) along with a permission agreement outlining the terms of your license. Alternatively, you may receive an invoice that functions as a permission agreement. The invoice or agreement will list the terms of your agreement (license), and should include the following information:

- the photograph (identified by title or catalog number)
- the nature and length of use (for example, the name of the publication or website in which the photo will be used)
- your name, or the name of your publisher or sponsor (the company paying for the publication or website)
- photographer's name or other photo credit requirements
- amount of the fee and to whom and when it should be paid, and
- samples (if you are required to furnish samples of your work when the photo is published).

2. The Small Print

The bottom or the back of the invoice will ordinarily contain additional terms and conditions for your use of the photos. These conditions often include the following:

- **Additional fees.** Image banks that furnish prints (not digital copies) request that you return the print. Usually, you can retain the originals for a period of 30 to 90 days, sometimes referred to as the "approval period." After you have copied the image for your use, you must return the images to the image bank before the end of the approval period. In some cases, a late fee may be charged ($1 or more per day). If you lose or damage the photo you might be stuck for a fee ranging from $50 to $1,500, depending on your agreement.
- **Late fees.** You may also have to pay late fees if your payment doesn't arrive on time. If your agreement states that "time is of the essence," you will have a harder time getting out of these late fee obligations. Despite the fact that you have a signed agreement, your failure to pay the fee on time may terminate your right to use the photo.
- **Model releases.** A model release is an agreement between the model and photographer allowing use of the model's image without violating the model's rights of privacy or publicity. (Model releases are discussed in detail in Chapter 12.) If the photo you're licensing has a model in it, it's a good idea to make sure the image bank has a model release on file. If the image bank says it has such a release, this should be stated somewhere in the permission agreement. Since many photo permission agreements are invoices (with contract language on the back), ask that the model release claim be stated on the invoice. For example, add language such as:

"Image Bank warrants that a model release is on file for the licensed photograph."

In addition, if possible, have the image bank provide you with a copy of the release so that you can compare it to the model release in Chapter 12. That chapter discusses how to analyze such a release agreement. These rules should apply regardless whether the photo is rights-protected or royalty-free.

- **Warranties and representations.** The image bank may want to be free from any legal claims resulting from: 1) unlicensed use of the photos, or 2) uses that are not included in the model release. These provisions typically include language such as "hold harmless" or "indemnify." For more information on these provisions, see Chapter 11. Review royalty-free shrink-wrap and click-wrap agreements for indemnity provisions as well.

- **Dispute resolution, attorney fees and jurisdiction.** The agreement may provide for methods of dealing with disputes, including arbitration or payment of attorney fees. In addition, the agreement may establish where you have to bring or defend a lawsuit. For more information on these dispute provisions, review Chapter 11. You won't likely find these provisions in a royalty-free agreement

Respect Photo Credits

Your agreement may require that you include certain credit information along with the photo. Recent court cases have held that a failure to provide proper credit may justify a lawsuit. Make sure that your credits conform to the requirements of your agreement.

Modifying a Photograph

Unless your agreement prohibits it, you can make minor modifications to the photograph, such as resizing the image or changing the resolution. However, major modifications—for example, colorizing a black-and-white image or digitally removing elements of a photo—require permission under copyright law. If the image bank or photographer discovers that you have made such major changes without permission, it may decide to sue you for copyright infringement. In this event, it's possible that you could defend yourself under fair use principles, arguing that you had a right to make changes and transform the image. However, this is an unpredictable defense. In addition, if you are distributing the work of a European photographer in Europe, you may violate certain moral rights (special European copyright rights) if you tinker with the photographer's aesthetic judgment.

To forestall lawsuits, we recommend that when seeking permission you notify the rights holder of your intent to modify the photo.

3. Basic Photo Permission Agreement

Th Photo Permission Agreement is included on the forms disk in the back of this book under the filename PICPERM.

Below we have provided a simple all-purpose photo permission agreement for rights-protected photos. A tear-out of this form is included in the Appendix, and a digital copy is included on the forms disk that comes with this book. Most likely, the image bank will provide you with its own agreement. If that is the case, you still can use the sample agreement below as a guide to help you understand the image bank's version. Or, in some cases the image bank may not furnish its own

Photo Permission Agreement

_____ ("Licensor") is the owner of rights for the photograph described below (the "Selection"). _____ ("Licensee") wants to acquire the right to use the Selection as specified in this agreement (the "Agreement").

Licensor Information

Title of work (the "Selection"): _____

Catalog number (if applicable): _____

Photographer: _____

Licensee Publication Information

The Selection will appear in the following publication(s) (the "Work"):

(check if applicable and fill in blanks)

☐   book—title: _____

☐   periodical—title: _____

☐   event handout—title of event: _____

☐   diskette–title: _____

☐   website—URL: _____

If to be used on a website, the Selection will appear on:

(check if applicable)

☐   home page

☐   internal page

Name of publisher or sponsor (if different from Licensee): _____

Estimated date(s) of publication or posting: _____

If applicable, the estimated number of copies to be printed or produced (if a book, the estimated first print run): _____

If for sale, the price: $ _____

If copies are free to attendees of a program, cost of program: _____

If a website, indicate the average number of visitors per month: _____

Grant of Rights

Licensor grants to Licensee and Licensee's successors and assigns, the:

(select one)

☐ nonexclusive

☐ exclusive

right to reproduce and distribute the Selection in:

(select all that apply)

☐ the current edition of the Work.

☐ all editions of the Work.

☐ all foreign language versions of the Work.

☐ all derivative versions of the Work.

☐ in all media now known or later devised.

☐ in promotional materials published and distributed in conjunction with the Work.

☐ other rights _____

Territory

The rights granted under this Agreement shall be for _____ (the "Territory").

Fees

Licensee shall pay Licensor as follows:

(select payment option and fill in blanks)

☐ **Flat Fee.** As full payment for all rights granted, Licensee shall pay Licensor a flat fee of:

$ _____ . Payment shall be made:

☐ upon execution of this Agreement.

☐ upon publication.

☐ **Royalties and Advance.** Licensee agrees to pay Licensor a royalty of____% of Net Sales. Net Sales are defined as gross sales (the gross invoice amount billed customers) less quantity discounts and returns actually credited. Licensee agrees to pay Licensor an advance against royalties of $_____ upon execution of this Agreement. Licensee shall pay Licensor within thirty

(30) days of the end of each quarter. Licensee shall furnish an accurate statement of sales during that quarter. Licensor shall have the right to inspect Licensee's books upon reasonable notice.

Credit & Samples

(check if applicable and fill in blanks)

☐   **Credit.** All versions of the Work that include the Selection shall contain the following statement: _____

☐   **Samples.** Upon publication, Licensee shall furnish _____copies of the Work to Licensor.

Warranty

Licensor warrants that it has the right to grant permission for the uses of the Selection as specified above and that the Selection does not infringe the rights of any third parties.

(check if applicable)

☐   Licensor warrants that a model release is on file for the Selection.

Miscellaneous

This Agreement may not be amended except in a written document signed by both parties. If a court finds any provision of this Agreement invalid or unenforceable, the remainder of this Agreement shall be interpreted so as best to effect the intent of the parties. This Agreement shall be governed by and interpreted in accordance with the laws of the State of _____. This Agreement expresses the complete understanding of the parties with respect to the subject matter and supersedes all prior representations and understandings.

Licensor	Licensee
By: _____	By: _____
Name: _____	Name: _____
Title: _____	Title: _____
Address: _____	Address: _____
Date: _____	Date: _____
	Tax ID # _____

agreement, in which case you can use ours. Our agreement lacks some provisions (such as dispute resolution and alternative payment systems) sometimes included in more complete artwork agreements. One reason for brevity is that it is often easier to negotiate and obtain permission using short agreements. Following the agreement is an explanation for its various provisions.

4. Explanation for Photo Permission Agreement

- In the introductory paragraph, insert the names of the licensor (the party who owns the material) and the licensee (you or the person who is seeking permission).
- In the Licensor Information and Licensee Publication Information section, complete the blank spaces.
- In the Grant of Rights section, complete the grant to reflect the rights that you have negotiated. More information on the rights associated with grants is provided in Chapter 11, "Art & Merchandise Licenses."
- Complete the Territory section to reflect the regions in which you have acquired rights. For more information about territory, review Chapter 11, Section C7.
- In the Fees section, indicate what type of fee has been negotiated, check the appropriate boxes and complete the information.
- Complete the Credit and Samples section to reflect your agreement with the licensor.
- As we explain in Chapter 11, Section C11, a warranty is a contractual promise made by the licensor. Some licensors do not want to make promises, particularly a promise that the work does not infringe any third parties' copyright or other rights. You may have to modify the Warranty section or strike it entirely if the licensor objects.
- If you have the bargaining power, you may want to include an indemnity provision in the agreement. Indemnity is a financial punish-

ment if the licensor breaks its promises. We have not included any indemnity provisions here. If you wish to add such a provision, samples and explanations are provided in Chapter 11, Section C11.
- Explanations for the Miscellaneous (also known as "boilerplate") provisions are provided in Chapter 11, Section C22). If you have the bargaining power, you may want to include an attorney fees or an arbitration provision.

⚠ Commercial uses may be more involved. If you are seeking permission to use a photograph on behalf of an advertising agency or a company selling a product or service (for example, Nike or American Airlines), your use is more likely to be categorized as a commercial endorsement which will trigger additional legal issues. Review Chapter 12 regarding the releases that may be required.

G. When the Photograph Includes Art, Trademarks or People

What if the photograph you intend to use includes copyrighted artwork, a trademark or a person? In that case you may need more than one permission, because certain uses—particularly commercial uses of people and trademarks—may trigger additional legal rights and claims. In other words, besides copyright permission from the photographer, you may need permission from the copyright owner or trademark owner of the subject of the photograph, or from a person appearing in it. This section offers a brief explanation of these issues. You also may want to refer to Chapter 10, "Getting Permission to Use Trademarks," and Chapter 12, "Releases."

1. When a Photograph Contains Copyrighted Art

You may need two permissions if you reproduce a photograph that contains copyrighted artwork. For example, if you wanted to use a photo that included a mural by Diego Rivera in the background, you may need permission from the copyright owner of the Rivera mural as well as from the owner of the photograph. Whether permission is in fact required from the owner of the artwork depends on whether your use of the artwork within the photo would be considered a fair use under copyright law. Fair use principles are discussed in more detail in Chapter 9, "Fair Use."

Generally speaking, you may not need permission if the artwork is incidental to your photo, such as artwork that appears in the far background of a street fair. A minimal use such as this may be deemed a fair use not requiring permission. For example, a court has ruled that the momentary appearance of an artist's work in a motion picture did not require permission. In another case, however, the appearance of a copyrighted poster in a television show did require permission. As explained in Chapter 9, relying on fair use principles can be risky as the final word can only be decided by a judge.

In Chapter 4, "Getting Permission to Use Artwork," information is provided regarding the relationship of photos and artwork. That chapter also discusses how to locate the copyright owners of artwork.

2. When a Photograph Contains Trademarks

A trademark is any word, photograph or symbol that is used to identify a product or service for sale. Familiar trademarks include Chevrolet, McDonald's and Apple Computer. Under trademark law, you do not need permission to reproduce a trademark if your use is informational (also referred to as "editorial"). An example of an editorial use would include using the trademark to illustrate a newspaper article, magazine feature or other literary statement. You do not need permission to use a trademark when making accurate, comparative product statements.

On the other hand, you are much more likely to need permission to use a trademark in a commercial context. Permission will likely be required if any of the following circumstances is true:

- *Your use is likely to create confusion among consumers.* For example, your use of a photo of a jogger wearing a Nike shirt in an ad for your sports equipment website may confuse viewers as to whether Nike is associated with or endorses your site. You would need permission from Nike to use its logo or name.
- *Your use diminishes the strength of the trademark.* A doctrine known as the "dilution doctrine" prohibits the use of trademarks which tends to weaken another famous mark by chipping away at its distinctiveness. In other words, the more just anyone is allowed to use the term "Nike," the less customers will make an automatic association between the term and actual Nike products. In addition, you may not be allowed to use a trademark if your use reflects poorly upon the trademark (also known as "tarnishing"). For example, if you use a photo of a woman wearing a Nike shirt on an X-rated website, the Nike company could stop the use.
- *You have modified the trademark.* Comparative advertising uses of trademarks are legal, but it is not permissible to modify the trademark when making comparisons. For example, a tractor company was found liable for animating the trademark of the John Deere Company in a television commercial.

It can be quite tricky to figure out whether or not permission may be required in a given situation. One thing to keep in mind is that even if you are legally entitled to use a trademark, some trademark owners (particularly owners of famous marks) will sue first and review the legal rules later.

For more information on trademark rules, review Chapter 10, "Getting Permission to Use Trademarks."

3. When Your Photograph Contains People

In general, you don't need permission to use a photograph of a person if your use is editorial and does not defame or invade the person's privacy (see below). An editorial use is an informational use—one in which the photo is used to elaborate or illustrate an article or story. For example, no permission is necessary to use a photo of a paratrooper in an article about the Vietnam War. However, you do need permission (known as a "release" or "consent"), for the uses described below. (Releases are discussed in Chapter 12.)

- *Your use is for commercial purposes such as advertising or to sell a product or service.* Under right of publicity laws, you cannot use a person's name or image for commercial (selling) purposes without obtaining a release. For example, if you sell sweaters from your website, you would need permission to use a photo of a model wearing one of your sweaters. This right of publicity can survive a person's death (sometimes for as long as 50 years depending on state law). There are some exceptions to these rules. If your use is editorial—for example, a photo of a fashion model in a book about the fashion industry—you can use the photo to advertise the book without obtaining a release.

- *Your use invades a person's privacy.* Every person has the right to be left alone. If you are using a photograph that was taken surreptitiously (for instance, using a hidden camera on private property) or if your photo depicts very personal or potentially embarrassing activities (for example, treatment at a mental institution), you should obtain a release. Without a release, your use might violate state right of privacy laws. Keep in mind that a person's right to privacy only exists while they are alive. This is not true of the right of publicity that survives death in some states.

- *Your use is defamatory.* If your use of a photograph creates a false impression injuring someone's reputation, you could be liable for defamation, sometimes known as libel. For example, say you use a stock photo of two doctors in an article on mercy killing. If you did not obtain a release as to that specific use, you may be subject to liability if the doctors sued you for damaging their reputations. There are some exceptions to these defamation rules for public figures such as politicians and celebrities who have voluntarily thrown themselves into the public eye and, to a limited extent, for people who have become subject of a public controversy. For these people, you will only be liable if the public figure can prove you acted with actual malice or reckless disregard for the truth—for example, you knowingly printed a damaging lie about someone. For non-public figures, truth is an absolute defense. Keep in mind, however, that dredging up old (but truthful) facts may invade a person's privacy. A more in-depth explanation of these principles is provided in Chapter 12.

H. Stock Photo Resources

This section lists the many companies, directories, organizations and other entities that may be able to help you in obtaining photographs and the rights to use them.

1. Image Banks

The image banks listed below are all accessible online. While we've categorized them according to whether they provide rights-protected or royalty-free images, note that some offer both. Selection may vary from company to company, so it's a good idea to check out a number of them to find the company that suits your needs. As with any online services, expect that some of these sites may change their website addresses.

a. Rights-Protected Image Banks

- AP/Wide World Photos: www.apwideworld.com.
- Archive Photos: www.history.com.
- Comstock: www.comstock.com.
- Corbis: www.corbisview.com (for professional use) or www.corbis.com (for personal use).
- Getty Images: www.getty-images.com.
- Liaison International: www.liaisonphoto.com.
- Muse: www.weststock.com.
- PictureQuest: www.picturequest.com.
- Pickerell Photo Services: www.pickphoto.com.
- Stock Solution: www.tssphoto.com.
- Stock, Boston, Inc.: www.stockboston.com.
- Time, Inc.: www.thepicturecollection.com.
- Tony Stone Images: www.tonystone.com.
- Vivid Details: www.vividdetails.com.
- Worldwide Photojournalism: www.blackstar.com.

b. Royalty-Free Image Banks

- Artville: www.artville.com.
- Comstock: www.comstock.com/72lies.
- Corbis/DigitalStock: www.digitalstock.com.
- Corel: www.corel.com.
- Cyberphoto: www.cyberphoto.com.
- Eyewire: www.eyewire.com.
- Photodisc: www.photodisc.com.
- PhotoEssentials: www.photoessentials.com.
- PhotoSource: www.photosource.com.
- PictureQuest: www.picturequest.com.
- Publishers Depot: www.publishersdepot.com.

2. Celebrity and Entertainment Image Banks

The image banks listed below have extensive collections of promotional photos, including images of celebrities, events and movie stills.

- Culver: 212-645-1672.
- The Everett Collection: 212-255-8610.
- Corbis/Outline: 212-226-8790.
- Photofest: 212-633-6330.
- Shooting Star: 323-469-2020.
- Star File: 212-929-2525.
- Motion Picture & Television Photo Archive: 818-997-8292.
- Liaison: 800-488-0484.

3. Resources for Locating Image Banks

The following websites are useful in finding image banks appropriate for your needs.

- Stock Photo Deskbook: www.stockphotodeskbook.com.
- AG Editions: www.agpix.com.
- Finding Images Online (Paula Berinstein's site): www.berinsteinresearch.com.
- 1StopStock.com: www.1stopstock.com.
- Arriba Vista: www.arribavista.com.
- Yahoo: ipix.yahoo.com.
- AltaVista: image.altavista.com.

A number of print resources are also available for locating image banks.

- *The Stock Photo Deskbook*, available from Exeter Company, 767 Winthrop Road, Teaneck, NJ 07666; 201-692-1743, fax 201-692-8173; email: exeter@Webspan.net.
- *The Green Book* and *The Blue Book* are available from AG Editions, 41 Union Square West, Ste. 523, New York, NY 10003; 212-929-0959, fax 212-924-4796; email: office@ag-editions.com.
- *Photograph Agency Council of America Directory*, P.O. Box 308, Northfield, MN 55057-0308; 800-457-PACA; email: paca@earthlink.net.
- *Finding Images Online*, by Paula Berinstein (Pemberton Press), is available from Berinstein Research, P.O. Box 1305, Woodland Hills, CA 91365; 818-865-0523.

4. Resources for Locating Photographers

- The American Society of Media Photographers, 14 Washington Road., Suite 502, Princeton Junction, NJ 08550; 609-799-8300; website: www.asmp.org.
- Professional Photographers of America, 229 Peachtree Street, NE, Suite 2200, International Tower, Atlanta, GA 30303; 404-522-8600, fax 404-614-6400; email: jhopper594@aol.com; website: www.ppa-world.org.
- National Press Photographers Association, 3200 Croasdaile Drive, Suite 306, Durham, NC 27705; 919-383-7246; website: www.sunsite.unc.edu/nppa.
- Advertising Photographers of America, 333 South Beverly Drive, Suite 216, Beverly Hills, CA 90212; 310-201-0781; website: www.apanational.org.
- Advertising Photographers of New York, 27 W. Twentieth Street, New York, NY 10011; 212-807-0399; website: www.apny.com.
- Yahoo! directory listing of photographers: dir.yahoo.com/Business_and_Economy/Companies/Photography/Photographers/.

5. Resources for Locating Picture Researchers

- American Society of Picture Professionals, 409 So. Washington Street, Alexandria, VA 22314; 703-299-0219; email: aspp1@idsonline.com; website: www.aspp.com.

You may also benefit by using the following texts.

- *Finding Images Online*, by Paula Berinstein (Pemberton Press).
- *Practical Picture Research*, by Hilary Evans (Routledge-Blueprint).

6. Photo Pricing Resources

- *Negotiating Stock Photo Prices and Selling Stock Online*, by Jim and Cheryl Pickerell (Pickerell). Order it online at www.pickphoto.com or call 301-251-0720, fax 301-309-0941.
- *Pricing Photography: The Complete Guide to Assignment and Stock Prices*, by Michael Heron and David MacTavish (Allworth Press). ■

Getting Permission to Use Artwork

This chapter explains how to obtain permission to reproduce artwork. By "artwork" we mean fine art or graphic art. Fine art includes one-of-a-kind or limited edition works, such as a limited edition silk-screen print by Andy Warhol, a mobile by Alexander Calder or a painting by Georgia O'Keeffe. Graphic artwork is any art intended for commercial reproduction such as an illustration, design, icon, clip art, cartoon or comic. We've grouped these works together into one chapter because the process of obtaining permission to use them is similar, the ways they are used are similar and the rights to use them are sometimes controlled by one company.

This chapter explains how to obtain permission to use fine art, graphic art and cartoons. Since the permissions process is slightly different for each of these types, we discuss each one in a separate section. We also offer tips for finding clip art (existing images available for license). At the end of the chapter you'll find two sample agreements: a basic license for acquiring permission to use artwork in a publication or website, and an agreement for using artwork in films and videos.

A. Acquiring Rights to Artwork

The way you approach the permssions process for any type of artwork will depend on what you want to use, and for what purpose. Also keep in mind that your budget will likely affect how you go about the permissions process.

Generally speaking, if you need to reproduce a specific item of artwork that's not in the public domain—for example, a painting by Pablo Picasso—you will need to negotiate with whoever owns copyright in the artwork (in this case, Picasso's estate) for the right to reproduce it. If, on the other hand, you want to use a fine art painting that is in the public domain—the Mona Lisa, for example—you won't have to acquire the rights to reproduce the work, since public domain works are free to copy. Remember, however, that unless you photograph the work yourself, you may have to obtain

the rights to use the reproduction of the work, such as from a photographer you hire, or from a gallery or artist rights organization who provides you with a photograph.

If you do not need a specific artwork and have a suitable budget, you may want to specially commission artwork and acquire rights to use it. For example, if you need illustrations for a book, you can hire a graphic artist and acquire exclusive and unlimited rights to the artwork. Ownership can be acquired under an employment arrangement, by an assignment or by using a work-for-hire agreement (acquiring ownership is explained in Chapter 15). Many artists prefer not to convey all rights and instead convey limited rights by granting a license. A sample license agreement is provided at the end of this chapter. When graphic artwork is used on merchandise such as T-shirts or ceramic cups, a special artwork merchandise license agreement is used (see Chapter 11) that provides for ongoing royalty payments.

If your budget is small, you may prefer to use clip art. The term "clip art" simply refers to existing graphic art images that are available either for a fixed fee or for free. Clip can often be used for unlimited purposes, so a permission agreement is not required. However, some clip art collections have limitations on use, and you should examine the shrink-wrap agreement accompanying the artwork. For information about clip art, see Section C.

B. Fine Art: Paintings, Sculptures and Limited Editions

The main thing to remember when seeking permission to use fine art is that one permission may not be enough. As with other forms of creative work, fine art is protected by a number of rights that may be held in different hands. To use just one work, you may need to obtain permission from two or more people or businesses, including:

- the copyright owner of the artwork. If the artwork is copyright protected, you need permission from the copyright owner—usually the artist or the artist's estate (if the artist is dead). Copyright protection for foreign works may last longer than works protected under U.S. law. If you are unsure whether a work is protected under copyright, review Chapter 8.

- the copyright owner of a photograph of the artwork. If you are using a photograph of artwork, you may need permission from the copyright owner of the photograph as well as from the copyright owner of the artwork itself (see Section B3).

- the people who appear in, or the owners of trademarks or other copyrightable art included in the fine art. Depending on your use, you may need a consent or release for any people, trademarks or copyrightable art included in the artwork. (Review Chapters 10 and 12.)

- the owner of the artwork. If you want to photograph a work of fine art, you may have to get permission from its owner, usually a museum or a private owner. Many museums won't allow you to photograph their art; instead they hire a photographer and charge you for the photograph.

In short, it's crucial to remember when seeking permission to use fine art to inquire what rights are being obtained. Never assume the person who "rents" you a fine art image controls the copyright in the underlying artwork, as it is often not the case.

1. Obtaining Photos of Fine Art

Photographs of fine art may often be obtained from the museum or gallery exhibiting the work or through museums affiliated with the Smithsonian Institution (see Sidebar in Section F2). Gallery resources are provided at the end of this chapter. Image banks (companies that license photos and artwork) sometimes also supply high-quality copies of copyrighted and public domain fine art. Both Corbis (www.corbisview.com) and Archive Photo (www.history.com) have an extensive collection of public domain fine art images. Another method of

searching for fine art images is by using the Stock Photo Deskbook database (www.stockphotodeskbook.com) or author Paula Berinstein's website (www.berinsteinresearch.com). For information on using image banks, see Chapter 3, Section A.

In addition to these sources, the Visual Artists and Galleries Association (VAGA) and Artists' Rights Societies (ARS) can, for a fee, assist in locating high quality photographs of public domain works. These organizations are discussed in more detail below.

2. Getting Permission to Use Copyrighted Fine Art

There are two organizations in the United States that manage permissions for copyrighted fine art: the Visual Artists and Galleries Association (VAGA) and Artists' Rights Societies (ARS), which is affiliated with Art Resource. These organizations represent many well-known American and European artists and galleries. They can grant permission for reproduction of copyrighted works for most common uses such as publications, websites, advertisements and merchandise. Contact information for VAGA and ARS is provided at the end of this chapter.

To locate the rights holder of copyrighted fine art, start by contacting VAGA or ARS. In the case of a fine artist who is not well-known, the best starting point is the institution or gallery in which the artist's work is exhibited. Often, the gallery can refer you to the rights holder.

EXAMPLE: We sought to reproduce a black-and-white copy of "Monogram," a fine artwork by Robert Rauschenberg. We wanted to use the art in a book with an initial pressing of 5,000 copies. We contacted VAGA and ARS and learned that VAGA controls the rights. A VAGA representative explained that the fee for our use would be $75.

Monogram © Robert Rauschenberg, Licensed by VAGA, New York NY

3. Photographs of Fine Art

Sometimes you must pay twice to reproduce a photograph of copyrighted artwork: once for permission to use the artwork and a second time for the right to use the photograph. This practice is derived from the principle that a photograph and artwork are two separate copyrighted works. Unfortunately, it's not always simple to figure out which photographs are protected by copyright and whether separate permissions are necessary.

One factor in determining whether a photo is protected by copyright (making it necessary to get permission to use it) is whether the subject of the photograph is itself protected by copyright. Another factor, which can be very subtle and difficult to measure, is the way in which the subject was photographed, including aspects such as lighting and camera angle.

In cases involving public domain works, the federal courts have ruled that "slavish" (nearly identical) copies of public domain works don't merit copyright protection. (*Hearn v. Meyer,* 664 F. Supp. 832 (S.D. N.Y. 1987).) In other words, a photographer cannot acquire protection for a perfect photographic reproduction of the Mona Lisa. (*Bridgeman Art Library Ltd. v. Corel Corp.,* 25 F.Supp.2d 412 (S.D. N.Y. 1997).

Unfortunately, there have not been enough cases to allow photographers, artists and academics to conclusively determine when a photograph of a painting acquires separate protection. In general, the more the photo is an exact reproduction of the original, the less likely it is protected by copyright (meaning you don't need permission to use the photograph). On the other hand, if the photograph has original elements in it such as unusual colored lighting, special effects or other additions to the piece of art itself, the more likely it is that the photographer owns copyright in the photo and that you'd need permission to use the photograph.

Regardless of the copyright rules (and regardless of whether the work is in the public domain), you may have to pay for the use of the photo owned by a museum, gallery or image bank. In some cases, you must even sign an agreement promising that you won't reproduce the photographic image other than for the agreed purposes. Such an agreement may not be legally enforceable—for example, in the case of a public domain work that's an exact reproduction without anything added by the photographer to create a separately copyrightable work. However, as a practical matter, you likely will not be able to afford the expense and aggravation of litigating the issue. For that reason, payment for photo reproductions of artwork is often a practical necessity.

Reproductions of Architecture

Under a copyright amendment passed in 1990, some works of architecture were granted copyright protection. You cannot reproduce the architectural plans, the architect's rendering renderings (the illustrations of the building) or mock-ups (the miniature constructions of the building). However, you can photograph a copyrighted building if it is visible from a public place, plus you can reproduce the photograph, without infringing copyright.

> EXAMPLE: Donald has acquired copyright protection for the architectural design of his new casino, Plump Towers. The building is visible from the public beach at Atlantic City. Shirley photographs the building and sells her photographs in postcard reproductions. Shirley is not infringing Donald's architectural copyright.

It is also possible that a unique building design may serve as a trademark—for example, the novel shape and appearance of a Fotomat kiosk may serve as a trademark. In this event, reproducing the commercial reproduction of the trademarked appearance of the building may trigger a lawsuit for trademark infringement. This is precisely what happened when a photographer shot and reproduced pictures of the Rock and Roll Hall of Fame—which the owners claimed was protected by trademark—though a federal appeals court ultimately ruled that the use was not a trademark infringement. For more information on this case and trademark laws, review Chapter 10, "Getting Permission to Use Trademarks."

C. Graphic Art

Graphic artwork is any illustration intended for commercial reproduction, whether in magazines or books, advertisements or websites. As with other types of artwork, how you obtain the right to use graphic art depends in part on whether you have the art created specifically for your use, or whether you've found existing artwork that you want to use.

1. Obtaining Rights to Works Created for You

If an artist creates a work for you, your right to use the work will be based either in an assignment, a work-for-hire agreement or a license.

- An assignment is a transfer of copyright ownership. In return for a payment (or ongoing payments) you acquire copyright ownership in the artwork. Acquiring ownership is explained in Chapter 15.
- A work made for hire is owned by the hiring party, not the artist. Works made for hire are created in a number of ways. If the artist is your employee and created the work within the course of employment, the work will be a work for hire. A work for hire can also be created if: 1) you commissioned the work, 2) the work falls into one of certain enumerated categories or 3) you entered into a written work-for-hire agreement. Assignments and works made for hire are discussed in more detail in Chapter 15.
- A license is the right to right to use the artwork for a specific purpose. A license does not transfer copyright ownership.

2. Obtaining Rights to Existing Artwork

If graphic artwork already exists and was not created for your use, you would usually acquire rights by license. Start by contacting the publisher (magazine, newspaper, or website, for example) in which the graphic art appeared. Since publishers generally try to acquire all rights from graphic artists, it's possible that the publisher may own the rights you need. If the publisher doesn't own the rights or is unable to help, you'll have to search for the graphic artist. Searching the Internet may do the trick, or you could try contacting the Graphic Artists Guild (GAG) (www.gag.org). The GAG has an artist locator service and publishes the *Graphic Artists Guild Handbook*.

Children's Book Illustrators

If you're looking for a graphic artist who has illustrated a children's book, contact the Society of Children's Book Writers and Illustrators, who can put you in touch with any member illustrator. Contact information for this organization appears in the resource section at the end of this chapter.

Reproducing U.S. Postage Stamps

Since 1970, U.S. postage stamps have been protected under copyright law. If you want to reproduce a copyrighted stamp image, you must obtain permission from the licensing division of the U.S. Postal Service, handled by Hamilton Projects. At the time of our inquiry, a minimum fee of $250 allowed the use of up to five stamp images, and each additional image cost $50. The fees are negotiated separately for publications related to stamp collecting. For more information call 212-333-9096 and select from the menu options.

D. Comics and Cartoons

Comics and cartoons include a variety of graphic artwork. Comics may be in strip or book form, both of which involve a series of drawings telling a story. Single-panel drawings telling a joke or gag are often called cartoons. Animated cartoons include shows like "The Simpsons," movies like *Toy Story* or *The Lion King*, old series like the "Bugs Bunny" or "Daffy Duck" cartoons, and basically any other animated images. Below we explain the process of obtaining rights to use various types of print or animated comics.

1. Comic Books

To obtain rights to reproduce images from comic books, you'll generally start with the publisher, as publishers typically own the rights for comic books. Rights for underground, experimental or other types of comics may be owned either by the publisher or by the individual artists. Sometimes ownership is indicated by the name located in the copyright notice. If the artist's name is in the notice, for example, "Copyright 1985 Steve Purcell," then the artist has probably retained reprint rights.

Determining the rights for comic books published before 1965 may prove complex, as many comic publishers have folded, sold rights to other companies or failed to renew copyright. Two sources of comic book information and links are Collecting Comics (www.collecting-comics.com/links/links.asp) and Comicon (www.comicon.com). A comprehensive listing of comic book publishers and contact information for them is located at the Indy Magazine site (www.nexilis-hobbies.com/indyworld/reference/industry.shtml). We list a number of major comic book publishers at the end of this chapter.

2. Comic Strips, Editorial Cartoons and Single-Panel Cartoons

Reprint rights for most newspaper comic strips and for many editorial cartoons (also known as political cartoons) are controlled by syndicates. Editorial cartoons or comic strips not owned by a syndicate are probably owned by the individual newspaper or magazine employing the cartoonist. Contact the syndicate or publication for information regarding permission. You'll usually find the name of the cartoonist and the syndicate printed vertically between the panels of the strip.

Besides the syndicates and publications, other resources exist to help in finding cartoonists. For example, a site called Politcalcartoons.com provides email addresses for many editorial cartoonists. For your reference, at the end of this chapter we offer a list of syndicates as well as other resources for finding editorial cartoonists.

Single-panel cartoons (not comic strips or editorial cartoons) are often owned by the publications in which they appear. If you're seeking rights for a single-panel cartoon from a magazine, start by contacting the publication. For example, if the cartoon first appeared in *Playboy*, contact that magazine's permission department. If calling the publication does not provide leads, you may be able to get contact information for the cartoonist through the National Cartoonists Society. Another source of single-panel cartoon information is the Cartoonbank, associated with *The New Yorker* magazine. Contact information for these and other resources are listed at the end of this chapter.

In the past few years, the syndicates have streamlined the licensing process and can accommodate a broad range of licensing from books to websites. Fees for a comic strip or single panel cartoon range from $35 to several hundred dollars depending on the type of use.

3. Animated Cartoons

Rights to an animated cartoon series such as "The Simpsons" or "The Flintstones" are usually owned by an entertainment production company. If the cartoon series is in syndication, you can find the production company by reviewing the credits at the end of any episode. Quite often, this is the last or next to last credit. The production company can also be determined online at the Internet Movie Database (www.imdb.com), a searchable database of thousands of films and television shows.

Most entertainment production companies can be found in the New York, Nashville or Los Angeles telephone listings, and through Internet directories such as Yahoo!, Internet Yellow Pages or search engines such as Infoseek and AltaVista. When you contact the company, ask for the publicity, media relations or public relations department.

⚠ **Reproducing cartoon characters may raise additional issues.** If you want to obtain permission to use a particular cartoon character such as Superman or Ren and Stimpy, review Chapter 10, "Getting Permission to Use Trademarks."

Medical Illustrations

Do you need medical imagery or anatomical imagery? Medical illustrators specialize in anatomical and health-related illustrations. Rights for illustrations are often controlled by the publishers or, if the publisher is unable to help, you can find a specific medical illustrator by contacting the Association of Medical Illustrators. You can also find medical clip art on the Web. One of the largest sites is provided by the medical publisher Williams & Wilkins Mediclip (www.lifeart.com), which offers medical clip art images at a cost of approximately $10 per image. Other websites offering medical images can be located using the search term "medical clip art."

E. Royalty-Free and Public Domain Clip Art

An alternative to paying licensing fees to use artwork is to use public domain artwork or artwork offered on a royalty-free basis. This type of artwork is sometimes referred to as clip art, royalty-free or copyright-free artwork and is sold in books, CD-ROM bundles or distributed free from websites.

1. The Terms

The terms clip art, public domain, royalty-free and copyright-free are often used interchangeably (and confusingly).

- Clip art is a general term used to refer to any artwork that is available in collections, either in book form or on computer disk. Clip art may be in the public domain or royalty-free.

- Public domain art is not protected by copyright. Many publishers, such as Dover Books, specialize in offering collections of public domain art. The image of the man and dog above is from a Dover publication entitled *Humorous Victorian Spot Illustrations.* You are free to copy and use the individual artwork in a public domain collection without permission. However, you are not free to copy and sell the collection.

- The term royalty-free is used to describe artwork that is available for a wide range of purposes. Unlike public domain art, royalty-free art is protected under copyright law and can't be used for free. However, once you buy the CD-ROM or pay for access to a website that contains royalty-free artworks, your license to use the images is usually largely unlimited, and you can use the works numerous times and in a broad range of uses. Keep in mind that uses for merchandising or commercial endorsements are often not allowed, which is a major exception to the rule that royalty-free images are free to use however you want. See Chapter 11 for the special rules surrounding merchandising and commercial uses.

- More often than not, the term copyright-free is used in confusing ways. Sometimes people use it to refer to public domain artwork. In other cases, it's used to refer to royalty-free artwork. Often, it's used to describe artwork that various websites offer for free to the public—though these works are essentially either public domain works or royalty-free works. We prefer not to use the term "copyright-free," and instead stick with the terms "royalty-free" for artwork that can be licensed for a wide range of uses, and the term "public domain work" for artwork that can be used for free.

2. Finding and Using Clip Art

Clip art is often available on CD-ROM or downloadable from the Web. To find websites that offer clip art, use the keywords "clip art," "royalty free" or "copyright free" with any Internet search engine. If you use America Online, type in the keywords "Image" or "Image Exchange" and you will be directed to stock art sources. Many of the royalty-free photo resources provided in Chapter 3 also provide royalty-free clip art.

Clip art—which generally includes royalty-free and public domain artwork—is fine for most standard business and personal uses. The only significant drawbacks to using this type of artwork is that the quality is often not very good and competitors are free to use the same image by accessing the same website or CD-ROM. If you are seeking exclusive rights to artwork, you should either hire an artist (see Chapter 15) or enter into an exclusive license to use a graphic work.

Sometimes clip art is sold for a flat fee or a subscription fee. Use is limited only by the terms of the shrink-wrap or click-wrap agreement (discussed below). Inexpensive clip art bundles are available on CD-ROM for $20 to $300.

⚠ Know your computer and what you're downloading. The three-letter extension on the graphic file, for example, "JPG," "TIF" or "GIF," tells you what type of file it is. Before downloading a digital image, make sure your computer and graphic programs can accommodate or convert that type of image file. For example, some TIF files are suitable for PCs and some are not. In addition, be aware that scanned artwork quality can vary widely. If you are seeking the highest quality scans, you should ask for drum-scanned artwork—a higher quality scanning process than used by flatbed scanners. If the image bank doesn't indicate the type of scan, ask.

3. Shrink-Wrap and Click-Wrap Agreements

Always read the shrink-wrap or click-wrap agreement accompanying a clip art collection. These agreements come in two forms: with software packages such as on the printed sticker under the plastic shrink-wrap; or contracts on the Web that require clicking on a button entitled "Okay" or "I Agree." These agreements contain a list of do's and don'ts—and sometimes the conditions are more restrictive than required under copyright law.

Clip art conditions are often similar to the following:

This software contains original clip art that is fully protected by copyrights. The original purchaser of the software is authorized to use individual items to produce copyright-free art for the printing of newsletters and the like. However this software collection may not be reproduced in whole or in part as a collection or individually as stock engravings, prints, negatives, positives, stock printing and the like.

In other words, you are free to use the clip art as a book illustration or in an ad, but you cannot reprint it in its entirety as a collection or sell individual images.

EXAMPLE: A company downloaded several volumes of fire-fighting clip art and then offered the clip art packages at its website. The company was found liable for copyright infringement for copying the three volumes of software clip art and placing it on a website for downloading without authorization of the clip art owner. *(Marobie-Fl, Inc. v. National Association of Fire Equipment Distributors,* 983 F. Supp. 1167 (E.D. Ill. 1997).)

Some courts have enforced these agreements but there is no definitive answer as to whether they are always enforceable. Legislation has been proposed by the software industry to end that uncertainty.

F. Researching Art

The methods of searching for artwork are similar to the searching techniques used for photo imagery discussed in Chapter 3, Section A. You can search online by using image search engines or exploring image bank websites. You can also hire an image researcher to assist you in locating art.

1. Online Searching

If you are seeking a particular work by an artist, it's usually simply a matter of typing in the artist's name or the name of the work into a search engine. Some image search engines such as the Clip Art Searcher (Webplaces.com/search/) allow you to use numerous image search engines such as HotBot, Lycos, and Yahoo!, and to search thousands of FTP files on the Web. (FTP stands for "file transfer protocol," and refers to files that are specifically for downloading from the Web.)

However, if you don't need a specific image but need a certain type of graphic image—such as a drawing of a horse—locating the right graphic image may be a little trickier. The problem is that search engines cannot distinguish between photographic images and graphic or "art" images, so you'll almost always have to sort through numerous photographic images to find the graphic image you want. As a general rule, you will do better to go directly to image banks that specifically provide artwork and search there. You can get a lengthy listing of websites providing clip art simply by typing the words "clip art" into a search engine.

EXAMPLE: Our goal was to find a classic image of an angel. We began our search using an image search engine, Clip Art Searcher, and typed in the word "angel." The search engine returned dozens of sites (including numerous photos from the TV show "Touched by an Angel") but only one site had graphic images of angels. Unfortunately, these were cartoon angels.

We abandoned the search engines and went to specific image sites and searched there. On AOL, we clicked on KEYWORD, and typed in "Image Exchange." We located a folder entitled "Angels From the Vatican" where we found several public domain angel images including an angel by Raphael Sanzio.

After that we used our Internet search engine and typed in "clip art" and found many free image clip art sites. At one of these sites, All Advantage, we downloaded another image of an angel.

2. Using Picture Researchers

If you are having difficulty locating a particular artwork item, consider using the services of professional picture researcher. Picture researchers are skilled at digging into a variety of resources such as the Library of Congress, the Smithsonian Institution or online image banks. These researchers are usually paid day rates (approximately $250) although some charge by the hour. As explained in Chapter 3, many picture researchers have specialties, so you may want to contact the American Society of Picture Professionals (listed in the resource section at the end of this chapter) in order to find someone appropriate for your needs.

Millions of Images: The Smithsonian

The Smithsonian Institution in Washington, D.C., is more than a single institution—it's an umbrella organization for national museums, libraries and archives. It provides an invaluable link to millions of photographic, fine art and historical images from sources such as the Archives of American Art, Freer Gallery of Art, Gem & Mineral Collection, Harvard-Smithsonian Center for Astrophysics, National Air & Space Museum, National Museum of African Art, National Museum of American Art, National Museum of American History, National Museum of Natural History, National Museum of the American Indian, National Portrait Gallery and the National Postal Museum.

There is no comprehensive Smithsonian guide explaining how to locate various materials. You may need to make several telephone calls until your request arrives at the correct curatorial or collecting unit. (The collecting unit is the museum or gallery controlling the rights to the work.) Permission to publish a photograph of an item can only be granted by the Smithsonian collecting unit holding the original object or image. That unit also provides you with the Smithsonian negative number, a necessary element if you need a copy of a photograph. To locate the right collecting unit, use the Public Inquiry Mail Service, the Smithsonian telephone book or one of the various Smithsonian websites that explain where collecting units are located. These resources are listed at the end of this chapter.

The Smithsonian and its affiliated institutions are not considered to be U.S. government agencies for copyright purposes. This means they are allowed to claim copyright in images they make of works in their collections.

G. Artwork Fees and Agreements

As a general rule, fees and agreements for using artwork are similar to those for using stock photography. One reason for this is that both photos and art are often licensed from the same source. As with photos, fees and agreements for licensing artwork vary depending on the work and your use, and increase for exclusivity, higher resolution and advertising and corporate uses. The fee for using a cartoon in a company newsletter may cost as little as $25, while the fee for reproducing fine art within a book may range from $75 to several hundred dollars. The detailed discussion in Chapter 3, Section E, of fee information for rights-protected photos also applies to artwork. Please refer to that section for in-depth fee information.

Below, we provide two sample agreements: a simple all-purpose artwork license agreement, as well as an agreement for using artwork in a film or video. If you want to reproduce artwork on posters, postcards, mugs or other merchandise, see Chapter 11, "Art & Merchandise Licenses."

Modifying Artwork

Modifications to artwork—for example, colorizing a black-and-white image or digitally removing elements of a picture—require permission under U.S. copyright law. In addition, under European and U.S. laws, artists possess special rights known as moral rights. You may violate these moral rights if you tinker with the artist's aesthetic judgments. When seeking permission, notify the rights holder of your intent to modify the work or seek a release granting you permission to make your intended alterations. A statement like: "Licensor grants to Licensee the right to modify the artwork as follows: [describe the modification]. . ." should suffice.

1. Sample Artwork Permission Agreement

Below you'll find a basic all-purpose artwork permission agreement. A tear-out copy of this agreement is included in the Appendix, and a digital copy is included on the forms disk at the back of this book. This agreement lacks some of the provisions (such as dispute resolution and alternative payment systems) sometimes included in more complete artwork agreements. One reason for brevity is that it is easier to negotiate and obtain permission using short agreements. Following the agreement is an explanation for the various provisions.

 The Artwork Permission Agreement is included on the forms disk that comes with this book under the file name ARTPERM.

Artwork Permission Agreement

_____ ("Licensor") is the owner of rights for the artwork described below (the "Selection"). _____ ("Licensee") wants to acquire the right to use the Selection as specified in this agreement (the "Agreement").

Licensor Information

Title of work (the "Selection"): _____

Catalog number (if applicable): _____

Artist: _____

Licensee Publication Information

The Selection will appear in the following publication(s) (the "Work"):

(check if applicable and fill in blanks)

☐ book—title: _____

☐ periodical—title: _____

☐ event handout—title of event: _____

☐ diskette–title: _____

☐ website—URL: _____

If to be used on a website, the Selection will appear on:

(check if applicable)

☐ home page

☐ internal page

Name of publisher or sponsor (if different from Licensee): _____

Estimated date(s) of publication or: _____

If applicable, the estimated number of copies to be printed or produced (if a book, the estimated first print run): _____

If for sale, the price: $ _____

If copies are free to attendees of a program, cost of program: _____

If a website, indicate the average number of visitors per month: _____

Grant of Rights

Licensor grants to Licensee and Licensee's successors and assigns, the:

(select one)

☐   nonexclusive

☐   exclusive

right to reproduce and distribute the Selection in:

(select all that apply)

☐   the current edition of the Work.

☐   all editions of the Work.

☐   all foreign language versions of the Work.

☐   all derivative versions of the Work.

☐   in all media now known or later devised.

☐   in promotional materials published and distributed in conjunction with the Work.

☐   other rights _____

Territory

The rights granted under this Agreement shall be for _____ (the "Territory").

Fees

Licensee shall pay Licensor as follows:

(select payment option and fill in blanks)

☐   **Flat Fee.** As full payment for all rights granted, Licensee shall pay Licensor a flat fee of:

    $ _____ . Payment shall be made:

    ☐   upon execution of this Agreement.

    ☐   upon publication.

☐   **Royalties and Advance.** Licensee agrees to pay Licensor a royalty of____% of Net Sales. Net Sales are defined as gross sales (the gross invoice amount billed customers) less quantity discounts and returns actually credited. Licensee agrees to pay Licensor an advance against royalties of $_____ upon execution of this Agreement. Licensee shall pay Licensor within thirty

(30) days of the end of each quarter. Licensee shall furnish an accurate statement of sales during that quarter. Licensor shall have the right to inspect Licensee's books upon reasonable notice.

Credit & Samples

(check if applicable and fill in blanks)

[ ] **Credit.** All versions of the Work that include the Selection shall contain the following statement: _____

[ ] **Samples.** Upon publication, Licensee shall furnish _____ copies of the Work to Licensor.

Warranty

Licensor warrants that it has the right to grant permission for the uses of the Selection as specified above and that the Selection does not infringe the rights of any third parties.

(check if applicable)

[ ] Licensor warrants that a model release is on file for the Selection.

Miscellaneous

This Agreement may not be amended except in a written document signed by both parties. If a court finds any provision of this Agreement invalid or unenforceable, the remainder of this Agreement shall be interpreted so as best to effect the intent of the parties. This Agreement shall be governed by and interpreted in accordance with the laws of the State of _____. This Agreement expresses the complete understanding of the parties with respect to the subject matter and supersedes all prior representations and understandings.

Licensor	Licensee
By: _____	By: _____
Name: _____	Name: _____
Title: _____	Title: _____
Address: _____	Address: _____
Date: _____	Date: _____
	Tax ID # _____

2. Explanation for Artwork Permission Agreement

- In the introductory paragraph, insert the names of the licensor (the party who owns the material) and the licensee (you or the person who is seeking permission).
- In the Licensor Information and Licensee Publication Information section, complete the blank spaces to describe the artwork you want to use, and the work in which you plan to use it.
- In the Grant of Rights section, complete the grant to reflect the rights that you have negotiated. More information on the rights associated with grants is provided in Chapter 11, "Art & Merchandise Licenses."
- Complete the Territory section to reflect the regions in which you are acquiring rights. For more help, review Chapter 11, Section C7.
- In the Fees section, indicate what type of fee has been negotiated, check the appropriate boxes and complete the information.
- Complete the Credit and Samples section to reflect your agreement with the licensor.
- As we explain in Chapter 11, Section C11, a warranty is a contractual promise made by the licensor. Some licensors do not want to make promises, particularly a promise that the work does not infringe any third parties' copyright or other rights. You may have to modify the Warranty section or strike it entirely if the licensor objects.
- If you have the bargaining power, you may want to include an indemnity provision in the agreement. Indemnity is a financial punishment if the licensor breaks its promises. We have not included any indemnity provisions here. If you wish to add such a provision, samples and explanations are provided in Chapter 11, Section C11.
- Explanations for the Miscellaneous or "boilerplate" provisions are provided in Chapter 11, Section C22). If you have the bargaining power, you may want to include an attorney fees or an arbitration provision.

Commercial endorsements may involve more complex issues. If you are seeking permission to use artwork on behalf of an advertising agency or a company selling a product or service (for example, Nike or American Airlines), your use is more likely to be categorized as a commercial endorsement which will trigger additional legal issues. Review Chapter 12, Section B, regarding the releases that may be required.

3. Using Artwork in Film and Video

Motion pictures, television programs and videos often include artwork such as a painting, poster, photograph or sculpture. As a general rule, permission should be obtained if the artwork is recognizable with sufficient detail so that the average viewer can clearly see the work.

For example, the appearance of a copyrighted poster in a television show for a total of 27 seconds required permission from the copyright owner. *(Ringgold v. Black Entertainment Television,* 126 F.3d 70 (2d Cir. 1997).) On the other hand, in a different case a court ruled that if the artwork appears fleetingly, is obscured, out of focus or virtually unidentifiable, permission is not required because the use is too small (or "de minimus"). *(Sandoval v. New Line Cinema Corp.,* 147 F.3d 215 (2d Cir. 1998).) For an analysis of fair use factors, see Chapter 9, "Fair Use."

If you perform clearance on a regular basis for motion pictures, television or video, review *Clearance and Copyright: Everything the Independent Filmmaker Needs to Know,* by Michael C. Donaldson (Silman-James Press).

Below is a basic permission agreement for using art within a motion picture. A tearout copy of this form is in the Appendix at the end of this book. A digital version is on the forms disk.

The Agreement to Use Artwork in a Motion Picture is on the forms disk under the file name ARTFILM.

Agreement to Use Artwork in Motion Picture

_____ ("Licensor") is the owner of rights for the artwork described below (the "Selection"). _____ ("Licensee") wants to acquire the right to use the Artwork as specified in this agreement (the "Agreement").

Use of the Artwork

The Artwork will appear in:

(choose one)

- [ ] motion picture
- [ ] television program
- [ ] music video
- [ ] other:
- [ ] entitled _____ (the "Picture").

Grant of Rights

Licensor grants to Licensee and Licensee's successors and assigns, the nonexclusive worldwide right (but not the obligation) to include the Artwork in the Picture for the unlimited distribution, advertising and promotion of the Picture in all languages and in all forms or devices now known or later devised. This use includes, but is not limited to, use of the Artwork in foreign language versions of the Picture, advertising, publicity or trailers of the Picture and music videos derived from the Picture.

Limitations on Use

Licensee will use the Artwork in a manner that is consistent with the general practices of the television and motion picture industry. Licensee will not materially alter the Artwork or depict it in any manner that conflicts with the restrictions below, without the consent of Licensor.

Restrictions: _____

Fees

As full payment for all rights granted, Licensee shall pay Licensor a flat fee of $_____. Payment shall be made upon execution of this agreement.

Credit

The Picture shall include the following credit for the Artwork: _____

Warranty & Release

Licensor warrants that it has the right to grant permission for use of the Artwork as specified above and that the Artwork does not infringe upon the rights of any third parties. Licensor waives any claims, known or unknown, arising out of Licensee's use of the Artwork. In the event that Licensee breaches this agreement, Licensor's relief shall be limited to damages and Licensor shall not be entitled to injunctive or equitable relief.

Miscellaneous

This Agreement may not be amended except in a written document signed by both parties. If a court finds any provision of this Agreement invalid or unenforceable, the remainder of this Agreement shall be interpreted so as best to effect the intent of the parties. This Agreement shall be governed by and interpreted in accordance with the laws of the State of_____ . This Agreement expresses the complete understanding of the parties with respect to the subject matter and supersedes all prior representations and understandings.

Licensor	Licensee
By:_____	By:_____
Name:_____	Name:_____
Title:_____	Title:_____
Address:_____	Address:_____
Date:_____	Date:_____
	Tax ID #_____

4. Explanation for Film and Video License Agreement

- In the introductory paragraph, insert the names of the licensor (the person or company who owns the copyright in the artwork) and the licensee (the person producing the motion picture or the authorized representative of the production company).
- In the Use of the Artwork section, indicate the type of program in which the artwork will appear, and the title of the program.
- The first sentence of the Grant of Rights section is intended to prevent any problems in the event that the scene with the artwork ends up on the cutting room floor. Our agreement grants the filmmaker broad rights—for example, to use the artwork in advertising and promotion. This means that additional permissions will not be required from the copyright owner of the artwork. More information on the concept of license grants is provided in Chapter 11, Section C4.
- If the copyright owner wants to place some limitations on use, they belong in the Limitations on Use section. The owner may write in a restriction such as "Artwork shall not be used in any scene depicting nudity or sexual activity."
- In the Fees section, indicate the fee amount, if any, that has been negotiated.
- Complete the Credit section if it applies.
- As we explain in Section C11 of Chapter 11, a warranty is a contractual promise made by the licensor. It's a promise that the the licensor does in fact have the rights to license the artwork, and that a the licensee won't be liable to a third party (for example, another artist) who claims that the artwork was ripped off. The waiver of claims is intended to prevent the licensor from subsequently claiming that the use violated some undisclosed right—for example, the use violated the artist's moral rights. There is also a limitation on the licensor's potential relief. If the film-

maker breaches the agreement—for example, fails to pay for the use—the licensor can sue for payment. However, the licensor cannot seek to prevent the release of the film.

- Explanations for the Miscellaneous or "boilerplate" provisions are provided in Chapter 11. You may want to include an attorney fees or arbitration provision (see Chapter 11, Section C22).

H. Artwork Resources

The following resources can assist in various aspects of the permissions process for fine art and graphic art.

1. Fine Art Resources

- Visual Artists and Galleries Association (VAGA): 350 Fifth Avenue, Ste. 6305, New York NY 10118; 212-736-6666, fax 212-736-6767. Email: rpanzer.vaga@erols.com.
- Artists' Rights Societies (ARS), a division of Art Resource: 65 Bleecker Street, 9th Floor, New York, NY 10012; 212-505-8700; email: requests@artres.co; Web: www.artres.com.

2. Online Fine Art Image Resources

The following websites provide access to a variety of fine art images:

- Gallery Guide Online: www.galleryguide.com/content/current/.
- Yahoo!: dir.yahoo.com/Arts/ Museums__Galleries__and_Centers/.
- America Online: type "Image Exchange" and go to "Museums and Exhibits Online."
- Image Directory: www.imagedir.com.
- Corbis: www.corbisview.com.
- Archive Photo: www.history.com.
- Stock Photo Deskbook: www.stockphotodeskbook.com.

- Paula Berinstein's Research Site: www.berinsteinresearch.com.
- Corel Corporation: www.corel.com or www.clipartdownload.com.
- World Art Treasures: sgwww.epfl.ch/berger/index.html.

3. Graphic Arts Resources

- Graphic Artists Guild: www.gag.org or write to GAG, 90 John Street, Suite 403, New York NY 10038; 800-878-2753.
- Society of Children's Book Writers and Illustrators (SCBWI): 345 No. Maple Drive #29, Beverly Hills, CA 90210; 310-859-9887; Web: www.scbwi.org.

4. Cartoon Resources

- Cartoonbank: 382 Warburton Avenue, Hastings on Hudson, NY 10706; 800-897-8666; Web: www.cartoonbank.com.
- The National Cartoonists Society: P.O. Box 20267, Columbus Circle Station, New York, NY 10023; 212-627-1550; Web: www.reuben.org/main.htm.
- The Association of American Editorial Cartoonists: Web: www.detnews.com/AAEC/AAEC.html.
- Politicalcartoons.com: Web: www.politcalcartoons.com.
- The Professional Cartoonist's Index: Web: www.cagle.com.

5. Comic Book Resources

- Marvel Comics: Marvel Entertainment Group, Inc., 387 Park Avenue South, New York, NY 10016; 212-576-8510, fax 212-576-9260; email: mail@marvel.com; Web: www.marvel.com.

- DC Comics and Mad Magazine: 1700 Broadway, New York, NY 10019; 212-636-5946, fax 212-636-5401; Web: www.dccomics.com.
- Harvey Comics: Harvey Comics Entertainment, 1999 Avenue of the Stars, #2050, Los Angeles, CA 90067-6068; 310-789-1190, fax 310-789-1191; Web: www.harvey.com.

6. Comic Syndicates

- King Features Syndicate: 235 E. 45th Street, New York, NY 10017; 212-455-4000, fax 212-682 9763 (reprints); email: kfs-us-licensingsales@hearst.com; Web: www.kingfeatures.com.
- United Media: 200 Park Avenue, New York, NY 10166; 800-221-4816 or 212-293-8500; Web: www.comiczone.com.
- Universal Press Syndicate: Permissions Director, Andrews McMeel Universal, 4520 Main Street, Kansas City, MO 64111-7701; 800-255-6734, fax 816-932-6684; email: msuggett@uexpress.com; Web: www.uexpress.com.
- Tribune Media Services Inc.: 435 No. Michigan Avenue, #1500, Chicago, IL 60611; 312-222-4444, fax 312-222-2581; Web: www.tms.tribune.com.
- Creators Syndicate, Inc.: 5777 W. Century Boulevard, # 700, Los Angeles, CA 90045-5677; 310-337-7003, fax 310-337-7625; Web: www.creators.com.
- Los Angeles Times Syndicate: 2 Park Avenue, Floor 18, New York, NY 10016-5675; 212-447-1450, fax 212-447-1455; Web: www.newscom.com (note: there is a fee to view the site).
- The Washington Post Writers Group: 1150 15th Street, NW, Washington, DC 20071-9200; 202-334-5666 (call 703-469-2504 for website uses), fax 202-334-7862; email: writersgrp@wshpoStreet.com.
- The Copley Press, Inc.: 800-238-6196.
- Ctoons: Web: www.ctoons.com.

7. Medical Image Resources

- Association of Medical Illustrators: 1819 Peachtree Street NE, Suite 620, Atlanta, GA 30309; 404-350-7900. email: assnhq@mindspring.com.
- Williams & Wilkins Mediclip: Web: www.lifeart.com.
- Custom Medical Stock Photo: The Custom Medical Building, Suite 100, 3660 West Irving Park Road, Chicago, IL 60618-4132; Web: www.cmsp.com.

8. Picture Researchers

- American Society of Picture Professionals: 409 So. Washington Street, Alexandria, VA 22314; 703-299-0219; email: aspp1@idsonline.com; Web: www.aspp.com.

9. Print Resources for Finding Artwork

- *Finding Images Online*, by Paula Berinstein (Pemberton Press).
- *Practical Picture Research*, by Hilary Evans (Routledge-Blueprint).

10. Smithsonian Institution

The resources below can assist in locating images affiliated with the Smithsonian Institution.

- Smithsonian Archives: A&I 2135, Washington, DC 20560-0414; 202-357-1420, fax 202-57-2395; email: osiaref@osia.si.edu; Web: www.si.edu.
- Graphic Services: The Office of Imaging offers a cross-section of the Smithsonian's photos in a Web database at photo2.si.edu. You can find the rules for use at www.si.edu/siphotos/CAPTIONS/oppsrules.html.
- Smithsonian Institution Research Information System (SIRIS): www.siris.si.edu. At this site you can search the holdings of the Smithsonian Institution Libraries, several Smithsonian archival repositories and other special collections areas.
- Yahoo! Smithsonian Internet directory: dir.yahoo.com/Government/U_S__Government/Agencies/Independent/Smithsonian_Institution/.

■

Getting Permission to Use Music

This chapter discusses common music permission situations, describes the options and fees for acquiring music rights and offers suggestions for locating and dealing with music copyright owners. Acquiring rights for music is often easier than for text or artwork because there are standardized fees and license agreements for most music uses. For example, in some cases, a music owner must permit a use if a fee is paid. It is also easier to track down the copyright owner of music and license rights because there are clearance services and organizations that assist in acquiring rights.

Despite the ease with music can be licensed, the fees are not always predictable and can escalate beyond similar text or artwork uses. In some cases, owners of music copyright are less receptive to permissions and refuse to negotiate. And with music, there's an additional copyright twist. Every musical recording includes two copyrights: one for the song or musical composition itself and the other for the particular recording of the song. Acquiring permission for music often means that you must obtain the permission of both of these copyright owners.

A. Acquiring Rights to Music

Music rights are generally acquired in one of the following ways:

- **Assignment or work-for-hire agreement.** If a musician or composer is hired to create music for a specific purpose—for example, a computer game—the music rights are transferred to the hiring party by an assignment or work made for hire agreement. An assignment is a transfer of ownership of the copyright in the music. A work made for hire arrangement occurs when the person paying for the music (the hiring party) acquires ownership because of an employer-employee relationship or through an independent contractor agreement. A sample assignment and an explanation regarding works made for hire is provided in Chapter 15. Under an assignment or work made for hire agreement, the company paying for the work becomes the owner of all music rights.

- **License.** If music already exists and is not created for a specific purpose—for example a Beatles song—the music rights are acquired by a license. This chapter explains how to license music and lyrics. We provide tips on determining the fees and finding the owner of a song or recording and provide typical license agreements for the use of music or lyrics in books, magazines, movies, videos, commercials, software, live performances, at businesses and in websites.

- **Production music.** Stock or generic music is available from production music libraries (known as PMLs), who provide pre-recorded compositions for fixed fees, blanket fees (for multiple uses) or per-use fees. Companies whose budgets prohibit hiring musicians or licensing popular music commonly use PML music for background and theme purposes. PMLs are discussed in Section B5.

If you are seeking permission to use music in conjunction with merchandise, review Chapter 11, "Art & Merchandise Licenses."

If performing music clearance on a regular basis, consult *Kohn on Music Licensing,* by Al Kohn and Bob Kohn (Aspen Law & Business), which provides a complete collection of music licensing agreements.

B. Song and Sound Recording Copyrights

This section explains the distinction between the two forms of copyright that protect music: song copyrights and sound recording copyrights.

Two copyrights exist when a song is recorded: 1) a song copyright, usually owned by a music publisher, and 2) a sound recording copyright, usually owned by a record company. The song copyright protects the words and music of the song. The sound recording copyright protects the musical performance and audio sound of the recording of the song. As we explain below, if you want to use a recorded song, permission is required from both the song and sound recording copyright owners.

1. Song Copyrights and Music Publishers

The songwriter is the initial owner of the song copyright. The only exception is if the songwriter writes songs as part of a job, in which case the employer would own the songs. Songwriters usually transfer their copyrights to music publishers who own and manage collections of songs. A music publisher may be a large multi-national company or a one-person operation run by the songwriter.

What Do Music Publishers Do?

A music publisher acts like a business agent for the songwriter, promoting songs, administering income from song licensing and paying the songwriter a royalty. The title "music publisher" refers to early days of the music business when the primary source of income for songwriters was the publication of sheet music. The concept of using music publishers has become so ingrained in the music business that in order to earn money from songs, a songwriter must either sell or license his or her rights to an established music publisher, or create his or her own music publishing business.

2. When Permission is Required From a Music Publisher

There are several common situations in which permission is required from a music publisher, including:

- when sheet music is reproduced
- when song lyrics are reproduced, and
- when a song is released on a recording, played publicly, used in an audiovisual work (such as a movie), or used in a digital format such as an MP3 music file.

Fortunately, some of these activities (such as releasing a recording or playing a song publicly) involve a streamlined process and fixed fees. For other activities, such as using music in a movie, there are no fixed fees and the costs can be quite high.

a. Reproducing Sheet Music or Lyrics

Permission is required from the music publisher when reproducing sheet music or song lyrics. The only exceptions to this rule would be if the song were in the public domain (see Chapter 8) or if your use qualifies as a fair use (see Chapter 9). In Section C we describe the procedure for reprinting sheet music and lyrics.

b. Songs Released on Recordings

Permission is required from the music publisher when a song is sold on an audio-only recording such as a compact disc or cassette recording. A fee must also be paid to the music publisher for recording and selling a song it owns. This payment is referred to as a mechanical royalty (the principles of mechanical royalty payments are further discussed in Section E). Music publishers either collect this money directly or delegate the responsibility to the Harry Fox Agency, an organization that negotiates and collects mechanical royalties. Information about contacting the Harry Fox Agency is provided at the end of this chapter.

c. Songs Played Publicly

Permission is required from the music publisher when songs are played in public—such as on the radio, television, at businesses, in concerts or at clubs. For example, radio stations must pay the music publisher that owns a particular song in order to play it on the air. The fees for these uses are referred to as performance royalties. Generally, radio stations, clubs and other places that play music regularly obtain blanket licenses instead of getting permission and paying the fee each time they play a song. The licenses are granted by performing rights societies such as BMI and ASCAP who execute the agreements, collect the fees and monitor performances on behalf of music publishers. Section D discusses this process in more detail.

What Is a Public Performance?

Public performances of music require permission from the music publisher; private performances do not. To perform a work publicly means that music is played at a place open to the public or where a substantial number of people outside the normal circle of a family and social acquaintances are gathered. The fact that a performance is not for profit does not affect this determination.

Transmission of music by a radio or television station is also a public performance. It does not matter if the public receives the music at the same time or place as when it was transmitted. For example, if one station transmits a work and another station receives the broadcast and re-transmits it later, the re-transmission would be a performance. Webcasting or audio streaming, the process of transmitting music over the Internet in real-time, is also considered a public performance (see Section I3).

Examples of public performance include:

- a disc jockey playing a record in a nightclub
- a band playing music during half-time at a football game
- a singer performing a song in a nightclub
- a business playing music through the office loudspeaker system
- a radio station playing music over the air
- a website webcasting music
- a television station broadcasting a television show containing music, and
- a cable company receiving a television station broadcast containing music and rebroadcasting it via cable transmission.

See Section D for more information on obtaining permission to play songs publicly.

d. Songs Used in Audiovisual Works

Permission is required from the music publisher to use music in a movie, television show or commercial or video. This is referred to as a synchronization license or a videogram license, depending on the use, and is either negotiated through the Harry Fox Agency or directly by the music publisher. More information about synchronization licenses is provided in Section G.

e. Songs Used in Digital Formats

Permission is required from the music publisher to upload, download and broadcast (sometimes referred to as webcasting or audio streaming) songs over the Internet. Depending on the use, permission agreements for digital uses are negotiated by the Harry Fox Agency, performing rights societies or directly by the music publisher. In Section I, information is provided about the rules regarding digital copies of songs.

3. Sound Recording Copyrights and Record Companies

Besides the copyright in the song composition itself, each recorded version of it (often referred to as a "master") is protected by a sound recording copyright. In other words, a sound recording is a separate and distinct work from the musical composition that is being performed. Since a song can be recorded in many different styles and arrangements, each recording is a record of the performance of the composition and as such is entitled to its own separate copyright protection. For example, the hundreds of different recorded versions of "White Christmas" are each protected by separate sound recording copyrights, while the song itself is protected by a single song copyright.

Generally speaking, the first owners of a sound recording are the individuals who created it, including the musicians, arrangers and producer of the recording session. More commonly, however, a musician or band signs a recording agreement, giving the record company the rights to the sound recording. Even without an official recording agreement, if somebody hires the musicians and recording engineers to record the songs, the employer would be the initial owner.

4. When Permission Is Required From a Record Company

When using a sound recording, permission is required from the record company in the following situations:

- **Duplicating or sampling a sound recording.** Examples of sound recording duplication include copying a compact disc or portion of it to cassette, using a sample in another recording, using a pop song in a video or motion picture soundtrack, or converting a sound recording into a digital format such as an MP3 file.
- **Digital broadcasting.** Digital broadcasting includes making a sound recording available over the Internet or over a cable music service. Section I provides more information on digital broadcasting.

Permission is not required from the record company (but well may be required from the music publisher, see Section A above) to reprint music or lyrics, to record the same song or to play or broadcast a recording—for example, on the radio or at a club, dance studio or retail business. (Note, this applies only to performances in the U.S. In some countries, permission is required from the record company to broadcast sound recordings.)

When contacting a record company for permission to use its recording, ask for the licensing or special markets department. Most record companies are prepared to issue the licenses described in this chapter and will furnish license agreements, usually known as "master use" licenses. More detailed information on getting permission to use copyrighted recordings is covered in Sections L and N. Information about locating record companies is included in the resources section at the end of this chapter.

5. Using Production Music Libraries

Production music libraries (PMLs) provide an inexpensive method of obtaining rights for original music and sound effects on a nonexclusive basis. PML music, which is primarily instrumental, is used in films, websites, slide shows, radio and television programming, commercials, software and multimedia, training videos, in-flight services and similar applications.

Like stock photography, PML music is categorized by genre or mood (old-time rock and roll, outer space, etc.) and is sold on compact disc collections on a royalty-free, blanket fee or per-use basis. A typical PML compact disc may contain ten to 15 original compositions, including a full-length version of each composition as well as shorter "tag" or "cue" version. Larger PMLs have hundreds of compact discs in their collections. Using the Internet, you can search through many of these collections and hear samples.

Since the PML owns music publishing and sound recording rights, obtaining permission to use the recordings is simple. A typical PML license permits use for most synchronization purposes, such as using the music in a film or software program. However, the PML license does not permit use of the music in audio recordings sold to the public. For example, while PML music may be used in a film, it cannot be sold to consumers in a commercial soundtrack album without special permission from the PML. PMLs generally prohibit the use of the music unless it is used in conjunction with other audio or visual elements. These limitations are usually expressed in the PML license as follows:

> The music may be used only in synchronization or mechanical reproduction with other audio and/or visual elements. The licensee must obtain prior written permission and negotiate a separate license if licensee intends to repackage or alter the music and make it available as commercial soundtracks or videos.

There are three methods of acquiring rights for PML music:

- Blanket agreements in which the user obtains unlimited use of all PML music on a compact disc or disc library for a specified time period, such as two years. If continued use is required, the license is renewed. Blanket licenses may range from several hundred dollars to four or five thousand dollars per year.
- Per-use agreements in which payments are made as compositions are used in a production. This method of payment is sometimes referred to as a "needle drop," in reference to the days of vinyl recordings when a radio or film producer paid each time the needle was dropped onto a piece of music. Per-use fees depend on the length and type of use and can range from $50 for a five-minute use in a local television show to $500 for the same music in a feature film.
- Buyout agreements in which the purchaser acquires unlimited rights by purchasing the PML's compact disc. Fees for buyout rights range from $50 to several thousand dollars.

PMLs offer a variety of fees and payment plans, making it possible to negotiate discounts based on use. Fees are often based on an estimate of per-unit sales. A list of PMLs is provided at the end of this chapter in the resources section.

Bypassing Sound Recording Rights

It's often more difficult to get permission from a record company than a music publisher. One reason is that record companies are obligated to many people, including recording artists and union musicians who receive a re-use fee for certain licensed uses of the master. Some record companies don't want to bother with master licensing unless there is a return of at least several thousand dollars.

This is one reason why many production companies pay for songs to be re-recorded instead of getting permission from a record company to use an existing recording. When this is done, permission is required only from the music publisher, not from the record company. Re-recorded sound recording masters may also be available from production music libraries on a one-time flat fee buyout basis (see Section B5).

It is not an infringement of the sound recording copyright to re-record a song so that it sounds exactly like the original recording. However, there may be other legal limitations. A performer's style cannot be imitated when the recording is used to sell a product or service or to sell recordings that confuse the public into believing they are buying the original recording. (See "Performer Rights" below.)

Researching Song and Sound Recordings in the Copyright Office

Song copyrights are registered in the Copyright Office using Form PA (performing arts). Sound recording copyrights are registered in the Copyright Office using Form SR (sound recording). Sound recording copyrights exist only for recordings created after 1971, before which sound recordings were protected by state laws. (See Chapter 13, "Copyright Research.")

Performer Rights

Under a legal principle known as the right of publicity, a performer's permission is required if his or her image, name or style is used to sell a product or service. Permission is also needed to imitate a performer's style if the imitation is likely to cause the public to believe that the performer is affiliated with or endorses a product. For example, an auto company was found liable for infringing the right of publicity when it imitated, without permission, the singing style of Bette Midler. A snack food company was similarly found liable for using an imitation of Tom Waits. If the performer is dead, you're not off the hook—in many states, permission is required from the performer's estate. For more information on rights of publicity and performer releases, see Chapter 12, "Releases."

Permission from a performer is also required to make an audio or video recording of a live performance or to distribute recordings of the performance. If the performer has signed an exclusive recording agreement with a record company, permission is required from the record company. These rules are based on copyright laws located in Section 1101 of the Copyright Act.

C. Reprinting Music or Lyrics

You may need permission to reprint music notation or lyrics, such as quoting lyrics at a website or reprinting music and lyrics in an instructional text. In these cases, you are not actually reproducing the sound of the music, only providing the words or musical notation. For that reason, you only need permission from the music publisher that owns copyright in the composition, not from any record company that may own a sound recording copyright for the song.

Generally, permission from the music publisher is required to reprint all or part of sheet music or lyrics. The fees for such uses are not fixed, so a music publisher can charge whatever the market will bear. In most cases, the fees are reasonable, such as $50 to reprint lyrics in a book. Below we discuss some common reprint situations and fees. You'll find information about locating music publishers in Section K.

Reprinting Lyrics Without Permission

In 1998, it was common to find websites such as the International Lyrics Server (ILS) devoted to reproducing pop music lyrics. Users could search these databases by title or artist and locate complete lyrics for thousands of songs. By 1999, most of these sites were closed because of failure to acquire permission. According to a message at the ILS site, the police confiscated the company's computers and the National Music Publishers' Association filed suit against the owners. (The ILS hopes to settle the lawsuit, acquire permission and return to its site, www.lyrics.ch.) Operators of websites featuring lyric databases should be aware that posting unauthorized lyrics may subject them to legal action.

1. Music and Lyric Reproduction

Music and lyrics are commonly sold as unbound sheet music, featuring piano notation, guitar chords and lyrics printed below the corresponding music. Sheet music is also sold or licensed in folios (collections of sheet music bound into a volume), fakebooks (a folio with hundreds of songs) or educational editions (sheet music for use in school instruction arranged for school performances). You'll also often find sheet music reproduced in specialty magazines, instructional booklets for musicians and on websites. Lyrics are often reproduced separately (without musical notation) for use in websites, books, greeting cards, advertisements and magazines.

Occasionally, music publishers permit the use of a few lyric lines for free, but more often they will charge a fee, as described below. To reproduce music and lyrics, contact the music publisher using the methods described in Section K. The reproduction of lyrics for a karaoke recording may require a synchronization license. This type of license is explained in Section G.

Also keep in mind that if a music publisher grants permission to record a song as explained in Section E, do not assume that also includes the right to reprint the lyrics, such as printing them in the liner notes to the compact disc booklet. Permission to print the lyrics must be acquired separately.

Don't assume that because sheet music is out of print that it is available for use. Unless it is in the public domain, sheet music is still protected under copyright law. (See Chapter 8 for an explanation of public domain rules). If you want to reproduce out-of-print sheet music, contact the Music Publisher Association (www.mpa.org/copyright/searchenter.html), as they have a procedure for locating and using out-of-print copyrighted music.

EXAMPLE: Our goal was to reproduce four lines from the song "Sneakers on a Rooster" performed by Bo Diddley. By searching online we determined that BMI is the performing rights society that represents the song. BMI provided contact information for the publisher, including an email address. We emailed the publisher, who okayed the request without requiring a fee. The publisher did provide a credit line for us to include with the use.

The clothes I buy for you is what I thought you always wanted
But the ones you buy for me, they feel like they're haunted
Girl I hope your love changes in the future

Cause lovin' you is like putting sneakers on a rooster.

"Sneakers on a Rooster," written by Sam Dees & David Camon. Lyrics reproduced courtesy of Ginn Music Group, Atlanta, Georgia.

2. Fees

Fees to reproduce music notation or lyrics vary quite widely depending on the use. Below are some general guidelines on what various uses may cost.

- Expect to pay $25 or more for the use of lyrics (or a portion of the lyrics) in a book or magazine.
- Fees for use of lyrics in a website may range from $50 to $1,000, depending on the site and how much traffic it gets. Fees for using lyrics in advertising depend on the type of advertisement, length of use and the territory in which the ad will appear. Fees range from several hundred to several thousand dollars per year.
- For use of lyrics in a greeting card or other merchandise, music publishers seek a royalty usually between 2% to 5% of the retail price of the merchandise.
- If music and lyrics are reprinted as part of a folio or educational publication, music publishers usually seek a royalty between 10% and 15% of the wholesale price. If the song is one of several within a publication the royalty is often pro-rated. Under a pro-rata arrangement, a music publisher would, for example, receive 1/10 of the royalty if it provided one of ten songs.
- Music publishers commonly charge $0.02 per copy to reproduce lyrics on liner notes, so that the cost to print lyrics on the liner notes of 1,000 copies would be $20.
- Fees for miscellaneous uses typically depend on the length of use, the popularity of the song—and often the publisher's whim.

Under limited conditions, music instructors are permitted to copy portions of sheet music and recordings without permission. For example, under fair use guidelines, a music instructor can copy excerpts of sheet music, provided that the excerpts do not constitute a "performable unit" such as a whole song, section, movement or aria. In no case can more than 10% of the whole work be copied and the number of copies may not exceed one copy per pupil. See Chapter 7, Section B, for more information on educational uses.

3. Lyric Permission Letter Agreement

Most publishers furnish a short license agreement or letter for use of lyrics. Some may okay the use on the telephone. If an oral "okay" is granted, follow it up with a letter confirming the arrangement, or use the Lyric Permission Letter Agreement below. This agreement is provided in the Appendix and on the forms disk. If you're seeking to use lyrics on merchandise such as a greeting card or poster, use the agreement provided in Chapter 11, "Art & Merchandise Licenses."

The Lyric Permission Letter Agreement is included on the forms disk in the back of this book under the file name LYRPRMLT.

Lyric Permission Letter Agreement

To _____ ("Music Publisher"):

I am writing to you to obtain permission to reprint portions of the lyrics (the "Lyrics") from the song _____ , written by _____ on behalf of _____ ("Licensee").

The lyrics will appear in the following publication(s) (the "Work"):

(check if applicable and fill in blanks)

☐ Book Use

Book title: _____

Name of publisher or sponsor: _____

Author(s): _____

ISBN: _____

Estimated date(s) of publication: _____

Estimated number of copies to be printed or produced (if a book, the estimated first print run): _____

Language editions: _____

Territory of publication: _____

Estimated price: $ _____

☐ Magazine

Magazine title: _____

Volume, issue, ISSN: _____

Estimated date of publication: _____

Circulation: _____

☐ Website

URL: _____

Name of publisher or sponsor: _____

Estimated dates of use: _____

Estimated visitors per day: _____

☐ Other (describe): _____

_____

Fee

Licensee shall pay a fee of $ _____ to Music Publisher at the following address: _____ upon publication of the Work or within 6 months of executing this Agreement, whichever is earlier.

Samples

Upon publication, Licensee shall furnish _____ copies of the Work to Music Publisher.

Credit

The following credit shall be included with the Work: _____

Signed by Licensee _____

Name: _____

Title: _____

Address: _____

Date: _____

Music Publisher's Approval of Request

Music Publisher warrants that it is the owner of rights for the lyrics and has the right to grant the permission to republish the lyrics as specified above. This license is for the nonexclusive worldwide right to republish the lyrics in all editions of the Work.

Signed by Music Publisher _____

Name: _____

Title: _____

Address: _____

Date: _____

4. Explanation for Lyric Permission Letter Agreement

This letter agreement should be used after you have contacted the music publisher and discussed the conditions of the use, the number of samples, the credit and the fee, if any. Once these details have been agreed upon, you should place that information in the agreement.

- Insert the names of the music publisher (generally, a company name), the song, the songwriter and the person who has responsibility for acquiring permission ("Licensee"). The licensee may be you; or, if you're acquiring permission on behalf of someone else, such as a publisher or employer, list that person or entity.
- In the next paragraphs, indicate where the reproduced lyrics will appear (book, magazine, website or other), and provide information about the fee, number of samples and any required credit (for example, "Lyrics by Kevin Teare reprinted courtesy of Electric Ladybug Music, Copyright 1999").
- Provide your address and sign the agreement.
- The Music Publisher's Approval of Request is an assurance that the music publisher has the legal ability to grant the rights in the agreement. A representative of the music publisher signs and dates this provision and provides his or her name and title at the company.
- It is possible that the music publisher will seek modifications in this agreement. For example, the music publisher may want to limit your rights to a specific print run of a book or for a specific time period at a website. If necessary, modify the Grant section to reflect your agreement with the music publisher.
- You may need more rights than provided by the standard language of this agreement—for example, rights for foreign translations, derivative rights and rights in all media. Either specify the additional rights needed or strike the last sentence of Music Publisher's Ap-

proval of Request and replace it with the broader grant of rights provided below. Be aware that a music publisher may object to the terms of a broad request, causing a delay in the permissions process.

I grant Licensee's successors, licensees and assigns, the nonexclusive worldwide right to republish the lyrics in all editions of the Work and in all versions derived from the Work in all media now known or hereafter devised.

Arranging a Copyrighted Musical Composition

Musical arrangements or orchestrations of copyrighted musical compositions are considered to be derivative works and cannot be used without permission. For example, if you intend to write and reproduce an arrangement of the Elvis song "Heartbreak Hotel," you will need permission from the music publisher. When we refer to an arrangement, we are referring to substantial modifications in the song such as intricate harmonies or re-workings of rhythm and chord structure. For an example of a sample request form and for more information on licensing for arrangements, see the "Request for Permission to Arrange" section of the Music Publisher's Association website (www.mpa.org/copyright/searchenter.html).

5. Using Lyrics Without Permission

If the music publisher cannot be located or permission is denied, the use of small portions of lyrics without permission may qualify as a fair use. Fair use rules for copyrighted materials are based in free speech principles. Permission is not required to use portions of a work if the use is for purposes of education, parody or disseminating a critical point of view. Unfortunately, there are no quantitative rules as to how many song lyrics can be used to qualify as fair use. However, if the following factors are present, your reproduction is more likely to be allowed without permission:

- the use is limited—for example, four lines or less
- the use is to comment upon or parody the song
- the music publisher is not deprived of income by the use, and
- a reasonable effort was made to locate the music publisher and secure permission.

The last factor, seeking permission, is not a necessity to qualify for fair use, but some courts have suggested that it demonstrates good faith. Fair use factors are discussed in more detail, along with real life examples, in Chapter 9, "Fair Use."

D. Playing Music at a Business or Event

As a general rule, when music is performed publicly at a business or event, permission must be obtained only from the music publisher. Remember, public performance encompasses more than just a musician playing a song (see Sidebar in Section B1); it also means the playing of recorded music. This means that permission is required for a disc jockey to play recordings either at a club or on the radio. Such permission is usually not granted directly by the music publisher, but instead by performing rights societies who handle the process on behalf of the music publishers. This process is described in more detail below.

EXAMPLE: The Emeryville Hotel plays tape recordings of popular music in its lobby. The hotel needs a blanket license from the performing rights societies for the public performance of the songs.

1. Performance Rights Blanket Licenses

The two major performance rights organizations are BMI and ASCAP. There is also a third company, SESAC, that accounts for a smaller share of the performance rights business. These nonprofit organizations collect fees from establishments where music is played (nightclubs, radio and TV stations, concert halls, restaurants, taverns, etc.), and distribute the money to the songwriters and music publishers who own the songs. All three performing rights societies—BMI, ASCAP and SESAC—issue licenses known as blanket licenses that permit the licensee to play all songs represented by that society. With a blanket license, separate permissions are not required for each play of each song.

Examples of some business uses for which blanket licenses are provided include:

- athletic clubs
- dance classes
- hotel or motel uses
- restaurants and bars, and
- retail establishments such as clothing stores.

Blanket licenses for uses other than radio and TV are usually only sought from BMI and ASCAP. Because of its smaller repertoire, SESAC's blanket licenses are geared more toward gospel and country music users. It's possible that a business could obtain a blanket license from only one performing rights society, but that may prove to be an inefficient approach because the business would have to make sure that only music from that society is played.

The annual fee for a blanket license is based on the manner in which music is performed and the potential audience for the music. For example, the ASCAP computes blanket licenses as follows:

- Restaurant, bar and nightclub rates are based on whether the music is live or recorded, whether it's audio only or audiovisual, the club's seating capacity, the number of nights of music per week, the number of musicians and whether admission is charged.
- Concert event rates are based on the seating capacity and ticket price.

- Corporate rates for playing music at a business are based upon the number of employees.
- Retail store rates depend on the number of speakers and square footage.
- Hotel rates are based on a percentage of entertainment expenses for live music and an additional charge if recorded music is used.

To obtain a blanket license, contact BMI, ASCAP or SESAC (contact information is included at the end of this chapter). Ask for the licensing department and explain your business use. The society's representatives will inquire as to the size and type of use and quote you a fee for an annual blanket license.

Permission for Music in Seminars and Training Programs

As explained in Chapter 7, permission is not required if music is played as part of a face-to-face teaching activity at a non-profit educational institution. Permission is required from BMI and ASCAP when music is used as part of instructional seminars, conventions or other commercial presentations.

How Is Harry Fox Different from BMI, ASCAP and SESAC?

The performing rights societies, BMI, ASCAP and SESAC, grant licenses to play songs on the radio and television, at concerts and public events, over the Internet and in movie theaters. These organizations are concerned only with the public performance of the song—that is, when the public hears songs. The Harry Fox Agency, a subsidiary of the National Music Publishers Association (NMPA) collects royalties for music publishers whenever a song is copied or reproduced (referred to as "mechanical royalties"), regardless of whether the public hears the song. Harry Fox provides licenses for reproducing songs in movies, videos, TV commercials, Internet commercials, corporate in-house presentations, trade shows, school shows, concerts, cabaret TV programs, products (such as music boxes or other devices incorporating songs), jukeboxes and karaoke systems.

There is some overlap between the territory covered by Harry Fox and performing rights societies. Both organizations grant licenses for songs used in film, radio, Internet and TV use. However, the purposes of the licenses are different. For example, when granting television rights, the performing rights license permits the playing of the song over a television broadcast. The Harry Fox license grants the right to copy the song (or synchronize it) onto the television program's soundtrack.

2. Additional Permissions

Additional permissions are required in the following situations:

- If the business is not just playing the music, but is also making a copy of it—for example, compiling songs on a tape or making a new recording—a mechanical license should be acquired through the Harry Fox Agency. Forms for these licenses are downloadable at the Harry Fox website as explained in Section N3.

- If the music is transmitted in a digital format such as over the Internet or via a digital cable music service, permission is required from the sound recording copyright owner. Digital rights are discussed in Section I.

- If the music is used at a corporate event to promote a product or service, permission of the performer is required in addition to permission from the music publisher and the record company. For example, if Microsoft debuts a new software product at a convention and plays a song recorded by the Rolling Stones, permission is required from the music publisher, the record company and from the Rolling Stones. (see Section F.)

Playing the Radio or Television at a Business

Before 1999, businesses using anything larger than a home stereo system had to pay performing rights societies for the right to play the radio or television for customers. However, under new rules, restaurants and bars of less than 3,750 square feet and retail establishments with less than 2,000 square feet don't have to pay any fees to play the radio or television in their establishments. (Note, establishments that play pre-recorded music, such as compact discs, are still subject to license requirements.)

In addition, regardless of size, all restaurants, bars and stores are exempt from paying fees if they have no more than six external speakers (but not more than four per room), or four televisions measuring 55 inches or less (but not more than one per room). These rules only apply to establishments that play radio and television. To learn more about these rules, consult the Copyright Office website at lcWeb.loc.gov/copyright/ and click on "The Copyright Term Extension and Music Licensing Act."

Press 1 for More Music

Music provided for a caller on hold constitutes a public performance because music is being transmitted to the public. The company providing on-hold music must obtain permission from the performing right societies, ASCAP and BMI (and in some cases, SESAC).

---

3. Nonprofit and Charitable Business Exemptions

Some nonprofit and charitable uses of music don't require permission. Below is a summary of some of the rules, which are located at 17 U.S.C. § 110 of the copyright law. Other educational permission rules are in Chapter 7, "Academic and Educational Permissions."

- **Free shows.** No permission is needed if music is performed before a live audience and the performers are not paid and admission is not charged.

- **Shows with admission fees.** No permission is needed if music is performed before a live paying audience, so long as the performers are not paid, the net proceeds are used exclusively for education, religious or charitable purposes and the music publisher is notified and given more than ten days to object. If the publisher objects, then the person seeking permission will have to pay for the use and acquire a license from the appropriate performing rights society.

- **Religious services.** No permission is needed to perform music in the course of religious services at a house of worship. However, permission is required to broadcast music performed at a religious service and to copy sheet music used for religious services.

- **Agricultural fairs.** Permission is not required for the performance of live music at nonprofit agricultural or horticultural annual fairs. However, see note below regarding concession and for-profit exhibits.

- **Fraternal and veterans events.** Permission is not required when nonprofit veterans' organizations or fraternal groups perform music provided that the general public is not invited and that the net profits are used exclusively for charitable purposes.
- **Fraternity and sorority events.** Permission is not required to perform music at college fraternity and sorority social functions provided that the purpose is solely to raise funds for a charitable purpose.
- **Concession stands.** Permission *is* required to play music at concession stands and for-profit exhibits regardless of whether the event at which the stand or exhibit is operating is exempt. For example, permission would be required to play music at a concession stand at a nonprofit agricultural fair.

E. Releasing Music for Sale

This section explains the rules behind obtaining permission to record and release a song as an audio recording—for example, where a singer wishes to record and release the Lou Reed song "Walk on the Wild Side" on compact disc. Thanks to federal laws, the process of acquiring permission to record a song is relatively simple and inexpensive (approximately 7 cents for each copy you distribute). In addition, the song owner must consent to your use if you follow the procedures in this section.

This section is only about using songs on audio recordings distributed to the public. Recording a song for use within a film or video is discussed in Section G. Recording and distributing a song over the Internet is described in Section I. Recording of a song for use in a software program is discussed in Section H.

To record a song for release to the public, a performer must obtain permission from the music publisher of the song and pay a fee, called a mechanical royalty. A mechanical royalty must be paid when songs are reproduced on cassettes, compact discs and records.

There are two ways to get permission and pay the mechanical royalty.

- use a compulsory license and pay the pre-set statutory mechanical royalty rate directly to the music publisher, or
- negotiate permission and the mechanical royalty directly with the music publisher or Harry Fox Agency.

Beware when proceeding without permission. Some musicians producing self-released recordings don't obtain compulsory licenses or pay mechanical royalties. For small pressings, this illegal activity usually goes undetected, but if the copyright owner learns of the unauthorized use, the musician could be forced to pay past due mechanical royalties, plus interest, or may be required to stop distributing the recording entirely. If the music publisher brings a lawsuit, there may be additional penalties including attorney fees.

1. Compulsory Licenses

One way to legally re-record a song is to use what's known as a compulsory license. Under this procedure the user doesn't actually ask for the music publisher's permission to make the recording or negotiate a license fee. Instead, the user merely informs the publisher of the recording (using the compulsory license procedure) and pays a license fee set by law. The music publisher can't prevent the recording of the song so long as the following requirements are satisfied:

- the song was previously released on a recording
- the performer making the new recording does not change the basic melody or fundamental character of the song

- the performer or record company making the new recording provides a Notice of Intention to Obtain Compulsory License (as described below) at least 30 days prior to distributing the recordings, and
- the performer or record company making the new recording pays the statutory mechanical royalty fee.

It's important to note that a compulsory license cannot be used the first time the song is distributed to the public—for example, if the songwriter never released a version of it and your version is the first. Nor can a compulsory license be used if the song was used on television or in a movie, but never released on an audio recording. In these cases, authorization must be acquired directly from the music publisher, or from the songwriter. Since the song has never been recorded, it's possible that the songwriter is still the owner and has not transferred it to a music publisher.

Compulsory licenses are used only when reproducing songs on records, compact discs or cassettes (that is, sound recordings). They do not apply if making copies for use on a website or for a video version. In addition, compulsory licenses are not available for video, laser disc, movies or any other use of music used in conjunction with other media.

a. Mechanical Royalty Rate

When using the compulsory license procedure, the music publisher must be paid a mechanical royalty rate set by the government (sometimes known as the "statutory rate"). This rate increases every few years.

Table of Statutory Mechanical Royalty Rates 1999-2003

1999	7.1 cents per copy
2000-2001	7.55 cents per copy
2002-2003	8 cents

For information on the current mechanical rate, call the Copyright Office Licensing Division at 202-707-8150.

EXAMPLE: Andrea, in the year 2000, records Lou Reed's "Walk on the Wild Side" and makes 1,000 compact discs of the recording. Andrea must pay $75.50 to the music publisher of the song (7.55 cents times 1,000 copies).

b. Notice of Intention to Obtain Compulsory License

For uses that meet the criteria described in this Section, a Notice of Intention to Obtain Compulsory License should be sent to the copyright owner of the song. An explanation for completing this form is provided below. A tear-out version of this notice appears in the Appendix.

Note: A compulsory license to record a song does not grant the right to reprint lyrics on the album artwork. Permission must be acquired separately from the publisher.

The Notice of Intention to Obtain Compulsory License is included on the forms disk in the back of this book under the name COMPLCNS.

Notice of Intention to Obtain Compulsory License for Making and Distributing Sound Recordings

To _____ , the copyright owner of _____ , written by _____ :

Pursuant to the compulsory license provisions of the U.S. Copyright Act (17 U.S.C.§ 1115), we apply

for a license to make and distribute phonorecords of _____ and provide the following

information:

Legal name or entity seeking the compulsory license:	
Fictitious or assumed names used for making and distributing phonorecords:	
Address:	
Business organization:	☐ corporation ☐ LLC ☐ partnership ☐ sole proprietor
Name of individuals who own a beneficial interest of 25% or more in the entity:	
If a corporation, names of the officers and directors:	
Configurations(s) to be made under the compulsory license (check all that apply):	☐ 7- or 12-inch vinyl single ☐ 12-inch long playing vinyl record ☐ cassette ☐ compact disc ☐ minidisc ☐ digital cassette recording
Catalog number(s):	
Label name(s):	
Principal recording artists:	
Anticipated date of initial release:	
We agree to pay the copyright owner royalties at the statutory rate provided by the Copyright Act. Date: _____ By:_____ Name/Title: _____	

c. Explanation for Notice to Obtain Compulsory License

- In the first blank of the first paragraph, insert the name of the song owner (usually the music publisher of the song). In the next blank insert the name of the song and then the songwriters. In the second paragraph, again insert the name of the song.

- In the first row of the table, insert the legal name of the company that owns your recording. If you or your company owns the recording, insert that name.

- Under "Fictitious or assumed names" insert the fictitious business name, if any, that you or your company uses.

- Insert your company's mailing address.

- Indicate the legal business structure of your company (corporation, LLC, partnership or sole proprietor).

- In the category "Names of individuals who own a beneficial interest," insert the names of anyone who has a 25% or more interest in the company. For example, if you and your partner own the recording equally (50%–50%), list both your names. If no one owns at least 25% of the company, leave this blank.

- If your company is a corporation, in the next row list the officers and directors.

- Check all the configurations that you expect to release.

- List any catalog number you may have created for the recording.

- Insert the name of your record label. If your company is putting out the record, the label name is probably the same as your company name.

- Insert the name of the recording artist.

- Insert the expected release date.

- The final paragraph establishes that the statutory rate will be paid. A company seeking a compulsory license (in this case, you or your company) is supposed to issue an accounting statement and pay statutory royalties every month. You can, however, contact the music publisher and ask if it is okay to make payments on a quarterly basis, rather than monthly.

- The compulsory license is signed by the licensee (you or your company, if you have one). The music publisher does not sign it because consent from the music publisher is not required. All that is required is that the publisher is notified and paid according to the rules. If you have a partnership, a partner should sign in the space next to the word "By" and below that, indicate the signer's partner status—for example, "Peggi Fournier, a general partner in the Grosse Point Partnership."

2. Negotiating a License Directly With the Music Publisher

Most major labels and established independent record companies do not use compulsory licenses or pay the statutory rate as described above. Instead, they obtain permission to make the recording directly from the music publisher and negotiate a rate lower than the compulsory license rate, usually three-quarters of the statutory rate. It is not a violation of the law to negotiate a rate lower than that provided in the Copyright Act if both parties consent.

As with performance royalties, many music publishers do not directly negotiate mechanical licenses; instead they delegate that authority to the Harry Fox Agency, an organization that negotiates and collects mechanical royalties on behalf of approximately 80% of the music publishers. Sample mechanical licenses can be downloaded from the Harry Fox website (see Section N3).

However, negotiating with the music publisher, either directly or through Harry Fox, may not work for you. Many music publishers won't negotiate a lower rate unless a substantial number of copies of the recording will be distributed or you agree to pay them an advance. If you can't do this, you'll have to use a compulsory license as outlined above.

Creating a Theatrical Musical: Grand Rights

Grand rights are the rights needed to create theatrical presentations such as Broadway-style musicals. For example, to create a musical drama using the songs of Bob Dylan, grand rights would be secured from either Bob Dylan's publisher or from the entity that he has designated to handle grand rights. Performance rights organizations such as ASCAP and BMI do not control grand rights. To find the company that controls grand rights for a song, start by contacting the music publisher of the song or the Harry Fox Agency.

Although performing rights societies do not control grand rights, these societies do grant performance permissions for songs from Broadway musicals, provided that the songs are not performed in a dramatic context. For example, playing a song from the musical *Rent* over the radio requires permission from a performing rights society but does not require grand rights clearance.

F. Using Music in a Commercial, Radio Show or Background Music Services

Pop music has become a common component of advertising and is used extensively in radio and television commercials. Using music in commercials, for syndicated radio shows or background music services such as Muzak requires permission from the music publisher and record company. We have grouped these uses together because the process of obtaining permission is similar.

If an advertising agency creates a new version of a song, permission may only be required from the music publisher. If a recording of the song is used, then permission will be required both from the music publisher and the record company. Using music in a radio or television commercial may also require

permission from the artist performing on the recording as described in Section D2. The same rule applies if an artist is imitated in a commercial.

1. Music Publisher Permissions and Fees

Music publishers grant "electrical transcription licenses" for the use of songs in radio commercials or syndicated radio programs. The music publisher either furnishes the electrical transcription license directly to the licensee, or uses the Harry Fox Agency to manage the licensing process. Electrical transcription licenses permit the copying of the songs for the particular use. When songs are played on the radio, performing rights societies also collect fees from the radio stations for the performance of the songs. In this case, permission is not needed from BMI or ASCAP as the radio station arranges for the performing rights permission.

Fees for using songs in radio ads often start at $1,000 per week for local radio uses and may go as high as $100,000 per year for national radio uses. If a song is used in a syndicated radio show, the fees are often based on the number of copies of the program broadcast by syndicated stations (for example, $100 per station).

2. Record Company Permissions and Fees

Sound recording rights for radio commercial and syndicated radio uses are negotiated directly with the sound recording owner (generally a record company), and usually involve a one-time fee for the right to make copies of the sound recording. The amount charged varies widely depending on the length and type of use. As noted earlier in this chapter, record companies can be difficult to negotiate with, and may charge exorbitant fees for authorizing the use of its recording. The result is that oftentimes it's easier to record a new version of the song—which will only require the music publisher's permission—rather than use the recording itself.

In some countries (not the U.S.), a payment must be made when a sound recording is played on the radio. In these countries, two performance payments are required each time a radio station plays a song: one payment to the music publisher and another to the record company.

G. Using Music With a Film, Television Show or Video

Music is an essential component of films, television shows or videos. The businesses that produce these audiovisual works (known as production companies) generally acquire music rights either by hiring musicians to record music or by obtaining the rights to use an existing recording. If the production company hires musicians to record existing songs—for instance, the hired musicians play Beatles songs—permission is only required from the music publisher. If a film or video production company wants to use an existing recording—for example, a Tom Petty recording—permission must be acquired from both the music publisher and the owner of the sound recording (the record company).

 You can also get music for a film, TV show or other type of program from production music libraries. PMLs, as they're typically called, have broad selections of music to which they own all rights. Licensing music from a PML is generally simple and inexpensive. See Section B5 for a more detailed description of PMLs. A list of PMLs appears at the end of this chapter.

In general, when you use a song in a movie—but not a particular recording of that song—you'll need to obtain a synchronization license from the music publisher. The term "synchronization" simply refers to the fact that the song is being synchronized with the video track of the program. If you're using your own recording of the song, keep in mind that you'll also need to obtain the rights to the re-recording.

EXAMPLE: Dave is making a movie about Los Angeles and wants to use the song, "I Love L.A." by Randy Newman. Dave cannot afford to pay for the Randy Newman master use rights (for the sound recording) so he hires a musician to re-record the song. He uses a work-for-hire agreement to acquire ownership of the master recording from the musician. To use the song in his movie, Dave only needs to obtain permission from the music publisher of the song.

On the other hand, when you use a specific recording in a movie, you'll also need what's called a master use license from the record company. The term "master use" refers to the fact that you're obtaining permission from the record company to use the master recording of the song.

It's important to understand that to use a particular recording, you'll generally need both a synchronization license (because you're using a song owned by the music publisher) and a master use license (because you're using the recording owned by the record company). An exception to this is if the song is in the public domain. In that case, you'd only need the master use license from the owner of the recording you're using.

This section explains the types of permissions that are required to use music in film, television or video, and the process of obtaining that permission. The section on synchronization licenses discusses the various ways to obtain permission to use a song, depending on how you plan to use it. The next section on master use licenses explains how to get the additional permission that's required if you want to use an existing recording.

 Acquiring permission for the use of music in motion pictures and videos can be complex. This is largely because older songs may be subject to copyright rules that resulted in a transfer of rights back to the original songwriter. If clearance is performed improperly, the costs of correcting permission errors can be substantial. For this reason, and to save time and money, many film and video production companies use music clearance services. These services are described in Section M, and a list of companies that perform these services is included at the end of this chapter.

Two helpful resources for clearing music for films are *Clearance & Copyright: Everything the Independent Filmmaker Needs to Know,* by Michael C. Donaldson (Silman-James Press), and *Kohn on Music Licensing,* by Al Kohn and Bob Kohn (Aspen Law & Business).

1. Synchronization Licenses

As mentioned above, permission must be obtained from the music publisher to use a song in a movie, television show or video. This is true whether an existing recording is used or a new recording is created. The general term for an agreement to use a song in conjunction with a series of visual images—for example, in a television show or movie—is a "synchronization license." There are more specific names for this agreement depending on the type of program that will include the music. For a movie, the specific type of license is a "theatrical motion picture synchronization license." If a song is used for a television commercial, the license is called a "television commercial synchronization license."

In addition, if the program will be released on videos for sale to the public, a "videogram license" is also necessary from the music publisher. In other words, the music publisher's permission to use the song in a movie or other program does not authorize the use of the song on subsequent video releases of the same program. See Section G1c below for more information on videogram licenses.

The essential terms of the various types of synchronization agreements are very similar. Synchronization licenses for films can also be tailored to specific purposes. For example, synchronization licenses can be granted specifically for student films or film festival uses.

Granting of synchronization permission is often delegated to the Harry Fox Agency, which maintains a website containing downloadable license agreements. For more information on contacting the Harry Fox Agency, see Section N3.

a. Videogram Licenses

If a song is used in a video distributed to the public, you will need an additional permission from the music publisher called a "videogram license." Videogram licenses are required for any programs—theatrical films, television shows, exercise videos—that are made available for sale to the public on video. This is true whether the program was originally made for video, or whether it was originally made for cinema or TV and later released on video. The key here is that the video is available for sale to the public. If a music video were made, for instance, and was only shown on MTV and not sold to the public, a videogram license would not be necessary.

b. Synchronization Fees

Fees for song rights in a film depend upon the nature of the film (documentary, independent or major studio release) and the use in the film—whether it is a background use, foreground use or a special use such as when a character sings the song. The fee for use of a song as background in an independent documentary may start at $500. Fees for a nontheatrical corporate video synchronization license range from $500 to $1,500. Fees for using a song in an independent theatrical release (an independent film) range from $5,000 to $15,000. Fees for a major motion picture use are generally between $10,000 and $25,000. These synchronization fees do not include the separate fee and royalty charged for the videogram license, described below.

If you plan to make your program available for sale on video, you'll have to pay videogram fees as well. Fees for song rights for a video release of a theatrical motion picture may be several thousand dollars or, on occasion, may be tied to sales of the video. For example, under certain arrangements, if sales pass a certain number an additional payment must be made. Corporate video uses may be charged a flat fee (for example, $500 to $2,000) or may be tied to the number of units manufactured or distributed.

c. Music Synchronization and Videogram License

Below is an agreement that provides for both synchronization and videogram rights from a music publisher. It can be used for any film or video that will be released theatrically (in theaters) or on video. This agreement can be used for purposes of comparison, since a music publisher or the Harry Fox Agency will likely provide its own license agreement.

If the work will only be released on video and not theatrically, the synchronization language can be removed, as described in the explanation following the agreement. Although this agreement is for films and videos, much of the language and license principles apply to other audiovisual uses as well.

A form for this agreement is provided in the Appendix and on the forms disk.

The Music Synchronization and Videogram License Agreement is included on the forms disk in the back of this book under the file name SYNCVID.

Music Synchronization and Videogram License Agreement

Music Synchronization and Videogram License Agreement (the "Agreement") is made between:

_____ ("Publisher") and _____ ("Producer").

Publisher is the owner of rights for the compositions listed below:

_____

_____

(the "Compositions").

Producer is the owner of rights for the Motion Picture tentatively entitled _____

(the "Motion Picture"). Producer desires to license the Compositions for use in the Motion Picture and in audiovisual devices for home use such as videotapes and laser discs ("Videograms"). The parties agree as follows:

Grant

(select one or more Grant provisions)

☐   **Grant of Audiovisual License.** Publisher grants to Producer and Producer's successors and assigns, the nonexclusive right to record the Compositions solely in synchronization with the Motion Picture (in any medium, now known or later created) within the Territory. Publisher grants to Producer the right to publicly perform the Compositions solely in synchronization to the Motion Picture within the Territory. These public performance rights include public exhibitions of the Motion Picture in theaters and other public places where motion pictures are customarily exhibited, provided that performances outside the United States are cleared by performing rights societies in accordance with customary practice and customary fees. The public performance rights also include television exhibition of the Motion Picture within the Territory, including all methods of television reproduction and transmissions, provided that the entities broadcasting those performances have licenses from the appropriate performing rights societies. Any television performance not licensed by performing rights societies must be cleared directly by the Publisher.

☐   **Grant of Videogram License.** Publisher grants to Producer and his successors and assigns, the nonexclusive right to record, copy and synchronize the Composition, solely as part of the Motion Picture, on audiovisual devices including, but not limited to video cassettes, video discs and similar compact audiovisual devices that reproduce the entire motion picture in substantially its original form ("Videogram"). This Videogram license is solely for the distribution of Videograms intended primarily for home use in the Territory.

☐ **Use in Trailers.** Publisher grants to Producer and his successors and assigns, the nonexclusive right to record, copy, synchronize and perform the Composition in connection with trailers used for the advertising and exploitation of the Motion Picture.

Reservation of Rights

Publisher reserves all rights not granted in this Agreement.

Modifications to Composition

Producer shall not make any change in the original lyrics, if any, or in the fundamental character of the music of the Composition or use the title or any portion of the lyrics of the Composition as the title or subtitle of the Motion Picture without written prior authorization from Publisher.

Territory

The rights granted in this Agreement are for the following: _____ (the "Territory").

Audiovisual License Payments

As payment for the rights granted for the Audiovisual License, Producer shall pay Publisher as follows:

(select payment option and fill in blanks)

☐ **One-Time Payment.** Producer shall pay Publisher one-time payment of $_____ upon first public performance of the Motion Picture or within nine (9) months of signing this agreement, whichever is earlier.

☐ **Advance and Royalties.** Producer shall pay Publisher nonrefundable advance ("Motion Picture Advance") in the sum of $_____ recoupable against royalties derived from the Audiovisual License ("Audiovisual Royalties"). Producer shall pay Publisher Audiovisual Royalties of ___% of net profits from the public exhibition and public performance of the Motion Picture.

☐ **Royalties.** Producer shall pay Publisher _____ % of the net profits from the public exhibition and public performance of the Motion Picture.

Videogram License Payments

As payment for the rights granted for the Videogram License, Producer shall pay Publisher as follows: (select payment option and fill in blanks)

[ ] **One-Time Payment.** Producer shall pay Publisher one-time payment of $_____ within nine (9) months of signing this agreement.

[ ] **Advance and Royalties.** Producer shall pay Publisher a nonrefundable advance ("Videogram Advance") in the sum of $_____ recoupable against royalties derived from the Videogram License ("Videogram Royalties"). Videogram Royalties for Videogram copies of the Motion Picture shall be paid as follows:

[ ] **Net Profits.** Producer shall pay Publisher _____ % of the Producer's net profits for all Videograms revenues including all sales, licenses, or other sources of revenue for Videogram distribution (not including shipping charges or taxes).

[ ] **Pro Rata Option.** Producer shall pay Publisher _____% ("Publisher's Pro-Rata Portion") of _____ % of the net revenue for all Videogram income including all sales, licenses, or other sources of revenue for Videogram distribution. Publisher's Pro-Rata Portion represents the proportion the Composition bears to the total number of Royalty-bearing compositions contained in the Motion Picture.

Payments; Statements

Within forty-five (45) days after the end of each calendar quarter (the "Royalty Period"), Producer shall furnish accurate statement of net revenues derived from the licenses granted in this agreement along with any royalty payments. Producer may withhold a reasonable reserve for anticipated returns, refunds, and exchanges of Videograms, and this reserve shall be liquidated no later than twelve (12) months after the respective accounting statement.

Favorable Rates

If a higher royalty rate than set forth in this Agreement becomes payable by operation of law with respect to Videograms sold in a particular country within the Territory, Producer shall either pay the higher royalty to Publisher with respect to that country, or delete the Compositions from the Motion Picture with respect to this country. In the event a musical composition is licensed for a substantially similar use in connection with the Videogram exploitation of the Motion Picture on a more favorable rate, Producer agrees that such favorable rate shall also be granted to Publisher for the licensing of the Composition.

Audit

Producer shall keep accurate books of account and records covering all transactions relating to the licenses granted in this Agreement, and Publisher or its duly authorized representatives shall have the right upon five (5) days prior written notice, and during normal business hours, to inspect and audit these accounts and records.

Warranty

Publisher warrants that it has the power and authority to grant the rights in this Agreement and that the Compositions do not infringe any third-party rights. In no event shall Publisher's liability for a breach of this Warranty exceed the amount of payments received under this Agreement.

Credits

Publisher shall receive credit in the following form: _____ .

This credit shall be provided as follows:

(select all that apply)

☐   credit similar to all other musical compositions used in the Motion Picture.

☐   a single card in the main titles on all prints of the Motion Picture and Videograms.

☐   in all paid advertising similar to all other musical compositions used in the Motion Picture.

Samples

Producer shall promptly furnish Publisher with _____ copies of each format of Videogram release.

Cue Sheets

Producer agrees to furnish Publisher a cue sheet of the Motion Picture within thirty (30) days after the first public exhibition of the Motion Picture.

Term

The term of this Agreement is for the term of United States copyright in the Composition including renewal terms, if any.

Termination and Breach

In the event that Producer (or Producer's assigns or licensees) breach this Agreement and fails to cure such breach within thirty (30) days after notice by Publisher to Producer, this license will automatically terminate and all rights granted under this Agreement shall revert to Publisher. Failure to make timely payments or to provide credit as provided in this Agreement shall be considered a material breach of this Agreement.

Miscellaneous

This Agreement may not be amended except in a writing signed by both parties. If a court finds any provision of this Agreement invalid or unenforceable, the remainder of this Agreement shall be interpreted so as best to effect the intent of the parties. This Agreement shall be governed by and interpreted in accordance with the laws of the State of _____ . This Agreement expresses the complete understanding of the parties with respect to the subject matter and supersedes all prior representations and understandings. Any controversy or claim arising out of or relating to this Agreement shall be settled by binding arbitration in accordance with the rules of the American Arbitration Association and judgment upon the award rendered by the arbitrator(s) may be entered in any court having jurisdiction. All notices provided for under this Agreement must be in writing and mailed to the addresses provided in the signature portion of this Agreement.

_____

PUBLISHER

_____

PRODUCER

d. Explanation for Music Synchronization and Videogram License

- The introductory paragraph identifies the companies entering into the agreement (the "parties"). Insert the name of music publisher ("Publisher") and producer ("Producer") of the film or video. Sometimes, a synchronization license may substitute the terms "Licensee" for Producer and "Licensor" for Publisher. The terms "Television Show" or "Audiovisual Work," if applicable, can be substituted for the term "Motion Picture." In this event, change all references throughout the agreement.

- The Grant provisions establish the rights under copyright law (the licenses) that the music publisher is granting to the film producer. The Grant of Audiovisual License establishes the right to use (synchronize) the music in conjunction with public presentations of the film or video—for example, in theaters or on a television broadcast. The Grant of Videogram License establishes the right to use (synchronize) the music with the video version of the motion picture, as well as to make copies for sale for home use. If the licensee is going "direct to video" and the film will not be shown in theaters, the The Grant of Audiovisual License is not needed (do not check the box). If no video rights are sought and the film will only be shown theatrically, then the Grant of Videogram License is not needed (do not check the box). The Use in Trailers section permits the use of the Composition in trailers advertising the film.

- The Reservation of Rights section establishes that any rights not covered in this agreement are held by the music publisher.

- The Modifications to Composition section provides that the producer must acquire written permission from the music publisher if modifications are made to the song. Failure to obtain permission may endanger the rights to use the music.

- As for the Territory, worldwide rights are preferred if the producer intends to show or distribute the film outside the U.S. If the publisher cannot grant worldwide rights, permission will be required from the holder of rights (usually a foreign music publisher) in each country in which the film will be distributed.

- There is a separate payment section for the audiovisual license and the videogram license. For each one, choose the payment method that reflects the agreement with the publisher. For the audiovisual license, you can choose either a one-time payment, an advance against royalties or royalties with no advance. For the videogram license, you can choose a one-time payment or an advance against royalties. You also can choose which type of royalties will be paid—royalties based on net profits, or pro-rated royalties. The pro-rata choice provides that a portion of income is paid to the publisher based upon the total number of songs being used in the video. For example if ten songs are used on a video, each publisher would receive 1/10 of the music royalty. If you choose this option, enter the composition's proportional share of the whole video in the first blank, and the overall royalty rate in the second blank. If there is no videogram license, do not check any options in the Videogram License Payments section.

- The provision entitled Favorable Rates is sometimes referred to as a "Most Favored Nation" clause and provides that if a country establishes a higher rate of payment for any of the uses described in this agreement, then the producer must pay the higher rate. Some film producers may not want to include this provision.

- The Warranty is a contractual promise that the publisher is legally capable to grant the rights in this agreement. The last sentence in the Warranty section limits the amount of damages to be paid by the publisher if the warranty is breached.

- In the Credits section, the publisher will establish the type and size of credit to be used. A failure to properly credit the composition may result in a loss of licensing rights. The term "single card" refers to a separate credit on a screen with no other credits.
- If the publisher wants samples to be provided, indicate the number you've agreed to provide in the Samples section.
- A cue sheet lists each separate musical use on a film or video. This provision simply provides that you will furnish one to the publisher within 30 days of the program's public premiere.
- For an explanation of the Term, Termination and Miscellaneous sections, see Chapter 11, "Art & Merchandise Licenses."
- The agreement must be signed by individuals with the authority to represent the music publisher and the film production company. For information about determining who has authority to sign (also known as "signing capacity"), see the explanation in Chapter 11, Section C22.

2. Master Use Licenses

A record company must grant a master use license to permit a recording to be used on a motion picture soundtrack. For instance, if a filmmaker wants to use a recording—not a re-make—of Johnny Cash's "Ring of Fire" in a film, the filmmaker will need to obtain a master use license from the record company that owns the recording. The license permits the filmmaker to duplicate the recording on the film soundtrack. The cost of the master use license depends on the size and type of production and the use within the film (foreground, background, etc.). The cost may range from a few hundred dollars for a student film to thousands of dollars for a feature film.

If a soundtrack album is released, the record company will seek a percentage, or royalty, based upon the album's sales. In some cases, a record

company may seek an advance payment plus a "rollover"—a payment made when a certain number of video or soundtrack copies have been sold. Costs are also affected by extra payments (known as reuse fees) that the record company must make to union and guild members who worked on the recording.

a. Videogram Licenses

If the program will be released on video, a videogram license is also necessary from the record company. In other words, the record company's permission to use the recording in a movie or other program does not authorize the use of the recording on video releases of the same program. If your program will be available for sale to the public on video, you'll need a videogram license whether the program was originally made for video, or whether it was originally made for cinema or TV and later released on video. The key here is that the video is available for sale to the public. If a music video were made, for instance, and was only shown on MTV and not sold to the public, a videogram license would not be necessary.

b. Master Use and Videogram License

Below is an agreement that provides for both master use and videogram rights from the owner of a recording. It can be used for any film or video that will be released theatrically (in theaters) or on video. Although this agreement is for films and videos, much of the language and license principles apply to other audiovisual uses as well. This agreement is provided in the Appendix and on the forms disk that comes with this book.

The Master Use and Videogram License is included on the forms disk in the back of this book under the file name MSTVIDLC.

⚠ **If you're obtaining a master use license, then you probably need a synchronization license as well.** For example, if the producer is obtaining master use rights to use the recording of "Stand By Me" in a film, he must also obtain synchronization rights from the music publisher of "Stand By Me." However, you won't need synchronization rights from the music publisher if the recorded song that you're using is in the public domain. In that case, you'd only need a master use license from the owner of the recording you're using.

Master Use and Videogram License

This Master Use and Videogram License Agreement (the "Agreement") is made between:

_____ ("Owner") and _____ ("Producer").

Owner is the owner of rights for the master recordings: _____

_____

_____

(the "Masters").

Producer is the owner of rights for the Motion Picture tentatively entitled _____

 (the "Motion Picture").

Producer desires to license the Masters for use in the Motion Picture and in audiovisual devices for home use such as videotapes and laser discs ("Videograms"). The parties agree as follows:

Grant

(select one or more Grant provisions if applicable)

☐ **Grant of Audiovisual License.** Owner grants to Producer and Producer's successors and assigns, the nonexclusive right to use and reproduce the Masters solely in synchronization with the Motion Picture in any medium, now known or later created within the Territory. Owner grants to Producer the right to publicly perform the Masters solely in synchronization to the Motion Picture within the Territory. These public performance rights include the public exhibitions of the Motion Picture in theaters and other public places where motion pictures are customarily exhibited and for television exhibition of the Motion Picture including all methods of television reproduction and transmissions within the Territory.

☐ **Grant of Videogram License.** Owner grants to Producer and Producer's successors and assigns, the nonexclusive right to record, copy and synchronize the Masters, solely as part of the Motion Picture, on audiovisual devices including, but not limited to video cassettes, video discs and similar compact audiovisual devices that reproduce the entire motion picture in substantially its original form ("Videogram"). This Videogram license is solely for the distribution of Videograms intended primarily for home use in the Territory.

☐ **Use in Trailers.** Owner grants to Producer and Producer's successors and assigns, the nonexclusive right to record, copy, synchronize and perform the Masters in connection with trailers used for the advertising and exploitation of the Motion Picture.

Reservation of Rights

Owner reserves all rights not granted in this Agreement.

Modifications to Masters

Producer shall not make any change in the Masters without written prior authorization from Owner.

Territory

The rights granted in this Agreement are for the following: _____
(the "Territory").

Union Re-use Fees

Owner agrees to provide Producer with all information regarding any re-use fees required by unions or guilds as a result of this license. Producer agrees to pay all such re-use payments including related pension or welfare payments and to indemnify Owner from claims arising from such payments.

Musical Works Synchronization Rights

Producer agrees to obtain all appropriate synchronization, performance and reproduction rights for the musical compositions embodied on the Masters and to indemnify Owner for any claims arising from such rights.

Audiovisual License Payments

As payment for the rights granted for the Audiovisual License, Producer shall pay Owner as follows:
(select payment option and fill in blanks)

[ ]　　**One-Time Payment.** Producer shall pay Owner one-time payment of $ _____ upon first public performance of the Motion Picture or within nine (9) months of signing this agreement, whichever is earlier.

[ ]　　**Advance and Royalties.** Producer shall pay Owner nonrefundable advance ("Motion Picture Advance") in the sum of $ _____ recoupable against royalties derived from the Audiovisual License ("Audiovisual Royalties"). Producer shall pay Owner Audiovisual Royalties of __% of net profits from the public exhibition and public performance of the Motion Picture.

☐ **Royalties.** Producer shall pay Owner _____% of the net profits from the public exhibition and public performance of the Motion Picture.

Videogram License Payments

As payment for the rights granted for the Videogram License, Producer shall pay Owner as follows: (select payment option and fill in blanks)

☐ **One-Time Payment.** Producer shall pay Owner one-time payment of $_____ within nine (9) months of signing this agreement.

☐ **Advance and Royalties.** Producer shall pay Owner a nonrefundable advance ("Videogram Advance") in the sum of $_____ recoupable against royalties derived from the Videogram License ("Videogram Royalties"). Videogram Royalties for Videogram copies of the Motion Picture shall be paid as follows:

☐ **Net Profits.** Producer shall pay Owner_____% of the Producer's net profits for all Videograms revenues including all sales, licenses, or other sources of revenue for Videogram distribution (not including shipping charges or taxes).

☐ **Pro Rata Option.** Producer shall pay Owner _____% ("Owner's Pro-Rata Portion") of _____% of the net revenue for all Videogram income including all sales, licenses, or other sources of revenue for Videogram distribution. Owner's Pro-Rata Portion represents the proportion the Composition bears to the total number of Royalty-bearing compositions contained in the Motion Picture.

Payments; Statements

Within forty-five (45) days after the end of each calendar quarter (the "Royalty Period"), Producer shall furnish accurate statement of net revenues derived from the licenses granted in this agreement along with any royalty payments. Producer may withhold a reasonable reserve for anticipated returns, refunds, and exchanges of Videograms, and this reserve shall be liquidated no later than twelve (12) months after the respective accounting statement.

Audit

Producer shall keep accurate books of account and records covering all transactions relating to the licenses granted in this Agreement, and Owner or its duly authorized representatives shall have the right upon five (5) days prior written notice, and during normal business hours, to inspect and audit these accounts and records.

Warranty

Owner warrants that it has the power and authority to grant the rights in this Agreement and that the Masters do not infringe any third-party rights. In no event shall Owner's liability for a breach of this warranty exceed the amount of payments received under this Agreement.

Credits

Owner shall receive credit in the following form: _____

This credit shall be provided as follows:

(select one or more if appropriate)

☐ credit similar to all other Masters used in the Motion Picture.

☐ in all paid advertising similar to all other musical Masters used in the Motion Picture.

Samples

Producer shall promptly furnish Owner with ___ copies of each format of Videogram release.

Cue Sheets

Producer agrees to furnish Owner a cue sheet of the Motion Picture within thirty (30) days after the first public exhibition of the Motion Picture.

Term

The term of this Agreement is for the term of United States copyright in the Masters including renewal terms, if any.

Termination and Breach

In the event that Producer (or Producer's assigns or licensees) breach this Agreement and fails to cure such breach within thirty (30) days after notice by Owner to Producer, then this license will automatically terminate and all rights granted under this Agreement shall revert to Owner. Failure to make timely payments or to provide credit as provided in this Agreement shall be considered a material breach of this Agreement.

Miscellaneous

This Agreement may not be amended except in a writing signed by both parties. If a court finds any provision of this Agreement invalid or unenforceable, the remainder of this Agreement shall be interpreted so as best to effect the intent of the parties. This Agreement shall be governed by and interpreted in accordance with the laws of the State of _____ . This Agreement expresses the complete understanding of the parties with respect to the subject matter and supersedes all prior representations and understandings. Any controversy or claim arising out of or relating to this Agreement shall be settled by binding arbitration in accordance with the rules of the American Arbitration Association and judgment upon the award rendered by the arbitrator(s) may be entered in any court having jurisdiction. All notices provided for under this Agreement must be in writing and mailed to the addresses provided in the signature portion of this Agreement.

_____

OWNER

_____

PRODUCER

c. Explanation for Master Use License and Videogram License

- The introductory paragraph identifies the companies entering into the agreement (the "parties"). In the Owner blank, insert the name of the owner of the masters (usually the record company), and in the Producer blank enter the name of the producer of the film or video. Sometimes, a synchronization license may substitute the terms "Licensee" for Producer and "Licensor" for Owner. The terms "Television Show" or "Audiovisual Work," if applicable, can be substituted for the term "Motion Picture." In this event, change all references throughout the agreement.

- For explanations of the sections regarding the Grant, Reservation of Rights, Modifications to Masters, Territory, License Payments, Payments & Statements, Audit, Warranty, Credits, Samples and Cue Sheet provisions, see the explanation provided to the Music Synchronization and Videogram License Agreement in Section G1 above. For an explanation of the Term, Termination and Miscellaneous sections, see Chapter 11, "Art & Merchandise Licenses."

- The Union Re-use Fees and Musical Works Synchronization Rights sections refer to obligations of the producer. Re-use fees are payments made to the union musicians and engineers who created the masters whenever the masters are used for additional purposes. Musical works synchronization rights are payments for use of the compositions and are acquired by use of the Music Synchronization and Videogram License in Section G1.

H. Using Music in Software, Videogames or Multimedia Programs

As the sound quality available on computers and video games has improved, so has the quality of music used in conjunction with software programs. Preparing or acquiring music for popular software products has become a major enterprise sometimes involving specially scored works by Hollywood film composers.

Software companies commonly acquire music rights by hiring musicians or purchasing music from production music libraries. When a software company hires musicians or composers, ownership rights are acquired by assignment or under work made for hire agreements as explained in Chapter 15.

On some occasions, software companies may use pre-existing songs or recordings for video games, educational software, multimedia presentations or MIDI software (MIDI is a format used for transmitting musical data). This section deals with situations in which a software company desires to acquire rights to pre-existing music.

1. Music Publisher Permission and Fees

If the software company is re-recording a song, permission is required from the music publisher (usually through the Harry Fox Agency).

> EXAMPLE: Softco creates a software program for guitar students and records a new version of "Layla." Softco must obtain permission from the music publisher of the song.

Licenses to incorporate music in software or multimedia programs are usually negotiated directly with the Harry Fox Agency, a company that represents music publishers for certain reproduction rights. A sample copy of the Harry Fox multimedia license (the MMERL License) can be downloaded from their website (listed in Section N3.)

If music is to be used in connection with audio-visual images, such as in an interactive video game, a multimedia synchronization license, similar to the agreement in Section G1, is required. If the music is intended for use in a karaoke program, drafting the license depends upon whether the device will display the lyrics, whether film or video imagery is synchronized with the music and whether the license is intended for private or public karaoke uses. Some publishers will charge an additional "fixing fee" for the right to synchronize the music with the visual imagery.

Most music publishers will demand an advance payment from you that you can deduct from any ongoing royalties you owe for the use of music. Advance payments may be several hundred to several thousand dollars depending on the song and the use. Royalty rates for multimedia uses depend upon the use. Use of a song in a video game may range from .5% to 1% of the retail price. Royalties for MIDI software may start at 5% of the retail price. These fees are often pro-rated based upon the number of songs included on the software. For typical multimedia CD-ROM uses, the royalty is between 5 and 15 cents per unit. Advances are often required for these uses and usually start at $250. Few publishers will allow multimedia uses for a flat fee. (Flat fee payments are common when using music from production music libraries, see Section B5.)

2. Record Company Permission and Fees

If a software company is duplicating a previously released recording, permission is required from the music publisher and record company.

EXAMPLE: Softco creates a software program for guitar students and incorporates the Eric Clapton recording of "Layla." Softco must obtain permission from the record company that owns the recording and from the music publisher of the song.

Permission from the record company is referred to as a multimedia or software master use license, and is usually supplied by the record company. This license is similar to the master use license in Section G2.

A software company should expect to pay a minimum of $500 to $1,000 as an advance fee for use of the master, plus a continuing royalty. Since royalties will often also be due to the music publisher, software companies often avoid paying two royalties by re-recording songs instead of using existing recordings.

I. Using Music at a Website

Using the Internet it is possible to preview music before buying a recording, to download a song by a pop artist, or to copy and send a song from one destination to the other, usually with perfect sound clarity. With these capabilities have come a new set of rules for Internet users. There are two common ways that music is transmitted over the Internet:

- the song is made available for digital downloading—that is, a copy is delivered from a website to users' computers. When downloading, the user obtains a copy. As of the writing of this book, the most popular downloading format is known as MP3. Or,

- the song is broadcast in real time (known as "webcasting" or "audio streaming") and the listener hears the song as it is played by an Internet website and may or may not have the opportunity make a digital copy.

Below we discuss both methods of transmitting music and the permissions required for each use.

1. MP3s and Downloading Music

The process of downloading music files, such as MP3 files, is called "digital phonorecord delivery." MP3 is a computer standard that enables a recording to be compressed so that it can be transmitted faster than uncompressed recordings. Other downloadable formats are being developed by the music industry.

> **EXAMPLE:** Kinksology is a website that features music of the rock group The Kinks. Don visits the site, clicks on the song title "You Really Got Me," and an MP3 file with The Kinks' song is downloaded onto Don's computer. Don can play this MP3 file on his computer or on a portable MP3 player. Kinksology is providing digital phonorecord delivery.

Any website providing digital phonorecord delivery must obtain permission from the owner of the song (music publisher) and owner of the sound recording (record company).

a. Music Publisher Permission

Permission is required from the music publisher to provide digital phonorecord delivery. The rules for how to pay the music publisher are evolving; music publishers currently are seeking to get paid in two ways (referred to as "double-dipping"): once for the reproduction of the MP3 file; and again for the transmission of the file over the Internet. Each of the payments and permission are discussed below.

- **Payment to music publisher for reproduction.** If a song was previously recorded and released in the U.S., permission can be obtained by using a compulsory license as described in Section E1 or by negotiating a digital delivery license directly with the Harry Fox Agency. See Section E2.
- **Payment to music publisher for transmission.** As of the writing of this book, a perfor-

mance license and fee must be negotiated with the appropriate performing rights societies (see Section I2a) for the right to transmit a digital recording such as an MP3. Contact the performing rights society and request a license for digital phonorecord delivery.

Both BMI and ASCAP grant blanket licenses for website uses. The minimum fees for these licenses range from $250 to $500, but total annual fees may be higher depending on the website's revenue. Both BMI and ASCAP offer formulas based on a percentage (ranging between 1.6% and 2.5%) of the net revenue of the website. To determine the amount, visit each performing society's website and download the society's website license. Rate calculations are located on the last page of each agreement. For information on determining whether BMI or ASCAP represents a music publisher, review Section K.

b. MP3 Sound Recording Permission

Digital phonorecord delivery, such as providing MP3 files for downloading, requires permission from the sound recording owner, usually a record company. This can prove to be an expensive and time-consuming procedure, as most record companies are wary of licensing rights for making digital copies of their sound recordings. For information about locating record companies, see Section L.

2. Webcasting and Audio Streaming

Webcasting and audio streaming are processes by which digital music is broadcast over the Internet, much like a radio station broadcasts music. The computer user hears the music simultaneously as it is being played by the website. Both webcasting and audio streaming are referred to as "digital audio transmissions." The music industry characterizes digital audio transmissions as either being interactive or noninteractive.

a. Interactive Digital Audio Transmissions

An interactive digital audio transmission is one in which a user requests a performance of a particular recording, usually by clicking on a song title. This type of transmission is popular for purposes of promoting recordings.

EXAMPLE: Kinksology is a website that features music of the rock group The Kinks. Don visits the site, clicks on the song title, "You Really Got Me," and hears the Kinks song. Don does not receive a copy of the song on his computer. He can only hear it by clicking on the button. Kinksology is providing interactive digital audio transmissions.

The rules for interactive digital audio transmission are the same as for MP3. The website must obtain two permissions from the music publisher: a blanket license from the performing societies, BMI and ASCAP (assuming songs are being played from the societies' repertoire); and a mechanical license, usually from the Harry Fox Agency. The website must also obtain permission from the sound recording owner, usually a record company. This permission must be directly negotiated with the record company.

The 30-Second Exception

Music publishers and record companies have reached an agreement between themselves to permit the interactive broadcast of a maximum of 30 seconds of a recording for promotional purposes. This agreement is solely between music publishers and record companies and can be used only to promote their own music and recordings. A website owner that does not own rights in either the sound recording or song cannot participate in this 30-second exception. However, as a practical matter, permission is routinely granted for 30-second digital audio segments of recordings used to promote the sale of those recordings.

b. Noninteractive Digital Audio Transmissions

A noninteractive digital audio transmission is one in which a website broadcasts various recordings over the Internet, much like a radio station, typically referred to as webcasting. A listener can request to hear a particular recording via email and, like a radio station, all listeners to the webcast will hear that requested recording.

EXAMPLE: 60s.com is a website that broadcasts music of the 1960s. Don visits the site and hears various songs. Don does not receive a copy of the songs on his computer. He emails a request, and when it is broadcast all listeners to 60s.com hear the song on their computers. 60s.com is providing noninteractive digital audio transmissions.

A website offering noninteractive digital audio transmission (or, a webcaster) must obtain permission from the music publisher in the form of a blanket performance license granted by the performing rights societies. Information about these blanket licenses is provided, above, in Section D1.

A webcaster must also follow certain rules and pay a fee, fixed by law, to the record company. This permits the webcasters to make single copies of recordings necessary in webcasting (known as "ephemeral recordings"). The rules to qualify are lengthy and include requirements such as:

- the digital broadcast cannot be interactive
- the broadcast cannot activate remote recording devices, and
- during a three-hour broadcast period, a site cannot program more than three songs from a single album, nor play two songs in a row from a single album.

More information on these rules can be obtained from the U.S. Copyright Office website.

c. Simulcasting

Local radio stations sometimes send their broadcast signal through the Internet, a practice known as "simulcasting." Simulcasting radio stations are required to follow a simpler set of rules than for noninteractive digital audio transmissions, and must pay a licensing fee. However, national radio broadcasting companies have announced their opposition to these rules and a court battle is expected to resolve the dispute. To learn more about the rules, visit the Copyright Office website at lcWeb.loc.gov/copyright/.

J. Using Music Samples

Sampling is the process of copying a piece of recorded music (usually on a device known as a sampler) and then reproducing it within another recording. Sometimes the sample is used repeatedly, such as a drumbeat or a vocal chorus. Sometimes a sample is used once or twice to accent a composition. Although there are some exceptions for trivial or unrecognizable samples, as a general rule, sampling is illegal without the authorization of the

owner of the recording (the record company) and the owner of the song (the music publisher).

There are no standardized fees or procedures for obtaining sampling permission and it can prove to be an expensive and time-consuming process. Some artists have had to give up one-third to one-half of their income in order to acquire sampling permissions. In this section we explain the basic rules and provide a model agreement for sampling permissions.

1. Sampling Licenses and Fees

While there are no standardized fees for sampling, as a general rule, the music publisher usually wants an advance payment (between $250 and $5,000) and a percentage of the income derived from the new recording, usually between 15% and 50%. In addition, the owner of the master recording may want an up-front payment (usually at least $1,000) plus a "rollover," a payment that must be made when a certain number of copies have been sold. Sometimes, instead of a rollover, the owner of the master may want a portion of future record royalties (although sampling consultants advise against this practice).

Record companies and music publishers typically provide sample clearance agreements. You'll also find copies of model sampling agreements in *Music Law: How to Run Your Band's Business* (Nolo.com), which also can be downloaded from the Nolo website (www.nolo.com) for a fee.

2. Reducing Sample Fees

Part of the sampling clearance fees can be avoided by re-recording the sampled section. Instead of sampling the original recording, a company can hire musicians to play the parts, creating a new recording that sounds very similar to the original. In that case, permission is only required from the music publisher. However, this imitation may require additional permissions if it is used to sell a service or product (see Section F).

Do not assume that sampling fees will be avoided by sampling public domain songs. The sound recording may be protected even though the song is in the public domain.

> **EXAMPLE:** In 1999, the singer P.J. Harvey records and releases the public domain song, "I Dream of Jeannie With the Light Brown Hair." George samples the recording and includes the sample on his new album. Although the song is in the public domain, the P.J. Harvey sound recording is not and George must obtain permission from P.J. Harvey's record company.

Of course, all sampling fees can be avoided by re-recording public domain songs. Companies also save money by using sample discs available from production music libraries and other sources. These recordings contain short musical parts that are "pre-cleared." Sample discs grant the user an "unlimited nonexclusive license" to use the samples once the disc is purchased. Always read the accompanying shrink-wrap or license agreement to verify this right before purchasing. Sample discs are not the same as PML music (see Section B5) and can be purchased through music stores and music supply catalogs. Advertisements for sample discs appear regularly in various music magazines such as *Keyboard* and *Electronic Musician.*

3. Operating Without Sample Clearance

Not every use of a sample constitutes an infringement. If an average listener comparing both works (the new composition and the source) can't hear any substantial similarities, there's no violation of the law. It is also possible that the use of a sample may qualify as fair use. The rap group 2 Live Crew's use of the musical tag and the opening lyric line from "Oh Pretty Woman," was considered to be a fair use because it was limited (the sampled section was used once) and it was for purposes of parody. *(Campbell v. Acuff-Rose Music,* 510 U.S. 569 (1994).) For more information on fair use, see Chapter 9, "Fair Use."

4. Using Samples to Sell a Product or Service

If a sample is used to sell or endorse a product (for example, using James Brown's voice in a Nike ad) and the sampled performer is identifiable, the performer's consent must be obtained. Without consent, the source artist could sue for violation of the right of publicity (see Chapter 12, "Releases"). The same rule would apply if the performer's voice is imitated by another singer.

K. Finding Music Publishers

The easiest method to locate the music publisher of a song is to search the online song databases at the three performing rights societies, BMI (bmi.com), ASCAP (www.ascap.com) and SESAC (www.sesac.com). Alternatively, you can search all three societies at the Music Publishers' Association at www.mpa.org/copyright/searchenter.html. These three societies represent all types of music, although SESAC's catalog is primarily gospel and country music.

Performing societies do not own songs; they represent music publishers for purposes of negotiating certain types of permissions. A song is usually listed with only one of the performing rights societies, although occasionally, songs written by more than one person may be listed in the catalogs for both societies. Online song databases can be searched by title, writer, performer or publisher. If you don't have access to the Internet, call the performing rights society and ask for writer/publisher information.

If a song cannot be located through BMI, ASCAP or SESAC, check the song database at the Harry Fox Agency (www.harryfox.com) which represents approximately 80% of U.S. music publishers (see Sidebar in Section D1). Harry Fox differs from the performing rights societies in that it deals with permission for copying a song onto a CD or tape (referred to as "mechanical rights") rather than performing a song publicly. Mechanical rights permissions are discussed in more detail throughout this chapter.

EXAMPLE: Our goal was to find the music publisher of "Ring of Fire." We started by searching BMI and ASCAP online databases. The BMI database provided three different songs entitled "Ring of Fire." Johnny Cash recorded the version we wanted. Searching the BMI database by artist, we discovered songs recorded by Johnny Cash including "Ring of Fire."

Writers: June Carter & Merle Kilgore
Publisher: Painted Desert Music Corporation, 640 Fifth Avenue, New York, NY 10019-6102; 212-957-0802, fax: 212-397-4638.

If you're unsure of a song's title, verify it through an online music store such as Amazon.com or CDNow. These sites contain databases searchable by song title, album title or artist and usually offer 30-second previews of the music to verify the correct version.

If a music publisher can't be located using the resources listed in this section, further research may be required. Try using some of the suggestions in Chapter 13, "Copyright Research," or use the services of a music clearance expert as described in Section M.

L. Finding Record Companies

The record company (the owner of the sound recording) can usually be determined by examining the cover artwork or liner notes and reviewing the sound recording copyright notice. The notice consists of the letter P in a circle, followed by the date the recording was published and the name of the recording copyright owner—for example: "℗ 1984, NBT Records."

If the recording was made before 1972, there will be no song recording copyright notice because recordings were not protected by copyright before that time. However, even in these cases the name of the record company usually appears prominently on the recording or artwork. Keep in mind that it is common for companies to transfer ownership of

sound recordings, so your information may be out of date if you're using an old recording.

If you're having trouble locating a sound recording owner try the following:

- Check online record stores or the Phonolog directory at a local record shop to determine the record company that is currently releasing the music, and contact that company.
- Find the publisher of a song featured on the recording and ask the publisher for information about the sound recording owner.
- If you're still unable to locate the sound recording owner, use the services of a music clearance expert (see Section M).

When contacting a record company, ask for licensing, clearance or the special products department. Most large record companies have departments that handle sound recording clearance. For example, Warner Special Products manages the licensing of sound recordings owned by Warner Bros., Elektra and Atlantic.

M. Music Clearance Companies

Music clearance companies assist in locating song and sound recording owners and acquiring permission to use music for a wide range of purposes including film, TV, multimedia and websites. Many clearance companies also help to clear sample rights. There is a wide variety of services offered and companies often specialize in a particular music clearance niche. A list of music clearance companies is provided at the end of this chapter.

N. Music Resources

This section lists a variety of resources that may be of help in the process of music licensing.

1. Production Music Libraries (PMLs)

Below is a list of PMLs. More can be located using an Internet search engine.

- Audio Palette: 800-454-1900, 818-718-9999, fax: 818-718-9990; www.smartsound.com/music.
- BMG Killer Tracks: See "Internet PML Licensing" below.
- British Audio Designs: P.O. Box 60631, Sunnyvale, CA 94088; 877-744-3742; email: ebritishaudio@intentscp.com; Web: www.intentscp.com.
- Chestnut Mills Musicraft: 12650 W. 64th Ave., Unit E #250, Arvada, CO 80004; Web: www.chestnutmills.com.
- Flying Hands Music: P.O. Box 19468, Louisville, KY 40259-0468; 800-536-6007, fax: 502-451-0090; Web: www.flyinghands.com.
- Gene Michael Productions: 441 Post Road, Buchanan, MI 49107-1051; 800-955-0619, fax: 616-695-4005 email: gmplibrary@genemichaelproductions.com; Web: www.genemichaelproductions.com.
- Impact Music: 800-779-6434; email: sales@studioland.com; Web: www.studioland.com.
- Lazertrax Production Music: P.O. Box 956009, Duluth, GA 30136-9501; 888-TRY-TRAX; fax: 888-879-8729; Web: www.lazertrax.com.
- Megatrax Production Music: 11684 Ventura Blvd., #978, Studio City, CA 91604; 888-MEGA-555, fax: 818-502-5244; email: megatrax@megatrax.com; Web: www.megatrax.com.
- Music Bakery: 800-229-0313; Web: www.musicbakery.com.
- Network Music: 15150 Avenue of Science, San Diego, CA 92128; 800-854 2075, fax: 619-451-6409; email: feedback@networkmusic.com; Web: www.networkmusic.com/prod.htm.
- ProBackground Theme Music (PBTM): 1350 Chambers Street, Eugene, OR 97402; 541-345-0212; fax: 541-345-8117; email:

info@pbtm.com; Web: www.pbtm.com/about.html.
- Production Music and Sound Effects Libraries: 941A Clint Moore Road, Boca Raton, FL 33487; 800-322-7879, fax: 561-995-8434; email: mail@Promusic-inc.com; Web: www.promusic-inc.com.
- Southern Library of Recorded Music: 4621 Cahuenga Blvd., Toluca Lake, CA 91602; 818-752-1530, fax: 213-656-3298.
- Valentino Production Music, Inc.: 500 Executive Blvd., Elmsford, NY 10523-0534; 800-223-6278, fax 914-347-4764; email: info@tvmusic.com; Web: www.tvmusic.com/index.html.
- Video Helper: 877-VIDEOHELPER, fax 212-633-9014; email: info@videohelper.com; Web: www.videohelper.com/index.html.
- Zomba Enterprises, Inc.: See "Internet PML Licensing" below.

Internet PML Licensing

As of the writing of this book, one of the largest libraries of production music, Zomba Music, was preparing a website designed specifically for Internet licensing. Information about the Zomba site and related PML Web music can be found at www.beatnik.com. It is expected that other companies will follow this trend including another large PML, BMG Killer Tracks.

2. Performing Rights Societies

- BMI: 320 W. 57th Street, New York, NY 10019; 212-586-2000; in L.A.: 310-659-9109; in Nashville: 615-401-2000; Web: bmi.com.
- ASCAP: One Lincoln Plaza, New York, NY 10023; 212-621-6000; in L.A.: 213-883-1000; in Nashville: 615-742-5000; Web: www.ascap.com.

- SESAC: 421 W. 54th Street, New York, NY 10019; 212-586-3450; in Nashville: 615-20-0055, fax 212-489-5699; Web: www.sesac.com.

3. Mechanical Rights Societies

- The Harry Fox Agency: 711 Third Avenue, 8th Flr., New York, NY 10017; 212-370-5330, fax: 212-953-2384; Web: www.harryfox.com.

4. Record Company Resources

The following resources provide contact information for record companies and are available at online bookstores and libraries.

- Album Network's Yellow Pages of Rock (The Album Network), 120 North Victory Boulevard, 3rd Floor, Burbank, CA 91502; 800-222-4382.
- The Recording Industry Sourcebook (Intertec Publishing), 6400 Hollis Street, Suite 12, Emeryville, CA 94608; 800-543-7771.
- Billboard Power Guide (Billboard Directories), P.O. Box 2016, Lakewood, NJ 08701; 800-344-7119.
- The Recording Industry Association of America (RIAA), a trade organization for record labels, may be able to provide more information regarding contact information for record labels. Its contact information is: 1020 19th St. NW, Suite 200, Washington, DC 20036; 202-775-0101, fax: 202-775-7253; Web: www.riaa.com.
- *Euro Pop Book* and *Euro Jazz Book* contain information on European record labels, music publishers and more. Available through Sound Marketing, 155 West 72nd Street, Suite 706, New York, NY 10023; 888-387-6249, fax 212-875-8648; email: soundmktg@earthlink.net; Web: home.earthlink.net/~soundmktg.

5. Music Clearance Companies

The services marked with an asterisk (*) also perform sampling clearance services.

- Arlene Fishbach Enterprises: 310-451-5916.
- BZ Rights and Permissions, Inc.: 212-924-3000, fax: 212-924-2525; Web: www.bzrights.com.
- *Clearance 13' 8" : 212-580-4654, fax 212-787-5834.
- Clearance Consultants: 310-441-2600, fax: 310-253-5086.
- Clearance Quest: 615-244-9305; email: photogal1@prodigy.net.
- Copyright Clearinghouse, Inc.: 818-558-3480, fax: 818-558-3474.
- Copyright Music and Visuals: 416-979-3333, fax: 416-979-2559 (Canada).
- *Diamond Time LTD.: 212-274-1006, fax: 212-274-1938; email: DTIMEMY@aol.com.
- Diane Prentice Music Clearance Inc.: 818-830-1270, 818-830-1274.
- *DMG, Inc.: 914-248-8319, 323-660-6116, fax: 914-248-8541.
- Fricon Entertainment Co., Inc.: 323-931-7323, fax: 323-938-2030; in Nashville: 615-826-2288, fax 615-826-0500.
- Jill Meyers Music Consultants: 310-441-2604, fax: 310-475-4323; email: jillmeyers@linkline.com.
- Longo Music Services: 818-368-4018, fax: 818-366-2968; email: longomusic@earthlink.com.
- Madeleine Smith Clearance Services: 661-257-1700, fax: 661-294-7836; email: madsong@earthlink.net.
- *Music Resources: 323-993-9915, fax: 323-993-9921.
- Parker Music Group: 818-905-9552, fax: 818-905-7807; Web: www.musicclearance.com.
- *Sample Clearance Limited: 212-586-3213, fax: 212-265-2033.
- Screenmusic International: 818-985-9997.
- *Signature Sound, Inc.: 212-989-0011, fax: 212-989-3576; Web: www.signature-sound.com.

- *Songwriter Services: 805-257-1700, fax 805-294-7836.
- Sound Thinking: 805-495-3306.

- Tulchin & Associates: 310-914-7979, fax: 310-914-7927; email: entesquire@aol.com; Web: www.medialawyer.com.

Website Permissions

The opportunities for inexpensive publishing on the Web have made "publishers" out of everyone who posts material online. While Web technology has made publishing more accessible to everyone, it's also brought potential copyright disputes to the masses. The rules for photos, text, music and artwork discussed in previous chapters (see Sidebar) apply just the same to websites and there is no reason to repeat them in this chapter. Instead, this chapter focuses on two specific problem areas for webmasters: unauthorized transfers of information to and from websites, and website linking.

- Copyright infringement occurs whenever copyrighted material is transferred to or from a website without authorization from the copyright owner. Transferring information to and from a website can be done in a few ways. A user can take information from a website by copying or downloading. Or, material can be placed (sometimes called "uploaded" or "posted") from a user's computer onto the website. Any time copyrighted information is transferred to or from a website without authorization from the owner, the owner may have a copyright infringement claim against the copier, the website or both. We'll discuss how to limit liability and what to do if confronted by an angry rights holder.

- Website links involve another potential area of copyright conflict. A link takes a user from one website page to another simply by clicking on a word or image. Although permission is not needed for a simple word link (also known as a "hypertext" link), it is required when the link comprises a trademark from the linked site (for example, using the Amazon logo without permission). Some other types of links known as deep links or framed links also require permission.

This chapter discusses these Web-specific permission issues and how to obtain the necessary permissions for website uses. We also provide a sample linking agreement for you to use. Since websites are becoming increasingly common targets for infringement lawsuits, we will focus on how website owners and people who manage websites (webmasters) can minimize their liability.

If you have hired a webmaster to maintain the site, the information in this chapter will be of use to both of you. While the webmaster will need to understand copyright rules in order to keep the site out of legal trouble, it's generally the owner of the site who will be liable for any claims of infringement. When we refer to the webmaster or the owner of a site in this chapter, keep in mind that both the webmaster and the owner should be aware of and compliant with copyright rules on the Web.

The underlying principles regarding various types of unauthorized uses are covered in previous chapters. Readers who turned directly to this chapter may want to cross-refer to these discussions:

- **Copyrighted material used without authorization.** Review Chapters 2 (text), 3 (photographs), 4 (artwork), 5 (music) and 15 (assignments and works for hire).
- **Trademarks used without authorization.** Review Chapter 10, "Getting Permission to Use Trademarks."
- **A person's image used for commercial purposes without authorization.** Review Chapter 12, "Releases."
- **A person is defamed or suffers invasion of privacy.** Review Chapter 12, "Releases."

A. Websites: Five Ways to Stay Out of Trouble

Since the Web is freely accessible and since it is quite easy to copy material from one site to another, many myths have developed regarding the right to use copyrighted materials and trademarks. Without repeating the copyright and trademark rules established in previous chapters, here are some simple rules for websites.

1. Assume It's Protected

As a general rule, it is wise to operate under the assumption that all works are protected by either copyright or trademark law unless conclusive information indicates otherwise. A work is not in the public domain simply because it has been posted on the Internet (a popular fallacy) or if it lacks a copyright notice (another myth). For information on these and other public domain issues, see Chapter 8, "The Public Domain."

2. Read Click-Wrap Agreements

Do not assume that clip art, shareware, freeware or materials labeled "royalty-free" or "copyright-free" can be distributed or copied without authorization. Read the terms and conditions in the "click to accept" agreement (often called a click-wrap agreement) or "Read Me" files ordinarily accompanying such materials to be certain that your intended use is permitted. One company failed to honor the terms of a click-wrap agreement and was found liable for illegally distributing three volumes of software clip art. *(Marobie-Fl, Inc. v. National Association of Fire Equipment Distributors,* 983 F. Supp. 1167 (E.D. Ill. 1997).)*

3. Remove Unauthorized Material

If someone complains about an unauthorized use at a website, the offending material should be removed immediately. In the case of unauthorized uploads, downloads or links, the webmaster should disable access to the offending material or link. This is not to imply that you should cave in to every complaint. However, the material should be removed during the period during which you investigate the claim and, if necessary, consult with an attorney. Attempts to "contain" the damage will likely help your case should it find its way into court. Continuing to use the offensive material after being notified may aggravate the claim and increase the chances of your being found liable—and increase the amount of damages you may have to pay.

Removal of infringing material is also an element of a 1998 law establishing that an Internet Service Provider (ISP, a company that provides Internet access to individuals and businesses) can avoid liability by following certain rules including speedy removal of infringing material. The text of this law is downloadable from the Copyright Office website at lcweb.loc.gov/copyright/. Click on "The Digital Millennium Copyright Act" and review Title II. The Copyright Office also offers information about how to deal with notices of infringement. You'll find this info at lcWeb.loc.gov/copyright/onlinesp/.

4. Investigate Claims Promptly

If someone complains about unauthorized use, investigate the claim quickly and seek evidence of copyright ownership and copyright validity from the complaining person. The webmaster can verify the facts through copyright research (see Chapter 13, "Copyright Research"). The webmaster must also investigate the transfer of the infringing material, if any, to and from the site. If copies were downloaded, how many and to whom? If copies were uploaded, by whom?

Below is a sample letter that can be adopted for use in response to a claim of infringement.

Sample Response to Infringement Claim

Dear Ms. Crancastle:

I received your certified letter of May 1, 2000, in which you state that my website, Chihuahua Planet, contains an unauthorized reproduction of a photo entitled "Jimmy the Flying Chihuahua." According to your letter, you are the copyright owner of the photo.

I have not had an opportunity to investigate your claim. However, pending resolution of the dispute, all copies of "Jimmy the Flying Chihuahua" have been removed from the site and access to the file containing the photo was disabled, thereby preventing downloading.

I would like to resolve this matter quickly and to do so will require some evidence of your copyright ownership. At your earliest convenience, please send me a copyright registration or some other evidence that you are the author of the photo. Once I have that information, I shall complete my investigation and promptly provide you with a response.

Sincerely,

Don Daly

5. When in Doubt, Seek Permission

Many webmasters manage personal websites or sites for small organizations such as a local tennis team. Do all of the rules on copyright and permissions apply to these intimate or personal uses? For example, is permission needed to reproduce a photo taken by a club member, a friend or a relative? The short answer is: "Legally, yes, practically, maybe."

Copyright protection extends to any original work regardless of who created it, and permission is required for reproduction, display or distribution of the work. One of the main reasons for acquiring permission is to avoid a lawsuit. If the webmaster is confident that a friend or family member has consented to the use, the concern over a lawsuit diminishes, as does the need for a formal written permission agreement. Oral consents are valid, although sometimes difficult to prove.

But, if you are in doubt about a use, always seek a written permission, even if the material comes from a friend or relative. Formal permission agreements are provided at the end of this book. However, in cases of cooperative friends and relatives, an informal release can be used, such as the following sentence:

I am the owner of rights to _____

[title of work] and I authorize its display and

reproduction at the _____

[name of website] website located at _____

[insert URL for site] for a period of _____

[insert length of time].

If you want to include additional items in the agreement, such as a requirement that a credit line for the work appear at the site, you can add them to this brief agreement.

EXAMPLE: Sally is the webmaster for the Jefferson Elementary School and intends to post student paintings. Sally has the parent of each child sign a one-sentence permission agreement stating, "I authorize the display and reproduction of the artwork entitled _____, credited to my child, _____, at the Jefferson Elementary School website for a period of one year."

The Likelihood of Getting Caught

As Web commerce increases, so does the likelihood of being caught for unauthorized uses. Many companies such as McDonald's, MTV, Levi's, Mattel, Walt Disney and Coca-Cola aggressively patrol the Web for infringement. New technology makes it possible for copyright owners to encode music, artwork, photographs and text with digital tags or marks that allow rapid tracking. Companies such as Markwatch (www.markwtch.com) and Datalytics, Inc. (www.datalytics.com) function as cyber bounty hunters. In addition, artist and writer organizations such as the Association for the Protection of Internet Copyright (also known as WebPossee, at a-w.org) seek out violations. If a website is controversial and angers some visitors, they may report perceived violations to copyright or trademark owners. Disgruntled employees are also common sources of infringement reports.

Besides the fact that the Web abounds with efficient ways of sniffing out copyright violations, the general rule is that the chances of an unauthorized use being discovered will increase as the site becomes more popular. Therefore, if the goal at a site is to increase traffic count, unauthorized uses should be avoided from the start as they rarely justify the potential aggravation and financial loss.

B. Transferring Information to and From a Website

Copyright infringement occurs whenever copyrighted material is copied from or posted to a website without authorization from the copyright owner. This section discusses the various ways that information can be transferred between your site and its users and the copyright conflicts that may arise with each.

1. Posting Information on a Website

Posting involves a user sending information from the user's computer to the website (sometimes referred to as "uploading"). Once posted, others can view or copy the material. If your site does not offer users a chance to post material, you can skip this section.

> EXAMPLE: A member of a discussion group posts a chapter from a John Grisham book to the group's chat room on the Web, making it available for others to copy.

While the person who uploaded the material is the actual infringer, whoever maintains the site can be held liable for allowing the material to be posted at the site. As with any unauthorized material, the wisest approach to dealing with unauthorized uploads at a site is to remove it quickly or disable access to the material pending resolution of the dispute. (See Section A.)

A site permitting uploading of material can post a notice prohibiting any unauthorized activities and require that perpetrators pay for any damages caused by such activities. The notice should be placed prominently so that persons performing uploads will see it. Alternatively, the site may include a "click to accept" agreement (often called a click-wrap agreement) setting forth similar terms. A click-wrap agreement is a page or window that appears before the user is allowed to perform a certain function (in this case, an upload) which states the terms of an agreement. The user will not be allowed to

proceed until he has clicked in a box to indicate he has read and accepts the agreement.

Below is an example of a "click to accept" agreement intended to prohibit unauthorized postings.

Uploading Restrictions

User agrees not to post:

- any materials protected under copyright, trademark or trade secret laws unless with the express authorization of the owner; or

- any material likely to defame or invade the privacy of any individual.

User agrees to indemnify the owners of the site and their affiliates and employees from any liability (including attorney fees) related to User's violation of this agreement.

CLICK TO ACCEPT

Unfortunately, notices and "click to accept" agreements are not enforceable in all states. And as a practical matter, a notice or agreement requiring a person who commits an illegal activity to pay your attorney fees is worthless if the person has no funds. Nevertheless, it's worthwhile to include some form of notice or "click to accept" agreement on your website. It may deter some users from making illegal uploads, and it may help to show your diligence in trying to prevent them.

2. Taking Information From a Website

Just as users can sometimes post information onto a website, in the reverse process a user may take material from the website and transfer it to the user's computer. This is typically done either by downloading or by copying. Many sites are set up for users to download material. Shareware sites, for example, allow users to download software they want by clicking on a downloadable file, which will then be transferred onto the user's computer. Another way of obtaining material from websites is simply by selecting text, copying and pasting it into a word processing document on the user's computer. Strictly speaking this is not downloading, but the effect is the same. The user has obtained material from the website and copied it onto her own computer.

EXAMPLE: A visitor to a Nirvana website that posts unauthorized copies of Kurt Cobain lyrics copies them and saves them in a Microsoft Word document on her computer.

a. Unauthorized Copying

If you don't offer material to download at your site, your main concern isn't whether you'll infringe someone else's copyright, but whether users will copy your material without your permission. Particularly if your site contains copyrightable works by outside authors—for instance, if you publish a Web magazine—you'll want to do everything you can to prevent users from unauthorized copying of the material. One common method (though not necessarily an effective one) is to prominently display a copyright notice on some or all of your Web pages clearly stating that the material is protected by copyright.

To deal with the fact that many users may copy information anyway, one option is to accept this fact and include in your copyright notice a prohibition on any commercial use of the material. In addition, you can require that the copyright notice must always be included with the material, so anyone who reads it knows who created it. Many webmasters are willing to accept some limited copying by users for personal use, especially if the copies show who originally generated the material.

EXAMPLE: Nolo.com, the publisher of this book, maintains a website with extensive self-help legal information. Since Nolo's goal is to empower people to take care of their own legal affairs, it is willing to accept some copying of the material at its site, with some limitations. Its copyright notice, which can be accessed from nearly every page, reads in part as follows:

Nolo's Copyright Policy

Nolo provides the information on this site to be read by anyone, but retains the copyright on all text and graphics. To use this information in any other way, you must strictly follow these guidelines.

Use by Individuals

As long as it is for your own personal use only, you may print copies of this information, store the files on your computer, and use hypertext links to reference the information.

However, if you publish material from the Nolo site on your website, you must follow the guidelines below, "Use by All Websites."

Licensing and Reprint Rights

If you wish to license or reprint any of the information on this site for non-Internet use (for example, as part of an article, book or pamphlet), contact us at: Webmaster@Nolo.com.

Use by All Websites

If you wish to place any information on this site on your site, Nolo hereby grants you limited permission for this in exchange for your adherence to these guidelines:

Sample Chapters

Sample chapters may not be used other than for personal use, that is, you may print copies of this information, store the files on your computer, and use hypertext links to reference the information. To obtain permission to use a sample chapter in any other way, you must contact us at: Webmaster@Nolo.com

Legal Encyclopedia Articles

1. You must not charge for the material used.

2. You may use no more than three Articles, FAQs, Auntie Nolo Questions & Answers, Legal Quizzes and/or Legal Dictionary entries on your site at any one time.

3. At the top of and in the same size font as text of the material used, you must display the Nolo website logo and this copyright notice: "Copyright © Nolo.com 1999" on each Article, FAQ, Auntie Nolo Question & Answer, Legal Quiz and/or Legal Dictionary entry.

4. You must include a link at the top of each Article, FAQ, Auntie Nolo Question & Answer, Legal Quiz and/or Legal Dictionary entry to the Nolo homepage at http://www.nolo.com (for instance, by making "Nolo" in the copyright notice a link) in the same size type as the text of the material used.

5. You must send an email message to Webmaster@Nolo.com with information about what content you are using and where the article appears.

We reserve the right to change the terms of and/or withdraw this permission at any time and for any reason.

If you take this more liberal approach, make sure that any contributors to your site who may retain copyright in their work understand and accept your policy. Otherwise, if they later discover that their article was copied, they might sue you for allowing their work to be infringed.

b. Unauthorized Downloading

The concept of unauthorized downloading may seem strange, considering that most sites that offer files for download are obviously consenting to the download. However, even if downloads are specifically allowed from your site, you still may have concerns over unauthorized uses of the downloaded material. For instance, if you offer free clip art for download at your site, you may want to prohibit users from selling the clip art, and limit their use to personal use. If the user violates the restriction, you may be able to sue for breach of contract. This approach has been successful in disputes based upon clip art and stock photos. Even if the agreement is not enforceable, its presence may defeat a claim of innocent infringement by the user.

A sample downloading restriction appears below. You can post it as a notice displayed where a downloader would clearly see it, or implement it as a "click to accept" agreement, as described in Section 1 above.

Downloading Restrictions

User agrees that the material provided for downloading is to be used solely for personal purposes such as on home computers and may not be reproduced, displayed or distributed for any commercial purposes.

CLICK TO ACCEPT

Liability for Other Website Issues

Websites may also get into disputes over domain names, obscenity and fraud. Issues may also arise based upon a website's content. For example, owners of sexually explicit sites may need to have warning notices; commercial sites must meet trade requirements such as posting refund and return policies; and sites offering stock trading should provide securities disclaimers. Sites providing downloads may want to disclaim liability for any potential viruses. These website issues are beyond the scope of a permissions book. Chapter 16, "Help Beyond This Book," directs you to additional resources to help you with these and other issues.

C. Connecting to Other Websites

One of the central features of the Web is the ability for each Web page to offer quick connections to other Web pages in the click of a button. There are a few different ways that websites connect with one another, each with different legal implications in the permissions context. This section discusses the issues raised when your site includes connections to other websites, and includes a sample linking agreement.

1. Linking and Framing

Two common ways websites connect to other sites are linking and framing.

a. Linking

Most often, a website will connect to another in the form of a link (also known as a "hypertext" link). A link is simply a specially coded word or image that when clicked upon, will take a Web user to another webpage. A link can take the user to another page within the same site (an "internal link"), or to another site altogether (an "external link").

> EXAMPLE: At the Nolo.com website, each page offers several links to other areas of the site. For example, from Nolo's Legal Encyclopedia area on Small Business information, you can link to Nolo's bookstore. These are internal links. Nolo.com also includes links to other sites such as Findlaw.com and the Small Business Administration's websites. These are external links.

Permission is not needed for a regular word link to another website's home page (however, see the warning about "deep linking" below). Even if your link appears perfectly legal, it is considered good online etiquette ("netiquette") to obtain consent for all links. Most linking issues can be squared away by having the linked site sign a linking agreement giving permission for the link as provided in Section C2.

⚠ **Linking to a page other than a website's home page sometimes angers Web owners.** The reason Web owners dislike this practice, known as deep linking, is that it allows users to bypass the home page, which often contains information the Web owner wants its users to see. Advertisements, for instance, are usually placed on a home page, and the fewer viewers that see it, the less the Web can charge for advertising space. In 1997, the Ticketmaster company sued Microsoft over deep links to Ticketmaster's ordering forms, and the case has not yet been resolved.

b. Framing

Besides external links, another way to access other sites is by framing. Framing is a lot like linking in that you code a word or image so that it will connect to another Web page when the user clicks on it. What makes framing different is that instead of taking the user to the next page, the information from that page is imported into the original page and displayed in a special "frame." Technically, when you're viewing framed information your computer is connected to the site doing the framing—not the site appearing in the frame.

EXAMPLE: John starts a site devoted to auto racing news called John's RacingVision. He offers a number of links to racing industry Web magazines like Autosport, and displays their content within a frame at his site. When users click on "Read Autosport News," for example, the content from the Autosport site is displayed within John's RacingVision website, in a frame. When the user reads the Autosport news, their computer is still connected to John's website, not Autosport's.

Framing is generally unpopular with websites whose content is framed at another site (unless they have agreed to it). Websites who frame the content of other sites are often seen as stealing the other site's content. One court found framing to be a copyright infringement because the process resulted in an unauthorized modification of the linked site. (*Futuredontics Inc. v. Applied Anagramic Inc.,* 45 U.S.P.Q. 2d 2005 (C.D. Cal. 1998).) In another case, *The Washington Post,* CNN and several other news companies sued a website, TotalNews, which framed news content. Under the terms of a settlement agreement, TotalNews agreed to stop framing and agreed to only use text-only links.

While case law hasn't developed definitive rules on the issue, a framer is more likely to be found liable for copyright (or trademark) infringement if copyrighted material is modified without authorization or if customers are confused as to the association between the two sites or the source of a product or service. For more information on trademark infringement, see Chapter 10, "Getting Permission to Use Trademarks."

Also beware of inlining content. Inlining (sometimes referred to as "mirroring"), which is similar to framing, involves the process of incorporating a graphic file from one website onto another website. As with framing, the site whose graphic is being used is likely to object. For example, United Media, the copyright owner of the "Dilbert" comic strip, pressured a computer user into halting daily inlining of daily comic strips taken from the United Media website.

Keep in mind that some forms of framing are perfectly legal. For instance, many sites use frames as a way of organizing their own content. When framing the content of another site, however, you are entering hazardous territory. Unless you know a site won't object (and preferably have their agreement in writing), you should proceed very carefully if you want to frame other websites' content.

2. Linking Agreements

The purpose of a linking agreement, like all permission agreements, is to avoid a dispute. If a webmaster is confident that a link will not create a dispute, then a linking agreement is probably not necessary.

However, the following types of links may create disputes:

- image links, particularly where the image is a trademark from the linked site
- deep links that bypass the site's homepage
- links that result in framing, and
- inlining links that only pull certain elements from a site, such as an image.

The permission may be informal, such as a written statement from the distant site stating, "You have permission to link to our website's homepage using the words *[insert the words in the link]*." Or, you can use a longer agreement that covers the terms more specifically.

The agreement provided below can be used to avoid disputes over any of these types of links. A copy of this form is in the Appendix at the end of this book and on the forms disk.

Linking Agreement

This Agreement (the "Agreement") is made between _____ ("Source Site")

with its homepage URL of _____ and _____ ("Destination

Site") with its homepage URL of _____ .

The parties agree as follows:

The Link

The Source Site will provide a link to the Destination Site as follows:: _____

_____ (the "Link")

The Link includes Destination Site's URL and:

(select if appropriate)

☐   Hypertext link—the words: _____ .

☐   Image link: _____ .

☐   Framed link: _____ .

Grant

Destination Site grants the right to display the Link at the Source Site and the nonexclusive right to

display publicly the trademarks or images in the Link. Source Site obtains no trademark rights under

this Agreement other than the right to display the marks. Any goodwill associated with the Source

Site's trademarks automatically vests in the Destination Site.

Standards and Notifications

(select if appropriate)

☐   Source Site shall maintain its site in accordance with industry standards and upon notice from
Destination Site shall promptly remove the Link if required. Source Site shall promptly notify
Destination Site of any change to the Link or changes to the Source Site affecting the Link.

By: _____   By: _____

Date: _____   Date: _____

Source Site Title: _____   Destination Site Title: _____

Source Site Mailing Address: _____   Destination Site Mailing Address: _____

email: _____   email: _____

The Linking Agreement is on the forms disk under the file name LINKAGR.

a. Explanation for Linking Agreement

- In the introductory section, insert the name of the company or person that owns the source site. The source site is the site where the link is located—that is, the starting point for the link. Once the link is clicked the user is taken to the destination site. Insert the URL (Web address—for example, www.address.com) for each site.

- In the section entitled "The Link," describe the pages that are linked. For example: "A link between the Source Site's 'Other References' page and Destination Site's internal page entitled 'Copyright Developments.'"
  Or,
  "A link between Source Site's home page and Destination Site's image entitled 'Two Chihuahuas' encapsulated as 2Chihua.JPG."
  Or,
  "A link between Source Site's home page and Destination Site's internal page entitled 'Today's News' resulting in a framed page with the frame incorporating Source site's trademarks and advertisements."
  Sometimes, the best way to describe a frame or inlined link is to provide a screen snapshot and attach it to the agreement. In that case, write in: "As attached and incorporated into this agreement" and attach the image to the agreement.

- In the next section, choose hypertext link or image link (or both if necessary). A hypertext link is a word link (usually viewed as color highlighted text). An image link should be described. If it is a trademark of the destination site, ask the destination site to supply it (usually in a GIF or JPG format).

- The Grant section permits the use of the link and related trademarks or images. The statement, "Any goodwill associated with the Source Site's trademarks automatically vests in the Destination Site" is a requirement of trademark law. It guarantees that the destination site preserves its trademark rights.

- The optional section entitled "Standards and Notification" is a further assurance sometimes required by a destination site that the source site won't operate in an unlawful manner or change the link dramatically. It offers the option of instant termination. Even if this section is not included, the Destination Site can probably force the removal of the link if it desires.

- Both parties should sign the agreement. For information regarding signing authority, see Chapter 11, "Art & Merchandise Licenses." Many of the miscellaneous provisions included in legal agreements, such as dispute resolution, are not included in order to keep the agreement lean and make it appealing for a quick signature.

b. Linking Disclaimers

To minimize liability for any activities that occur when a visitor is taken to a linked website, a webmaster may want to include a disclaimer on the home page. A disclaimer is a statement denying an endorsement or waiving liability for a potentially unauthorized activity. A sample disclaimer appears below.

Linking Disclaimer

By providing links to other sites, *[name of site]* does not guarantee, approve or endorse the information or products available at these sites.

A disclaimer is not a cure-all for infringement, but if a disclaimer is prominently displayed and clearly written a court may take it into consideration as factor limiting damages (see Chapter 12, "Releases"). For example, in a case involving a dispute between two websites for restaurants named Blue Note, one factor that helped the lesser-known restaurant avoid liability was a prominently displayed disclaimer stating that it was not affiliated with the more famous restaurant. *(Benusan Restaurant v. King,* 937 F. Supp. 295 (S.D. N.Y. 1996).)

Academic and Educational Permissions

This chapter is intended to assist educators seeking permission to use copyrighted works for academic purposes. We provide information about assembling academic coursepacks and discuss issues that arise when using copyrighted material in the classroom. The chapter includes form agreements you can use to obtain clearances for coursepacks, and outlines some established and proposed educational fair use guidelines. We have included this information in a separate chapter because there are some special legal rules for academic uses and there are special services that assist in providing academic permissions.

The first half of this chapter focuses on the most common form of academic permission, the coursepack, a collection of copyrighted materials used for teaching. The second half of the chapter is devoted to an analysis of academic fair use guidelines. These guidelines establish principles in which permission is not required for educational use of copyrighted materials.

A. Academic Coursepacks

An academic coursepack is a collection of materials (usually photocopied) used in the classroom, distributed either in book format or as class handouts. Coursepacks are commonly offered for sale in campus bookstores, although professors may arrange to sell them in class. Most publishers grant "clearances" for coursepacks—that is, for a fee, publishers give permission for their books or articles to be copied and distributed in educational contexts. Such clearances normally last for one semester or for one school term. After that, the instructor must seek clearance again. In addition to these paper coursepacks, some companies now assist in the assembly of electronic coursepacks used in distance learning and electronic teaching programs.

1. Coursepacks and Copyright

Until 1991, many instructors and photocopy shops assembled and sold coursepacks without permission and without compensating the authors or publishers. This was based on the assumption that educational copying qualified as a "fair use" under copyright law, which, legally speaking, is a particular kind of use that is exempt from the permissions requirements that normally apply to copyrighted materials. (For a full explanation of fair use principles, see Chapter 9, "Fair Use.") However, in 1991 a federal court ruled that a publisher's copyright was infringed when a Kinko's copy shop reprinted portions of a book in an academic coursepack. *(Basic Books Inc. v. Kinko's Graphics Corp.,* 758 F.Supp. 1522 (S.D. N.Y. 1991).) The court said that reprinting copyrighted materials in academic coursepacks was not a fair use and that permission was required.

The owner of a copy shop in Ann Arbor, Michigan, began a personal crusade to prove that the Kinko's case was wrongly decided by advertising that he would copy course materials for students and professors. As a result, he was sued by several book publishers. A federal Court of Appeals decided against the copy shop owner, ruling that the copying did not qualify as a fair use. This ruling was based on the amount and substantiality of the portions taken and because academic publishers were financially harmed—they lost licensing revenues—while the copy shop was making money on the coursepacks. *(Princeton Univ. v. Michigan Document Servs.,* 99 F.3d 1381 (6th Cir. 1996).)

This and similar court rulings establish the rule that you need to obtain permission before reproducing copyrighted materials for an academic coursepack. Many campus copy shops still perform coursepack assembly. However, these copy shops have either affiliated with established clearance services or are prepared to obtain clearance on behalf of instructors.

2. Obtaining Clearance for Coursepacks

It's the instructor's obligation to obtain clearance for materials used in class. Instructors typically delegate this task to one of the following:

- Clearance services. These services are the easiest method of clearance and assembly and more information about them is provided in Section A3.
- University bookstores or copy shops. University policies may require that the instructor delegate the task to the campus bookstore, copy shop or to a special division of the university that specializes in clearances. Or,
- Department administration (generally, the instructor's secretary). In Section A4, we offer some suggestions for these kinds of administrators on how to assemble a coursepack without a clearance service.

3. Using a Clearance Service

It can be time-consuming to seek and obtain permission for 20 to 30 or more articles used in a coursepack. Fortunately, private clearance services will, for a fee, acquire permission and assemble coursepacks on your behalf. After the coursepacks are created and sold, the clearance service collects royalties and distributes the payments to the rights holders. Educational institutions may require that the instructor use a specific clearance service. As noted earlier in this chapter, some clearance companies also provide clearance for non-paper electronic coursepacks used in distance learning.

The largest copyright clearing service is Copyright Clearance Center (CCC) and it clears millions of works from thousands of publishers and authors. Among CCC's services are the Academic Permissions Service (APS) for granting permission for paper coursepacks and the Electronic Course Content Service (ECCS), a new service providing permissions for "electronic coursepacks," "electronic reserves" and other new uses of copyrighted material

in the distance education and academic electronic environments.

Contact information for several clearance companies is provided in the resource section at the end of this chapter. The rest of this section discusses the details of working with a clearance company to assemble a coursepack.

a. Clearance Company Fees

The total fees that clearance companies charge for assembling a coursepack are based upon the cost of copyright permission for the material to be copied, plus copying, binding, the clearance service's processing fee and, if sold in a campus bookstore, the store's markup (usually 20%, sometimes 25%). Permission fees vary, but most publishers charge approximately 8 cents per copied page (for example, $4.80 for a 60-page coursepack). Ultimately, the cost of the permission is absorbed by the student buying the coursepack. One advantage of using a coursepack service is that fees are based on the number of copies sold, not printed.

Some clearance services cap their processing fees, which means that the fee for their service (not including other costs like the publisher's fee or printing) will not exceed a certain amount. For example, Campus Custom Publishing (CCP) caps its processing fees at $3 per coursepack. One clearance company, CAPCO/Follett, estimates that a 60-page coursepack would cost students approximately $15 per coursepack (including printing, binding, permission fees and the standard bookstore markup). CCP provided a similar estimate. Note that these rates were applicable at the time of writing this book and may have subsequently changed.

The Copyright Clearance Center (CCC) ordinarily charges customers an annual service fee of $120, regardless of the number of services in which a customer participates, although CCC has been known to clear individual permissions for professors and other individuals who don't have accounts without charging them the annual service fee.

Clearance companies will sometimes work on a "copyright only" basis. This means the company acquires permission to include the material in the coursepack, but does not assemble the coursepacks themselves. This task is usually left to the bookstore, copy shop or academic support staff. Most clearance services provide free estimates for coursepack permissions and assembly.

b. Coursepack Application Forms

To begin the clearance process, you must complete and submit a coursepack application form to the clearance service. Each clearance service has its own application form. Most clearance services have websites from which you can download the forms. You must print the form, complete it and fax it back (clearance companies don't accept email requests). As with all permissions, if you don't make the payment as required under the agreement, the permission may be terminated.

ISBNs and ISSNs

When filling out a coursepack permission request, you'll need to provide the ISBN or ISSN for the publications you want to copy. ISBNs and ISSNs are part of a standardized numbering system all publishers use. ISBNs (International Standard Book Numbers) are used for books. ISSNs (International Standard Serial Numbers) are for magazines, journals, newsletters and other serialized publications. These numbers can be found on or near the title or copyright page or near the publication's UPC bar code. Since several numbers may be printed on the bar code, make sure the number is preceded either by ISSN or ISBN.

c. Clearance Company Agreements

In addition to filling out and submitting an application, you must enter into a written agreement with a clearance company. The agreement establishes that the company will act as your agent to acquire permissions and assemble the coursepack, and details your obligations regarding payment and copyright law.

As noted above, the Copyright Clearance Center's Academic Permissions Service (APS) provides photocopy permissions for paper and electronic coursepacks. In order to use CCC services, a coursepack producer must sign the appropriate APS agreement (see below) that lists the general terms which govern all permissions. Various limitations are included in the agreement which are based on the CCC's years of experience in the industry, and tend to be the same as those you would receive if you asked the author or publisher directly. Thus, for example, 1) no more than 25% may ordinarily be copied from a single book or journal issue, 2) a coursepack will ordinarily be cleared for sale at only one institution, and 3) no permission takes legal effect until payment is made (although this does not mean that payment must be made in advance).

Reprinted below is CCC's latest version of its User Agreement for its Academic Permissions Service. Check CCC's website (www.copyright.com) to be sure that this is the latest version of the document. The website provides additional information about copyright and CCC services, many of which can be conducted over the Internet.

The APS/CCC Coursepack Agreement is included on the forms disk that comes with this book under the file name CCCPERM.

APS/CCC Coursepack Agreement (courtesy Copyright Clearance Center)

PERMISSIONS AGREEMENT made this ____ day of _____ , _____ , between the Copyright Clearance Center, Inc. ("CCC") and _____ ("User").

1. Nature and Form of Program. This Agreement provides for participation by User in CCC's Academic Permissions Service ("APS"). The APS grants authorizations to photocopy and to create photocopy anthologies for sale and/or distribution to students and other academic customers. The copies and anthologies may be made and assembled by faculty members individually or at their request by on-campus bookstores or copy centers, or by off-campus copy shops and other similar entities. It does not permit "publishing ventures" where any particular anthology would be systematically marketed at multiple institutions. User acknowledges that the holders of copyright rights have complete discretion under the United States Copyright Act, 17 United States Code, whether to grant any permission, and whether to place any limitations on any grant, and that CCC has no right to supersede or to modify any such discretionary act by a rightsholder.

2. Grant of Permissions. In order to receive a permission to photocopy a portion of a printed publication, User must first submit to CCC a form as prescribed in CCC's published APS Guidelines. CCC shall not accept any form that is not complete. Within CCC's published response time (measured from CCC's receipt of a completed form), CCC shall notify User whether or not a permission has been granted and the royalty fee due, if any. CCC shall notify User of any limitations imposed by a rightsholder on that permission and, unless User notifies CCC of its intention to decline any particular permission, User shall pay the amount due as set forth in the notification and shall be bound by any such limitation. Any act by User that involves copying beyond that set forth in the notification shall be deemed in its entirety to be an unpermitted act of copying. Separate portions of a work, even if they are to be included in the same anthology, shall require a separate permission under the APS.

3. Payment for Permissions. User shall pay to CCC the amount set forth in the permissions notification in full payment for any permission set forth therein (which will include both the amount due to the rightsholder and the service fee payable to CCC), within the time set forth therein. In the event of a failure by User to pay any such amount by the due date, the applicable permission shall be null and void. In the event that User sells fewer copies than the number for which permissions were granted, User shall pay CCC only for the total number of copies sold, and permissions for the unsold copies shall be null and void.

4. General Terms and Conditions of the Program. Subject to any further limitations determined by any particular rightsholder, the copying permitted under the APS is limited as follows:

(i)   no more than 25% of the text of a book or of the items in a published collection of essays, poems or articles may be copied;

(ii)   no more than the greater of (A) 25% of the text of an issue or of a journal or other periodical, or (B) two articles from such an issue, may be copied;

(iii)   no User may sell or distribute any particular anthology at more than one institution of learning;

(iv)   each copy sold by User must contain a proper copyright notice, identifying the copyright rightsholder in whose name CCC has granted permission and a statement to the effect that such copy was made pursuant to permission; and

(v)   no materials may be entered into electronic memory by User except in order to produce an identical copy of a work before or during the academic term (or analogous period) as to which any particular permission is granted.

In the event that User shall choose to retain the materials in electronic memory for purposes of producing identical copies more than one day after such retention (but still within the scope of any permission granted), User must notify CCC of such fact in the applicable permission request form and such retention shall constitute one copy actually sold for purposes of calculating permissions fees. No permission granted under the APS shall in any way include any right by User to create a non-identical copy of the work or to edit or in any other way modify the work (except by means of deleting material immediately preceding or following the entire portion of the work copied).

5. Term and Termination. This Agreement shall be in force beginning as of the date hereof and shall continue for an initial period of one year. This Agreement is automatically renewable for subsequent one year periods in the absence of timely notice of termination. Either party may terminate this Agreement for any reason by giving 90 days' prior written notice thereof to the other party. In the event of termination of this Agreement for any reason, any permissions the periods of which have not yet ended shall remain in effect until their respective terminations. Termination of this Agreement shall have no effect on any party's obligation to pay money to the other party.

6. Warranty. Each copyright rightsholder which has granted CCC the right to grant permission under the APS to use any particular Work has warranted that it has all rights necessary to authorize CCC to act on its behalf.

7. Books and Records; Right to Audit. As to each permission granted under the APS, User shall maintain for at least four full calendar years books and records sufficient for CCC to determine the numbers of copies made by user under such permission. CCC and any representatives it may designate shall have the right to audit such books and records at any time during User's ordinary business hours, upon two days' prior notice. If any such audit shall determine that User shall have underpaid for, or underreported, any copies sold by three percent (3%) or more, then User shall bear all the costs of any such audit; otherwise, CCC shall bear the costs of any such audit. Any amount determined by such audit to have been underpaid by User shall immediately be paid to CCC by User, together with interest thereon at the rate of 10% per annum from the date such amount was originally due. The provisions of this paragraph shall survive the termination of this Agreement for any reason.

8. Notices. All notices and communications under this Agreement shall be in writing addressed, in the case of User, to the person designated below, and in the case of CCC, its President, and shall be deemed to have been given on the day of delivery or transmission if delivered by hand or if sent by electronic mail or facsimile transmission (with receipt confirmed), or on the fifth business day following the day of mailing if mailed, postage prepaid:

Person and/or title: _____

Address: _____

(if different from that set forth at end of Agreement)

Telephone Number: _____

Facsimile Number: _____

Email Address: _____

9. No Assignment; Integrated Agreement; Governing Law. Neither party to this Agreement shall have the right to assign or sublicense any of its rights or obligations hereunder without the prior written consent of the other party. This agreement constitutes the entire agreement between the parties with respect to the subject matter hereof and may not be modified or amended except in a writing signed by the parties hereto. This Agreement shall be interpreted, construed, governed and enforced in accordance with and under the laws of the State of New York, without giving effect to the principles thereof of conflicts of law.

User's Name: _____

Address: _____

Signature: _____

Printed Name: _____

Title: _____

Copyright Clearance Center, Inc.

222 Rosewood Drive

Danvers, Massachusetts 01923 USA

Signature: _____

4. Assembling Your Own Coursepack

Instead of hiring a clearance company to obtain clearance and assemble a coursepack, you (or your secretary) can do it. Why take on this extra work? There may be two good reasons: 1) a clearance company may be unable to obtain permission for certain items that you may be able to obtain yourself; and 2) by doing it yourself you can save students' money by minimizing your fees.

It's not unusual for a clearance company to be unable or unwilling to acquire permission for certain works. Here's why: Clearance companies typically enter into affiliations with academic publishers—that is, they get permission in advance to use all the material in the publisher's catalog. This avoids having to spend the time and bother of asking permission to use each individual item. This works fine so long as the material you want to use comes from publishers who have affiliated with the coursepack company. But if the material is not from one of these pre-cleared publishers, the clearance company often will not even try to get permission, or will be unable to obtain permission if they do try.

For example, Nolo.com, the publisher of this book, has not authorized APS to grant rights for its works. Therefore, APS could not acquire permission for Nolo books in its coursepacks. In these cases, if you wanted to obtain permission to use Nolo's material, you may want to pursue clearance independently. Before paying membership or annual fees, inquire whether the clearance service is affiliated with the publishers of the articles or books you want to include in your coursepack.

Librarians at Wake Forest University have established the Copyright Permission Pages (www.law.wfu.edu/library/copyright/), an extensive coursepack-assistance website with links to publishers, copyright information sources and related educational organizations. The Association of American Publishers (AAP) website (www.publishers.org) also provides sample request forms and information on coursepack requests.

Here are some suggestions for preparing your own coursepack:

- Start with the publisher (not the author) of the item you want to use and direct your request to the publisher's permissions, licensing or clearance department. If the publisher doesn't control the rights you need, they can probably direct you to the rights holder. Information about locating publishers is provided in Chapter 2, Section A2.
- Obtain permission for works whether or not they are in print. Even if a work is out of print, you still need permission to use it unless it is in the public domain.
- Fax or mail your request at least three to nine weeks before your class begins (most publishers will not accept email requests for permission).

What Copyright Notice Is Used on a Coursepack?

A copyright notice must identify the copyright owners of the materials included in your coursepack. A clearance company can assist in creating the notices. If you are handling clearance on your own, your clearance agreement should require each rightsholder to provide the format for their notice. Below is an example of a notice for a coursepack:

"Dangerous Similarities" by Stan Soocher is excerpted from *They Fought the Law* © Schirmer Books (1998);

"Who Will Own Your Next Good Idea" by Charles C. Mann is excerpted from *Atlantic Monthly* © Atlantic Monthly (Sept. 1998).

a. Sample Coursepack Request Form

Below is a sample coursepack permission request form prepared by the Association of Academic Publishers.

Coursepack Permission Request Form
(Association of Academic Publishers)

To:

Publisher Contact: _____

Publisher: _____

Fax Number: _____

Date of Request: _____

From:

Your Name: _____

Department: _____

School name: _____

Address: _____

City: _____

State: _____

Zip code: _____

Phone #: _____

Fax #: _____

Course name and number: _____

Number of copies needed: _____

Instructor: _____

Semester and year: _____

ISBN/ISSN number: _____

Book or journal title: _____

Author: _____

Translator: _____

Editor: _____

Edition: _____

Volume: _____

Copyright year: _____

Publication year: _____

Chapter/article title: _____

Chapter/article author: _____

Page numbers: _____

Total pages: _____

Is it an out-of-print work? _____

Have you included a copy of the material with this request? _____

Are you the author? _____

Permission is requested for use during one term only. _____

A tear-out copy is included in the Appendix, and a digital copy is in the forms disk at the back of this book. Mail or fax this to the publisher or other rights holder. If you have already discussed rightswith the copyright owner and agreed upon the terms, bypass the request form and send the Coursepack Permission Agreement.

The Coursepack Permission Request Form is included on the forms disk that comes with this book under the file name CRSRQST.

b. Coursepack Permission Agreement

Ordinarily, when you create your own coursepack you will be seeking permission to photocopy the material. You should always obtain written permission from the copyright owner for this. Use the agreement below for this purpose. A tear-out copy of this form is included in the Appendix, and a digi-

tal copy is on the forms disk in the back of this book. In the section entitled "Number of Copies & Assembly," indicate the number of copies to be produced for the class and check the box that indicates how the coursepack will be assembled. Coursepack agreements are almost always limited to one semester and to one institution. Unlike the non-negotiable coursepack agreements provided by clearance companies, you can modify this agreement if you wish to negotiate a multi-term agreement.

The Coursepack Permission Agreement is included on the forms disk that comes with this book under the file name CRSPERM.

Coursepack Permission Agreement

_____ ("Licensor")

_____ ("User")

Department: _____

School Name: _____

Course name and number: _____ ("the Course").

Date when Course starts: _____ (the "Course date").

Authorization

Licensor authorizes User to photocopy the Selection, as defined below, for purposes of creating a photocopy anthology (the "Coursepack") for sale or distribution to students and academic customers in the Course.

Number of Copies & Assembly

_____ copies of the Coursepack shall be assembled and distributed for the Course:

☐   by User

☐   by on-campus bookstores or copy centers, or

☐   by off-campus copy shops.

Number of pages (or actual page numbers) to be used _____ .

The permission granted in this Agreement is limited to the Course and institution listed above and to be used for one semester only. Any further rights must be negotiated separately.

Material for Which Permission Is Sought

Title of text or artwork: _____ (the "Selection").

Author: _____ .

Source publication (or product from which it came): _____ .

If from a periodical, the ISSN, volume, issue and date. If from a book, the ISBN: _____ .

If from the Internet, the entire URL address: _____ .

Credit

A standard credit line including User's name will appear where the Selection is used. If you have a special credit line you would prefer, indicate it here: _____ .

Fee

User shall pay a fee of $ _____ to Licensor at the following address: _____

_____ within 30 days of commencement date, listed above.

Warranty

Licensor warrants that it is the owner of rights for the Selection and has the right to grant the permission to republish the materials as specified above.

_____ (User signature)

Name: _____

Title: _____

Address: _____

Date: _____

Permission Granted By:

_____ (Licensor signature)

Name: _____

Title: _____

Address: _____

Date: _____

B. Educational Uses of Non-Coursepack Materials

Unlike academic coursepacks, other educational materials can be used without permission in certain circumstances. Some of these uses are permitted under the copyright law and others are considered as a fair use. Fair use is the right to use portions of copyrighted materials for purposes of education, commentary or parody. While we've devoted a chapter (Chapter 9) to explain fair use principles, we discuss the special fair use rules for educational purposes in this chapter because these rules are more specific and because compliance with them will generally avoid lawsuits—something which cannot be guaranteed under general fair use principles.

1. Educational Fair Use Guidelines

Publishers and the academic community have established a set of educational fair use guidelines to provide "greater certainty and protection" for teachers. While the guidelines are not part of the federal Copyright Act, they are recognized by the Copyright Office and by judges as minimum standards for fair use in education. A teacher or pupil following the guidelines can feel comfortable that a use falling within these guidelines is a permissible fair use and not an infringement. Many judges look to these guidelines when making related fair use determinations. The educational use guidelines can be found in Circular 21, provided by the Copyright Office (lcWeb.loc.gov/copyright/circs/circ21.pdf). More information on educational guidelines is provided in the resource section at the end of this chapter.

Keep in mind that none of these guidelines permit creation of coursepacks as described in Section A, but they do allow uses that involve copying much less material than is used in a coursepack. Below we answer some basic questions about these guidelines. In Section C we discuss proposed guidelines that have yet to be adopted.

a. What Is the Difference Between the Guidelines and General Fair Use Principles?

The educational guidelines are similar to a treaty that has been adopted by copyright owners and academics. Under this arrangement, the copyright owners will permit uses that are outlined in the guidelines. In other fair use situations, there are no adopted guidelines and the only way to prove that a use is permitted is to submit the matter to court or arbitration. In other words, in order to avoid lawsuits, the various parties have agreed in these guidelines as to what is permissible for educational uses.

b. What Is an "Educational Use"?

The educational fair use guidelines apply to material used in educational institutions and for educational purposes. Examples of educational institutions include K-12 schools, colleges and universities. Libraries, museums, hospitals and other nonprofit institutions also are considered educational institutions under most educational fair use guidelines when they engage in nonprofit instructional, research, or scholarly activities for educational purposes.

"Educational purposes" means:
- non-commercial instruction or curriculum-based teaching by educators to students at nonprofit educational institutions
- planned non-commercial study or investigation directed toward making a contribution to a field of knowledge, or
- presentation of research findings at non-commercial peer conferences, workshops or seminars.

2. Rules for Reproducing Text Materials for Use in Class

The guidelines permit a teacher to make one copy of any of the following: a chapter from a book; an article from a periodical or newspaper; a short story, short essay or short poem; a chart, graph, diagram, drawing, cartoon or picture from a book, periodical or newspaper.

Teachers may photocopy articles to hand out in class, but the guidelines impose restrictions. Classroom copying cannot be used to replace texts or workbooks used in the classroom. Pupils cannot be charged more than the actual cost of photocopying. The number of copies cannot exceed more than one copy per pupil. And a notice of copyright must be affixed to each copy.

Examples of what can be copied and distributed in class include:

- a complete poem if less than 250 words or an excerpt of not more than 250 words from a longer poem
- a complete article, story or essay if less than 2,500 words, or an excerpt from any prose work of not more than 1,000 words or 10% of the work, whichever is less; or
- one chart, graph, diagram, drawing, cartoon or picture per book or per periodical issue.

Not more than one short poem, article, story, essay or two excerpts may be copied from the same author, nor more than three from the same collective work or periodical volume (for example, a magazine or newspaper) during one class term. As a general rule, a teacher has more freedom to copy from newspapers or other periodicals if the copying is related to current events.

The idea to make the copies must come from the teacher, not from school administrators or other higher authority. Only nine instances of such copying for one course during one school term are permitted. In addition, the idea to make copies and their actual classroom use must be so close together in time that it would be unreasonable to expect a timely reply to a permission request. For example, the instructor finds a newsweekly article on capital punishment two days before presenting a lecture on the subject.

Teachers may not photocopy workbooks, texts, standardized tests or other materials that were created for educational use. The guidelines were not intended to allow teachers to usurp the profits of educational publishers. In other words, educational publishers do not consider it a fair use if the copying provides replacements or substitutes for the purchase of books, reprints, periodicals, tests, workbooks, anthologies, compilations or collective works.

3. Rules for Reproducing Music

A music instructor can make copies of excerpts of sheet music or other printed works, provided that the excerpts do not constitute a "performable unit" such as a whole song, section, movement or aria. In no case can more than 10% of the whole work be copied and the number of copies may not exceed one copy per pupil. Printed copies that have been purchased may be edited or simplified provided that the fundamental character of the work is not distorted or the lyrics altered (or added).

A single recording of a performance of copyrighted music may be made by a student for evaluation or rehearsal purposes, and the educational institution or individual teacher may keep a copy. In addition, a single copy of a sound recording owned by an educational institution or an individual teacher (such as a tape, disc or cassette) of copyrighted music may be made for the purpose of constructing aural exercises or examinations, and the educational institution or individual teacher can keep a copy.

Instructors may not:

- copy sheet music or recorded music for the purpose of creating anthologies or compilations used in class
- copy from works intended to be "consumable" in the course of study or teaching such as workbooks, exercises, standardized tests and answer sheets and like material

- copy sheet music or recorded music for the purpose of performance, except for emergency copying to replace purchased copies which are not available for an imminent performance (provided purchased replacement copies are substituted in due course); or
- copy any materials without including the copyright notice which appears on the printed copy.

If copyrighted sheet music is out of print (not available for sale), an educator can request permission to reproduce it from the music publisher. Information about contacting music publishers is provided in Chapter 5. A library that wants to reproduce out-of-print sheet music can use a system established by the Music Publishers' Association (www.mpa.org/copyright/searchenter.html). Download the "Library Requisition for Out-of-Print Copyrighted Music."

4. Rules for Recording and Showing Television Programs

Nonprofit educational institutions can record television programs transmitted by network television and cable stations. The institution can keep the tape for 45 days, but can only use it for instructional purposes during the first ten of the 45 days. After the first ten days, the video recording can only be used for teacher evaluation purposes, to determine whether or not to include the broadcast program in the teaching curriculum. If the teacher wants to keep it within the curriculum, permission must be obtained from the copyright owner. The recording may be played once by each individual teacher in the course of related teaching activities in classrooms and similar places devoted to instruction (including formalized home instruction). The recorded program can be repeated once if necessary, although there are no standards for determining what is and is not necessary. After 45 days, the recording must be erased or destroyed.

A video recording of a broadcast can be made only at the request of, and used by, individual teachers. A television show may not be regularly recorded in anticipation of requests—for example, there can't be a standing request to record each episode of a PBS series. Only enough copies may be reproduced from each recording to meet the needs of teachers, and the recordings may not be combined to create teaching compilations. All copies of a recording must include the copyright notice on the broadcast program as recorded, and as mentioned above, must be erased or destroyed 45 days after having been recorded.

C. Proposed Educational Guidelines on Fair Use

The guidelines discussed in the previous Section have been approved by a consensus of educators, scholars and publishers (copyright owners). Since these educators and copyright owners have come to an agreement, it is unlikely that a publisher will sue an educator who uses material in a manner that is permitted by the guidelines. Besides these guidelines, there are others that have been discussed and proposed, but not formally approved. These proposed guidelines lack the official consensus of the adopted guidelines described in Section B. However, the parties created some standards which were included in a report and it is hoped that these proposed guidelines will eventually be adopted. This section discusses these proposed educational guidelines.

We provide the proposed guidelines because they give you a ballpark idea of what may be permissible. For example, these standards may help you formulate a fair use analysis, as described in Chapter 9. You can access the full report from which these proposed guidelines originated at the Patent and Trademark Office's Conference on Fair Use (CONFU) site at www.uspto.gov/web/offices/dcom/olia/confu/confurep.htm. For current information as to whether any of these proposed guidelines have been adopted, check Christine Sundt's Art and Copyright website at oregon.uoregon.edu/~csundt/cWeb.htm. For further information on the proposed guidelines, see the resources section at the end of this chapter.

1. Proposed Guidelines for Digital Copying

Under proposed guidelines, educators can digitize analog images (non-digital photographic prints or paintings). Digitizing is traditionally accomplished by scanning a printed photo. In this process, an analog image (that is, a three dimensional printed photograph or slide created by a non-computer photo processing method) is converted into a digital format known as binary code. This digital format is stored in a computer file. Under the proposed guidelines, educators can digitize a lawfully acquired analog image for educational use unless the image is readily available in usable digital form at a fair price. The proposed guidelines for digital imaging are located at the Patent and Trademark Office's CONFU site at the Web address listed above.

Under the proposed guidelines, an educational institution may use digital thumbnail images created from analog images for inclusion in a searchable catalog used by the institution. A thumbnail is a small scale, typically low resolution, digital reproduction which has no commercial or reproductive value.

An educational institution may display images digitized under the proposed guidelines through its own secure electronic network, provided that notice is included stating that the images shall not be downloaded, copied, retained, printed, shared, modified or otherwise used, except as provided in the educational use guidelines.

2. Proposed Guidelines for Using Digitized Images in Lectures, Scholarly Presentations or Publications

Under proposed guidelines, an educator may display a digital image prepared from an analog image if the display is for educational purposes such as face-to-face teaching or research and scholarly activities at a nonprofit educational institution. An educational institution may compile digital images for display on the institution's secure electronic net-

work to students enrolled in a course given by that educator for classroom use, after-class review or directed study. Educators, scholars, and students may use or display digital images in connection with lectures or presentations in their fields, including uses at non-commercial professional development seminars, workshops and conferences.

The proposed guidelines do not permit reproducing and publishing images in publications, including scholarly publications in print or digital form, for which permission is generally required.

AMICO—A System for Educators to Negotiate Digital Images

In an attempt to provide educational access to copyrighted images, a consortium of art museums and archives created the Art Museum Image Consortium (AMICO). AMICO maintains and licenses a collective digital library of images and documentation. AMICO enables its members to negotiate digital rights with artists, artists' estates and museums in other countries, and provides members with access to each others' holdings for their own educational uses. AMICO's website is located at www.amico.net/amico.html.

3. Proposed Guidelines for Students or Instructors Preparing Multimedia Works

There are extensive proposed guidelines for the creation and use of multimedia works. Multimedia works include any combination of music, text, graphics, illustrations, photographs and audiovisual imagery combined into an integrated presentation, along with accompanying projection and playback equipment. For example, an instructor in copyright law may use a software program such as Microsoft Power Point to create a class presentation that includes still and moving imagery as well as music and spoken words. If you are contemplating preparing multimedia works for classroom instruction you should download the CONFU Report (website listed above) and review Appendix J in that report.

In general, students and instructors may create multimedia works for face-to-face instruction, directed self-study or for remote instruction provided that the multimedia works are used only for educational purposes in systematic learning activities at nonprofit educational institutions. Instructors may use their multimedia works for teaching courses for up to two years after the first use.

There are also certain "portion limitations." An educational multimedia presentation may include:

- up to 10% or 1,000 words, whichever is less, of a copyrighted text work. For example, an entire poem of less than 250 words may be used, but no more than three poems by one poet, or five poems by different poets from any anthology.
- up to 10%, but in no event more than 30 seconds, of the music and lyrics from an individual musical work.
- up to 10% or three minutes, whichever is less, of a copyrighted motion media work (for example, an animation, video or film image).
- a photograph or illustration may be used in its entirety but no more than five images by an artist or photographer may be reproduced. When using photographs and illustrations from a published collective work, no more than 10% or 15 images, whichever is less. Or,
- up to 10% or 2,500 fields or cell entries, whichever is less, from a copyrighted database or data table may be reproduced. A field entry is defined as a specific item of information, such as a name or Social Security number in a record of a database file. A cell entry is defined as the intersection where a row and a column meet on a spreadsheet.

Only two copies of an educational multimedia project may be made, only one of which may be placed on reserve. An additional copy may be made for preservation purposes, but may only be used or copied to replace a copy that has been lost, stolen or damaged. If an educational multimedia project is

created by two or more people, each creator may retain one copy for the educational purposes described in the proposed guidelines. Permission is needed for uses that are commercial or go beyond the limitations in the proposed guidelines.

D. Library Photocopying

The Copyright Act at 17 USC § 108 provides a set of rules regarding library reproductions. In general, a library or archive open to the public (or whose collection is available to specialized researchers other than those affiliated with the institution) will not be liable for copyright infringement based upon a library patron's unsupervised use of reproducing equipment located on its premises, provided that the copying equipment displays a notice that the making of a copy may be subject to the copyright law. The notice must appear in a specific form, as shown below.

NOTICE WARNING CONCERNING COPYRIGHT RESTRICTIONS

The copyright law of the United States (Title 17, United States Code) governs the making of photocopies or other reproductions of copyrighted material. Under certain conditions specified in the law, libraries and archives are authorized to furnish a photocopy or other reproduction. One of these specified conditions is that the photocopy or reproduction is not to be "used for any purpose other than private study, scholarship, or research." If a user makes a request for, or later uses, a photocopy or reproduction for purposes in excess of "fair use," that user may be liable for copyright infringement. This institution reserves the right to refuse to accept a copying order if, in its judgment, fulfillment of the order would involve violation of copyright law.

When copies of text works are requested (the library is making the copies), the warning notice must be printed within a box located prominently on the order form, either on the front side of the form or immediately adjacent to the space for the name and signature of the user. The library may make only one copy of such works per patron. Copying a complete work from the library collection is prohibited unless the work is not available at a "fair price." This is generally the case when the work is out of print and used copies are not available at a reasonable price. If a work, located within the library's collection, is available at a reasonable price, the library may reproduce one article or other contribution to a copyrighted collection or periodical issue, or a small part of any other copyrighted work, for example, a chapter from a book. This right to copy does not apply if the library is aware that the copying of a work (available at a fair price) is systematic. For example, if 30 different members of one class are requesting a copy of the same article, the library has reason to believe that the instructor is trying to avoid seeking permission for 30 copies.

The copying, whether performed by the library or whether unsupervised by the library patron, cannot be for a commercial advantage. This means that the library (or a copying service hired by the library) cannot profit from the copying. In addition, the copying for the patron must be done for purposes of private study, scholarship or research.

If a library or educational institution makes a copy of a work for a patron, the actual copyright notice (for example, "© 1953, Grove Press") from the material being copied must be included. If the material contains no copyright notice, the material should be stamped with the notice "This material may be protected by copyright law (Title 17 U.S. Code)." 17 USC § 108(a). In addition to limiting the library's liability, the use of the warning notice will defeat an infringer's defense that the copying was an "innocent infringement" and might even support an argument that the infringement was willful, thereby increasing the damages paid to the copyright owner.

Library Copying After 75 Years

In 1998, the Sonny Bono Copyright Term Extension Act extended the period of copyright protection for an additional 20 years. As part of the Act, Congress provided that during the last 20 years of any term of copyright of a published work, a library or archives may reproduce a copy of the work for purposes of preservation, scholarship or research provided that: the work is not being commercially distributed; the work cannot be obtained at a reasonable price; or the copyright owner or its agent provides notice that either of the above conditions applies.

E. Academic Permission Resources

The following resources can assist with obtaining permission to use materials for academic purposes.

1. Coursepack Resources

- The Copyright Permission Pages: www.law.wfu.edu/library/copyright/.
- The Association of Academic Publishers: www.publishers.org.
- Copyright Clearance Center (Academic Permissions Service): APS c/o Copyright Clearance Center, 222 Rosewood Drive, Danvers, MA 01923; 978-750-8400, fax: 978-750-4470; Web: www.copyright.com.
- CAPCO (Academic Publishing Company/ Follett Custom Publishing): CAPCO, 913 North Broadway, Oklahoma City, OK 73102; 800-364-0010; fax: 800-364-0500; Web: www.capco.com.
- CCP (Campus Custom Publishing): CCP, 4355 D International Blvd., Norcross, GA 30093; 800-459-2679, 770-717-1710, fax: 770-717-1948: email: ccp@campuscp.com; Web: menus.atlanta.com/ccp/.

2. Educational Fair Use Guidelines

- The established educational guidelines, as well as other regulations and rules regarding libraries are available in Copyright Office Circular 21, "Reproduction of Copyrighted Works by Educators and Librarians," which can be downloaded from lcWeb.loc.sgov/copyright/circs/circ21.pdf. See Chapter 13 for more information about Copyright Office circulars and contacting the Copyright Office.

- Copies of proposed guidelines may be downloaded from www.uspto.gov/web/offices/dcom/olia/confu/appendix.htm, or may be obtained, free of charge, by mailing or faxing a written request to: CONFU Report, Office of Public Affairs, U.S. Patent and Trademark Office, Washington, DC 20231; fax: 703-308-5258.

- Information about established and proposed guidelines can also be found in the extensive list of links regarding educational uses of copyrighted material at Christine Sundt's Art and Copyright website located at oregon.uoregon.edu/~csundt/cWeb.htm.

■

8

The Public Domain

ABSOLUTELY FREE! MUSIC, TEXT AND ART!! COPY ALL YOU WANT!! If you saw an advertisement like this, you might wonder, "What's the catch?" When it comes to the public domain, there is no catch. If a book, song, movie or artwork is in the public domain, then it is not protected by intellectual property laws (such as copyright, trademark or patent law)—which means it's free for you to use without permission.

As a general rule, most works enter the public domain because of old age. This includes any work published in the United States before 1923. Another large block of works are in the public domain because they were published before 1964 and copyright was not renewed. (Renewal was a requirement for works published before 1978.) A smaller group of works fell into the public domain because they were published without copyright notice (copyright notice was necessary for works published in the United States before March 1, 1989). Some works are in the public domain because the owner has indicated a desire to give them to the public without copyright protection. The rules establishing the public domain status for each of these types of works are different and more details are provided throughout this chapter.

For a detailed analysis of public domain rules and issues, see *The Copyright Handbook,* by Stephen Fishman (Nolo).

A. Welcome to the Public Domain

The term "public domain" refers to creative materials that are not protected by intellectual property laws such as copyright, trademark or patent laws. The public owns these works, not an individual author or artist. Anyone can use a public domain work without obtaining permission, but no one can ever own it.

An important wrinkle to understand about public domain material is that collections of it may be protected by copyright. If, for example, someone has collected public domain images in a book or at a website, the collection as a whole may be protectible, even though individual images are not protected. You are free to copy and use individual images but copying and distributing the complete collection may infringe what is known as the "collective works" copyright. Collections of public domain material will be protected if the person who created it has used creativity in the choices and organization of the public domain material. This usually involves some unique selection process, for example, a poetry scholar compiling a book, *The Greatest Poems of e.e. cummings.*

There are four common ways that works arrive in the public domain:

- expiration of copyright: the copyright has expired.
- failure to renew copyright: the owner failed to follow copyright renewal rules.
- dedication: the owner deliberately places it in the public domain.
- no copyright protection available: copyright law does not protect this type of work.

Let's look at each of these routes into the public domain more closely.

1. Expired Copyright

Copyright has expired for all works published in the United States before 1923. In other words, if the work was published in the U.S. before January 1, 1923, you are free to use it in the U.S. without permission. As an example, the graphic illustration of the man with mustache was published sometime in the 19th Century and is in the public domain, so no permission is required to include it within this book. These rules and dates apply regardless of whether the work was created by an individual author, a group of authors or by an employee (the latter sometimes referred to as a "work made for hire.")

Because of legislation passed in 1998, no new works will fall into the public domain until 2019 when works published in 1923 will expire. In 2020, works published in 1924 will expire and so forth. If a work was written by a single author and published after 1977, the copyright will not expire until 70 years after the author's death. If a work was written by several authors and published after 1977, it will not expire until 70 years after the last surviving author dies.

Year-End Expiration of Copyright Terms

Copyright protection always expires at the end of the calendar year of the year it's set to expire. In other words, the last day of copyright protection for any work is December 31. For example, if an author died on June 1, 2000, protection of the works would continue through December 31, 2070.

2. The Renewal Trapdoor

Thousands of works published in the United States before 1964 fell into the public domain because the copyright was not timely renewed under the law in effect at that time. If a work was first published before 1964, the owner had to file a renewal with the Copyright Office during the 28th year after publication. No renewal meant a loss of copyright.

If you plan on using a work that was published after 1922, but before 1964, you should research the records of the Copyright Office to find if a renewal was filed. Chapter 13 describes methods of researching copyright status.

3. Dedicated Works

If, upon viewing a work, you see words such as "This work is dedicated to the public domain," then it is free for you to use. That's because sometimes an author deliberately chooses not to protect a work and dedicates the work to the public. This type of dedication is rare and unless there is express authorization placing the work in the public domain, do not assume that the work is free to use. For example, many people mistakenly assume that shareware and freeware are in the public domain (see Sidebar).

An additional concern is whether the person making the dedication has the right to do so. Only the copyright owner can dedicate a work to the public. Sometimes, the creator of the work is not the copyright owner and does not have authority. If in doubt, contact the copyright owner to verify the dedication. Information about locating copyright owners is provided in Chapter 13.

Shareware and Freeware

Shareware is a system of marketing software. It is distributed at no charge on a trial basis and if the recipient likes the software and intends to use it, a fee is paid. Freeware is software that is made available to the public for free. Unlike shareware, there are no fees. Both of these forms of software are protected under copyright law and you cannot reproduce or distribute these programs unless authorized by the copyright owners—even if you got them for free. For example, in one case, a company gathered various shareware programs and offered them in a CD-ROM collection, despite warnings on the shareware prohibiting such use. A court ruled that the shareware, originally placed on the Internet for free distribution, was entitled to copyright protection. Therefore, do not assume because you acquired a work for free that it is in the public domain.

Clip Art Compilations

Generally clip art is sold in books, CD-ROM bundles or from websites, and is often offered as "copyright-free." As explained in Chapter 3, the term "copyright-free" is usually a misnomer, and actually refers to either royalty-free artwork or work in the public domain. Keep in mind that much of the artwork advertised as copyright-free is actually royalty-free artwork, which *is* protected by copyright. Your rights and limitations to use such artwork are expressed in the artwork packaging or in the shrink-wrap agreement or license that accompanies the artwork. These principles are discussed in more detail in Chapter 3.

If the artwork is in the public domain you are free to copy items without restriction. However, even if the artwork is in the public domain, the complete collection may not be reproduced and sold as a clip art collection since that may infringe the unique manner in which the art is collected (known as a compilation or collective work copyright).

4. Copyright Does Not Protect Certain Works

There are some things that copyright law will not protect. Copyright will not protect the titles of a book or movie, nor will it protect short phrases such as "Make my day." Copyright protection also doesn't cover facts, ideas or theories. These things are free for all to use without authorization.

a. Short Phrases

Phrases such as "Show me the money" or "Beam me up" are not protected under copyright law. Short phrases, names, titles or small groups of words are considered common idioms of the English language and are free for anyone to use. In subsequent chapters we'll explain how this rule applies to specific types of works. However, a short phrase used as an advertising slogan is protectible under trademark law. In that case, you could not use a similar phrase for the purpose of selling products or services. For more information on trademarks, see Chapter 10.

b. Facts and Theories

A fact or a theory—for example, the fact that a comet will pass by the Earth in 2027—is not protected by copyright. If a scientist discovered this fact, anyone would be free to use it without asking for permission from the scientist. Similarly, if someone creates a theory that the comet can be destroyed by a nuclear device, anyone could use that theory to create a book or movie. However, the unique manner in which a fact is expressed may be protected. Therefore, if a filmmaker created a movie about destroying a comet with a nuclear device, the specific way he presented the ideas in the movie would be protected by copyright.

> EXAMPLE: Neil Young wrote a song, "Ohio," about the shooting of four college students during the Vietnam War. You are free to use the facts surrounding the shooting but you may not copy Mr. Young's unique expression of these facts without his permission.

In some cases, you are not free to copy a collection of facts because the collection of facts may be protectible as a compilation (see Section B5). For more information on how copyright applies to facts, refer to Chapter 2, Section F3.

c. Ideas

Copyright law does not protect ideas; it only protects the particular way an idea is expressed. What's the difference between an idea and its expression? In the case of a story or movie, the idea is really the plot in its most basic form. For example, the "idea" of the movie *Contact* is that a determined scientist, seeking to improve humankind, communicates with alien life forms. The same idea has been used in many motion pictures, books and television shows including *The Day the Earth Stood Still, The Abyss* and *Star Trek*. Many paintings, photographs and songs contain similar ideas. You can always use the underlying idea or theme—such as communicating with aliens for the improvement of the world—but you cannot copy the unique manner in which the author expresses the idea. This unique expression may include literary devices such as dialogue, characters and subplots.

The Merger Doctrine

There is an exception to the principle that you cannot copy the unique expression of a fact or idea. If there is a limited number of ways to express the fact or idea, you are permitted to copy the expression. This is known as the merger doctrine and means that the idea and the expression are merged or inseparable. For example, in the case of a map, there may be very few ways to express the symbol for an airport, other than by using a small image of an airplane. In that case, you are free to use the airport symbol. Similarly, there may be a limited way of expressing a rule about the public domain, for example, the statement, "Works published in the U.S. before 1923 are in the public domain." In that case the fact and the expression are inseparable and you are free to copy the expression. As you can imagine this is a heavily litigated area and many companies have butted heads to determine the boundaries of the merger doctrine. For example, Microsoft and Apple litigated over the right to use the trash pail icon as a symbol for deleting computer materials. A federal court of appeals ruled that design constraints made the trash can an unprotectible element of the graphic interface and that Apple could not claim infringement solely based on another company's use of a similar icon. (*Apple Computer, Inc. v. Microsoft Corp.*, 35 F.3d 1435 (9th Cir. 1994).)

d. U.S. Government Works

Any work created by a U.S. government employee or officer is in the public domain, provided that the work is created in that person's official capacity. For example, during the 1980s a songwriter used words from a speech by then-President Ronald Reagan as the basis for song lyrics. The words from the speech were in the public domain and permission was not required from Ronald Reagan. Keep in mind that this rule applies only to works created by federal employees, and not to works created by state or local government employees. However, state and local laws and court decisions are in the public domain.

Some federal publications (or portions of them) are protected under copyright law and that fact is usually indicated on the title page or in the copyright notice. For example, the IRS may acquire permission to use a copyrighted chart in a federal tax booklet. The document may indicate that a certain chart is "Copyright Dr. Matt Polazzo." In that case, you could not copy the chart without permission from Dr. Polazzo.

Legal Cases and Pagination

As noted above, federal, state and local laws and court decisions are in the public domain. However, legal publishers have attempted to get around the public domain status by claiming that unique page numbering systems are copyrightable. These publishers argued that you can copy and distribute a court decision, but you cannot copy the page numbering, which is crucial to the official citation system used by the courts. For many years, Lexis and other computerized legal research systems could not cite to the official page numbering system used by West publications. In a 1994 case, West Publishing Company sued when a legal publisher, Matthew Bender, incorporated West's page numbering system on a CD-ROM product. A court of appeals ruled that the use of West's pagination was not protectible and in any case, the page citation copying was permitted as a fair use. As a result of this ruling, you are free to copy a publisher's reproduction of court decisions and page numbering. *(Matthew Bender & Co. v. West Publishing Co.,* 158 F.3d 693 (2d Cir. 1998). But see also *West Publishing Company v. Mead Data,* 799 F.2d 1219 (1986).)

Loss of Copyright From Lack of Copyright Notice

Under copyright laws that were in effect before 1978, a work that was published without copyright notice fell into the public domain. If the work did not include the word "Copyright" or a © (a "c" in a circle) and the name of the copyright owner, the work would be injected into the public domain. This rule was repealed and copyright notice is not required for works first published after March 1, 1989 (although works first published prior to that date must still include notice). Just because you find a copy of a book without a copyright notice doesn't mean that the work is in the public domain. It's possible that the copy you are viewing is unauthorized or that the notice has only been removed from a very small number of copies, both of which are excusable. It is also possible that the author followed a copyright law procedure for correcting the error. Finally, if you're using text from a journal, anthology, newsletter or magazine published before March 1, 1989, check to see if there is a copyright notice either for the individual article or for the whole publication. Either type of notice will prevent the work from falling into the public domain.

The table below may assist you in determining public domain status.

Table for Determining Public Domain Status

Works published in the U.S. before 1923	In the public domain
Works published in the U.S. after 1922 through 1963	Initial term of 28 years. If not renewed during the 28th year, the work falls into the public domain.
Works published in the U.S. after 1922 but before March 1, 1989	Generally, if a work is published without copyright notice under the authorization of the copyright owner and the law does not provide an exception for the omission, the work is in the public domain.

B. Public Domain Trouble Spots

While it's true that no strings are attached to using public domain materials, you should be aware of certain potholes on the public domain highway.

1. Multi-Layered Works

Works such as movies or sound recordings use and contain many underlying works such as musical soundtracks, painted illustrations or other works. There has been a disturbing trend by some copyright owners to assert protection in an element of a public domain work. For example, the film *It's a Wonderful Life* fell into the public domain because of a failure to renew copyright. For years, anyone was free to copy and sell the movie on videotape. However, a production company recently acquired rights to the musical sound track that is used in the movie. That soundtrack is not in the public domain. The copyright owner of the soundtrack can now prevent anyone from copying the music, thereby effectively stopping anyone from copying the film (unless the soundtrack is removed). This process can create confusion when making a determination of public domain status.

Usually you don't have to be concerned with this type of legal maneuver as it is only used in connection with a popular and older multi-layered works such as a film. It would be difficult, if not impossible, to apply this procedure to a public domain book or painting.

EXAMPLE: A movie musical containing songs by Cole Porter is in the public domain because of a failure to renew copyright. However, the Cole Porter songs were timely renewed so they are still protected by copyright and cannot be reproduced without permission. Therefore, you must obtain permission from the copyright owner of the Cole Porter songs in order to copy the public domain film. If you do not want to obtain permission from the owner, you must delete the songs from the film.

2. Public Domain Works That are Modified

Modifications to a public domain work may be protected by copyright and cannot be used without permission. A famous example used in many copyright classes is of the artist who paints an elaborate hat and mustache on the Mona Lisa. Even though anyone is free to copy the Mona Lisa image, the modified image (with mustache and hat) is protected under the artist's copyright.

EXAMPLE: Color has been added to the black-and-white public domain film *God's Little Acre*. This colorization process is copyrightable. Therefore, the colorized version of *God's Little Acre* cannot be copied without permission.

3. Works Protected by Trademark Law

It is possible that a work may not be protected by copyright, but is still protected by trademark laws. In Chapter 10, we provide more trademark information.

> EXAMPLE: The gold-colored top of the New York Life building is in the public domain and anyone can photograph it. However, that image also functions as a trademark for the New York Life Company, and a competing company could not use the image if it would be likely to confuse life insurance consumers.

4. Works Protected in Other Countries

Before 1978, most countries had different periods of copyright protection than the United States. As a result, many works that are public domain in the United States are still protected by copyright in foreign countries and vice versa. Therefore, you may have to research public domain status in each country in which you plan to publish your work.

5. Compilations

Often an author creates a work by selecting various public domain components and grouping them together. If the selection, coordination and arrangement of the material is unique it will be protected as a copyrightable compilation.

> EXAMPLE: The owners of the book *Bartlett's Familiar Quotations* selected and arranged famous quotes. Anyone may copy a few quotes from *Bartlett's Familiar Quotations,* but no one may copy the arrangement and selection of all the quotes.

6. Works First Published Outside the U.S.

Some works first published outside the United States have been resurrected from the public domain. As a result of international treaties signed in the 1990s, public domain works that meet certain qualifications are now protected. (For a detailed discussion, see *The Copyright Handbook*, by Stephen Fishman (Nolo).)

You may be able to do some public domain detective work yourself (we offer research tips in Chapter 13) or you can hire private companies or individuals who perform public domain searches and furnish public domain reports. Information about these companies is included in Chapter 13.

Fair Use

Fair use is a copyright principle based on the belief that the public is entitled to freely use portions of copyrighted materials for purposes of commentary and criticism. For example, if you wish to criticize a novelist, you should have the freedom to quote a portion of the novelist's work without asking permission. Absent this freedom, copyright owners could stifle any negative comments about their work.

Unfortunately, if the copyright owner disagrees with your fair use interpretation, the dispute will have to be resolved by courts or arbitration. If it's not a fair use, then you are infringing upon the rights of the copyright owner and may be liable for damages.

The only guidance is provided by a set of fair use factors outlined in the copyright law. These factors are weighed in each case to determine whether a use qualifies as a fair use. For example, one important factor is whether your use will deprive the copyright owner of income. Unfortunately, weighing the fair use factors is often quite subjective. For this reason, the fair use road map is often tricky to navigate.

This chapter explains the various rules behind the fair use principle. To help you get a feel for which uses courts consider to be fair uses and which ones they don't, we provide several examples of fair use lawsuits at the end of this chapter.

 For educational fair use guidelines, see Chapter 7, which deals with academic permissions.

A. What Is Fair Use?

In its most general sense, a fair use is any copying of copyrighted material done for a limited and "transformative" purpose such as to comment upon, criticize or parody a copyrighted work. Such uses can be done without permission from the copyright owner. Another way of putting this is that fair use is a defense against infringement. If your use qualifies under the definition above, and as defined more specifically later in this chapter, then your use would not be considered an illegal infringement.

So what is a "transformative" use? If this definition seems ambiguous or vague, be aware that millions of dollars in legal fees have been spent attempting to define what qualifies as a fair use. There are no hard-and-fast rules, only general rules and varying court decisions. That's because the judges and lawmakers who created the fair use exception did not want to limit the definition of fair use. They wanted it—like free speech—to have an expansive meaning that could be open to interpretation.

Most fair use analysis falls into two categories: commentary and criticism; or parody.

1. Comment and Criticism

If you are commenting upon or critiquing a copyrighted work—for instance, writing a book review—fair use principles allow you to reproduce some of the work to achieve your purposes. Some examples of commentary and criticism include:

- quoting a few lines from a Bob Dylan song in a music review
- summarizing and quoting from a medical article on prostate cancer in a news report
- copying a few paragraphs from a news article for use by a teacher or student in a lesson, or
- copying a portion of a *Sports Illustrated* magazine article for use in a related court case.

The underlying rationale of this rule is that the public benefits from your review, which is enhanced by including some of the copyrighted material. Additional examples of commentary or criticism are provided in the examples of fair use cases in Section C.

2. Parody

A parody is a work that ridicules another, usually well-known work, by imitating it in a comic way. Judges understand that by its nature, parody demands some taking from the original work being parodied. Unlike other forms of fair use, a fairly extensive use of the original work is permitted in a parody in order to "conjure up" the original.

B. Measuring Fair Use: The Four Factors

Unfortunately, the only way to get a definitive answer on whether a particular use is a fair use is to have it resolved in federal court. Judges use four factors in resolving fair use disputes, which are discussed in detail below. It's important to understand that these factors are only guidelines and the courts are free to adapt them to particular situations on a case-by-case basis. In other words, a judge has a great deal of freedom when making a fair use determination and the outcome in any given case can be hard to predict.

The four factors judges consider are:

1. the purpose and character of your use
2. the nature of the copyrighted work
3. the amount and substantiality of the portion taken, and
4. the effect of the use upon the potential market.

Educational Fair Use Guidelines

Since the current copyright law was adopted, various organizations and scholars have established guidelines for educational uses. These guidelines are not part of the Copyright Act. However, the guidelines establish the standards for uses and copying in education. These guidelines, as well as other regulations and rules regarding educational uses are summarized in Chapter 7, which deals with academic and educational permissions.

1. The Transformative Factor: The Purpose and Character of Your Use

In a 1997 case, the Supreme Court emphasized this first factor as being a primary indicator of fair use. At issue is whether the material has been used to help create something new, or merely copied verbatim into another work. When taking portions of copyrighted work, ask yourself the following questions:

- Has the material you have taken from the original work been transformed by adding new expression or meaning?
- Was value added to the original by creating new information, new aesthetics, new insights and understandings?

In a parody, for example, the parodist transforms the original by holding it up to ridicule. Purposes such as scholarship, research or education may also qualify as transformative uses because the work is the subject of review or commentary.

EXAMPLE: Roger borrows several quotes from the speech given by the CEO of a logging company. Roger prints these quotes under photos of old-growth redwoods in his environmental newsletter. By juxtaposing the quotes with the photos of endangered trees, Roger has transformed the remarks from their original purpose and used them to create a new insight. The copying would probably be permitted as a fair use.

2. The Nature of the Copyrighted Work

Because the dissemination of facts or information benefits the public, you have more leeway to copy from factual works such as biographies than you do from fictional works such as plays or novels.

In addition, you will have a stronger case of fair use if the material copied is from a published work than an unpublished work. The scope of fair use is narrower for unpublished works because an author has the right to control the first public appearance of his expression.

3. The Amount and Substantiality of the Portion Taken

The less you take, the more likely that your copying will be excused as a fair use. However, even if you take a small portion of a work, your copying will not be a fair use if the portion taken is the "heart" of the work. In other words, you are more likely to run into problems if you take the most memorable aspect of a work. For example, it would not probably not be a fair use to copy the opening guitar riff and the words "I can't get no satisfaction" from the song, "Satisfaction."

This rule—less is more—is not necessarily true in parody cases. In a parody, the parodist is borrowing in order to comment upon the original work. A parodist is permitted to borrow quite a bit, even the heart of the original work, in order to conjure up the original work. That's because, as the Supreme Court has acknowledged, "the heart is also what most readily conjures up the [original] for parody, and it is the heart at which parody takes aim." (*Campbell v. Acuff-Rose Music*, 510 U.S. 569 (1994).)

4. The Effect of the Use Upon the Potential Market

Another important fair use factor is whether your use deprives the copyright owner of income or undermines a new or potential market for the copyrighted work. As we indicated previously, depriving a copyright owner of income is very likely to trigger a lawsuit. This is true even if you are not competing directly with the original work.

For example, in one case an artist used a copyrighted photograph without permission as the basis for wood sculptures, copying all of the elements of the photo. The artist earned several hundred thousand dollars selling the sculptures. When the photographer sued, the artist claimed his sculptures were a fair use because the photographer would never have considered making sculptures. The court disagreed, stating that it did not matter whether the photographer had considered making sculptures; what mattered was that a potential market for sculptures of the photograph existed. (*Rogers v. Koons*, 960 F.2d 301 (2d Cir. 1992).)

Too Small For Fair Use: The De Minimis Defense

In some cases, the amount of material copied is so small (or "de minimis") that the court permits it without even conducting a fair use analysis. For example, in the motion picture *Seven*, several copyrighted photographs appeared in the film, prompting the copyright owner of the photographs to sue the producer of the movie. The court held that the photos "appear fleetingly and are obscured, severely out of focus, and virtually unidentifiable." The court excused the use of the photographs as "de minimis" and a fair use analysis was not required. (*Sandoval v. New Line Cinema Corp.*, 147 F.3d 215 (2d Cir. 1998).)

As with fair use, there is no bright line test for determining a de minimis use. For example, in another case, a court determined that the use of a copyrighted poster for a total of 27 seconds in the background of the TV show, "Roc" was not de minimis. What distinguished the use of the poster from the use of the photographs in the *Seven* case? The court stated that the poster was clearly visible and recognizable with sufficient observable detail for the "average lay observer" to view the artist's imagery and colorful style. (*Ringgold v. Black Entertainment Television, Inc.* 126 F.3d 70 (2d Cir. 1997).)

Parody is given a slightly different fair use analysis with regard to the impact on the market. It's possible that a parody may diminish or even destroy the market value of the original work. That is, the parody may be so good that the public can never take the original work seriously again. Although this may cause a loss of income, it's not the same type of loss as when an infringer merely appropriates the work. As one judge explains, "The economic effect of a parody with which we are concerned is not its potential to destroy or diminish the market for the original—any bad review can have that effect—but whether it fulfills the demand for the original." (*Fisher v. Dees*, 794 F.2d 432 (9th Cir. 1986).)

5. The "Fifth" Fair Use Factor: Are You Good or Bad?

When you review fair use cases, you may find that they sometimes seem to contradict one another or conflict with the rules expressed in this chapter. Fair use involves subjective judgments and are often affected by factors such as a judge or jury's personal sense of right or wrong. Despite the fact that the Supreme Court has indicated that offensiveness is not a fair use factor, you should be aware that a morally offended judge or jury may rationalize its decision against fair use.

For example, in one case a manufacturer of novelty cards parodied the successful children's dolls, the Cabbage Patch Kids. The parody card series was entitled the Garbage Pail Kids and used gruesome and grotesque names and characters to poke fun at the wholesome Cabbage Patch image. Some copyright experts were surprised when a federal court considered the parody an infringement, not a fair use. (*Original Appalachian Artworks, Inc. v. Topps Chewing Gum, Inc.*, 642 F. Supp. 1031 (N.D. Ga. 1986).)

Does It Help to Use a Disclaimer?

A disclaimer is a statement that "disassociates" your work from the work that you have borrowed. For example, if you write an unauthorized biography of Mickey Mouse, you may include a disclaimer such as "This book is not associated with or endorsed by the Walt Disney Company." Will it help your position if you use a disclaimer? In close cases where the court is having a difficult time making a fair use determination, a prominently placed disclaimer may have a positive effect on the way the court perceives your use. However, a disclaimer by itself generally will not help. That is, if the fair use factors weigh against you, the disclaimer won't make any difference. For example, in a case involving a "Seinfeld" trivia book (see Section C), the publisher included a disclaimer that the book "has not been approved or licensed by any entity involved in creating or producing Seinfeld." Despite the disclaimer, the court held that the use of the "Seinfeld" materials was an infringement, not a fair use.

What If You Acknowledge the Source Material?

Some people mistakenly believe it's permissible to use a work (or portion of it) if an acknowledgment is provided. For example, they believe it's okay to use a photograph in a magazine as long as the name of the photographer is included. This is not true. Acknowledgment of the source material (such as citing the photographer) may be a consideration in a fair use determination, but it will not protect against a claim of infringement. In some cases, such as advertisements, acknowledgments can backfire and create additional legal claims, such as a violation of the right of publicity. When in doubt as to the right to use or acknowledge a source, the most prudent course may be to seek permission of the copyright owner.

C. Summaries of Fair Use Cases

The best method of understanding the flexible principle of fair use is to review actual cases decided by the courts. Below are summaries of a series of fair use cases.

1. Cases Involving Text

- **Not a fair use.** An author copied more than half of an unpublished manuscript to prove that someone was involved in the overthrow of the Iranian government. **Important factors:** A substantial portion was taken (half of the work) and the work had not yet been published. (*Love v. Kwitny*, 772 F. Supp. 1367 (S.D. N.Y. 1989).)

- **Fair use.** A biographer of Richard Wright quoted from six unpublished letters and ten unpublished journal entries by Wright. **Important factors:** No more than 1% of Wright's unpublished letters were copied and the purpose was informational. (*Wright v. Warner Books, Inc.*, 953 F.2d 731 (2d Cir. 1991).)

- **Not a fair use.** A biographer paraphrased large portions of unpublished letters written by the famed author J.D. Salinger. Although people could read these letters at a university library, Salinger had never authorized their reproduction. In other words, the first time that the general public would see these letters was in their paraphrased form in the biography. Salinger successfully sued to prevent publication. **Important factors:** The letters were unpublished and were the "backbone" of the biography—so much so that without the letters the resulting biography was unsuccessful. In other words, the letters may have been taken more as a means of capitalizing on the interest in Salinger than in providing a critical study of the author. (*Salinger v. Random House*, 811 F.2d 90 (2d Cir. 1987).)

- **Not a fair use.** *The Nation* magazine published excerpts from ex-President Gerald Ford's unpublished memoirs. The publication in *The Nation* was made several weeks prior to the date of serialization of Mr. Ford's book in another magazine. **Important factors:** *The Nation's* copying seriously damaged the marketability of Mr. Ford's serialization rights. (*Harper & Row v. Nation Enters.*, 471 U.S. 539 (1985).)

- **Not a fair use.** A company published a book entitled *Welcome to Twin Peaks: A Complete Guide to Who's Who and What's What*, containing direct quotations and paraphrases from the television show "Twin Peaks" as well as detailed descriptions of plot, character and setting. **Important factors:** The amount of the material taken was substantial and the publication adversely affected the potential market for authorized books about the program. (*Twin Peaks v. Publications Int'l, Ltd.* 996 F.2d 1366 (2d Cir. 1993).)

- **Not a fair use.** A company published a book of trivia questions about the events and characters of the "Seinfeld" television series. The book included questions based upon events and characters in 84 "Seinfeld" episodes and used actual dialogue from the show in 41 of the book's questions. **Important factors:** As in the "Twin Peaks" case, the book affected the owner's right to make derivative "Seinfeld" works such as trivia books. (*Castle Rock Entertainment, Inc. v. Carol Publ. Group*, 150 F.3d 132 (2d Cir. 1998).)

- **Fair use.** Publisher Larry Flynt made disparaging statements about the Reverend Jerry Falwell on one page of *Hustler* magazine. Rev. Falwell made several hundred thousand copies of the page and distributed them as part of a fund-raising effort. **Important factors:** Rev. Falwell's copying did not diminish the sales of the magazine (since it was already off the market) and would not adversely affect the marketability of back issues. (*Hustler Magazine, Inc. v. Moral Majority, Inc.*, 606 F. Supp. 1526 (C.D. Cal. 1985).)

2. Artwork and Audiovisual Cases

- **Not a fair use.** A television news program copied one minute and 15 seconds from a 72-minute Charlie Chaplin film and used it in a news report about Chaplin's death. **Important factors:** The court felt that the portions taken were substantial and part of the "heart" of the film. (*Roy Export Co. Estab. of Vaduz v. Columbia Broadcasting Sys., Inc.*, 672 F.2d 1095, 1100 (2d Cir. 1982).)

- **Fair use.** The makers of a movie biography of Muhammad Ali used 41 seconds from a boxing match film in their biography. **Important factors:** A small portion of film was taken and the purpose was informational. (*Monster Communications, Inc. v. Turner Broadcasting Sys. Inc.*, 935 F. Supp. 490 (S.D. N.Y. 1996).)

- **Not a fair use.** A television station's news broadcast used 30 seconds from a four-minute copyrighted videotape of the 1992 Los Angeles beating of Reginald Denny. **Important factors:** The use was commercial, took the heart of the work and affected the copyright owner's ability to market the video. (*Los Angeles News Service v. KCAL-TV Channel 9*, 108 F.3d 1119 (9th Cir. 1997).)

- **Fair use.** In a lawsuit commonly known as the Betamax case, the Supreme Court determined that the home videotaping of a television broadcast was a fair use. This was one of the few occasions when copying a complete work (for example, a complete episode of the "Kojak" television show) was accepted as a fair use. Evidence indicated that most viewers were "time-shifting" (taping in order to watch later) and not "library-building" (collecting the videos in order to build a video library). **Important factors:** The Supreme Court reasoned that the "delayed" system of viewing did not deprive the copyright owners of revenue. (*Universal City Studios v. Sony Corp.*, 464 U.S. 417 (1984).)

- **Not a fair use.** A poster of a "church quilt" was used in the background of a television series for 27 seconds. **Important factors:** The court was influenced by the prominence of the poster, its thematic importance for the set decoration of a church and the fact that it was a conventional practice to license such works for use in television programs. (*Ringgold v. Black Entertainment Television, Inc.*, 126 F.3d 70 (2d Cir. 1997).)

3. Internet Cases

- **Not a fair use.** Entire publications of the Church of Scientology were posted on the Internet by several individuals without Church permission. **Important factors:** Fair use is intended to permit the borrowing of portions of a work, not complete works. (*Religious Technology Center v. Lerma*, 40 U.S.P.Q. 2d 1569 (E.D. Va. 1996).)

- **Fair use.** *The Washington Post* used three brief quotations from Church of Scientology texts posted on the Internet (see previous case). **Important factors:** Only a small portion of the work was excerpted and the purpose was for news commentary. (*Religious Technology Center v. Pagliarina*, 908 F. Supp 1353 (E.D. Va. 1995).)

4. Music Cases

- **Fair use.** A person running for political office used 15 seconds of his opponent's campaign song in a political ad. **Important factors:** A small portion of the song was used and the purpose was for purposes of political debate. (*Keep Thomson Governor Comm. v. Citizens for Gallen Comm.*, 457 F. Supp. 957 (D. N.H. 1978).)

- **Fair use.** A television film crew, covering an Italian festival in Manhattan, recorded a band playing a portion of a copyrighted song "Dove sta Zaza." The music was replayed during a news broadcast. **Important factors:** Only a portion of the song was used, it was incidental to the news event and did not result in any actual damage to the composer or to the market for the work. (*Italian Book Corp, v. American Broadcasting Co.*, 458 F. Supp. 65 (S.D. N.Y. 1978).)

5. Summaries of Parody Cases

- **Fair use.** The rap group 2 Live Crew borrowed the opening musical tag and the words (but not the melody) from the first line of the song "Pretty Woman" ("Oh, pretty woman, walking down the street"). The rest of the lyrics and the music were different. **Important factors:** The group's use was transformative and borrowed only a small portion of the "Pretty Woman" song. The 2 Live Crew version was essentially a different piece of music and the only similarity was a brief musical opening part and the opening line. (Note: The rap group had initially sought to pay for the right to use portions of the song but were rebuffed by the publisher who did not want "Pretty Woman" used in a rap song.) (*Campbell v. Acuff-Rose Music*, 510 U.S. 569 (1994).)

- **Fair use.** The composers of the song, "When Sunny Gets Blue," claimed that their song was infringed by "When Sonny Sniffs Glue," a 29-second parody that altered the original lyric line and borrowed six bars of the song. A court determined this parody was excused as a fair use. **Important factors:** Only 29 seconds of music were borrowed (not the complete song). (*Fisher v. Dees,* 794 F.2d 432 (9th Cir. 1986).) (Note: As a general rule, parodying more than a few lines of a song lyric is unlikely to be excused as a fair use. Performers such as Weird Al Yankovic, who earn a living by humorously modifying hit songs, seek permission of the songwriters before recording their parodies.)

- **Fair use.** Comedians on the late-night television show "Saturday Night Live" parodied the song "I Love New York" using the words "I Love Sodom." Only the words "I Love" and four musical notes were taken from the original work. **Important factors:** The "Saturday Night Live" version of the jingle did not compete with or detract from the original song. (*Elsmere Music, Inc. v. National Broadcasting Co.*, 482 F. Supp. 741 (S.D. N.Y.), aff'd 632 F.2d 252 (2d Cir. 1980).)

- **Not a fair use.** An author mimicked the style of a Dr. Seuss book while re-telling the facts of the O.J. Simpson murder trial in *The Cat NOT in the Hat! A Parody by Dr. Juice.* The Ninth Circuit Court of Appeals determined that the book was a satire, not a parody, because the book did not poke fun at or ridicule Dr. Seuss. Instead, it merely used the Dr. Seuss characters and style to tell the story of the murder. **Important factors:** The author's work was nontransformative and commercial. (*Dr. Seuss Enterprises, L.P. v. Penguin Books USA, Inc.*, 109 F.3d 1394 (9th Cir. 1997).)

- **Fair use.** A movie company used a photo of a naked pregnant woman and superimposed the head of actor Leslie Nielsen. The photo was a parody using similar lighting and body positioning of a famous photograph taken by Annie Leibovitz of the actress Demi Moore for the cover of *Vanity Fair* magazine. **Important factors:** The movie company's use was transformative because it imitated the photographer's style for comic effect or ridicule. (*Leibovitz v. Paramount Pictures Corp.*, 137 F.3d 109 (2d Cir. N.Y. 1998).)

- Not a fair use. An artist created a cover for a *New Yorker* magazine that presented a humorous view of geography through the eyes of a New York City resident. A movie company later advertised their film Moscow on the Hudson using a similar piece of artwork with similar elements. The artist sued and a court ruled that the movie company's poster was not a fair use. Important factors: Why is this case different than the previous case involving the Leslie Nielsen/Annie Leibovitz parody? In the Leibovitz case, the use was a true parody, characterized by a juxtaposition of imagery that actually commented on or criticized the original. The Moscow on the Hudson movie poster did not create a parody; it simply borrowed the New Yorker's parody (the typical New York City resident's geographical viewpoint that New York City is the center of the world). (*Steinberg v. Columbia Pictures Industries, Inc.*, 663 F. Supp. 706 (S.D. N.Y. 1987).)

D. Disagreements Over Fair Use: When Are You Likely to Get Sued?

The difficulty in claiming fair use is that there is no predictable way to guarantee that your use will actually qualify as a fair use. You may believe that your use qualifies—but, if the copyright owner disagrees, you may have to resolve the dispute in a courtroom. Even if you ultimately persuade the court that your use was in fact a fair use, the expense and time involved in litigation may well outweigh any benefit of using the material in the first place.

EXAMPLE: Sam quotes from four pages of a biography in his documentary film about poet Allen Ginsberg. He believes that his use qualifies as a fair use and he does not seek permission from Barbi, the author of the biography. Barbi does not think that Sam's copying is a fair use and wants to be paid for having her work used in his film. She sues Sam for copyright infringement, and Sam is forced to hire a lawyer to defend him in the lawsuit. Even though the court ultimately rules that Sam's use was a fair use, Sam's lawyer fees exceed $20,000, which far exceeds any profits he earned from the film.

Because there is a sizable gray area in which fair use may or may not apply, there is never a guarantee that your use will qualify as a fair use. The fair use doctrine has been described as a murky concept in which it is often difficult to separate the lawful from the unlawful. Two types of situations are especially likely to cause legal problems:

- Your work causes the owner of the original work to lose money. For example, you borrow portions of a biology text for use in a competing biology text.
- The copyright owner is offended by your use. For example, you satirize the original work and your satire contains sexually explicit references or other offensive material.

Remember, these criteria do not determine whether you will prevail in a fair use lawsuit—they simply indicate whether you are likely to trigger a lawsuit. When you use someone's work and deprive them of money or offend them, the chances of a lawsuit increase.

Just as there are situations that are more likely to cause lawsuits, there are some situations that may lower the risk:

- You use a very small excerpt, for example, one or two lines from a news report, of a factual work and your use is for purposes of commentary, criticism, scholarship, research or news reporting.
- You diligently tried to locate the copyright owner but were unsuccessful, and after analyzing the fair use factors (see Section B), you became convinced that your use would qualify as a fair use.

If in doubt about your fair use assessment, consult with a copyright attorney. For information on dealing with attorneys, see Chapter 16, "Help Beyond This Book."

■

CHAPTER

10

Getting Permission to Use Trademarks

This chapter is about obtaining permission to use trademarks—words, symbols or devices used to help identify products and services. It includes an explanation of when trademark permission is necessary, how to find a trademark owner and how to license a trademark for commercial purposes.

In many ways, the use of a trademark is trickier to manage than use of copyrighted material. Even though certain informational and parody uses of trademarks are permitted without permission, there is no guaranteed shield from trademark disputes. Trademark owners are notoriously protective of their business interests and often use trademark law as a means to bully competitors and those critical of the company.

Trademark rights are also complex because there is an overlap with copyright law. For example, a fictional character such as Superman can be protected and registered under both trademark and copyright laws. We'll provide some guidance in sorting out the differences.

At the end of the chapter we have provided an agreement for licensing a trademark for merchandise purposes. Although there are a few minor differences, you will notice that this agreement is similar to the merchandise agreement in Chapter 11.

Even if your use is legally permissible, an aggressive trademark owner might file a lawsuit to intimidate you and get you to stop using the mark. As explained below, sometimes you may be legally entitled to use a trademark without permission on the grounds of free speech (see Section B1). But defending your right to free speech can be expensive, easily costing tens of thousands of dollars. The chances of a legal confrontation increase when using a famous trademark without permission. Review the rules in this chapter carefully and weigh the benefits against the potential risk before making unauthorized uses of famous trademarks.

A. Trademark Basics

This section provides an overview of trademark basics. Readers familiar with basic trademark principles may skip it and proceed to Section B.

For more trademark information, consult *Trademark: Legal Care for Your Business & Product Name,* by Kate McGrath and Stephen Elias (Nolo).

1. What Is a Trademark?

A trademark is any word, symbol or device that identifies and distinguishes a product or service. For example, the word "McDonalds," the distinctive yellow arches and the Ronald McDonald character are all trademarks of the McDonald's company.

Trademarks used to identify services are also known as service marks. For example, the service mark "UPS" represents a company that provides package delivery services; the mark "The Eagles" identifies a band that provides music services. Service marks have the same legal rights and follow the same rules as trademarks. For this reason, the term "trademark" or sometimes simply "mark" is often used when discussing either trademarks or service marks.

Most trademarks, such as brand names, slogans and logos, are easy to spot because the trademark owner displays them in a distinct manner, often using stylized lettering. A trademark may also be explicitly identified with the symbols ®, TM or SM (see Section A5). While most trademarks are easily identifiable, some are more difficult to discern, particularly trade dress, product configurations, colors and other nontraditional trademarks. The next section discusses the different kinds of trademarks in more depth.

2. Types of Trademarks

There are many different types of trademarks, including:

- **Brand names.** The most common form of trademark is a brand name—for example, Sweet 'n' Low or FedEx. Brand names are usually words, although they can be a combination of words, letters and numbers such as 7-Up.
- **Slogans.** A combination of words used as a slogan qualifies as a trademark—for example, "Where do you want to go today?" for Microsoft computer products, or "Hair Color So Natural Only Your Hairdresser Knows for Sure" for Miss Clairol hair products.
- **Logos.** A graphic image or symbol may serve as a trademark—for example, the open-banded cross used by Chevrolet.
- **Sounds.** A sound can function as a trademark—for example, the foghorn sound used by San Francisco radio station, KFOG.
- **Trade dress.** Any distinctive combination of elements may serve as a trademark—for example, the combination of yellow and black colors and distinctive lettering used in the Cliff's Notes books.

Websites and Trade Dress

A website using a distinctive combination of colors, graphic borders and buttons can stop a competitor from imitating this combination of trade dress elements under trademark law. Although website designers are free to incorporate animations, java applets and other eye-catching features, the chances of litigation increase if you copy a competitor's distinctive combination of website elements such that consumers confuse the two websites.

- **Product configurations.** Distinctive product packaging that is primarily nonfunctional is protected as a trademark—for example, the shape of the Mrs. Butterworth syrup bottle (resembling a female cook).
- **Fictional characters.** Trademark law protects a fictional character used to sell a product or service. Rules about acquiring permission to use characters are explained in Section B6.

EXAMPLE: The Pebble Beach Company incorporated a distinctive Cypress tree growing on its golf course into an abstract design. This graphic image became a logo distinguishing the Pebble Beach Company's golf services and products from other golf courses. The public is free to photograph the tree and other golf courses can grow cypress trees, but only the Pebble Beach Company is free to use this distinctive tree image to identify its golfing services and goods.

3. Trademark Rights

Trademark protection is granted to the first company to use a particular trademark in the marketplace. Trademark rights are created only when the mark is actually used in commerce—that is, in an effort to sell a product or service. Trademark protection lasts for as long as a business continuously uses a trademark to help sell goods or services. Many trademarks have been protected for over a century.

On rare occasions, however, trademark rights end if the public believes that the trademark is a generic term. For example, the terms "aspirin" and "escalator" were trademarks that lost protection once the public used the term to describe all versions of these products, not one manufacturer's version. Nowadays, companies such as Kimberly-Clarke (manufacturer of Kleenex) and Dow Chemical (manufacturer of Styrofoam) aggressively oppose this loss of trademark rights (known as "genericide") by educating the public. For example, a journalist who mistakenly writes "styrofoam cup" will probably receive a letter from Dow indicating that its trademarked Styrofoam products are not used in drinking cups (they are used primarily in boat and house insulation.)

4. Trademark Registration

A trademark owner can register the mark with the federal or state government. Registration is not required to obtain trademark protection, but it strengthens and broadens your rights, which is especially important if someone infringes your trademark.

The United States Patent and Trademark Office (PTO) administers federal registrations. The PTO can be accessed on the Web at www.uspto.gov. State registrations are handled by the Secretary of State offices of the 50 states. For an index of all state and federal trademark law websites, see the All About Trademarks website at www.ggmark.com/welcome.html.

5. Trademark Symbols

Typically, the symbols ®, TM or SM are used along with trademarks—for example, NIKE®. The symbol ® indicates that a trademark has been registered at the U.S. Patent and Trademark Office (PTO). It is illegal to use the ® symbol if the trademark in question has not been registered with the PTO. There is no legal requirement that the ® be used, but the failure to use it may limit the amount of damages that the trademark owner can recover in an infringement lawsuit. If the trademark hasn't been registered, the TM symbol can be used. Similarly, the SM symbol can be used for service marks that have not been registered. The TM and SM have no legal significance other than to indicate the fact that the owner is claiming trademark rights.

6. Violations of Trademark Owners' Rights

Trademark owners' rights can be violated in two ways: by direct infringement and by dilution.

a. Direct Infringement

Infringement occurs when one company uses another company's trademark (or a substantially similar mark) in a manner that is likely to confuse consumers into believing that there is some connection, affiliation or sponsorship between the two companies. Usually this occurs when a trademark is used on similar goods—for example a counterfeit Rolex watch. The counterfeiter is relying on the unauthorized Rolex trademark to confuse consumers into believing that the watch came from the Rolex company. Subtler forms of consumer confusion occur when companies use similar but nonidentical marks or use similar marks on related but nonidentical products or services.

EXAMPLE: A comic book store uses the name "The Batcave" without authorization. Because "Batcave" is a trademark of DC Comics, consumers may believe that the comic book publisher endorses or is connected with the store. On this basis the owners of the "Batcave" trademark can bring a trademark infringement lawsuit against the comic book store to stop the unauthorized use.

b. Trademark Dilution

Trademark dilution occurs when the integrity of a trademark is "muddied" by an unwanted commercial association, either by a vulgar or insulting affiliation (tarnishment) or by a connection with a lesser product (blurring).

- **Tarnishment.** A company may tarnish the image of a famous trademark if it uses the trademark to promote a product or service that may be considered offensive. For example, if an X-rated website named itself Candyland, its use may tarnish the image of the trademark "Candyland" used on children's games.

- **Blurring.** Normally, the rules of trademark prohibit someone from commercially using a trademark that's owned by someone else if the use is likely to cause customer confusion. However, sometimes even if there's little likelihood of customer confusion, one company can stop another company who commercially uses its famous trademark in a manner that blurs the two companies in the customers' minds. For example, say a toilet paper maker named its product Rolls Royce Toilet Paper. Even though most people wouldn't think that Rolls Royce toilet paper was produced by the famous luxury car maker, the Rolls Royce car company might pursue the toilet paper maker for diluting its trademark.

Dilution is a vague concept, often used by companies to justify going after an offensive use of a trademark. Dilution does not result from informational uses such as a critical product review (see Section B). However, dilution can result from a commercial use such as a comparative advertisement.

Altering a Trademark

Besides blurring and dilution, the alteration of a trademark in a comparative advertisement has also been found to be a dilution. In a television advertisement, a competitor of John Deere, a farming equipment company, animated the John Deere "deer" logo and appeared to make it run from the competition. The competitor was found liable for trademark dilution. (*Deere & Company v. MTD Prods. Inc.*, 34 U.S.P.Q. 1706 (S.D. N.Y. 1995).) Based on this ruling, it would be unwise to modify another company's trademark unless it can be justified under free speech or parody rules. See section B for more information on these rules.

---

7. Disparagement and Defamation

There is yet another way you can get sued by a trademark owner: if you commit disparagement or defamation. Disparagement involves making false statements that interfere with a company's business relations. Defamation involves making false statements that injure a business's reputation. Disparagement affects a company's ability to do business; defamation affects the manner in which the public perceives the company's trademarked products.

Unlike infringement and dilution, defamation and disparagement do not have to occur in a commercial context. For example, using a trademark in a newspaper article, if based on false statements, can result in a claim of disparagement or defamation. Disparagement and defamation are not claims under trademark law; they fall into a broad category of laws known as business torts. For more information on basic defamation principles, see Chapter 12.

B. When You Need Permission to Use a Trademark

This section describes when permission is required for various types of trademark uses. In certain situations you can use a trademark without obtaining the owner's permission. In others, you'll need to do a bit more analysis before using a trademark without an okay from the owner. The answer to whether a given use is legally okay will usually depend on a number of factual issues, and can sometimes be tricky to figure out.

Below we discuss the various ways that trademarks are typically used, and whether permission is required for each type of use. Keep in mind, however, that even if you're legally entitled to use a trademark, that doesn't mean that the trademark owner will always be agreeable. If you're forced into court to prove that your use is allowed by law, in a sense you've already lost the battle. Take care to make sure your use is in fact within the bounds of the law, and be aware of the trademark owner's likely response. You'll need to carefully weigh the benefits of using the trademark if you suspect the owner will fight you with legal action.

Remember also that what might be permitted under trademark law might not be permitted under copyright law. Therefore, if the trademark contains some copyrightable elements, analyze your use under both trademark and copyright rules.

1. Informational Uses

Informational (or "editorial") uses of a trademark do not require permission. These are uses that inform, educate or express opinions protected under the First Amendment of the United States Constitution (protecting freedom of speech and of the press). For example, permission is not required to use the Chevrolet logo in an article describing Chevrolet trucks, even if the article is critical of the company. Similarly if you were preparing a documentary film on the history of American trucks, permission would not be required to include the Chevrolet logo. However, the use of the logo must have some relevance to the work. For example, it would not be wise to publish an article critical of overseas auto manufacturing practices and include the Chevrolet logo unless Chevrolet were mentioned in the article.

Whether to Use Trademark Symbols

When using a trademark in a text format for informational purposes, it is not necessary to include the ®, TM or SM symbols. However, it is good trademark etiquette to distinguish a trademark by capitalizing or italicizing it—for example, "The house was constructed with Styrofoam insulation," or "He used a Nordic Trak exercise machine."

---

2. Comparative Advertising

It's permissible to use a trademark when making accurate comparative product statements in advertisements. However, since comparative advertisements tend to provoke trademark owners, an attorney knowledgeable in trademark or business law should review the advertisement before publication. As noted in Section A, modification of another company's trademark may result in a claim of dilution.

3. Commercial Uses

Commercial uses of a trademark include advertising, promotion or marketing, and require permission (except for cases of comparative advertising as explained in the previous section). Commercial uses include business-sponsored promotional activities such as public presentations, informational advertisements (known as "advertorials") and merchandise.

EXAMPLE: An auto insurance company publishes a booklet on drunk driving. The booklet includes the logo for a beer company. The use of the logo would be considered a commercial use and permission should be obtained.

Include Trademark Symbols for Commercial Uses

When using a trademark in a commercial context, such as in an advertisement, product manual or in connection with the sale of a product or service, include the ®, TM or SM symbols adjacent to trademark—for example, Adobe® PageMaker®. Remember—the ® symbol should only be used if the trademark is federally registered. This may be evident from the trademark's owner's use or can be learned by researching the federal trademark database. A statement such as "Adobe and PageMaker are registered trademarks of the Adobe Corporation" is also recommended. Place the statement on the index page of a website, the copyright page of a publication or at the end of a movie.

4. Parodies: Laughing All the Way to Court

A trademark parody occurs when someone imitates a trademark in a manner that pokes fun at the mark. A newspaper called *The San Francisco Chomical*, meant to poke fun at *The San Francisco Chronicle*, is an example of a parody. In Chapter 9, dealing with fair use of copyrighted materials, we provided some general rules as to when parodies are permissible and when they infringe copyright. Below we have provided some specific rules for trademark parodies.

Keep in mind the general rule which applies to both types of parodies—offensive parodies often

trigger lawsuits. Therefore, weigh the legal consequences carefully before proceeding.

Generally speaking, a trademark parody is less likely to run into problems if it:

- *Doesn't compete*. The use of the parody product does not directly compete with the trademark product.
- *Doesn't confuse*. The parody does not confuse consumers; they get the joke and do not believe the parody product comes from the same source as the trademarked goods.
- *Does parody*. Not all humorous uses are parodies. To avoid trouble, the use should specifically poke fun at the trademark.

Below are some trademark parody court cases.

- **Allowable trademark parody.** A college student sold T-shirts at Myrtle Beach depicting a red, white and blue beer can with the phrase, "This Beach is for You." Anheuser-Busch, the owners of the Budweiser trademark, filed a lawsuit, seized all of the T-shirts and raided the college student's home and his mother's business. A jury determined that the T-shirts were a parody, but the judge overturned the jury verdict and ruled for Anheuser-Busch. An appeals court ruled that the use was a parody. Seven years and several lawsuits later, the parties reached a settlement in which Anheuser-Busch granted a license for sales of the T-shirt. (*Anheuser-Busch, Inc. v. L & L Wings, Inc.*, 962 F.2d 316 (4th Cir.), cert. denied, 113 S. Ct. 206 (1992).)

- **Allowable trademark parody.** During a half-time show, the San Diego Chicken mascot initiated a fistfight with Barney, the popular purple dinosaur. A court held the use of the Barney trademark a permissible parody because the aggressive manner in which Barney behaved was not likely to cause consumer confusion. (*Lyons Partnership L.P. v. Giannoulas*, 14 F. Supp. 2d 947 (N.D. Texas).)

- **Not an allowable trademark parody.** A gaudy, '60s style nightclub in Houston used the trademark "The Velvet Elvis" and, after being sued by the owner of the Elvis trademark, claimed that the club's name was an Elvis parody. A court disagreed, pointing out that the intent of the club's name and decor was to parody the Las Vegas lounge scene and the velvet painting craze, not to parody Elvis. (*Elvis Presley Enterprises v. Capece*, 141 F.3d 188 (5th Cir. 1998).)

Conflicting case law and the discretionary power of judges make it difficult to predict the outcome of a lawsuit based on trademark parody. It is also difficult to predict when a company will take action against a parodist. Some companies, like Anheuser-Busch, prefer to fight to the end while others believe that chasing parodists generates negative publicity and prefer to let the parody run its course.

5. Using a Trademark Containing Copyrightable Elements

Use of a trademark containing a copyrightable image such as a character, photograph or illustration may be prohibited under copyright law even if permitted under trademark law. Examples of copyrightable trademarks include:

- animated logos such as the Microsoft Internet Explorer spinning globe
- logos containing artwork or photos, such as the floral bouquet in the Herbal Essence logo, and
- characters such as Mr. Peanut or Betty Crocker.

Characters are discussed in the next section.

Before proceeding with the unauthorized use of a trademark containing copyrightable elements, compare trademark and copyright rules to minimize potential liability. Certain elements such as fonts, simple geometric shapes, individual words and short phrases are not protected under copyright law.

6. Using Characters

In previous chapters dealing with artwork and photographs, we indicated that literary and pictorial characters such as Sam Spade and Fred Flintstone are protected under copyright law. In addition, these characters may be protected under trademark law, which protects a wide range of text and images that are used to sell products or services. Trademarked characters can be either graphic (for example, Snoopy or Spiderman) or human (for example, Rambo or Mr. Whipple). Characters may have an association with a specific product or service, such as Mr. Clean and home cleaning products. Or, a character may be used to sell a variety of merchandise—such as the Mutant Ninja Turtle characters that were used to sell breakfast cereal, T-shirts and a wide range of assorted merchandise.

Since nowadays characters often simultaneously tell stories and sell products, the difference between the two forms of legal protection is often indistinct. If this overlap seems confusing, take solace in the fact that it has often confounded attorneys and the courts. In the real world, this overlap is sometimes an academic issue, since the owner of the fictional character usually controls both copyright and trademark rights. Therefore, the company will tailor your license to permit all appropriate uses. If there are a number of owners involved, however, obtaining permission to use the character may become somewhat trickier.

Below, we offer guidance on how to deal with using various types of characters, particularly when trademark and copyright rules may overlap.

a. Graphic Character; Informational Use

Trademark permission is not required to reproduce a graphic character such as Woody Woodpecker for informational purposes. Copyright authorization, on the other hand, is required. In Chapter 4, "Getting Permission to Use Artwork," we provide information on getting permission to use cartoon and comic characters. Keep in mind that copyright permission is not required if the character is in the public domain or if the reproduction qualifies as a fair use. For example, the use of Mickey Mouse (a character owned by the Disney Corporation) in a news story qualifies as a fair use, but the use of Mickey Mouse in a trivia book about Disney characters requires permission. See Chapter 9 for detailed information on which uses of copyrighted material qualifies as fair use.

b. Human Character; Informational Use

Using a photograph of a human character such as Captain Kirk for an informational use such as in a news story does not require trademark permission. However, copyright authorization from the owner of the photograph is required. The copyright owner is usually an entertainment production company. In Chapter 3, "Getting Permission to Use Photographs," we explain how to locate production companies. Permission is not required from the actor portraying the character.

c. Graphic Character; Commercial Use

Trademark permission is required for the commercial use of a graphic character in an advertisement or on merchandise. For example, reproducing the Road Runner character in an advertisement for an auto race would require permission from the owners of Road Runner. Follow the rules in this chapter. As we mentioned earlier, the trademark owner almost always controls the copyright as well and they will tailor the license to permit both uses.

d. Human Character; Commercial Use

Trademark permission is required to reproduce an image of a human character such as James Bond for commercial uses. Permission must also be obtained from the person portraying the character. In Chapter 12, "Releases," we provide model releases that can

be used to obtain permission from actors who portray fictional characters. Failure to obtain permission from the human who portrayed the character may prove expensive. For example, a federal court permitted two actors from the TV show "Cheers" to sue a company that sold robots based on their characters without obtaining their permission. The case eventually settled. (*Wendt v. Host Int'l, Inc.*, 125 F.3d 806 (9th Cir. 1997).) Based on the "Cheers" litigation, a company that uses fictional characters personified by human actors should obtain permission from the actors or risk a lawsuit.

7. Using a Trademark in a Title

Permission should be obtained to use a trademark on the cover of a book, in the title of a film or song or in the advertising for an informational work. The following cases illustrate that failure to obtain such permission can easily result in a lawsuit.

- The owner of the Godzilla trademark successfully stopped a book publisher from selling a film-study book entitled *Godzilla*. The court ruled that the use of the name without a prominent disclaimer amounted to a trademark infringement. (*Toho Inc. v. William Morrow and Co.*, 33 F. Supp. 2d 1206 (C.D. Cal. 1998).)
- A film company producing a movie satirizing Minnesota beauty queens was prohibited from using the title *Dairy Queen* even though no Dairy Queens or Dairy Queen trademarks were seen in the film. The court ruled that consumers would be confused as to the source of the film and would believe that the owner of the Dairy Queen trademark had permitted the use. (*American Dairy Queen Corp. v. New Line Productions Inc.*, 35 F. Supp. 2d 727 (Minn. 1998).)
- The makers of Tron fuses sued the makers of the film *Tron*. The company did not sue about the use of the name in the film, but instead sued because the Tron name was used on video games and telephones, two prod-

ucts that might cause confusion among consumers of Tron fuses. This case was ultimately settled. (*McGraw-Edison Co. v. Walt Disney Productions*, 787 F.2d 1163 (7th Cir. 1985).)

8. Using a Trademark as a Character Name

You don't need permission to name a fictional character in a story or movie after a trademark—for example, naming a character Nerf or Advil. However, this practice is likely to provoke the trademark owner if the character is unsavory or is used to sell merchandise. In one case, Hormel, the makers of Spam, sued the makers of a Muppet movie because a pig character was named Sp'am. The court ruled against Hormel, noting that it did not tarnish Spam's trademark to be associated with a pig, and that Spam had been so maligned in popular culture that the association with the film character, a helpful boar who befriends Muppet characters, could not possibly tarnish the trademark. (*Hormel Foods Corp. v. Jim Henson Productions Inc.*, 73 F.3d 497 (2d Cir. 1996).)

9. Trademark Practices: Books, Movies, Songs and Websites

Acquiring trademark permissions differs within various media industries. Some of these rules are provided below. Often, permission is not legally required and a court will permit an unauthorized use. However, since book publishers, software companies, Internet providers and movie companies do not want to risk a lawsuit, they seek permission anyway. Some short model permission forms are provided.

a. Book Publishing

Although publishers ordinarily don't have to obtain permission for informational uses of trademarks, many seek authorization anyway. Note that authorization is required to use a trademark in a book published as a means of promoting a product or service. For example, a computer company publishing a manual on desktop publishing should obtain permission to reproduce trademarks from software companies whose products are mentioned in the manual.

An example of a simple permission statement is provided below.

The Basic Permission to Use a Trademark in a Book or Magazine is included on the forms disk under the file name TMBKMAG.

Basic Permission to Use a Trademark in a Book or Magazine

_____ ("Owner) is the owner of rights in the trademark _____ (the "Trademark"). Owner grants permission for the Trademark's reproduction in the format indicated below in the publication, _____ , and in any subsequent editions or derivative versions in any media. Any goodwill associated with the Trademark vests in Owner.

Owner Name _____

Signature _____

Date _____

Insert Sample of Trademark

b. The Film Industry

Most film, video and television production companies obtain permission for the use of trademarks that appear in their movies and videos. This includes trademarks on signs in public locations. Below we have provided a sample permission agreement for use of a trademark in a film, television show or video.

Companies with trademarks are sometimes eager to see their products in films and enter into special permission agreements known as "product placement agreements." Under these agreements, the companies may provide free products, services or cross-promotions. For example, America Online allowed use of its trademarks, including the phrase "You've Got Mail" in the film of the same name. On the other hand, the FCC prohibits the use of product placements in programming made for television. Clearance companies in Los Angeles and New York review scripts and prepare clearance reports. For further information regarding film clearance, see *Clearance and Copyright*, by Michael C. Donaldson (Silman-James Press).

The Basic Permission to Use a Trademark in a Movie is included on the forms disk under the file name TMFILMAG.

Basic Permission to Use a Trademark in a Movie

_____ ("Owner") is the owner of rights in the trademark, _____ (the Trademark"). Owner grants permission for the Trademark's reproduction in the format indicated below in all versions of the film, _____ (the "Film"), and any derivative versions in any media. Any goodwill associated with the Trademark vests in Owner.

Owner Name _____

Signature _____

Date _____

Insert Sample of Trademark

c. Artwork and Photography

Artwork and photographs sometimes include trademarks. Permission from the trademark owner is required if the art or photograph are created and reproduced for commercial purposes, such as in advertising or on merchandise. For example, a company that sold trading cards of collectible cars was prohibited from reproducing Chrysler trademarks and trade dress because Chrysler licensed similar collectible products. (*Chrysler Corp. v. Newfield Publications Inc.*, 880 F. Supp. 504 (E.D. Mich. 1995).)

A photograph that portrays a trademark in a morally offensive manner is liable to trigger a trademark dispute. For example, lawsuits were filed over lewd photos of the Pillsbury Doughboy and of photos showing the Barbie and Ken dolls in compromising positions. Below we have provided a sample permission form for use of a trademark in artwork.

The Basic Permission to Use a Trademark in a Photograph or Artwork is in the appendix and on the forms disk under the file name TMPHTART.

Basic Permission to Use a Trademark in a Photograph or Artwork

_____ ("Owner") is the owner of rights in trademark _____ (the "Trademark"). Owner grants permission for the Trademark's reproduction in the format indicated below in all versions of the artwork, _____ , (the "Artwork"), and any derivative versions in any media. Any goodwill associated with the Trademark vests in Owner.

Owner Name _____

Signature _____

Date _____

Insert Sample of Trademark

d. The Internet

Using a word trademark as a link on a website (known as a hypertext link) is permitted without authorization. For example, no authorization is needed to link to the General Motors website by using a text link "General Motors." However, use of another company's trademark as a graphic or visual link requires authorization. In Chapter 6, "Website Permissions," we provide a linking agreement and discuss additional website issues. In Chapter 12, "Releases," we explain how to figure out whether a site is primarily informational or commercial. For information about domain name and related trademark uses, review Chapter 16, "Help Beyond This Book."

e. The Music Industry

The unauthorized use of a trademark in a song title or album title may be permitted under First Amendment principles provided the title does not confuse or dilute the mark. Regardless of the law, however, this type of use is likely to provoke a trademark dispute. For example, toymaker Mattel Inc. sued MCA Records over a song entitled "Barbie Girl" by the Danish pop group Aqua. A federal court ruled in favor of the record company based upon First Amendment issues and refused to halt the sale of the song. (*Mattel, Inc. v. MCA Records, Inc.*, 28 F. Supp. 2d 1120 (C.D. Cal. 1998).) The band Motley Crue was sued by the owner of the Dr. Feelgood trademark, used primarily on hospital scrubs. In that case, the band prevailed by demonstrating there was no customer confusion. (*Reeves v. Motley Crue Inc.*, 21 U.S.P.Q.2D (BNA) 1587, (N.D. Ala. 1991).)

10. Using a Trademark in Connection With an Award

A business receiving an award or a favorable review from an organization needs authorization to use the organization's trademark. For example, if a software company received an award from a *MegaSoft* computer magazine, the software company could state it received an award from *MegaSoft*, but permission would have to be obtained in order to use the magazine's graphic awards trademark in an advertisement.

Generally, companies that provide ratings or create awards have guidelines for how their trademarks are used in advertising—for example one computer magazine requires that a company using its trademarks include the issue date of the award as well as the version of the software. Some consumer companies do not permit the use of their trademarks for other companies' products regardless of the rating, review or award.

The person at a publication who grants trademark permission is usually in the company's business department. Larger companies have departments for managing trademark rights and permission. For help locating trademark owners, see Section C.

11. Using a Certification Mark

Certain trademarks certify that a product or service meets a certain standard. For example, the CCOF logo guarantees that produce is from a California Certified Organic Farm. These certification marks may also establish standards for the materials used in a product, the accuracy of a product, source of labor or the region of origin.

If your company or business wants to be certified to use the mark, you must contact the certification mark owner and obtain the standards. For example, if you were a potato farmer in Idaho, you would contact the respective certification mark owner to learn the standards for using the "Idaho Potatoes" certification mark. Information about locating trademark owners is provided in Section C.

12. Trademark Disclaimers

A disclaimer is a statement intended to minimize confusion in consumer's minds or deflect liability. A disclaimer is only effective if it is prominently placed, permanently affixed, can be read and understood and really minimizes confusion. A disclaimer, by itself, will not provide a shield against litigation but, when properly done, a disclaimer can minimize confusion and prevent dilution.

EXAMPLE: An individual publishes a parody of the newspaper *Newsday*, entitled *Snoozeday*. A prominently displayed disclaimer such as "This newspaper is intended as a parody of *Newsday* and no claim is made to *Newsday*'s trademarks or related proprietary rights" may minimize potential liability.

C. Locating a Trademark Owner

Locating a trademark owner can be accomplished through business directories, by contacting the trademark owner's website or searching trademark records to locate the name and address of the trademark owner. Many large companies such as Coca-Cola, General Motors and FedEx have departments that handle the licensing and permission arrangements.

1. Business Directories

There are several general business directories on the Internet. Your Internet search engine should be capable of finding them. For example, Big Yellow, the NYNEX business directory (www.bigyellow.com), enables the user to search by business category, name, street address, state or zip code.

2. Federally Registered Marks

Ownership of federally registered trademarks can be researched at the PTO website, which provides free access to records of registered marks and marks that are pending (applications undergoing examination at the PTO). Searching tips and techniques are provided at the site. The PTO's database can be accessed at www.uspto.gov/tmdb/index.html.

EXAMPLE: A movie company wants permission to include a Tower Records sign in a film. Accessing the PTO Trademark database and typing in Tower Records uncovers the following information:

> Word Mark: TOWER RECORDS
> Owner Name (REGISTRANT): MTS, Incorporated
> Owner Address: 2500 Del Monte Street
> West Sacramento CALIFORNIA 95691 CORPORATION CALIFORNIA
> Attorney of Record: Rochelle D. Alpert

The PTO trademark database has limitations. It may not include applications filed during the last two to four months, nor does it contain information on state, foreign or common law trademarks or inactive applications and registrations (that is, abandoned applications or canceled or expired registrations). The database may be as much as four months out of sequence with the PTO's internal trademark database, so it may not be possible to locate the owner of a mark for which an application was recently filed. For more up-to-date federal registration trademark information, consider using the Micropatent database described in Section 4, below.

3. Common Law Marks

Trademark owners do not have to register their trademarks to obtain trademark rights. These unregistered trademarks are sometimes referred to as "common law marks." The owners of these marks are harder to locate than registered mark owners since they don't appear in government databases. It may be possible to locate common law marks using Internet search engines (type in the mark as a keyword) or in online business directories.

4. Private Trademark Databases

Private trademark databases such as Micropatent are the most current and comprehensive trademark research sources. They include state trademarks, international marks, and inactive, canceled and abandoned marks. Micropatent's website is located at www.micropatent.com.

5. Owners of Characters

Locating the owner of a character may be accomplished by contacting the business's owner directly, searching trademark databases (see example below) or searching specialized journals that concentrate on character and trademark licensing.

> EXAMPLE: A nonprofit children's organization wants permission to use Daffy Duck on fundraising posters. Accessing the PTO trademark database and typing in Daffy Duck produces the following information:
>
> DAFFY DUCK
> Owner Name (REGISTRANT): Time Warner Entertainment Company, L.P.
> Owner Address: 75 Rockefeller Plaza New York NEW YORK 10019 LIMITED PARTNERSHIP DELAWARE
> Attorney of Record: Elise A. Tenen

6. Character Resources

The following resources can help you locate the owners of trademarked characters.

- Licensing Journal: 1185 Avenue of the Americas, New York, NY 10046; 212-597-0200; Web: www.aspenpub.com.
- The EPM Licensing Letter Sourcebook, EPM Entertainment Marketing Sourcebook, and The Licensing Letter: EPM Communications, 160 Mercer Street, 3rd Floor, New York, NY 10012-3212; 212-941-0099; fax: 212-941-1622.

7. Trademark Services

For a listing of companies that provide trademark research services, review the resources at the Yahoo! Trademarks directory at dir.yahoo.com/ Business_and_Economy/Companies/Law/ Intellectual_Property/Trademarks/Services/.

D. Trademark Licensing

This section deals with trademark licensing, primarily the use of a trademark on merchandise in return for periodic payments known as royalties. The underlying principle of trademark licensing is that consumers are more likely to buy merchandise if it includes a familiar trademark. Trademarks are often licensed in the following situations:

- Characters such as Barney or the Power Rangers are often licensed to merchandise producers, and provide lucrative licensing income.
- Collegiate trademark licensing provides an important revenue source for universities. In 1999, Ohio University and Ohio State settled a bitter dispute over which university could license the word "Ohio."
- Companies such as Harley-Davidson and Jack Daniels earn income by licensing their corporate trademarks.

- Designers such as Calvin Klein have created a billion dollar enterprise placing their names on a wide array of products.
- Entertainment trademarks such as MTV or Late Night With David Letterman provide additional earnings for entertainment companies.
- Annual festivals and activities such as the Gilroy Garlic Festival license their trademarks to augment income for the event.
- State and municipal tourism offices license trademarks such as "Ski Colorado."
- Trademark licensing earns revenue for nonprofit causes—for example the Audubon Society licenses its name for a clock that provides birdcalls.
- Licensing league and sports team trademarks such as the Chicago Bulls or San Francisco Forty-Niners is probably the greatest single generator of trademark licensing revenue.

The rest of this section describes the trademark licensing process in more detail, and provides a sample licensing agreement.

1. Overview of the Licensing Process

The trademark licensing process is usually more challenging than the licensing of copyrighted works. One reason is that the trademark owner often has a stronger interest in controlling the quality and consistency of the merchandise. The trademark owner is concerned about misuse of the mark or that shoddy goods will diminish the trademark's goodwill.

The trademark licensing process is initiated in one of three ways: a licensee locates a trademark owner, the trademark owner contacts the licensee or a third-party agency facilitates the licensing arrangement. Many famous trademarks such as Harley-Davidson are represented by agencies who seek out suitable merchandise partners. After the parties make contact, the basic terms of the agreement are sorted out. In Chapter 11, we have pro-

vided a worksheet that may be helpful in negotiating the aspects of the license agreement.

It is quite common for owners of well-known trademarks to dictate the terms and furnish the agreements for merchandise licensing. Often these terms are on a "take it or leave it" basis and if the licensee does not agree, the trademark owner will go elsewhere. In other cases, a licensee will furnish the trademark license agreement. Usually, prior to furnishing the agreement, the licensee and the licensor have worked out all of the business terms. Even after the terms are agreed upon and the license is furnished, there may be additional changes.

2. Royalty Payments

Payment of royalties depends on the industry trends. Royalties are usually paid for use of a trademark on merchandise such as clothing or ceramic goods, and range from 2% to 10% of the net sales. A trademark owner may accept a lump-sum payment for a one-time license—for example, the use of the image on 10,000 T-shirts at a sporting event.

 For more information on trademark licensing, review *A Primer on Licensing,* by Jack Revoyr (Kent Press).

3. Sample Trademark License Agreement

Below is a sample trademark license agreement, followed by an explanation of selected provisions. This trademark license is very similar to the merchandise license provided in Chapter 11, "Art & Merchandise Agreements." The primary distinctions relate to quality control standards and ownership rights related to the trademarks. These distinctions are explained in Section 4.

 The Trademark License Agreement is on the forms disk under the file name TMLICNS.

Trademark License Agreement

Introduction

This Trademark License Agreement (the "Agreement") is made between _____ (referred to as "Licensor") and _____ (referred to as "Licensee").

The parties agree as follows:

The Trademarks

The "Trademarks" refer to any trademark, service mark, trade name, logo, or other device and its associated good will used to identify and distinguish Licensor's products and services as included in Exhibit A. Licensor is the owner of all rights to the Trademarks and Licensee shall not claim any right to use the Trademarks except under the terms of this Agreement.

Licensed Products

Licensed Products are defined as the licensee's products incorporating the Trademarks specifically described in Exhibit A (the "Licensed Products").

Grant of Rights

Licensor grants to Licensee:

(select one)

☐   an exclusive license

☐   a nonexclusive license

to reproduce and distribute the Trademarks on the Licensed Products.

Sublicense

(select one)

☐   **Consent required.** Licensee may sublicense the rights granted pursuant to this Agreement provided: Licensee obtains Licensor's prior written consent to such sublicense; and Licensor receives such revenue or royalty payment as provided in the Payment section below. Any sublicense granted in violation of this provision shall be void.

☐   **No sublicensing permitted.** Licensee may not sublicense the rights granted under this Agreement.

Reservation of Rights: Assignment of Good Will

Licensor reserves all rights other than those being conveyed or granted in this Agreement. Licensee assigns to Licensor any good will from the Trademarks that may accrue under this Agreement or from the distribution of the Licensed Products. Licensee's rights to the Trademarks are only in connection with the Licensed Products and Licensee shall not assert any other association with Licensor or the Trademarks. Licensee acknowledges the validity of the Trademarks and agrees not to challenge Licensor's ownership of the Trademarks or their validity.

Territory

The rights granted to Licensee are limited to _____ (the "Territory").

Term

The "Effective Date" of this Agreement is defined as the date when the agreement commences and is established by the latest signature date.

(select one)

☐   **Specified term with renewal rights.** This Agreement shall commence upon the Effective Date and shall extend for a period of _____ years (the "Initial Term"). Following the Initial Term, Licensee may renew this Agreement under the same terms and conditions for____consecutive _____ periods (the "Renewal Terms") provided that Licensee provides written notice of its intention to renew this Agreement within thirty (30) days before the expiration of the current term.

☐   **Term with renewal based upon sales.** This Agreement shall commence upon the Effective Date and shall extend for a period of _____years (the "Initial Term") and may be renewed by Licensee under the same terms and conditions for consecutive_____year periods (the "Renewal Terms"), provided that:

(a) Licensee provides written notice of its intention to renew this Agreement within thirty days before the expiration of the current term; and

(b) Licensee has met the sales requirements as established in Exhibit A.

☐   **Indefinite term.**This Agreement shall commence upon the Effective Date and shall continue until terminated pursuant to a provision of this Agreement.

☐   **Fixed term.**This Agreement shall commence upon the Effective Date and shall continue for _____ unless sooner terminated pursuant to a provision of this Agreement.

☐   **Term for as long as Licensee sells Licensed Products.**This Agreement shall commence upon the Effective Date as specified in Exhibit A and shall continue for as long as Licensee continues to offer the Licensed Products in commercially reasonable quantities or unless sooner terminated pursuant to a provision of this Agreement.

Approval of Samples & Quality Control

Pre-Production. Licensee shall submit to Licensor a reasonable number of pre-production designs and prototypes at no cost prior to production as well as production samples of every Licensed Product to assure that the product meets Licensor's quality standards. Licensee agrees not to distribute any Licensed Product until receipt of Licensor's written approval of such Licensed Product.

Production and Promotion. At least once every six (6) months, Licensee shall submit to Licensor two (2) production samples of each Licensed Product for review. Licensee shall pay all costs for delivery of these materials. In the event that any production sample does not meet Licensor's quality standards, licensee agrees to immediately correct such deficiencies. Licensor shall have the right to inspect Licensee's premises upon reasonable notice for purposes of observing the manufacturing process. Licensee shall submit all advertising and promotional materials to Licensor and shall not distribute such materials until receipt of written approval from Licensor.

Royalties

All royalties ("Royalties") provided for under this Agreement shall accrue when the respective Licensed Products are sold, shipped, distributed, billed or paid for, whichever occurs first.

Net Sales

"Net Sales" are defined as Licensee's gross sales (i.e., the gross invoice amount billed customers) less quantity discounts or rebates and returns actually credited. A quantity discount or rebate is a discount made at the time of shipment. No deductions shall be made for cash or other discounts, commissions, manufacturing costs, uncollectible accounts, or for fees or expenses of any kind which the Licensee may incur in connection with the Royalty payments.

Fees

(select one or more provisions)

☐ **Advance Against Royalties.** As a nonrefundable advance against royalties (the "Advance"), Licensee agrees to pay to Licensor upon execution of this Agreement the sum of $ _____ .

☐ **Licensed Product Royalty.** Licensee agrees to pay a Royalty of ____ % percent of all Net Sales revenue of the Licensed Products ("Licensed Product Royalty").

☐ **Per Unit Royalty.** Licensee agrees to pay a Royalty of $ ___ for each unit of the Licensed Product that is ☐ manufactured ☐ sold [select one].

☐ **Guaranteed Minimum Annual Royalty Payment.** In addition to any other advances or fees, Licensee shall pay an annual guaranteed royalty (the "GMAR") as follows: $ _____ . The GMAR shall be paid to Licensor annually on _____ . The GMAR is an advance against royalties for the twelve-month (12-month) period commencing upon payment. Royalty payments based on Net Sales made during any year of this Agreement shall be credited against the GMAR due for the year in which such Net Sales were made. In the event that annual royalties exceed the GMAR, Licensee shall pay the difference to Licensor. Any annual royalty payments in excess of the GMAR shall not be carried forward from previous years or applied against the GMAR.

☐ **License Fee.** As a nonrefundable, nonrecoupable fee for executing this license, Licensee agrees to pay to Licensor upon execution of this Agreement the sum of $ _____ .

☐ **Sublicensing Revenues.** In the event of any sublicense of the rights granted pursuant to this Agreement, Licensee shall pay to Licensor _____ % percent of all sublicensing revenues.

Payments and Statements to Licensor

Within thirty (30) days after the end of each calendar quarter (the "Royalty Period"), an accurate statement of Net Sales of Licensed Products along with any royalty payments or sublicensing revenues due to Licensor shall be provided to Licensor, regardless of whether any Licensed Products were sold during the Royalty Period. All payments shall be paid in United States currency drawn on a United States bank. The acceptance by Licensor of any of the statements furnished or royalties paid shall not preclude Licensor questioning the correctness at any time of any payments or statements.

Audit

Licensee shall keep accurate books of account and records covering all transactions relating to the license granted in this Agreement, and Licensor or its duly authorized representatives shall have the right upon five days prior written notice, and during normal business hours, to inspect and audit Licensee's records relating to the Licensed Products under this Agreement. Licensor shall bear the cost of such inspection and audit, unless the results indicate an underpayment greater than $ _____ for any six-month (6-month) period. In that case, Licensee shall promptly reimburse Licensor for all costs of the audit along with the amount due with interest on such sums. Interest shall accrue from the date the payment was originally due and the interest rate shall be 1.5% per month, or the maximum rate permitted by law, whichever is less. All books of account and records shall be made available in the United States and kept available for at least two years after the termination of this Agreement.

Late Payment

Time is of the essence with respect to all payments to be made by Licensee under this Agreement. If Licensee is late in any payment provided for in this Agreement, Licensee shall pay interest on the payment from the date due until paid at a rate of 1.5% per month, or the maximum rate permitted by law, whichever is less.

Licensor Warranties

Licensor warrants that it has the power and authority to enter into this Agreement and has no knowledge as to any third-party claims regarding the proprietary rights in the Trademarks that would interfere with the rights granted under this Agreement.

Indemnification by Licensor

(select one if appropriate)

☐ **Licensor indemnification without limitations.** Licensor shall indemnify Licensee and hold Licensee harmless from any damages and liabilities (including reasonable attorney fees and costs), arising from any breach of Licensor's warranties as defined in Licensor's Warranties, above.

☐ **Licensor indemnification limited to amounts paid.** Licensor shall indemnify Licensee and hold Licensee harmless from any damages and liabilities (including reasonable attorney fees and costs), arising from any breach of Licensor's warranties as defined in Licensor's Warranties, above. Licensor's maximum liability under this provision shall in no event exceed the total amount earned by Licensor under this Agreement.

Licensee Warranties

Licensee warrants that it will use its best commercial efforts to market the Licensed Products and that their sale and marketing shall be in conformance with all applicable laws and regulations, including but not limited to all intellectual property laws.

Indemnification by Licensee

Licensee shall indemnify Licensor and hold Licensor harmless from any damages and liabilities (including reasonable attorney fees and costs), arising from any breach of Licensee's warranties and representation as defined in the Licensee Warranties above, or arising out of any alleged defects of the Licensed Products, any product liability claims or any claims arising out of advertising, distribution or marketing of the Licensed Products.

Intellectual Property Rights

The license granted in this Agreement is conditioned on Licensee's compliance with the provisions of the intellectual property laws of the United States and any foreign country in the Territory.

Proprietary Notices

Licensee shall identify Licensor as the owner of rights to the Trademarks and shall include the notices provided in Exhibit A on all copies of the Licensed Products.

Infringement Against Third Parties

In the event that either party learns of imitations or infringements of the Trademarks or Licensed Products, that party shall notify the other in writing of the infringements or imitations. Licensor shall have the right to commence lawsuits against third persons arising from infringement of the Trademarks or Licensed Products. In the event that Licensor does not commence a lawsuit against an alleged infringer within sixty (60) days of notification by Licensee, Licensee may commence a lawsuit against the third party. Before filing suit, Licensee shall obtain the written consent of Licensor to do so and such consent shall not be unreasonably withheld. Licensor will cooperate fully and in good faith with Licensee for the purpose of securing and preserving Licensee's rights to the Trademarks.

Any recovery (including, but not limited to a judgment, settlement or licensing agreement included as resolution of an infringement dispute) shall be divided equally between the parties after deduction and payment of reasonable attorney fees to the party bringing the lawsuit.

Exploitation Date

Licensee agrees to manufacture, distribute and sell the Licensed Products in commercially reasonable quantities during the term of this Agreement and to commence such manufacture, distribution and sale by _____ . This is a material provision of this Agreement.

Advertising Budget

(select if appropriate)

☐   Licensee agrees to spend at least _____% of estimated annual gross sales for promotional efforts and advertising of the Licensed Products.

Licensor Copies and Right to Purchase

Licensee shall provide Licensor with _____copies of each Licensed Product. Licensor has the right to purchase from Licensee, at Licensee's manufacturing cost, at least_____copies of any Licensed Product and such payments shall be deducted from royalties due to Licensor.

Confidentiality

The parties acknowledge that each may have access to confidential information that relates to each other's business (the "Information"). The parties agree to protect the confidentiality of the Information and maintain it with the strictest confidence, and no party shall disclose such information to third parties without the prior written consent of the other.

Insurance

(select if appropriate)

☐   Licensee shall, throughout the Term, obtain and maintain, at its own expense, standard product liability insurance coverage, naming Licensor as an additional named insured. Such policy shall provide protection against any claims, demands and causes of action arising out of any alleged defects or failure to perform of the Licensed Products or any use of the Licensed Products. The amount of coverage shall be a minimum of $_____ with no deductible amount for each single occurrence for bodily injury or property damage. The policy shall provide for notice to the Licensor from the insurer by Registered or Certified Mail in the event of any modification or termination of insurance. The provisions of this section shall survive termination for three (3) years.

Licensor's Right to Terminate

Licensor shall have the right to terminate this Agreement in the following situations:

(select one or more provisions)

☐ **Failure to Make Timely Payment.** Licensee fails to pay Royalties when due or fails to accurately report Net Sales, as defined in the Payment Section of this Agreement, and such failure is not cured within thirty days after written notice from the Licensor.

☐ **Failure to Introduce Product.** Licensee fails to introduce the product to market by the date set in the Exploitation section of this Agreement or to offer the Licensed Products in commercially reasonable quantities during any subsequent year.

☐ **Assignment or Sublicensing.** Licensee assigns or sublicenses in violation of the Agreement.

☐ **Failure to Maintain Insurance.** Licensee fails to maintain or obtain product liability insurance as required by the provisions of this Agreement.

☐ **Failure to Meet Quality Standards for Submit Samples.** Licensee fails to provide Licensor with samples for approval or fails to meet the quality standards established by Licensor.

Licensor shall have the right to terminate the grant of license under this Agreement with respect to any country or region included in the Territory in which Licensee fails to offer the Licensed Products for sale or distributions or to secure a sublicensing agreement for the marketing, distribution and sale of the product within two years of the Effective Date.

Effect of Termination

Upon termination of this Agreement, all Royalty obligations as established in the Payments Section shall immediately become due. After the termination of this license, all rights granted to Licensee under this Agreement shall terminate and revert to Licensor, and Licensee will refrain from further manufacturing, copying, marketing, distribution, or use of any Licensed Product or other product which incorporates the Trademarks. Within thirty (30) days after termination, Licensee shall deliver to Licensor a statement indicating the number and description of the Licensed Products that it had on hand or is in the process of manufacturing as of the termination date.

Sell-Off Period

Licensee may dispose of the Licensed Products covered by this Agreement for a period of ninety (90) days after termination or expiration, except that Licensee shall have no such right in the event this agreement is terminated according to the Licensor's Right to Terminate, above. At the end of the post-termination sale period, Licensee shall furnish a royalty payment and statement as required under the Payment Section. Upon termination, Licensee shall deliver to Licensor all original designs or reproductions of Trademarks used in the manufacture of the Licensed Products. Licensor shall bear the costs of shipping for these materials.

Attorney Fees and Expenses

The prevailing party shall have the right to collect from the other party its reasonable costs and necessary disbursements and attorney fees incurred in enforcing this Agreement.

Dispute Resolution

(select one if appropriate)

☐   **Mediation & Arbitration.**The Parties agree that every dispute or difference between them, arising under this Agreement, shall be settled first by a meeting of the Parties attempting to confer and resolve the dispute in a good faith manner. If the Parties cannot resolve their dispute after conferring, any Party may require the other Parties to submit the matter to nonbinding mediation, utilizing the services of an impartial professional mediator approved by all Parties. If the Parties cannot come to an agreement following mediation, the Parties agree to submit the matter to binding arbitration at a location mutually agreeable to the Parties. The arbitration shall be conducted on a confidential basis pursuant to the Commercial Arbitration Rules of the American Arbitration Association. Any decision or award as a result of any such arbitration proceeding shall include the assessment of costs, expenses and reasonable attorney's fees and shall include a written record of the proceedings and a written determination of the arbitrators. An arbitrator experienced in trademark and merchandising law shall conduct any such arbitration. An award of arbitration shall be final and binding on the Parties and may be confirmed in a court of competent jurisdiction.

☐   **Arbitration.** If a dispute arises under or relating to this Agreement, the parties agree to submit such dispute to binding arbitration in the state of _____ or another location mutually agreeable to the parties. The arbitration shall be conducted on a confidential basis pursuant to the Commercial Arbitration Rules of the American Arbitration Association. Any decision or award as a result of any such arbitration proceeding shall be in writing and shall provide an explanation for all conclusions of law and fact and shall include the assessment of costs, expenses and reasonable attorney fees. An arbitrator experienced in trademark and merchandising law shall conduct any such arbitration. An award of arbitration may be confirmed in a court of competent jurisdiction.

Governing Law

This Agreement shall be governed in accordance with the laws of the State of _____ .

Jurisdiction

The parties consent to the exclusive jurisdiction and venue of the federal and state courts located in _____ in any action arising out of or relating to this Agreement. The parties waive any other venue to which either party might be entitled by domicile or otherwise.

Waiver

The failure to exercise any right provided in this Agreement shall not be a waiver of prior or subsequent rights.

Invalidity

If any provision of this Agreement is invalid under applicable statute or rule of law, it is to be considered omitted and the remaining provisions of this Agreement shall in no way be affected.

Entire Understanding

This Agreement expresses the complete understanding of the parties and supersedes all prior representations, agreements and understandings, whether written or oral. This Agreement may not be altered except by a written document signed by both parties.

Attachments & Exhibits

The parties agree and acknowledge that all attachments, exhibits and schedules referred to in this Agreement are incorporated in this Agreement by reference.

No Special Damages

Licensor shall not be liable to Licensee for any incidental, consequential, punitive or special damages.

Notices

Any notice or communication required or permitted to be given under this Agreement shall be sufficiently given when received by certified mail, or sent by facsimile transmission or overnight courier.

No Joint Venture

Nothing contained in this Agreement shall be construed to place the parties in the relationship of agent, employee, franchisee, officer, partners or joint ventures. Neither party may create or assume any obligation on behalf of the other.

Assignability

(select one)

☐ **Assignment Requires Licensor Consent.** Licensee may not assign or transfer its rights or obligations pursuant to this Agreement without the prior written consent of Licensor. Any assignment or transfer in violation of this section shall be void.

☐ **Licensor Consent Not Required for Assignment to Parent or Acquiring Company.** Licensee may not assign or transfer its rights or obligations pursuant to this Agreement without the prior written consent of Licensor. However, no consent is required for an assignment or transfer that occurs: (a) to an entity in which Licensee owns more than fifty percent of the assets; or (b) as part of a transfer of all or substantially all of the assets of Licensee to any party. Any assignment or transfer in violation of this Section shall be void.

Each party has signed this Agreement through its authorized representative. The parties, having read this Agreement, indicate their consent to the terms and conditions by their signature below.

By: _____   By: _____

Date: _____   Date: _____

Licensor Name: _____   Licensee Name/Title: _____

EXHIBIT A

The Property _____

_____

Licensed Products _____

_____

Sales Requirements

$ _____ in Gross Sales per year.

Proprietary Notices

All licensed products shall bear the following

proprietary notice: _____

_____

4. Explanation for Trademark License Agreement

The Trademark License Agreement is essentially identical to the Merchandise License Agreement provided in Chapter 11. All of the explanations provided in that chapter apply to this agreement, with the exception of three items: good will, quality control and proprietary notices.

a. Reservation of Rights: Assignment of Good Will

This section of the license provision establishes that the trademark owner is only delivering a narrow group of rights and is retaining everything else. This section also provides that the trademark owner always owns the good will associated with the mark. Good will is an intangible item—a measurement of the consumer's attitude towards the trademark. The stronger the good will, the more momentum that the trademark maintains. For example, Coca-Cola trademarks have extraordinary good will, demonstrated by the fact that consumers insist on Coca-Cola product over other products that may claim to have similar ingredients.

This license provision guarantees that only the trademark owner earns the good will. If the licensee accumulates any good will, it is automatically transferred to the trademark owner. In the real world, this simply means that the licensee can't make any claims to the trademark.

This license provision also provides that the licensee won't attack the licensor's ownership of the trademarks. This is to avoid the possibility of a successful licensee attempting to destroy the trademark owner's rights.

b. Approval of Samples & Quality Control

Failure of a trademark owner to maintain quality standards over trademark uses can result in the loss of trademark rights (known as "abandonment"). For this reason, every trademark license agreement includes reasonable quality control standards. The important issue for trademark owners is not simply that the agreement provides for quality control, but that the control is actually exercised.

The license provision provides for written approval both prior to production and during production. The termination section of the agreement permits the licensor to terminate if these quality control standards are not met.

c. Proprietary Notices

The Proprietary Notices provision, included on Exhibit A, establishes what notices must be included on the licensed products. For example, if the licensor wants the products to include a registered trademark notice such as "™ Meathead Designs," this should be indicated here.

■

11

Art & Merchandise Licenses

This chapter is about merchandising: the business of affixing an image or text to products you plan to sell, such as T-shirts, buttons, caps and posters. Nowadays, it is difficult to escape the presence of licensed merchandise. Sweatshirts, posters, postcards, shower curtains, tote bags and even underwear are covered with copyrighted images.

The process of merchandising is similar to other permission arrangements in that a copyright owner must consent to a specific use. The primary difference between merchandising and other permission situations is the payment system. The copyright owner usually negotiates an arrangement for continuing periodic payments known as royalties.

In this chapter we analyze the principles of merchandise licensing and analyze two merchandise agreements, a long form merchandise agreement and an abbreviated merchandise agreement.

A. Merchandise Licensing Overview

Acquiring permission to sell merchandise that incorporates copyrighted material is similar to other permission arrangements—you need to locate the copyright owner, negotiate an agreement and execute the agreement in writing. However, the agreement used in merchandise licensing is usually more complex than a typical permission agreement and contains additional responsibilities for the parties.

Under the terms of a merchandise license, the owner of the image or text (the licensor) is usually paid an advance and a royalty based on a percentage of income from sales. The company selling the merchandise (the licensee) must meet certain obligations including payments, quality control and enforcement of rights. If the licensee fails to do so, the license can be terminated. Termination can be very expensive for both parties due to the loss of income for the licensor and the loss of a substantial investment for the licensee.

There are alternatives to licensing rights under a merchandise agreement. One alternative is to purchase the copyright in the artwork (known as an assignment). The other choice is to hire an artist,

photographer or musician to create the material and acquire ownership under a work-for-hire agreement. These options are explained in Chapter 15.

Copyright-Free Artwork and Merchandise Agreements

Some artwork is labeled "copyright-free" or "royalty-free" to indicate that it can be used without permission after a one-time payment is made. Can this type of artwork be used freely on merchandise? Not necessarily. Despite the name, copyright-free artworks are often protected under copyright laws and there are limitations on their use. (We try to avoid such confusion in this book by using the term "royalty-free artwork" to refer to a work that does have copyright protection, but which can be used in a wide range of uses once a fee is paid.) Only public domain artworks are truly free to use however you want. In order to determine if permission is required, read the shrink-wrap, click-wrap or other license agreement supplied with the royalty-free artwork. These principles and rules are explained in Chapter 3.

---

1. What Is Merchandise?

Licensable merchandise is any consumer product on which an image or text can be affixed. In general, merchandise has some utility or function, such as clothing, jewelry or stationery. However, there are no limitations on what can be merchandise; artwork can be placed on anything that can be reproduced. Products that are commonly the subject of merchandise licenses include: auto sunshades, auto tire covers, backpacks, badges, bank checks, beach mats, bed sheets, belt buckles, belts, blankets, bumper stickers, caps, casual shoes, calendars, ceramic cups, children's wear, clocks, cuff links, decals, desk sets, dress shirts, drink holders, fabric, flags, gift wrap, golf bags, golf club covers, greeting cards, handkerchiefs, hats, heat transfer patches, jackets, jerseys, jewelry, key rings, knit shirts, lamps, letter openers, license plate frames, loose-leaf binders, magnets, mittens, napkins, neckties, notebooks, pennants, pens, pins, polo shirts, postcards, posters, pot holders, rings, running shorts, running shoes, scarves, shower curtains, sleepwear, snack trays, socks, squeeze bottles, stationery, stuffed animals, sunglasses, sweatpants, sweatshirts, sweaters, swimwear, tablecloths, tie clips, tote bags, towels, toys, training suits, T-shirts, umbrellas, underwear, wallpaper, watches and wind-breakers.

Information about locating copyright owners of text, photos, art and music is provided in Chapters 2 through 5.

2. Different Types of Materials Used on Merchandise

Most merchandise licenses are for artwork or photographs. However, text and music are also licensed in connection with merchandise. In general, the rules are the same. However, when it comes to licensing music there are some additional issues that arise depending on whether you are licensing a recorded composition or whether you will be re-recording a previously written composition.

a. Using Art on Merchandise

Using art on merchandise generally consists of using an artistic image such as a drawing or painting on items you plan to sell. Examples include reproducing a Keith Haring painting on a T-shirt or using images from Georgia O'Keeffe paintings on notecards. Of course, if the image is in the public domain, such as the Mona Lisa, no permission is required. If the artwork is labeled "royalty-free," you will need to review the license or agreement that accompanies the purchase of the artwork (see

Sidebar above) to determine if your merchandise use is permitted.

Agreements for the use of art on merchandise are sometimes called "art licenses" or "design licenses." Whatever such an agreement is called, it is essentially a merchandise license as described in this chapter. You may occasionally find unique provisions in some art licenses for the use of fine artworks—for example, a clause permitting the artist to enter and inspect a poster-making facility to ensure a quality production process. While special provisions such as these are sometimes included to protect the artist, they don't change the basic character of the agreement as a merchandise license.

b. Using Music on Merchandise

The ability to place music onto computer chips has made it possible to include music in merchandise such as greeting cards, watches, toys, musical equipment, music boxes and even clothing.

Most songs used on merchandise are not copied directly from an existing recording; instead, they are re-recorded in order to be embedded on a computer chip. Since the recording of the song isn't being used, permission is not needed from the record company. Similarly, if lyrics will be reprinted on merchandise but no recording will be reproduced, permission is required from the music publisher, not the record company. Rules for using music are explained in detail in Chapter 5.

The merchandise license agreements provided in this chapter can be used for licensing music or for the reprinting of lyrics on merchandise. However, the licensor (the music publisher) may want to incorporate additional requirements—for example, that the music cannot be used in advertisements for the merchandise. The music publisher usually provides the language for such provisions.

An example of a music merchandise license is also available at the Harry Fox Agency website. (Harry Fox is an organization that represents music publishers.) Although the license agreement provided by Harry Fox is intended for use with agency-affiliated publishers, it establishes basic music licensing standards and can be adopted for your purposes. In Chapter 5 we explain how to locate copyright owners of songs and sound recordings.

c. Using Trademarks, Fictional Characters or Celebrities on Merchandise

A trademark is any word, photograph or symbol that is used to identify a business's products or service. Trademarks are commonly licensed for merchandise—for example, the licensing of a university's trademark (the school name or the name of its mascot) on sports equipment or apparel.

Fictional characters include characters from books, television or movies such as Mickey Mouse, Sabrina the Witch or Daffy Duck. A fictional character may be animated (Homer Simpson) literary (Willie Loman) or cinematic (James Bond). The rules for licensing characters may change if a real person has portrayed the character (John Goodman as Fred Flintstone). In that case, additional permission is required as explained in Chapter 10.

Most of the provisions contained in a merchandise agreement are also used in trademark, character and celebrity licenses. However, there are some unique aspects to these agreements, some of which require knowledge of trademark law or the right of publicity. For example, character licensing involves overlapping trademark, copyright and design patent laws. These types of licenses are often handled by special licensing agencies that represent trademark owners, fictional characters and celebrities. A sample trademark license and additional trademark licensing information is provided in Chapter 10, "Getting Permission to Use Trademarks."

d. Using Short Phrases on Merchandise

Merchandise, by its nature, can generally only accommodate small amounts of text. Since copyright law does not protect short phrases, most of the text used on merchandise—for example, "Honk if you like Prune Tacos"—can be used without permission.

However, in the following situations, permission should be obtained to use a short phrase.

- **The phrase is associated with a fictional character.** For example, the unauthorized use of the phrase "E.T., Phone Home." on a ceramic cup was found to be a copyright infringement. (*Universal City Studios, Inc. v. Kamar Indus.*, 217 U.S.P.Q. (BNA) 1162, (S.D. Texas 1982).) In this case, the outcome was directly related to use of E.T. in the phrase. The use of "Phone Home" without E.T. would not require authorization.

- **The phrase is a trademark.** You should always obtain permission to use a phrase on merchandise if it is used as a trademark or is taken from an advertising campaign, such as Coke's "It's the Real Thing" or Microsoft's "Where Do You Want to Go Today?" Permission is also needed to use a phrase that is used to indicate a product or service such as the Marlboro Man. (See Chapter 10, "Getting Permission to Use Trademarks.")

- **The phrase is extremely inventive.** An extremely clever phrase such as Ashleigh Brilliant's epigram, "I may not be perfect but parts of me are excellent," or Lewis Caroll's phrase, "Twas brillig and the slithy toves," are protectible. There is no hard and fast rule for how inventive the phrase must be, but it's best to avoid phrases that appear highly inventive to you. Additional rules on the protection of text are provided in Chapter 2, "Getting Permission to Use Text."

3. Royalty Rates for Merchandise Licensing

When you license text, art, graphics or music for use on merchandise, you are ordinarily required to pay the owner of the licensed material a royalty—that is, a continuing payment based upon a percentage of the income you earn from the sale of the merchandise.

Royalty rates for merchandise licensing vary depending on the merchandise involved. Below are some royalty estimates:

- Greeting cards and gift wrap: 2% to 5%.
- Household (cups, sheets, towels): 3% to 8%.
- Fabrics, apparel (T-shirts, caps, etc.) decals, bumper stickers: 5% to 10%.
- Posters and prints: 10% or more.

4. Additional Information About Merchandise Licensing

Many libraries contain general business directories such as the multi-volume publication *Thomas Register of American Manufacturers* (Thomas Register Publishing) or the *Directory of Corporate Affiliations (DCA)* (Reed Reference Publishing Company). The *Thomas Register* lists manufacturers by subject and provides profiles and phone numbers. It is also searchable online at www5.thomasregister.com. The *DCA* lists companies by name, brand name product or service, geographic location or by SIC code, a four-digit number created by the Department of Commerce used to classify a business by the type of service or product it provides.

General business directories on the Internet can identify merchandise manufacturers, and a search engine should be capable of finding them. One website that may be helpful is BigYellow, the NYNEX business directory located at www.bigyellow.com. It enables the user to search by business category, name, street address, state or zip code. Most online services have general business directories, which perform the same functions.

If you're pursuing merchandise licensing on a regular basis, consider a subscription to *The Licensing Journal* (Aspen Law & Business), 212-597-0200. Although pricey at $225 a year, the journal contains thorough information on current trends in art, merchandise, trademark and toy licensing.

B. Merchandise License Agreement

Occasionally, a seasoned copyright owner who has licensed many properties may furnish the merchandise license agreement. However, most of the time, the licensee—the company that is manufacturing and selling the merchandise—furnishes the merchandise license agreement. Usually, prior to furnishing the agreement, the licensee and the licensor have worked out all of the business terms. For example, they have already determined the royalty rate, the rights being transferred, the length of time for the agreement and other financial terms.

As a means of helping you prepare this information, we have included a Merchandise License Worksheet in Section D. In addition to helping you determine the essential elements of the license agreement, the worksheet is also helpful for monitoring the license arrangement after it is signed. Sometimes essential elements from the worksheet are included on a special sheet known as an exhibit that is attached to the agreement and incorporated into its provisions. Our model agreement includes such an exhibit.

Even after the terms are agreed upon and the license is furnished, there may be additional changes. For example, the licensor may want to modify provisions about sublicensing or dispute resolution. Be prepared to make modifications, to cut and paste provisions or to restructure the agreement so that the sections are in a different order. These types of changes are common.

Below is a long-form merchandise license agreement for licensing artwork, text or music for use with merchandise. A tear-out copy of this form is in the Appendix at the end of this book and a digital version is on the forms disk.

 The Merchandise License Agreement is on the forms disk under the file name MRCHLIC.

Merchandise License Agreement

Introduction

This License Agreement (the "Agreement") is made between _____ (referred to as "Licensor") and _____ (referred to as "Licensee").

The parties agree as follows:

The Work

The Work refers to the work described in Exhibit A. Licensor is the owner of all rights to the Work and Licensee shall not claim any right to use the Work except under the terms of this Agreement.

Licensed Products

Licensed Products are defined as the licensee's products incorporating the Work specifically described in Exhibit A (the "Licensed Products").

Grant of Rights

Licensor grants to Licensee:

(select one)

☐   an exclusive license

☐   a nonexclusive license

to reproduce and distribute the Work in or on the Licensed Products.

Licensor grants to Licensee:

(select if appropriate)

☐   the right to modify the Work to incorporate it in or on the Licensed Products provided that Licensee agrees to assign to Licensor its rights, if any, in any derivative works resulting from Licensee's modification of the Work. Licensee agrees to execute any documents required to evidence this assignment of copyright and to waive any moral rights and rights of attribution provided in 17 USC § 106A of the Copyright Act.

☐   the right to publicly display the Work as incorporated in or on the Licensed Products.

☐   the right to publicly perform the Work as incorporated in or on the Licensed Products.

Sublicense

(select one)

☐ **Consent required.** Licensee may sublicense the rights granted pursuant to this agreement provided: Licensee obtains Licensor's prior written consent to such sublicense; and Licensor receives such revenue or royalty payment as provided in the Payment section below. Any sublicense granted in violation of this provision shall be void.

☐ **Consent to sublicense not unreasonably withheld.** Licensee may sublicense the rights granted pursuant to this agreement provided: Licensee obtains Licensor's prior written consent to such sublicense. Licensor's consent to any sublicense shall not be unreasonably withheld, and Licensor receives such revenue or royalty payment as provided in the Payment section below. Any sublicense granted in violation of this provision shall be void.

☐ **No sublicensing permitted.** Licensee may not sublicense the rights granted under this agreement.

Reservation of Rights: Assignment of Good Will

Licensor reserves all rights other than those being conveyed or granted in this Agreement.

Territory

The rights granted to Licensee are limited to _____ (the "Territory").

Term

The "Effective Date" of this Agreement is defined as the date when the agreement commences and is established by the latest signature date.

(select one)

☐ **Specified term with renewal rights.** This Agreement shall commence upon the Effective Date and shall extend for a period of__years (the "Initial Term"). Following the Initial Term, _____ Licensee may renew this agreement under the same terms and conditions for ___consecutive _____ periods (the "Renewal Terms") provided that Licensee provides written notice of its intention to renew this agreement within thirty (30) days before the expiration of the current term. In no event shall the Term extend beyond the period of United States copyright protection for the Work.

☐   **Term with renewal based upon sales.** This Agreement shall commence upon the Effective Date and shall extend for a period of ___ years (the "Initial Term") and may be renewed by Licensee under the same terms and conditions for consecutive _____ year periods (the "Renewal Terms"), provided that:

(a) Licensee provides written notice of its intention to renew this agreement within thirty days before the expiration of the current term; and

(b) Licensee has met the sales requirements as established in Exhibit A.

☐   **Indefinite term.** This Agreement shall commence upon the Effective Date and shall continue until terminated pursuant to a provision of this Agreement.

☐   **Fixed term.** This Agreement shall commence upon the Effective Date and shall continue for _____ unless sooner terminated pursuant to a provision of this Agreement.

☐   **Term for as long as Licensee sells Licensed Products.** This Agreement shall commence upon the Effective Date as specified in Exhibit A and shall continue for as long as Licensee continues to offer the Licensed Products in commercially reasonable quantities or unless sooner terminated pursuant to a provision of this Agreement. In no event shall the Term extend beyond the period of U.S. copyright protection for the Work.

Payments

All royalties ("Royalties") provided for under this Agreement shall accrue when the respective Licensed Products are sold, shipped, distributed, billed or paid for, whichever occurs first.

Net Sales

Net Sales are defined as Licensee's gross sales (i.e., the gross invoice amount billed customers) less quantity discounts or rebates and returns actually credited. A quantity discount or rebate is a discount made at the time of shipment. No deductions shall be made for cash or other discounts, commissions, manufacturing costs, uncollectible accounts, or for fees or expenses of any kind which the Licensee may incur in connection with the Royalty payments.

Fees

(select one or more provisions)

☐   **Advance Against Royalties.** As a nonrefundable advance against royalties (the "Advance"), Licensee agrees to pay to Licensor upon execution of this Agreement the sum of $ _____.

☐ **Licensed Product Royalty.** Licensee agrees to pay a Royalty of____% percent of all Net Sales revenue of the Licensed Products ("Licensed Product Royalty").

☐ **Per Unit Royalty.** Licensee agrees to pay a Royalty of $__ for each unit of the Licensed Product that is: (select one)

    ☐ manufactured.

    ☐ sold.

☐ **Guaranteed Minimum Annual Royalty Payment.** In addition to any other advances or fees, Licensee shall pay an annual guaranteed royalty (the "GMAR") as follows: $_____ . The GMAR shall be paid to Licensor annually on _____. The GMAR is an advance against royalties for the twelve-month period commencing upon payment. Royalty payments based on Net Sales made during any year of this Agreement shall be credited against the GMAR due for the year in which such Net Sales were made. In the event that annual royalties exceed the GMAR, Licensee shall pay the difference to Licensor. Any annual royalty payments in excess of the GMAR shall not be carried forward from previous years or applied against the GMAR.

☐ **License Fee.** As a nonrefundable, nonrecoupable fee for executing this license, Licensee agrees to pay to Licensor upon execution of this Agreement the sum of $_____ .

☐ **Sublicensing Revenues.** In the event of any sublicense of the rights granted pursuant to this Agreement, Licensee shall pay to Licensor_____% percent of all sublicensing revenues.

Payments and Statements to Licensor

Within thirty (30) days after the end of each calendar quarter (the "Royalty Period"), an accurate statement of Net Sales of Licensed Products along with any royalty payments or sublicensing revenues due to Licensor shall be provided to Licensor, regardless of whether any Licensed Products were sold during the Royalty Period. All payments shall be paid in United States currency drawn on a United States bank. The acceptance by Licensor of any of the statements furnished or royalties paid shall not preclude Licensor questioning the correctness at any time of any payments or statements.

Audit

Licensee shall keep accurate books of account and records covering all transactions relating to the license granted in this Agreement, and Licensor or its duly authorized representatives shall have the right upon five days prior written notice, and during normal business hours, to inspect and audit

Licensee's records relating to the Work licensed under this Agreement. Licensor shall bear the cost of such inspection and audit, unless the results indicate an underpayment greater than $ _____ for any six-month (6-month) period. In that case, Licensee shall promptly reimburse Licensor for all costs of the audit along with the amount due with interest on such sums. Interest shall accrue from the date the payment was originally due and the interest rate shall be 1.5% per month, or the maximum rate permitted by law, whichever is less. All books of account and records shall be made available in the United States and kept available for at least two years after the termination of this Agreement.

Late Payment

Time is of the essence with respect to all payments to be made by Licensee under this Agreement. If Licensee is late in any payment provided for in this Agreement, Licensee shall pay interest on the payment from the date due until paid at a rate of 1.5% per month, or the maximum rate permitted by law, whichever is less.

Licensor Warranties

Licensor warrants that it has the power and authority to enter into this Agreement and has no knowledge as to any third-party claims regarding the proprietary rights in the Work that would interfere with the rights granted under this Agreement.

Indemnification by Licensor

(select one if appropriate)

☐ **Licensor indemnification without limitations.** Licensor shall indemnify Licensee and hold Licensee harmless from any damages and liabilities (including reasonable attorney fees and costs), arising from any breach of Licensor's warranties as defined in Licensor's Warranties, above.

☐ **Licensor indemnification limited to amounts paid.** Licensor shall indemnify Licensee and hold Licensee harmless from any damages and liabilities (including reasonable attorney fees and costs), arising from any breach of Licensor's warranties as defined in Licensor's Warranties, above. Licensor's maximum liability under this provision shall in no event exceed the total amount earned by Licensor under this Agreement.

☐ **Licensor indemnification with limitations.** Licensor shall indemnify Licensee and hold Licensee harmless from any damages and liabilities (including reasonable attorney fees and costs), arising from any breach of Licensor's warranties as defined in Licensor's Warranties, above, provided:

(a) such claim, if sustained, would prevent Licensee from marketing the Licensed Products or the Work;

(b) such claim arises solely out of the Work as disclosed to the Licensee, and not out of any change in the Work made by Licensee or a vendor;

(c) Licensee gives Licensor prompt written notice of any such claim;

(d) such indemnity shall only be applicable in the event of a final decision by a court of competent jurisdiction from which no right to appeal exists; and

(e) that the maximum amount due from Licensor to Licensee under this paragraph shall not exceed the amounts due to Licensor under the Payment Section from the date that Licensor notifies Licensee of the existence of such a claim.

Licensee Warranties

Licensee warrants that it will use its best commercial efforts to market the Licensed Products and that their sale and marketing shall be in conformance with all applicable laws and regulations, including but not limited to all intellectual property laws.

Indemnification by Licensee

Licensee shall indemnify Licensor and hold Licensor harmless from any damages and liabilities (including reasonable attorney fees and costs),

(a) arising from any breach of Licensee's warranties and representation as defined in the Licensee Warranties, above;

(b) arising out of any alleged defects or failures to perform of the Licensed Products or any product liability claims or use of the Licensed Products; and

(c) any claims arising out of advertising, distribution or marketing of the Licensed Products.

Intellectual Property Registration

Licensor may, but is not obligated to, seek in its own name and at its own expense, appropriate copyright registrations for the Work. Licensor makes no warranty with respect to the validity of any copyright that may be granted. Licensor grants to Licensee the right to apply for registration of the Work or Licensed Products provided that such registrations shall be applied for in the name of

Licensor and licensed to Licensee during the Term and according to the conditions of this Agreement. Licensee shall have the right to deduct its reasonable out-of-pocket expenses for the preparation and filing of any such registrations from future royalties due to Licensor under this Agreement. Licensee shall obtain Licensor's prior written consent before incurring expenses for any foreign copyright applications.

Compliance With Intellectual Property Laws

The license granted in this Agreement is conditioned on Licensee's compliance with the provisions of the intellectual property laws of the United States and any foreign country in the Territory. All copies of the Licensed Product as well as all promotional material shall bear appropriate proprietary notices.

Licensor Credits

Licensee shall identify Licensor as the owner of rights to the Work and shall include the following notice on all copies of the Licensed Products: "_____. All rights reserved."

Licensee may, with Licensor's consent, use Licensor's name, image or trademark in advertising or promotional materials associated with the sale of the Licensed Products.

Infringement Against Third Parties

In the event that either party learns of imitations or infringements of the Work or Licensed Products, that party shall notify the other in writing of the infringements or imitations. Licensor shall have the right to commence lawsuits against third persons arising from infringement of the Work or Licensed Products. In the event that Licensor does not commence a lawsuit against an alleged infringer within sixty days of notification by Licensee, Licensee may commence a lawsuit against the third party. Before filing suit, Licensee shall obtain the written consent of Licensor to do so and such consent shall not be unreasonably withheld. Licensor will cooperate fully and in good faith with Licensee for the purpose of securing and preserving Licensee's rights to the Work. Any recovery (including, but not limited to a judgment, settlement or licensing agreement included as resolution of an infringement dispute) shall be divided equally between the parties after deduction and payment of reasonable attorney fees to the party bringing the lawsuit.

Exploitation Date

Licensee agrees to manufacture, distribute and sell the Licensed Products in commercially reasonable quantities during the term of this Agreement and to commence such manufacture, distribution and sale by _____ . This is a material provision of this Agreement.

Advertising Budget

(select if appropriate)

[ ]   Licensee agrees to spend at least _____% of estimated annual gross sales for promotional efforts and advertising of the Licensed Products.

Approval of Samples & Quality Control

Licensee shall submit a reasonable number of pre-production designs, prototypes, and camera-ready artwork prior to production as well as pre-production samples of the Licensed Product to Licensor to assure that the product meets Licensor's quality standards. In the event that Licensor fails to object in writing within ten (10) business days after the date of receipt of any such materials, such materials shall be deemed to be acceptable. At least once during each calendar year, Licensee shall submit two (2) production samples of each Licensed Product for review. Licensee shall pay all costs for delivery of these approval materials. The quality standards applied by Licensor shall be no more rigorous than the quality standards applied by Licensor to similar products.

Licensor Copies and Right to Purchase

Licensee shall provide Licensor with ____ copies of each Licensed Product. Licensor has the right to purchase from Licensee, at Licensee's manufacturing cost, at least _____copies of any Licensed Product and such payments shall be deducted from royalties due to Licensor.

Confidentiality

The parties acknowledge that each may have access to confidential information that relates to each other's business (the "Information"). The parties agree to protect the confidentiality of the Information and maintain it with the strictest confidence, and no party shall disclose such information to third parties without the prior written consent of the other.

Insurance

Licensee shall, throughout the Term, obtain and maintain, at its own expense, standard product liability insurance coverage, naming Licensor as an additional named insured. Such policy shall provide protection against any claims, demands and causes of action arising out of any alleged defects or failure to perform of the Licensed Products or any use of the Licensed Products. The amount of coverage shall be a minimum of $_____with no deductible amount for each single occurrence for bodily injury or property damage. The policy shall provide for notice to the Licensor from the insurer by Registered or Certified Mail in the event of any modification or termination of insurance. The provisions of this section shall survive termination for three years.

Licensor's Right to Terminate

Licensor shall have the right to terminate this Agreement for the following reasons:

(select one or more provisions)

- [ ] **Failure to Make Timely Payment.** Licensee fails to pay Royalties when due or fails to accurately report Net Sales, as defined in the Payment Section of this Agreement, and such failure is not cured within thirty (30) days after written notice from the Licensor.

- [ ] **Failure to Introduce Product.** Licensee fails to introduce the product to market by the date set in the Exploitation section of this Agreement or to offer the Licensed Products in commercially reasonable quantities during any subsequent year.

- [ ] **Assignment or Sublicensing.** Licensee assigns or sublicenses in violation of this Agreement.

- [ ] **Failure to Maintain Insurance.** Licensee fails to maintain or obtain product liability insurance as required by the provisions of this Agreement.

- [ ] **Failure to Submit Samples.** Licensee fails to provide Licensor with pre-production samples for approval.

- [ ] **Termination As to Unexploited Portion of Territory.** Licensor shall have the right to terminate the grant of license under this Agreement with respect to any country or region included in the Territory in which Licensee fails to offer the Licensed Products for sale or distribution or to secure a sublicensing agreement for the marketing, distribution and sale of the product within two (2) years of the Effective Date.

Effect of Termination

Upon termination of this Agreement ("Termination"), all Royalty obligations as established in the Payments Section shall immediately become due. After the Termination of this license, all rights granted to Licensee under this Agreement shall terminate and revert to Licensor, and Licensee will refrain from further manufacturing, copying, marketing, distribution, or use of any Licensed Product or other product which incorporates the Work. Within thirty (30) days after Termination, Licensee shall deliver to Licensor a statement indicating the number and description of the Licensed Products that it had on hand or is in the process of manufacturing as of the Termination date.

Sell-Off Period

Licensee may dispose of the Licensed Products covered by this Agreement for a period of 90 days after Termination or expiration except that Licensee shall have no such right in the event this agreement is terminated according to the Licensor's Right to Terminate, above. At the end of the post-Termination sale period, Licensee shall furnish a royalty payment and statement as required under the Payment Section. Upon termination, Licensee shall deliver to Licensor all original artwork and camera-ready reproductions used in the manufacture of the Licensed Products. Licensor shall bear the costs of shipping for the artwork and reproductions.

Attorney Fees and Expenses

The prevailing party shall have the right to collect from the other party its reasonable costs and necessary disbursements and attorney fees incurred in enforcing this Agreement.

Dispute Resolution

(select one if appropriate)

☐ **Mediation & Arbitration.** The Parties agree that every dispute or difference between them, arising under this Agreement, shall be settled first by a meeting of the Parties attempting to confer and resolve the dispute in a good faith manner. If the Parties cannot resolve their dispute after conferring, any Party may require the other Parties to submit the matter to nonbinding mediation, utilizing the services of an impartial professional mediator approved by all Parties. If the Parties cannot come to an agreement following mediation, the Parties agree to submit the matter to binding arbitration at a location mutually agreeable to the Parties. The arbitration shall be conducted on a confidential basis pursuant to the

Commercial Arbitration Rules of the American Arbitration Association. Any decision or award as a result of any such arbitration proceeding shall include the assessment of costs, expenses and reasonable attorney's fees and shall include a written record of the proceedings and a written determination of the arbitrators. An arbitrator experienced in copyright and merchandising law shall conduct any such arbitration. An award of arbitration shall be final and binding on the Parties and may be confirmed in a court of competent jurisdiction.

☐ **Arbitration.** If a dispute arises under or relating to this Agreement, the parties agree to submit such dispute to binding arbitration in the state of_____or another location mutually agreeable to the parties. The arbitration shall be conducted on a confidential basis pursuant to the Commercial Arbitration Rules of the American Arbitration Association. Any decision or award as a result of any such arbitration proceeding shall be in writing and shall provide an explanation for all conclusions of law and fact and shall include the assessment of costs, expenses and reasonable attorney fees. An arbitrator experienced in copyright and merchandising law shall conduct any such arbitration. An award of arbitration may be confirmed in a court of competent jurisdiction.

Governing Law

This Agreement shall be governed in accordance with the laws of the State of_____.

Jurisdiction

The parties consent to the exclusive jurisdiction and venue of the federal and state courts located in _____ in any action arising out of or relating to this Agreement. The parties waive any other venue to which either party might be entitled by domicile or otherwise.

Waiver

The failure to exercise any right provided in this Agreement shall not be a waiver of prior or subsequent rights.

Invalidity

If any provision of this Agreement is invalid under applicable statute or rule of law, it is to be considered omitted and the remaining provisions of this Agreement shall in no way be affected.

Entire Understanding

This Agreement expresses the complete understanding of the parties and supersedes all prior representations, agreements and understandings, whether written or oral. This Agreement may not be altered except by a written document signed by both parties.

Attachments & Exhibits

The parties agree and acknowledge that all attachments, exhibits and schedules referred to in this Agreement are incorporated in this Agreement by reference.

No Special Damages

Licensor shall not be liable to Licensee for any incidental, consequential, punitive or special damages.

Notices

Any notice or communication required or permitted to be given under this Agreement shall be sufficiently given when received by certified mail, or sent by facsimile transmission or overnight courier.

No Joint Venture

Nothing contained in this Agreement shall be construed to place the parties in the relationship of agent, employee, franchisee, officer, partners or joint ventures. Neither party may create or assume any obligation on behalf of the other.

Assignability

(select one)

☐ **Assignment Requires Licensor Consent.** Licensee may not assign or transfer its rights or obligations pursuant to this Agreement without the prior written consent of Licensor. Any assignment or transfer in violation of this section shall be void.

☐ **Licensor Consent Not Unreasonably Withheld.** Licensee may not assign or transfer its rights or obligations pursuant to this Agreement without the prior written consent of Licensor. Such consent shall not be unreasonably withheld. Any assignment or transfer in violation of this section shall be void.

☐ **Licensor Consent Not Required for Assignment to Parent or Acquiring Company.** Licensee may not assign or transfer its rights or obligations pursuant to this Agreement without the prior written consent of Licensor. However, no consent is required for an assignment or transfer that occurs: (a) to an entity in which Licensee owns more than fifty percent of the assets; or (b) as part of a transfer of all or substantially all of the assets of Licensee to any party. Any assignment or transfer in violation of this Section shall be void.

Each party has signed this Agreement through its authorized representative. The parties, having read this Agreement, indicate their consent to the terms and conditions by their signature below.

By: _____   By: _____

Date: _____   Date: _____

Licensor Name: _____   Licensee Name/Title: _____

EXHIBIT A

The Property _____

_____

Licensed Products _____

_____

Sales Requirements

$ _____ in Gross Sales per year.

C. Explanation for Merchandise License Agreement

Every merchandise license agreement contains essential elements including a grant of rights, territory, term and identification of the parties. Most, like the model merchandise license agreements in this chapter, contain additional provisions such as warranties, indemnity, termination and miscellaneous clauses.

What If the Licensor Furnishes the Agreement?

If the licensor furnishes the merchandise license agreement, the licensee will need to read and review its provisions. Deciphering a license agreement can be a challenge, even for experienced attorneys. Unfortunately, there are no rules for the ordering and placement of provisions in a license agreement. Many agreements seem haphazardly organized. In order to analyze a new agreement, we suggest the following strategies:

- Be prepared to spend several hours making an analysis.
- Make a photocopy of the agreement.
- Locate the major provisions (as discussed below) and label them in the margin.
- Compare each provision with the language suggested in this book.
- Underline everything you don't like or don't understand.
- Prepare a chart, listing the number of the provision and your concerns about that section.
- Convert the chart into a response letter detailing your requested changes for the licensee.

---

1. The Introductory Paragraph: Identifying the Parties

The introductory paragraph identifies the people or companies entering into the agreement, known as the "parties." The licensor (the copyright owner) grants permission. The licensee is the person or company seeking permission. The introductory paragraph may also include the parties' business form (corporation, sole proprietor, etc.) and business address. Insert that information, if desired, following the name of each party—for example, "Artco Printing, a California corporation located at 434 W. Oakdale Avenue, Los Angeles, California."

Whereas Provisions

In some license agreements, the introductory information is referred to as the "Whereas" provisions, for example: "Whereas DTK publishing (the licensee) desires to acquire rights." The use of the term "whereas" has no particular legal significance and we have abandoned it in our model agreements.

Instead of licensee and licensor, the agreement can be drafted to use the names of the parties throughout the agreement or terms such as "Artist" for the licensor and "Manufacturer" for the licensee, as long as this terminology is used consistently within the agreement.

2. The Work

The licensor's material (the art, text or music licensed) is referred to as the "Work." Any term can be substituted instead of "Work"—for example, the "Photograph" or the "Book"—as long as this terminology is used consistently within the agreement. If more than one work is being licensed from the licensor, each work can be identified separately, such as "Work #1," "Work # 2," etc. In Exhibit A, each work should be described or, if possible, a photocopy of the artwork or text should be attached to the agreement and referenced in Exhibit A. (Exhibit A is an attachment to the agreement, described below in Section C23.)

3. The Licensed Product

A licensed product is any merchandise that incorporates the work. If the definition of the product is too narrow, the licensee may be precluded from certain markets. For example, if the licensed product is described as "T-shirts" then other shirts like tank tops could not be sold. Similarly, the term "ceramic cups" precludes the sale of plastic cups. If you don't want large categories of items to be excluded from the merchandise you can sell, be sure to define your licensed product broadly enough. For instance, instead of "T-shirts" you could define your licensed product as "upper body apparel." Any plain language definition is suitable. Consider some of the examples in Section A1. The definitions should be inserted in Exhibit A.

4. The Grant of Rights

The grant of rights (also known as simply the "grant") officially permits use of the work, describes the rights under copyright law that the copyright owner is licensing and establishes whether the rights are exclusive or nonexclusive. In a merchandise license agreement, the grant must include the following rights:

- **The right to reproduce.** This refers to the right to make copies on merchandise. This is similar to the grant of rights for a regular license agreement that gives the right to make copies on various media such as print or film. This right is essential for the merchandise agreement and without it, the material cannot be duplicated. Note that the right to reproduce is not unlimited. The agreement specifi-

cally limits it to the use of the material on "Licensed Products." In other words, the artwork can only be used on specific products as defined in the attached exhibit.

- **The right to distribute copies.** This refers to the right to sell or give away the work.

Reproduction and distribution are closely related, and every merchandise license agreement requires both rights.

Other rights, however, are optional. Below we discuss what optional rights may be granted and the difference between exclusive and non-exclusive rights.

a. Optional Rights

The following rights may be included in a merchandise agreement:

- **The right to adapt or create derivatives.** This refers to the right to modify the work—for example, to alter a photograph so that only a portion is used. The result of the modification is referred to as a derivative work. If you plan to create a derivative work, the grant of rights must reflect that permission has been granted to modify the original work. For example, if the licensee plans on creating a series of T-shirts based upon a character, each modification of the character would be a derivative. The language in the model agreement allows the licensor to own any modifications or contributions the licensee makes to the work. If this language is not included, the licensee and licensor may become co-authors of any jointly created derivative work.

- **The right to display publicly.** This refers to the right to publicly exhibit or display a licensed product. As a general rule, the licensee should always acquire this right, as it permits activities such as displaying the work—for example, to sell posters of artwork over the Internet. However, even without this right the licensee can display the artwork (as it is included on the merchandise) in connection with advertisements. That's because the copyright act (17 USC § 113) permits the reproduction of artwork or photographs on "useful articles" in advertisements. A useful article includes clothing, totebags or most other merchandise that has a utilitarian function.

- **The right to perform publicly.** This refers to the right to publicly perform the work—for example, if music is licensed for use in a toy and the toy is demonstrated in a television or radio commercial. In cases of music licenses, this right would always be necessary. For more information on public performance of music, see Chapter 5, "Getting Permission to Use Music."

b. Exclusive vs. Non-Exclusive Rights

Every merchandise license agreement is either exclusive or nonexclusive. Exclusive means that only the licensee will have the rights granted in the agreement—no one else can be given those same rights during the term of the agreement. Nonexclusive means that the licensor (the copyright owner) can give the same rights to someone else. The primary reason for seeking exclusive rights is to prevent a competitor from using the same material.

An exclusive license is usually more expensive than a nonexclusive license, but not always. For example, the fee for an exclusive license to use an image on auto seat covers may be the same as a nonexclusive license simply because the seat cover market is limited and there are few manufacturers. However, an exclusive license for T-shirts or calendars may be two or three times the cost of a nonexclusive license.

An important rule to understand is that if you're seeking exclusive rights, you must obtain the consent of all owners of the work, not just one. Sometimes more than one person or entity is the owner of a copyrighted work. For nonexclusive rights, you need only the consent of one owner. But all owners must agree to grant exclusive rights.

5. Sublicenses

A sublicense allows the licensee to license its rights to another company. Often, a licensee will sublicense rights to foreign companies. Retaining or granting sublicensing rights depends on each situation. For example, if a licensee has experience in foreign markets and can handle the licensing abroad, then the licensee would want to prohibit foreign sublicensing and retain those rights. If the licensor was unsure of whether it could license rights abroad, then the licensor may want a provision requiring written consent. That way, the licensor could review each sublicensing arrangement to determine its relative advantages and disadvantages.

Our model agreement provides three choices:
- no sublicensing is permitted
- sublicensing is permitted with written consent of licensor, and
- sublicensing is permitted with written consent of licensor, but the consent cannot be unreasonably withheld. This is the preferred option for most licensees because it means that the licensor can only withhold consent for a valid business reason.

6. Reservation of Rights

If a licensor does not grant a specific right, the licensor has retained (also known as "reserved") that right. Although it is not essential to state this fact, most licensors prefer to include this statement.

7. Territory

Geographic limits ("territory") determine where the licensee can exercise rights. The territory can be as small or as large as desired. Worldwide rights are always desirable. This allows the licensee to exercise rights in every country in the world. If the territory is the world, insert the word "worldwide" into this section. If the territory is a specific region or country, insert that information. Many merchandise licenses are only for the U.S. and Canada. Since the cost of a worldwide license is usually greater than for rights in an individual country, review the sales potential in any country before including it in the territory.

8. Term

Term refers to the length of the merchandise license. As a general rule, the licensee wants permission for as long as possible while the licensor prefers a short time period. The date that an agreement commences is usually referred to as the effective date. If the agreement has a fixed date of termination, say ten years, the agreement would end ten years from the effective date.

The agreement prohibits a term that is longer than United States copyright protection because once copyright expires, the licensee should not have to pay to use the licensed materials. Even if no time limit is expressed, United States copyright law, under some circumstances, allows the copyright owner to terminate the merchandise license after 35 years. This is true even if the agreement contains a statement that the license is "forever" or "in perpetuity."

9. Payments

Most merchandise licenses are based upon a royalty payment system. A royalty is a continuing payment based upon a percentage of the income from the licensed product. The advantage of a royalty system is that the licensee only has to pay if the licensed product is earning money. The disadvantages are that royalty obligations often also include advance or guaranteed annual payments and continuing accounting responsibility. Below are definitions of some royalty terms.

- Gross sales are the total amount billed to customers. Net sales are usually defined as the licensee's gross sales minus certain deductions. In other words, the licensee calculates the total amount billed to customers, and deducts certain items before paying the royalty. It is generally acceptable to deduct from gross sales any amounts paid for shipping, freight, taxes, credits, returns and discounts made at the time of sale.

- An advance against royalties is an up-front payment to the licensor, usually made at the time the license agreement is signed. An advance is almost always credited or "recouped" against future royalties unless the agreement provides otherwise. It's as if the licensee is saying, "I expect you will earn at least $1,000 in royalties so I am going to advance you that sum at the time we sign the agreement." When the licensor starts earning royalties, the licensee keeps the first $1,000 to repay the advance. If the licensor doesn't earn the $1,000 in royalties, the licensee takes a loss. A licensor generally doesn't have to return the advance unless the licensor breaches the agreement.

- The licensed product royalty is the most common form of royalty payment—a percentage of net sales. Net sales royalty payments are computed by multiplying the royalty rate against net sales. For example, a royalty rate of 5% multiplied by net sales of $1,000 equals a net sales royalty of $50. Estimates of merchandise royalties are provided in Section A3.

- A per-unit royalty is tied to the number of units sold or manufactured, not the total money earned by sales. For example, under a per-unit royalty a licensor might receive 50 cents for each licensed product sold or manufactured. (Note that the licensee cannot choose both per-unit and net sales royalties.) If the licensor is using the merchandise as part of a free distribution, for example, giving out hundreds of the products at a promotion for a restaurant, check the "manufactured" box. If the merchandise will be offered for sale, check the "sold" box. Generally, net sales royalties are used instead of per-unit because revenue may come from sources such as sublicensing, in which case, the total net sales will be easier to track.

- The guaranteed minimum annual royalty payment (GMAR) is an annual payment that guarantees that the licensor receives a specific payment, regardless of how well the merchandise sells in any year. At the end of each year, the earned royalties are totaled and if they are more than the GMAR, the licensor is paid the difference. If the earned royalties are less than the GMAR, the licensee takes a loss. In some cases, a licensee may not want to take the loss and will insist that this difference be carried forward and deducted against the next year's royalties. If a license agreement includes a GMAR, the licensee may want to limit the initial term of the agreement. Otherwise, the licensee risks being locked into paying GMARs when the merchandise is not selling.

- A license fee is a one-time fee usually paid at the time of signing the agreement. The licensee may arrange to make the payment when the licensed product is first distributed. That way, if the licensed product is not produced, the licensee does not have to pay.

- The provision for sublicensing revenue should be included in the agreement if the licensor permits sublicensing. (See the section of the agreement entitled "Sublicensing.")

10. Audits

The audit provision describes when the licensor (or the licensor's representative) shall have access to the licensee's records. If the licensee has failed to properly pay the licensor, the audit will detect that information. The licensee will have to pay for the audit if the audit detects an error of a certain magnitude, usually anywhere from $500 to $2,000 dollars. Insert an amount in the blank space.

11. Warranties and Indemnity

Warranties are contractual promises. If the licensor breaches a warranty, under an indemnity provision the licensee will have to pay for certain costs that result from the breach. In this way warranties and indemnity work together. They are each discussed in more detail below.

Keep in mind that the merchandise license can be executed without including warranties or indemnity. They are recommended but not essential for the agreement.

a. Warranties

In some agreements, warranties are labeled as Covenants or Representations. Regardless of the title, they are essentially the same things: promises made between the parties regarding certain aspects of the contract. A common warranty, for instance, is that the licensor owns the rights to the work and has the power to grant them to the licensee. In addition, the licensee should seek a promise that the work doesn't infringe third-party rights (rights of people who are not part of the agreement). Since licensors are often wary of making this type of assurance, the model agreement provides a more palatable warranty that the licensor "has no knowledge as to any third-party claims." This means that a reasonable person in the licensor's position would know whether the work is infringing someone else's rights.

A licensor may ask that the licensee provide a warranty that sales and marketing of the licensed product will conform to applicable laws. A sample provision is included in the model merchandise agreement.

If an agreement includes a warranty but no indemnity provision, the parties can still sue for "breach of warranty," however, a judge or jury must decide whether the breaching party must pay the costs or attorney fees associated with the breach.

b. Indemnity

A licensor who provides indemnity is agreeing to pay for the licensee's damages for certain situations. For example, if the licensor indemnifies the licensee against infringement, the licensor will have to pay damages (and legal fees) if the licensee is sued for infringement for use of the work. In this way, indemnity acts like a powerful shield. The licensee can deflect a lawsuit and make the licensor pay for the damages and legal fees. Indemnity provisions are also sometimes referred to as "hold harmless" provisions because the language for an indemnity provision often states that the "Licensor shall hold the Licensee harmless from any losses, etc."

Licensors are often unwilling to provide indemnity and often don't want to be legally obligated to pay legal costs. Since indemnification involves a financial risk, licensors avoid it completely, or will only agree to it with further limitations. For example, a licensor may agree to pay indemnity but only if the amount is not larger than any amounts they received under the agreement. The licensor may request that the licensee provide indemnification as well—for example, that the licensee will market and distribute the licensed product in a legal manner.

It is also important to remember that indemnity is only worthwhile if the party has money or insurance to cover the costs. An indemnity provision is useless if the indemnifier (the person who is supposed to indemnify) is broke.

12. Intellectual Property Rights

If the licensor has not filed a copyright registration and does not plan to do so, the licensee may register for protection under this provision. It is common for the licensee to deduct the reasonable costs of registration from future royalties.

13. Credits

The licensor should insert any credit they want to appear on the merchandise. For instance, a photographer who wanted to be credited for his photograph he's licensing could insert the following desired credit line:

Tom Bamberger Photo Studios

If the credit is not displayed on the merchandise, it could provide a basis for the licensor to terminate the agreement. The credit section also provides the licensee with the right to use the licensor's name and trademark in advertising for the merchandised product. This is essential if the licensor is an established artist or writer and the licensee intends to use their name or image in promotional materials.

14. Infringement Against Third Parties

If the licensed product is successful, unethical competitors may create imitations. If the licensor does not have the financial resources to fight the infringer, this provision allows the licensee to deal with infringers. It provides for funding of a lawsuit and for determining how to divide any money that is recovered from the infringer. The provision in our model agreement establishes a 50/50 division of any award money after payment of attorney fees.

15. Exploitation Date

This provision establishes the date by which the licensee must release the licensed product. Without this assurance, a licensor may be worried that the licensee will simply sit on the work and not exploit it. Sometimes the release date coincides with a specific trade show or a seasonal catalog. If the licensee fails to meet this date, the licensor can claim that there has been a "material breach" which is a basis for termination of the license agreement.

16. Approval of Samples and Quality Control

The licensor needs to guarantee that the work is being reproduced properly and that the licensed product is not inferior to competing products. This provision permits the licensor to review the pre-production artwork and prototypes and to provide approval within a ten-day period.

17. Licensor Copies and Right to Purchase

The licensor will want free copies of the licensed product and the right to purchase more at wholesale cost. If the licensee is concerned that the copies will be sold or transferred to a competitor, a statement can be added to this provision preventing the licensor from selling the copies.

18. Confidentiality

It's possible that the licensee or licensor may be disclosing confidential information in the course of the merchandise license. Confidential information includes any information that gives the business an advantage and is maintained in confidence. This clause requires that each party to the agreement preserve the confidential information. For example, if the licensor has a secret marketing plan and the licensee discloses that information in an interview, that would be a breach of the agreement.

19. Insurance

If a consumer is injured using the licensed product and claims it's defective, the licensee and licensor may be sued for product liability. It is for this reason that the sellers of merchandise acquire product liability insurance. By naming the licensor in the policy, the licensor is shielded from claims of product injuries. The minimum amount of coverage inserted for the policy should be $1,000,000. Note that this type of insurance usually does not cover infringement lawsuits. A separate business policy is often required for protection against claims of infringement.

20. Termination

Even without a termination provision, either party can terminate a merchandise license agreement if there is a material breach. A "material breach" is a substantial abuse of the agreement—for example, the licensee used the work for purposes that were not described in the agreement. However, most licensors will insist upon a written termination provision and will seek some or all of the rights listed in the agreement including the right to terminate as to a specific portion of the territory if it is not exploited.

21. Effect of Termination

At the time of termination, the licensee may have boxes of licensed products left in the warehouse. If the agreement has ended amicably, it is reasonable to allow the licensee a period of time to sell off the remaining inventory. Naturally, the licensor is entitled to royalties for these products. A period between three and six months is probably sufficient for sell-off. In addition, the licensor should obtain an accounting of the remaining inventory. If the licensee is not paying royalties or has breached the agreement, the licensee is not permitted to sell off inventory.

22. Miscellaneous Provisions

Many agreements contain provisions entitled "Miscellaneous" or "General." These provisions actually have little in common with one another except for the fact that they don't fit anywhere else in the agreement. They're contract orphans, and for that reason they are usually dumped at the end of the agreement. Lawyers often refer to these provisions as "boilerplate."

Don't be misled by the fact that boilerplate is buried in the back of the agreement. These provisions can affect how disputes are resolved and how a court enforces the agreement. However, even though they are important, they are not mandatory—they can be removed without affecting the validity of the agreement. Below is a summary of common boilerplate provisions.

a. Attorney Fees

In the event of a legal dispute between the licensee and licensor, the attorney fees provision establishes that the winner of the dispute will receive payment for legal fees. Without this provision, neither party will be reimbursed for attorney fees unless the lawsuit is for infringement of copyright. Even in that case, the award is not mandatory; it is at the judge's discretion.

b. Dispute Resolution

Arbitration is like going to court with less formality and expense. Instead of filing a lawsuit, the parties hire one or more arbitrators to evaluate the dispute and make a determination. The arbitrators are trained to evaluate disputes and many of them are retired judges.

Mediation is similar to arbitration except that instead of making a determination, a neutral evaluator attempts to help the parties settle their dispute themselves. That is, the mediator offers advice so that the parties reach a solution together. Mediation and arbitration are often referred to as alternative dispute resolution or ADR.

The model agreement includes two alternative dispute resolution provisions. The first provides for mediation first, then arbitration if mediation fails. The second is only for arbitration.

Pros and Cons of Arbitration

Arbitration has both good and not-so-good aspects. Here is an overview of the pros and cons of arbitration:

- **Pros:** Arbitration is usually less expensive and more efficient than litigation. Moreover, the parties can select an arbitrator who has knowledge in the merchandising field.
- **Cons:** There is no right to discovery (the process by which the parties must disclose information about their cases). However, the licensee can include a requirement for discovery in the arbitration provision. Unlike a court ruling, a binding arbitration ruling is not appealable. It can only be set aside if it can be demonstrated that the arbitrator was biased or that the ruling violated public policy. Arbitrators must be paid (unlike state and federal judges) and these fees can often run to $10,000 or more. Most participants hire attorneys so the licensee will still have to pay attorney fees (although probably lower than in a lawsuit).

Private arbitration is offered by a number of organizations, the best known of which is the American Arbitration Association (AAA). For information on arbitration and the American Arbitration Association, check the AAA website at www.adr.org.

c. Governing Law

In the event of a dispute, this provision (sometimes called "Choice of Law") determines which state law will govern the lawsuit. Every state has laws regarding contract interpretation. The licensor usually favors the state where its headquarters are located, often New York or California. Does it matter which state is chosen? Some states have a reputation as being favorable for certain kinds of disputes, but generally, the differences in state law are not great enough to make this a major negotiating issue.

d. Jurisdiction

In the event of a dispute, this provision establishes in which state (and, if you want to specify, which county) the lawsuit or arbitration must be filed. Each party will prefer having jurisdiction in its home location, and therefore this section is sometimes a matter of negotiation.

If the section creates contention, remove it. If there is no reference to jurisdiction, the location is usually determined by whoever files a lawsuit. If a jurisdiction clause is used, it should conform to the governing law section (as discussed above) and include the same state.

In Some States, Jurisdiction Clauses Are Invalid

In the past, many courts believed that citizens should not be able to bargain for jurisdiction (sometimes referred to as forum shopping) and would not enforce jurisdiction provisions. Today, only three states—Idaho, Montana and Alabama—refuse to honor jurisdiction provisions in agreements. In those states if the licensee uses a jurisdiction provision, it will be invalid.

---

e. Waiver

This provision permits the parties to waive (forego or give up claim to) a portion of the agreement without establishing a precedent—that is, without giving up future claims under the same portion of the agreement.

f. Invalidity

This provision (sometimes referred to as "Severability") permits a court to sever (or take out) an invalid provision and still keep the rest of the agreement intact. Otherwise, if one portion of the agreement is invalid, a court may rule that the whole agreement is invalid.

g. Entire Understanding

This provision (sometimes referred to as "Integration") establishes that the agreement is the final version and that any further modification must be in writing.

h. Attachments

This provision guarantees that any attachments (documents sometimes referred to as "Exhibits" which are attached to the agreement) will be included as part of the agreement.

i. No Special Damages

If either party breaches the agreement, state laws provide that the nonbreaching party can recover the amount of the loss resulting from the breach. For example, if the licensee fails to pay royalties accurately, the licensor can sue to recover the unpaid amount, and attorney fees if the agreement provides for such fees (see Section 22a). Under some state laws, claims may be made for additional damages—for example, special or punitive damages that are awarded to punish the breaching party. This provision prevents either party from claiming any damages than those actually suffered directly from the breach.

j. Notices

If a dispute arises, each party is entitled to be notified of the problem and the purpose of the notice provision is to establish the method of notification. If the notice procedures are not followed, claims against either party may be delayed until proper notification is provided.

k. No Joint Venture

The relationship between the parties is defined by the agreement. But to an outsider, it may appear that a licensee and licensor have a different relationship, such as a partnership or joint venture. It's possible that an unscrupulous licensor will try to capitalize on this appearance and make a third-party deal. That is, a licensor may claim to be a partner of the licensee and obtain a benefit from a distributor or sublicensee. In order to avoid liability for such a situation, most agreements include a provision disclaiming any relationship other than licensee/licensor.

l. Assignability

It is possible that the licensee may, at some point, want to transfer the rights under this agreement to another company. For example, say the licensee has two agreements with a licensor, one for shirts and another for hats. The licensee later decides it only wants to concentrate on shirts, so it wants to assign its rights in the hat agreement to a company that specializes in hat merchandising. Since agreements are only binding between the parties who sign them, the hat company can only acquire the rights of the contract if the licensee assigns those rights. The licensor may not be happy with the change. For example, the new company may have a bad reputation when it comes to paying royalties. Since assignability can be a sensitive issue, three choices are provided in our agreement.

The first option requires that the licensor's written consent be given for an assignment. In that case, the licensor can review the deal and decide, for any reason, if it wants to participate with the new licensee. The second choice also requires written consent, but that consent cannot be unreasonably withheld. In that situation, the licensor can review the prospective arrangement and if there is a valid business reason for refusing to consent, the licensor can refuse. A valid business reason usually relates to some financial quality of the new licensee. The third provision permits the transfer without consent provided that it is to a company who is purchasing the licensee. In this arrangement, another company is acquiring all of the licensee's interests. Some licensees insist on this because they want the freedom to sell the whole company (and its licenses).

m. Signatures

Each party must sign the agreement. The people who sign on each party's behalf must have the authority to do so. Use the following rules to determine how the agreement should be signed:

- **Sole Proprietorship.** If either party is a sole proprietorship, that party signs using his or her own name. If either party is using a fictitious business name (sometimes known as a d.b.a.), list the name of the business above the signature line.

EXAMPLE: Tom Lennon is a sole proprietor calling his business Lennonism. He would sign as follows:

Lennonism
By: _____
Tom Lennon, sole proprietor

- **Partnership.** If either party is a general or limited partnership, the only person authorized to sign the agreement is a general partner or someone who has written authority from a general partner (usually in the form a partnership resolution). The name of the partnership must be mentioned above the signature line or the partnership will not be bound (only the person signing the agreement will be bound).

EXAMPLE: Cindy Peacock is a general partner in Speculative Ventures Partnership. She would sign as follows:

Speculative Ventures Partnership
By: _____
Cindy Peacock, general partner

- **Corporation or LLC.** If either party is a corporation or limited liability company (LLC), only a person authorized by the corporation can sign the agreement. The president or chief operating officer (CEO) usually has such power, but not every officer of a corporation has the authority to bind the corporation. If in doubt, ask for written proof of the authority. This proof is usually in the form of a corporate resolution. The name of the corporation should be mentioned above the signature line or the corporation may not be bound (only the person signing the agreement would be bound).

EXAMPLE: Matthew LaNotta is CEO of Sunday Marketing. He would sign as follows:

Sunday Marketing, Inc., a New York corporation
By: _____
Matthew LaNotta, CEO

If either party has doubts about any person's authority to sign the agreement, don't proceed until satisfied that the person has full authority to represent the company.

May a Signature Be Faxed?

A faxed signature is suitable assuming that both parties accept the authenticity of the signature. If there is a dispute about the signature (that is, one party claims a forgery) there may difficulty proving the signature is authentic from a fax. If executing the agreement by fax, follow up the fax by mailing signed copies.

23. Exhibit A

Agreements often have attachments known as "exhibits" that are separate documents stapled to the agreement. In license agreements, the exhibit summarizes some of the essential business elements. For example, in the model agreement, Exhibit A includes a description of the work, the licensed product, and, if applicable, the sales minimum required to renew the agreement.

The advantage of using an exhibit is that if you are dealing with multiple licensees or if you are licensing more than one item to one licensee, you may be able to keep the body of the agreement the same and only change the exhibit.

Right of First Refusal

Some merchandise agreements include a provision known as a right of first refusal. The purpose of this provision is to give the licensee the first shot at licensing any new works from the licensor. For example, if the licensor creates new illustrations, the licensee will have the first opportunity to license those new works. If another company makes a better offer than the licensee, the licensee has a period of time to match the offer. A sample right of first refusal provision reads as follows:

Right of First Refusal. Licensor may identify and develop new works suitable to be used as Licensed Products ("New Works"). Licensee shall have the first right to license such New Works and the parties shall negotiate in good faith to reach agreement as to the terms and conditions for such license. In the event that the parties fail to reach agreement and Licensor receives an offer from a third party for the New Works, Licensee shall have 30 days to notify Licensor whether Licensee desires to execute a license on similar terms and conditions. In the event that Licensee matches any third-party terms and conditions, Licensor shall enter into a License Agreement with Licensee and terminate negotiations with any third parties.

D. Merchandise License Worksheet

We've provided the Merchandise License Worksheet below to help you (the licensee, presumably) keep track of the merchandise license agreement elements discussed throughout this chapter. It can function in two ways: It can be a record of the elements that the parties agreed upon; or it can be a method of deciphering an agreement furnished by the licensor. A tear-out copy of this form is in the Appendix at the end of this book and a digital version is on the forms disk.

A copy of the Merchandise License Worksheet is on the forms disk under the file name MRCHWK.

Merchandise License Worksheet

Licensor	Name of licensor business: _____ Licensor address: _____ Licensor business form: ☐ sole proprietorship ☐ general partnership ☐ limited partnership ☐ corporation ☐ state of incorporation _____ ☐ limited liability company ☐ state of organization _____ Name and position of person signing for licensor: _____
The Work(s)	Source: _____ Description: _____ Page Number: _____ Relevant data (e.g., ISBN, copyright notice): _____
Licensed Product(s)	Tentative title: _____ Format: _____
Grant of Rights (check those rights needed)	☐ reproduce ☐ distribute ☐ modify, adapt ☐ display ☐ perform
Market and Format Limitations	☐ specific market _____ ☐ specific format _____
Territory	☐ worldwide ☐ countries or states (name which): _____
Exclusivity	☐ exclusive ☐ nonexclusive

Merchandise License Worksheet (cont.)

Term	☐ no time limits
	☐ fixed term (how long: _____)
	☐ unlimited term until one party terminates
	☐ an initial term with renewals (see below)
	☐ other _____
Renewals	If the parties have agreed upon an initial term with renewals: _____
	How many renewal periods? _____
	How long is each renewal period? _____
	What triggers renewal? _____
Fee	☐ one time fee $ _____
	date due: _____
	☐ recurring fee $ _____
	date due/trigger _____
	☐ advance against royalties $ _____
	date due: _____
	☐ royalty rate(s): _____% of
	☐ net sales
	☐ gross sales
	☐ If royalty payments, are there any
	☐ deductions: _____
	☐ audits. How many per year: _____
Warranties	☐ licensor warranty conditions _____
	☐ licensee warranty conditions _____
Indemnity	☐ licensor indemnity conditions _____
	☐ licensee indemnity conditions _____
Credit	☐ licensor credit _____
Furnished Samples	☐ licensor samples required. How many: _____
	When _____
Miscellaneous	☐ jurisdiction state _____
	☐ governing law state _____
	☐ arbitration
Termination	☐ conditions _____

E. Short-Form Merchandise License Agreement

Below is a short-form merchandise license agreement. It is intended primarily for licensing an image on merchandise such as a T-shirt. The short-form merchandise agreement eliminates many of the choices in the longer agreement and substitutes the most commonly used provisions. You should consider using this agreement if your arrangement is limited to one or two years or limited to a specific number of copies (for example, 2,000 T-shirts). This agreement is suitable if you have a good relationship and sense of trust with the licensee such that you do not feel that the increased formality of a full-length agreement is necessary.

A tear-out copy of this form is in the Appendix at the end of this book. A digital version is on the forms disk. For an explanation of the various provisions, review Section C.

The Short-Form Merchandise License Agreement is on the forms disk under the file name SHMRCHLC.

Short-Form Merchandise License Agreement

Introduction

This License Agreement (the "Agreement") is made between _____ (referred

to as "Licensor") and _____ (referred to as "Licensee").

The parties agree as follows:

Grant of Rights

The "Work" is defined as follows: _____ .

Licensed Products are Licensee products incorporating the Work, specifically

("Licensed Products").

Licensor is the owner of all rights to the Work and Licensee shall not claim any right to use the

Works except under the terms of this Agreement. Licensor grants to Licensee:

(select one)

☐   an exclusive license

☐   a nonexclusive license

to reproduce and distribute the Work in or on the Licensed Products.

Sublicense

Licensee may sublicense the rights granted pursuant to this agreement provided: Licensee obtains

Licensor's prior written consent to such sublicense, and Licensor receives such revenue or royalty

payment as provided in the Payment section below. Licensor's consent to any sublicense shall not be

unreasonably withheld. Any sublicense granted in violation of this provision shall be void. Licensor

reserves all rights other than those being conveyed or granted in this Agreement.

Territory

The rights granted to Licensee are limited to _____ (the "Territory").

Term

This Agreement shall commence upon the "Effective Date," established by the latest signature date, and shall extend for a period of____ years (the "Initial Term"). Following the Initial Term, Licensee may renew this agreement under the same terms and conditions for_____consecutive _____ periods (the "Renewal Terms") provided that Licensee provides written notice of its intention to renew this agreement within thirty (30) days before the expiration of the current term.

Royalties

All royalties ("Royalties") provided for under this Agreement shall accrue when the respective Licensed Products are sold, shipped, distributed, billed or paid for, whichever occurs first.

Net Sales

Net Sales are defined as Licensee's gross sales (i.e., the gross invoice amount billed customers) less quantity discounts or rebates and returns actually credited. A quantity discount or rebate is a discount made at the time of shipment. No deductions shall be made for cash or other discounts, commissions, manufacturing costs, uncollectible accounts, or for fees or expenses of any kind which the Licensee may incur in connection with the Royalty payments.

Advance Against Royalties

As a nonrefundable advance against royalties (the "Advance"), Licensee agrees to pay to Licensor upon execution of this Agreement the sum of $ _____ .

Licensed Product Royalty

Licensee agrees to pay a Royalty of_____% percent of all Net Sales revenue of the Licensed Products ("Licensed Product Royalty").

Sublicensing Revenues

In the event of any sublicense of the rights granted pursuant to this Agreement, Licensee shall pay to Licensor _____% percent of all sublicensing revenues.

Payments and Statements

Within thirty (30) days after the end of each calendar quarter (the "Royalty Period"), an accurate statement of Net Sales of Licensed Products along with any royalty payments or sublicensing revenues shall be due to Licensor. The acceptance by Licensor of any of the statements furnished or royalties paid shall not preclude Licensor questioning the correctness at any time of any payments or statements.

Audit

Licensee shall keep accurate books of account and records covering all transactions relating to the license granted in this Agreement, and Licensor or its duly authorized representatives shall have the right upon five (5) days prior written notice, and during normal business hours, to inspect Licensee's records relating to the Work licensed under this Agreement.

Late Payment

If Licensee is late in any payment provided for in this Agreement, Licensee shall pay interest on the payment from the date due until paid at a rate of 1.5% per month, or the maximum rate permitted by law, whichever is less.

Warranties

Licensor warrants that it has the power and authority to enter into this Agreement and has no knowledge as to any third-party claims regarding the proprietary rights in the Work that would interfere with the rights granted under this Agreement.

Licensee warrants that it will use its best commercial efforts to market the Licensed Products and that their sale and marketing shall be in conformance with all applicable laws and regulations, including but not limited to all intellectual property laws.

Licensor Credits

Licensee shall identify Licensor as the owner of rights to the Work and shall include the following notice on all copies of the Licensed Products:

"_____ . All rights reserved."

Licensee may, with Licensor's consent, use Licensor's name, image or trademark in advertising or promotional materials associated with the sale of the Licensed Products.

Exploitation

Licensee agrees to manufacture, distribute and sell the Licensed Products in commercially reasonable quantities during the term of this Agreement and to commence such manufacture, distribution and sale by _____ . This is a material provision of this Agreement.

Approval of Samples & Quality Control

Licensee shall submit a reasonable number of pre-production samples of the Licensed Product to Licensor to assure that the product meets Licensor's quality standards. In the event that Licensor fails to object in writing within ten (10) business days after the date of receipt of any such materials, such materials shall be deemed to be acceptable.

Licensor Copies and Right to Purchase

Licensee shall provide Licensor with ___ copies of each Licensed Product. Licensor has the right to purchase from Licensee, at Licensee's manufacturing cost, at least _____copies of any Licensed Product and such payments shall be deducted from royalties due to Licensor.

Licensor's Right to Terminate

Licensor shall have the right to terminate this Agreement for the following reasons:

(select one or more provisions)

☐ **Failure to Make Timely Payment.** Licensee fails to pay Royalties when due or fails to accurately report Net Sales, as defined in the Payments and Statements section of this Agreement, and such failure is not cured within thirty (30) days after written notice from the Licensor.

☐ **Failure to Introduce Product.** Licensee fails to introduce the product to market by the date set in the Exploitation section of this Agreement or to offer the Licensed Products in commercially reasonable quantities during any subsequent year.

Effect of Termination

After the termination of this license, all rights granted to Licensee under this Agreement shall terminate and revert to Licensor, and Licensee will refrain from further manufacturing, copying, marketing, distribution, or use of any Licensed Product or other product which incorporates the Work. Licensee may dispose of the Licensed Products covered by this Agreement for a period of 90 days after termination or expiration except that Licensee shall have no such right in the event this agreement is terminated according to the Licensor's Right to Terminate, above.

Miscellaneous

The prevailing party shall have the right to collect from the other party its reasonable costs and attorney fees incurred in enforcing this Agreement. This Agreement expresses the full, complete and exclusive understanding of the parties with respect to the subject matter and supersedes all prior proposals, representations and understandings. If a dispute arises between the parties arising under or relating to this Agreement, the parties agree to submit such dispute to arbitration conducted under the rules of the American Arbitration Association. An arbitration award may be confirmed in a court of competent jurisdiction. The waiver or failure of any party to exercise in any respect any right provided for in this Agreement shall not be deemed a waiver of any further right under this Agreement. No party shall represent themselves to be the employee, franchisee, franchiser, joint venturer, officer or partner of the other party and nothing in this Agreement shall be construed to place the parties in the relationship of partners or joint venturers. If any provision of this Agreement is invalid under any applicable statute or rule of law, it is to that extent to be deemed omitted and the remaining provisions of this Agreement shall in no way be affected or impaired. Licensee may not assign or sublicense the rights granted under this Agreement without the written consent of Licensor. Such consent shall not be unreasonably withheld. Each party has signed this Agreement through its authorized representative. The parties, having read this Agreement, indicate their consent to the terms and conditions by their signature below.

By: _____   By: _____

Date: _____   Date: _____

Licensor Name: _____   Licensee Name/Title: _____

Releases

A release is an agreement by which someone waives (gives up) any rights to sue arising from a certain activity. A release is usually needed because a publication (or broadcast) of a person's name or image may trigger legal claims such as defamation, invasion of privacy or violation of the right of publicity. These types of legal claims are personal and relate to false statements, intrusions into personal affairs or commercial uses. The person signing the release usually foregoes any right to sue over these claims.

Traditionally, these personal releases (sometimes known as model releases) are needed when a person's name or image is used for commercial purposes. However, there may be other instances as described within this chapter in which it may be prudent to obtain a signed release. In addition to two types of personal releases, we have provided a release enabling you to use interview statements and another release permitting the use of property, such as a photo of a building, in an advertisement.

A. What Is a Release?

A release is a binding contract in which someone foregoes a right to sue you for specific types of claims. Without a written release, if you reproduce photos, video or other representations of an individual, that person might be able to bring you into court for various violations of personal rights. These include defamation, the right to privacy and the right of publicity. Each of these legal claims is discussed in more detail below.

It's generally best to keep releases as short and simple as possible. That's because people are often asked to sign releases under short notice and may balk if the document is complex or intimidating.

There are many instances in which releases are not required, and these are discussed in Section B. As a general rule you will not need a release for the use of a person's name or image if your use is not defamatory, does not invade privacy and is not for a commercial purpose. For example, a celebrity's photo can be used in a news story without a release. Remember, however, that you often will need to obtain copyright permission from the owner of the photograph. See Chapters 1 through 7 for more information on obtaining permission from copyright owners.

1. Invasion of Privacy

Every person has a right to be left alone—this is called the right of privacy. A release is needed to use a living person's name or image in a manner that constitutes an invasion of the person's right to privacy. Releases are vital because a person whose privacy is invaded can sue for monetary damages. Generally, invasion of privacy isn't an issue for individuals who are dead.

There are several different ways a person's right to privacy can be invaded, including any of the following:

- **False Light.** This type of invasion of privacy occurs when an individual is falsely portrayed in a highly offensive manner—for example, posting a photograph of a man who has never committed a crime at the "America's Most Wanted" website.

- **Disclosure of Private Facts.** This invasion of privacy occurs when private or embarrassing facts are disclosed about an individual without relation to a legitimate public concern.

EXAMPLE: A man who had served time for a robbery 20 years earlier rehabilitated himself and is now a pastor. Publication of the facts of the 20-year-old robbery would be an invasion of privacy unless there was a related public interest—for example, the pastor was again arrested for a crime.

- **Intrusion.** Intruding upon situations in which people have a reasonable expectation of privacy—for example, spying on a person at home, secretly eavesdropping on conversations or opening mail—can give rise to an invasion of privacy claim. However, it is not an invasion of privacy to photograph someone in a public place or at any event where the public is invited. Such photos can be used freely for informational purposes, provided that the use does not defame or hold the individual up to a false light.

EXAMPLE: Mary is photographed sleeping on a bench in a public park. The photo appears in the newspaper under the caption, "A Sunny Day in the Park." No release is required. However, if the caption were "Crack Addicts Seek Refuge in Park," Mary would have a claim for invasion of privacy and defamation (provided she was not a crack addict).

2. Right of Publicity

The right of publicity grew out of the general principles of invasion of privacy that prohibited the appropriation of a person's name or likeness to gain some benefit. Within the past few decades, the right of publicity has emerged as an independent type of claim that can be made when a person's name or likeness is used for commercial purposes. Although the right of publicity is commonly associated with celebrities, every person, regardless of how famous, has a right to prevent unauthorized use of their name or image to sell products. The right of publicity extends beyond the commercial use of a person's name or image and includes the use of any personal element that implies an individual's endorsement of a product, provided that the public can identify the individual based upon the use.

The right of publicity extends to a performer's identifiable voice. For example, in two separate cases, advertisements that used vocal performances that sounded like singers Tom Waits and Bette Midler were found to violate the singers' rights of publicity. In both of these cases, the advertising agency had sought permission from the performer and when it was not granted, the singer's voice was deliberately imitated—a good example of what not to do. As rule of thumb, if the performer's voice mimics a well-known performer, either accidentally or intentionally, avoid using it.

In many states, the right of publicity survives death and can be exercised by the person's estate.

3. Defamation

Defamation occurs when information is published about a person that creates a false impression and injures the person's reputation. Defamation is often divided into two categories: slander, which is an oral comment made to others, and libel, which is a fixed statement, whether printed, broadcast or published electronically. The rules for both types of defamation are similar. A deceased person cannot be defamed but a false statement that reflects on a living relative can cause defamation. In addition to personal defamation, a corporation or partnership can also be defamed if a false statement affects the business's integrity, credit or solvency.

The key to determining defamation is the injury caused to the victim's reputation in the community. The term "community" can be interpreted to mean a narrow group of persons acquainted with the injured person. Courts have permitted claims for statements that ridicule, humiliate or subject the victim to contempt.

If the information that is published is true, there is no defamation. Or, as some courts have stated, the truth is an absolute defense to defamation. Literal truth in every element is not required, provided that the statement is substantially true.

There are exceptions to defamation rules for politicians and celebrities and, to a limited extent, for people who have become the subjects of a public controversy. These people, because they are in the public eye, are expected to have tougher skins and can only be defamed if it is proven that the false statements were made with actual malice and a reckless disregard for the truth—for example, a website owner posting what he knows to be false information about a celebrity's sex life.

B. When to Use a Release

Whether you need to obtain a release depends on why you want to use a person's name or image. If your use is for commercial purposes—for example, using a person's photo in an advertisement—you should acquire a release. If your use is for informational purposes such as a documentary film or news article, a release is not required. However, even if a release is not required, you should be careful that your use does not defame or invade the privacy of the individual. If there's any potential that your use might violate these laws, a release will provide legal protection. Sorting out these differences can be confusing, and we provide some examples in the sections below. When in doubt, however, we recommend that you obtain a signed release.

1. Informational Uses

A release is not needed to use a person's name or image for informational purposes. An informational (or "editorial") purpose is anything that informs, educates or expresses opinions protected under the First Amendment of the United States Constitution (protecting freedom of speech and of the press). An informational use would include using a person's name or photograph in a newspaper or magazine article, an educational program, film, nonfiction book, or informational webzine (a magazine published on the World Wide Web).

If a person's name or image is used in an informational publication, that name or image may be used in incidental advertising for the publication. For example, you may state in an advertisement, "Featuring an interview with Johnny Depp." However, advertisements posing as informational publi-

cations require a release. (See Section 3 below for examples.)

Even if your use is informational, a release may be required if the person's name or image is used in a defamatory manner (see Section A3) or invades the person's privacy (see Section A1). It may seem odd to seek a release for a use that may defame a person or invade privacy. After all, why would anyone sign a release for a use that would create a false impression? Such releases are usually used in cases where a model or actor is posing to illustrate an article, such as "The Horror of Date Rape."

2. Commercial Uses

A release is needed for the commercial use of a person's name or image. A "commercial use" occurs when selling or endorsing a product or service. For example, if your website offers haircutting products and you feature pictures of people using the products, you would need a release from the people in the photos. A release is not required if the person cannot be recognized in the photo, for example, if the photo only includes the person's hands.

Several decades ago, the failure to obtain the release would have led to an invasion of privacy lawsuit. However, the "right of publicity" has now become the claim de jour for those whose name or image is used for commercial purposes.

3. Is Your Use Commercial or Informational?

Unfortunately, there is no definitive test that tells you whether your intended use is informational or commercial. Below are summaries of cases that straddle the border between informational and commercial uses. Cases with similar facts may seem to have different results often because a judge has broad discretion in making a determination.

- **Informational use.** A photo of football player Joe Namath was featured on the cover of *Sports Illustrated* and later used in advertisements to sell subscriptions to *Sports Illustrated*. No permission was required because the initial use of the photo was editorial and the subscription ads were "merely incidental," indicating the nature of the magazine contents. (*Namath v. Sports Illustrated*, 371 N.Y.S.2d 10 (1975).)

- **Informational use.** *The National Enquirer* and *USA Today* held telephone survey polls about the musical group New Kids on the Block. Use of the names and images of the group in connection with the newspapers' profit-making 900 numbers did not require permission because it was primarily for purposes of "news gathering and dissemination." (*New Kids on the Block v. News America Publishing Inc.*, 971 F.2d 302 (9th Cir. 1992).)

- **Informational use.** Public domain film clips of Fred Astaire were used as a prologue to an instructional dance video. The use of the Astaire name was permitted in the prologue based on the informational content of the video. (*Astaire v. Best Film & Video Corp.*, 136 F.3d 1208 (9th Cir. 1998).)

- **Informational use.** A film company acquired the rights to re-release 1950s films featuring actress Betty Page and commissioned drawings of Ms. Page to promote the films. Ms. Page sued to prevent the use of her image and name to promote the films. A court permitted the use because the advertising was incidental to the re-release and was "newsworthy" due to the reemergence of the two 1950s movies. (*Page v. Something Weird Video*, 960 F. Supp. 1438 (C.D. Ca. 1996).)

- **Informational use.** Following a Superbowl victory, a San Jose newspaper sold posters of quarterback Joe Montana. Mr. Montana sued but, in a surprising ruling, a court permitted the use, claiming it was newsworthy because of the "relatively contemporaneous" publication of the posters with the news event. (*Montana v. San Jose Mercury News*, 34 Cal.App.4th 790 (1995).)

- **Commercial use.** During the NCAA tournament broadcast, an ad for Oldsmobile featured a voice asking who held the record for being voted the most outstanding player of the tournament. The answer printed onscreen "Lew Alcindor, UCLA, '67, '68, '69." (The basketball player Kareem Abdul-Jabbar was previously known as Lew Alcindor.) The ad stated that Oldsmobile was the winner of a *Consumer's Digest* award three years in a row and ended with the statement "A Definite First Round Pick." Abdul-Jabbar sued, claiming that his name was used without permission. The court decided in his favor, ruling that although the advertisement provided information, the overall effect was commercial and required permission. (*Abdul-Jabbar v. General Motors Corp.*, 85 F.3d 407 (9th Cir. 1996).)

- **Commercial use.** *Los Angeles Magazine* contained a fashion article which featured a digitally modified photograph combining Dustin Hoffman's head with a photograph of a male model's body in a gown and woman's shoes. The text stated: "Dustin Hoffman isn't a drag in a butter-colored silk gown by Richard Tyler and Ralph Lauren heels." Although the photo was used in an informational article, the overall effect of the use was commercial, promoting the specific designers. (*Hoffman v. Capital Cities/ABC Inc.*, 33 F. Supp.2d 867 (C.D. Ca. 1999).)

- **Commercial use.** A photo of Cher was featured in *Forum Magazine* and was later used in advertisements for subscriptions to the magazine. Beneath Cher's photo in the advertisements was a caption implying Cher's endorsement of the magazine. The implied endorsement created a commercial use of the name and distinguished this use from the case involving Joe Namath, above. (*Cher v. Forum Inter. Ltd.*, 692 F.2d 634 (9th Cir. 1982).)

4. Websites: Informational or Commercial?

Can a website be informational if its primary purpose is to promote a business? Websites raise many of the issues in the borderline cases in the previous section. Several factors are weighed to determine whether the use of a name or image on a website is commercial or informational:

- If the use of the name or image at the website relates to a newsworthy event, the use is more likely to be informational.
- The more website space devoted to selling, the less likely the use is informational.
- The longer the person's name or image remains at the site, the use is less likely to be informational.
- The more separation between the informational content and the sponsorship of the site and related advertisements, the more likely the use is informational.

5. Free Speech May Obviate Need for Release

A person's name or image can be used for commercial purposes without permission if the commercial use qualifies as free speech. This generally occurs when the use is categorized as a parody. (For more information on trademark parodies see Chapter 10. For more information on copyright parodies, see Chapter 9).

For example, a company sold trading cards featuring caricatures of major league baseball players. Text on the cards ridiculing player salaries and egos included a statement: "Cardtoons baseball is a parody and is NOT licensed by Major League Baseball Properties or Major League Baseball Players Association." A federal court permitted the use of player's names and caricatured images as free speech. (*Cardtoons v. Major League Baseball Players Assn.*, 838 F. Supp. 1501 (N.D. Okla. 1993).)

However, individuals wary of litigation should weigh the consequences and costs of a lawsuit before claiming a free speech right to use an individual's name or image.

What Good Are Disclaimers?

Disclaimers are statements advising readers about potential confusion or danger and disavowing legal responsibility. When using a person's name or image, some businesses attempt to avoid liability for breaching a person's publicity or privacy rights by providing a disclaimer such as "Woody's One-Liners is not associated with or endorsed by Woody Allen."

The important thing to remember is that a disclaimer by itself will never shield a business from liability. In many cases, disclaimers have been found to add to rather than reduce confusion in the minds of customers or readers as to whether or not a celebrity is endorsing a product or service. Moreover, a disclaimer is an acknowledgment that the business admits the potential for confusion, a fact that may be used against the business in a lawsuit.

To have any legal effect, a disclaimer must be in close proximity to the person's image or name and as prominent as the name or image. It must also disclaim any sponsorship, endorsement or association with the product or service involved. Because of the legally tenuous value of disclaimers, it is generally not wise to rely on them for protection.

C. Personal Release Agreements

In this section we provide and discuss personal release agreements that permit the use of a person's name and image. Personal releases are often referred to as model releases, although the term "model" can be used for anyone, not just professional models. There are two classes of personal releases: blanket releases and limited releases.

- A blanket release permits any use of the photographic image of the person signing the release and is suitable if the company or photographer needs an unlimited right to use the image. Stock photographers who sell their photos for unlimited purposes commonly use blanket releases.

- Celebrities and professional models usually sign limited releases that specify the particular ways their image and name may be used. If a use exceeds what's permitted under the limited release, the person can sue for breach of the agreement. For example, a model that signed a release limiting use of her image for a museum brochure sued when the photo appeared on a Miami transit card.

Later, in Section D, we will introduce two other types of releases: a release for an interview and release to use an image of building.

1. General Rules for Releases

In addition to the specific legal rules for releases discussed throughout this chapter, some general advice is helpful when dealing with release situations.

a. Get It in Writing

Although oral releases are generally valid, you should always try to get a release in writing. This way, the model can't claim he or she never agreed to the release. In addition, the terms of an oral release can be hard to remember and even harder to prove in court if a dispute arises.

b. Make It Clear

When a release is sought for a specific purpose, do not hide or misrepresent facts to get the signature. A fraudulently obtained release is invalid. For example, a model was told that his image would be used by an insurance company and signed a blanket release based upon that statement. However, a viaticals company that pays cash for life insurance policies owned by AIDS victims used the photo. A Florida court permitted the model to sue.

c. Keep It Simple

Release agreements usually do not include many of the legal provisions found in other agreements in this book. Instead, releases are usually "stripped down," and pose less likelihood of triggering a discussion or negotiation. So keep your release short and simple (see tip below).

 You may find it easier to obtain a signed release if you shrink the release information to the size of a 3x5 or 5x7 card. Photographers have found that photo subjects find the smaller documents less intimidating. Some photographers reduce the material to a font size that fits on the back of a business card. However, if the contract is difficult to read, it will be less likely to be enforceable.

d. Get the Right Signatures

There are two requirements for the signature on a release: it must be an informed consent, which means that the person signing the release understood it; and the person signing must have the authority to grant the release.

In the majority of states, a minor is any person under 18 years of age, although in some the age may be 19 or 21. Since a minor may not understand the terms of a release, the signature of a parent or guardian is required before using a minor's name or image.

EXAMPLE: A 16-year old boy was photographed on the beach at Cape Canaveral and signed a release; his parents did not. The photo was later used on the cover of a novel about a gay adolescent. The father sued the publisher and settled out of court.

In some cases, an agent representing the person may have the authority to sign a release. For example, an agent signed a release granting an unlimited time period for use of a model's image in a

Nintendo advertisement. The model had intended that the image only be used for one year. A court held that the agent had the authority to sign the release on behalf of the model and the release was binding.

It is always preferable to have a release signed by the subject, not an agent. When dealing with an agent, seek an assurance that the agent has the legal authority to sign. This can be done by including the statement, "I am the authorized agent for [name of model]" above the agent's signature line.

Get a release signed ASAP. It is sometimes difficult to track down a subject after a photo has been created and there is less incentive for the subject to sign a release later at a later date. Therefore, most photographers obtain releases prior to or directly after a photo session or when the model is paid.

Consideration: Paying for a Release

A contract is legally binding only if each party obtains something of value (referred to as "consideration") in return for performance of obligations. For this reason, releases traditionally stipulated payment of a nominal amount such as one dollar. However, most courts now take a modern approach to contract law and accept the fact that consideration can be implied and an actual payment is not mandatory. Each release in this chapter establishes that the contract has met the consideration requirement by beginning with the statement, "For consideration which I acknowledge...." However, to fortify this position, you may wish to make a payment—even if nominal—to the person signing the release and indicate the amount of the payment somewhere in the release.

---

2. Unlimited Personal Release Agreement

The following form is an unlimited or blanket release agreement. It permits you to use the model's image and name in all forms of media throughout the world forever.

A tear-out copy of this form is in the Appendix at the end of this book. A digital version is on the forms disk.

The Unlimited Personal Release Agreement is on the forms disk under the file name PRSRLSUL.

Unlimited Personal Release Agreement

Grant

For consideration which I acknowledge, I irrevocably grant to _____ ("Company") and Company's assigns, licensees and successors the right to use my image and name in all forms and media including composite or modified representations for all purposes, including advertising, trade or any commercial purpose throughout the world and in perpetuity. I waive the right to inspect or approve versions of my image used for publication or the written copy that may used in connection with the images.

Release

I release Company and Company's assigns, licensees and successors from any claims that may arise regarding the use of my image including any claims of defamation, invasion of privacy, or infringement of moral rights, rights of publicity or copyright. Company is permitted, although not obligated, to include my name as a credit in connection with the image.

Company is not obligated to utilize any of the rights granted in this Agreement.

I have read and understood this agreement and I am over the age of 18. This Agreement expresses the complete understanding of the parties.

Name: _____ Date: _____

Signature: _____

Address: _____

Witness Signature: _____

Parent/Guardian Consent [include if the person is under 18]

I am the parent or guardian of the minor named above. I have the legal right to consent to and do consent to the terms and conditions of this model release.

Parent/Guardian Name: _____ Date: _____

Parent/Guardian Signature: _____

Parent/Guardian Address: _____

Witness Signature: _____

3. Limited Personal Release Agreement

The following form is a limited personal release agreement. It allows you to use the model's name or image only for the purposes specified in the agreement.

A tear-out copy of this form is in the Appendix at the end of this book. A digital version is on the forms disk.

 The Limited Personal Release Agreement is on the forms disk under the file name PRSRELLT.

Limited Personal Release Agreement

Grant

For consideration which I acknowledge, I grant to _____ ("Company") and

Company's assigns, licensees and successors, the right to use my image for the following purposes:

_____

_____ in the following territory

_____ for a period of _____ year(s) (the "Term").

I grant the right to use my name and image for the purposes listed above in all forms and media including composite or modified representations and waive the right to inspect or approve versions of my image used for publication or the written copy that may be used in connection with the images.

Payment

(select if appropriate)

☐   For the rights granted during the Term, Company shall pay $_____ upon execution of this release.

Renewal

(select if appropriate)

☐   Company may renew this agreement under the same terms and conditions for _____ year(s) provided that Licensee makes payment of $ _____ at the time of renewal.

Release

I release Company and Company's assigns, licensees and successors from any claims that may arise regarding the use of my image including any claims of defamation, invasion of privacy, or infringement of moral rights, rights of publicity or copyright. Company is permitted, although not obligated, to include my name as a credit in connection with the image.

Name: _____ Date: _____

Signature: _____

Address: _____

Witness Signature: _____

Parent/Guardian Consent [include if the person is under 18]

I am the parent or guardian of the minor named above. I have the legal right to consent to and do consent to the terms and conditions of this model release.

Parent/Guardian Name: _____ Date: _____

Parent/Guardian Signature: _____

Parent/Guardian Address: _____

Witness Signature: _____

4. Explanation for Limited and Unlimited Personal Releases

- The grant paragraph establishes the rights granted by the person. In the unlimited agreement, a "blanket" grant is used. This grant is broad and intended to encompass all potential uses whether informational, commercial or otherwise. In the limited agreement, the uses must be listed—for example, "For use on the cover of trade book and for related advertisements." This release also has limitations regarding territory and term. Insert the appropriate geographic region and term—for example, "North America with a two-year term."
- The release is the person's promise not to sue the company for legal claims such as libel and invasion of privacy.
- If the person is a minor, the parent or guardian should sign where it is marked parent/guardian consent (see Section C1). Since issues about release authenticity often crop up many years after a photo was made, a witness should sign the agreement to verify the person's signature or the signature of the parent. The witness should be an adult. An employee or assistant is suitable.

invasion of privacy. In addition, many interview subjects don't have the ability or inclination to execute a written release—for example, a person interviewed by telephone for a deadline newspaper story.

Nevertheless, a written interview release can be useful. It can help avoid lawsuits for libel, invasion of privacy or even copyright infringement (since the speaker's words may be copyrightable). It's wise to obtain a signed release if the interview is lengthy, will be reprinted verbatim (for example, in a question and answer format) or if the subject matter of the interview is controversial.

It is common for an interview subject to ask to read or edit the interview or to have some comments removed or kept "off the record." Any agreement that is made with the interview subject (including an agreement for anonymity) should be documented. Failure to honor the arrangement may give rise to a lawsuit for monetary damages.

If the interview subject is willing to proceed with the interview, but does not want to sign a release, ask if he or she will make an oral consent into a tape or video recorder or video. Although not as reliable as a written release, a statement such as "I consent to the use of my statements for use in the *Musician's Gazette*" will provide some assurance of your right to use the statement.

D. Interview and Property Releases

There are occasions when a release is required for a purpose other than using someone's name or image. Below we present two other forms of release: a release to use statements from an interview; and a release permitting to use of images of a building.

1. Interview Releases

Most reporters and writers do not obtain signed interview releases because they presume that by giving the interview, the subject has consented to the interview and, therefore, there can be no claim for

a. Interview Release Agreement

An interview release is a hybrid agreement, part release and part license. The release below is suitable if permission is sought to use an existing interview or to conduct a new interview.

A tear-out copy of this form is in the Appendix at the end of this book. A digital version is on the forms disk.

 The Interview Release Agreement is on the forms disk under the file name INTVRLS.

Interview Release Agreement

Grant

For consideration which I acknowledge, I consent to the recording of my statements and grant to

_____ ("Company") and Company's assigns, licensees and successors the right to

copy, reproduce, and use all or a portion of the statements (the "Interview") for incorporation in the

following work _____ (the "Work").

I permit the use of all or a portion of the Interview in the Work in all forms and media including

advertising and related promotion throughout the world and in perpetuity. I grant the right to use my

image and name in connection with all uses of the Interview and waive the right to inspect or

approve use of my Interview as incorporated in the Work.

Release

I release Company and Company's assigns, licensees and successors from any claims that may arise

regarding the use of the Interview including any claims of defamation, invasion of privacy, or

infringement of moral rights, rights of publicity or copyright. I acknowledge that I have no ownership

rights in the Work.

Company is not obligated to utilize the rights granted in this Agreement.

I have read and understood this agreement and I am over the age of 18. This Agreement expresses

the complete understanding of the parties.

Name: _____ Date: _____

Signature: _____

Address: _____

Witness Signature: _____

Parent/Guardian Consent [include if the person is under 18]

I am the parent or guardian of the minor named above. I have the legal right to consent to and do

consent to the terms and conditions of this model release.

Parent/Guardian Name: _____ Date: _____

Parent/Guardian Signature: _____

Parent/Guardian Address: _____

b. Explanation for Interview Release Agreement

- It's possible that the interview may already have been recorded, in which case the language "consent to the recording of my statements and" can be stricken from the Grant section. If the interview will be included in more than one work, list all works and change the term "Work" to "Works" throughout the agreement. Unlimited or blanket releases for interviews are not common, partly because subjects usually are not prepared to relinquish unlimited rights.
- If seeking unlimited rights (the interview can be used for any purpose) substitute the following Grant section:

Grant

For consideration which I acknowledge, I consent to the recording of my statements and grant to

_____ ("Company") and Company's assigns, licensees and successors the right to copy, reproduce, and use all or a portion of the statements (the "Interview") for all purposes, including advertising, trade or any commercial purpose throughout the world and in perpetuity.

I grant the right to use my image and name in connection with all uses of the Interview and waive the right to inspect or approve any use of my Interview.

If the interview subject does not wish to waive the right to inspect the final work, strike that sentence and arrange for the interview subject to provide approval.

- If the release is executed after the interview has been transcribed, it is helpful to attach a transcription of the interview to the release agreement. This provides an assurance that the interview subject has notice of what was said in the interview. Add a sentence to the grant section such as, "A complete transcription of the interview is attached and incorporated in this Agreement." The release section provides protection against subsequent legal claims.
- If the interview subject is under 18, a parent or guardian's consent is required (see Section C1).

2. Property Releases

In some cases, you'll need to obtain a release for using pictures of places. You may find this odd—after all if a building can be viewed publicly why is permission required to use an image of it? Over the last few decades some buildings have earned protection under both trademark or copyright laws or both. Trademark law will protect a building's appearance under very limited circumstances. If a distinctive-looking building is used to signify a business's services, then you cannot use an image of that building in a manner that will confuse consumers. For example, the Sears Tower in Chicago functions as a trademark, and if you intend to use it in the foreground of an advertisement, permission should be obtained from the Sears Company. Use of the building's image for informational purposes, such as in magazine article, does not require permission.

Is permission needed to use the image of a trademarked building on a postcard or poster? That issue arose when a photographer sold images of the Rock and Roll Hall of Fame. A federal court of appeals permitted the use of the trademarked building on posters and did not consider it to be trademark infringement. (*Rock and Roll Hall of Fame v. Gentile*, 134 F.3d 749 (6th Cir. 1998).)

Copyright protection also extends to architectural works, specifically for architectural works created after March 1, 1989. However copyright protection also has limitations. A release is not needed to photograph a building or property visible from a public place. However, permission is needed to photograph and reproduce images of a building protected by copyright and not visible from a public place. Entering private property to photograph a building or related private property may also trigger a claim of trespass. To avoid such claims, photographers, publishers and filmmakers use a property release, sometimes known as a location release.

a. Property Release Agreement

This form may be used for a property release.

A tear-out copy of this form is in the Appendix at the end of this book. A digital version is on the forms disk.

 The Property Release Agreement is on the forms disk under the file name PROPRLS.

Property Release Agreement

The Property: _____

Grant

For consideration which I acknowledge, I irrevocably grant to _____
("Company") and Company's assigns, licensees and successors the right to enter onto the property listed above and to photograph, copy, publish, display and use images of the property in all forms and media including composite or modified representations throughout the world and in perpetuity for the following purposes: _____

    I waive the right to inspect or approve the manner in which the images of the property are used and waive the right to inspect any text that is used in connection with the images of the property.

Dates of Use

Company shall enter onto the property on the following dates and times: _____

    In consideration for the rights granted under this Agreement, Company shall pay me $ _____ upon execution of this Agreement.

    Company is not obligated to utilize any of the rights granted in this Agreement.

    Warranty, Indemnity & Release I warrant that I am the owner of the property and have the authority to grant the rights under this agreement and agree to indemnify Company from any claims regarding my ownership of the property. I release Company and Company's assigns, licensees and successors from any claims that may arise regarding the use of the images of the property.

    I have read and understood this agreement. This Agreement expresses the complete understanding of the parties.

Owner's Signature: _____

Owner's Name: _____

Owner's Address: _____

Date: _____

b. Explanation for Property Release

- The Grant section allows access to photograph the property (on the dates provided in the Dates of Use section) and the right to use the photographs for the purposes listed in the agreement.
- If payment is required for the release, indicate the amount in the paragraph after the Dates of Use section.
- The owner provides an assurance of ownership in the Warranty, Indemnity & Release section and also agrees to defend the Company from anyone else with a property ownership claim.

■

Copyright Research

Most of the chapters in this book discuss the different rules for when and how to seek permission from a copyright owner when using a copyrighted work. But what if you don't know who the copyright owner is, or how to find them? This chapter explains how to conduct a very specific type of research: finding information about ownership and copyright validity. This information is usually contained in Copyright Office and Library of Congress records such as copyright registrations, assignments, renewals and related documents. This chapter will explain how to go about searching these documents, including how to gather information to prepare for your searches.

It's possible you may not have to perform copyright research. You may be able to locate all the copyright information you need through other sources. However, if you seek permissions on a regular basis, there may come a time when you will have to to trace copyright ownership (known as "the chain of title"), determine the first date of publication or determine if copyright for a work has been renewed.

We'll walk you through the basics of copyright research and explain some common approaches. But first we'll start with answers to some common questions regarding copyright ownership and transfers.

⚠️ **This chapter does not cover other types of research such as locating stock photos or private databases of art or music.** For more media-specific research, review the relevant chapter covering that type of media.

⚠️ **Copyright Office records are not always conclusive.** Records of the Copyright Office and Library of Congress are helpful for locating ownership information and for determining copyright status. Unfortunately, these records are not always conclusive, because copyright registration and the filing of copyright assignments (documents that transfer copyright ownership) are not mandatory. Since these documents don't have to be filed, it's possible that there is no Copyright Office record regarding a particular work.

Despite this fact, we still recommend performing copyright research because the Copyright Office and the Library of Congress are still the largest repositories of copyrighted materials. In addition, even if you can't find records of ownership, your research will demonstrate that you acted in good faith in the event that you are later sued for an unauthorized use. This "innocent infringement" categorization will limit the damages that you may have to pay in a court case.

A. Copyright Ownership and Transfers FAQ

When performing copyright research, questions may arise as to copyright rules or terminology related to ownership or transfers. For example, you may uncover a registration indicating the work is "made for hire" or you may find a document indicating that the copyright has been "reclaimed" by the author. Before we begin explaining how to conduct copyright research, let's go through some answers to frequently asked questions (FAQ) about ownership and transfers.

📖 For a more detailed discussion of these copyright issues, refer to *The Copyright Handbook*, by Stephen Fishman (Nolo).

1. What Is a Work Made for Hire?

Usually, the person who creates a work is also the initial owner of the copyright in the work. But this isn't always the case. Under some circumstances, a person who pays another to create a work becomes the initial copyright owner, not the person who actually created it. The resulting works are called "works made for hire" (or sometimes simply "works for hire"). There are two distinct types of work that will be classified as made for hire:

- a work created by an employee within the scope of employment, or

- a commissioned work that falls within a special list of works and that is the subject of a written agreement. The types of works that qualify and the other relevant requirements are explained in more detail in Chapter 15.

If the work qualifies under one of these two methods, the person paying for the work (the hiring party) is the author and copyright owner. If you want to use the work, you should seek permission from the employer or hiring party, not the person who created the work. If in doubt, you may be able to determine work-for-hire status by examining the copyright registration, as explained in Section C.

2. What Is a Transfer of Title?

The person who owns a copyright is sometimes referred to as having "title" to the copyright. A "title" is often simply the document that establishes ownership to property, like the title to your car or house—but even in the absence of an official document, the owner of property such as a copyright is often said to have title to it.

Just like title to your car or house, title to a copyright can be sold or otherwise transferred. A person or company can have ownership ("title") of a copyright transferred to it by means of an assignment (essentially a sale in which all or part of a copyright is transferred) or by means of a will or through bankruptcy proceedings. Since title to a copyright can be transferred, you may have to search copyright records to determine the current owner of a work you want to use.

There are two ways that you can learn whether copyright ownership has been transferred: by reviewing the copyright registration certificate issued by the Copyright Office or by locating an assignment or transfer agreement. By reviewing the copyright registration you can find out who is currently claiming copyright and on what basis. For example, if a publisher has been assigned copyright to the work, it will file a copyright registration in its own name and indicate on the registration that copyright was acquired through a legal transfer. Also, many

companies file with the Copyright Office the agreement that establishes the assignment, license or transfer. For example, if an artist assigned his work to a company, the company could file the assignment document with the Copyright Office. (See Section C for guidance on how to check these Copyright Office records.)

3. What Is a Termination of a Transfer?

Sometimes an author transfers copyright to someone and then later the author re-acquires it through a process known as "terminating a transfer." Copyright laws provide a method by which authors can reclaim rights after a number of years. This termination and reclamation process is complex and the rules differ depending on when the work was first published. As a very general rule, transfer terminations occur between 28 and 56 years of first publication. Terminations are filed with the Copyright Office and can be located by researching Copyright Office records.

> **EXAMPLE:** In June of 1996, the author J.D. Salinger terminated his transfer to the publisher Little, Brown and Company, and reacquired ownership rights to the story, "A Perfect Day for Bananafish." The termination notice was filed with the Copyright Office (and located through Internet research).

Below is the information from the termination notice as displayed in the Copyright Office's online records.
RECORDED: 11Jun96
PARTY 1: Phyllis Westberg, as agent for J. D. Salinger.
PARTY 2: Little, Brown and Company.
NOTE: A perfect day for bananafish & 5 other titles; stories.

From Nine stories. By J. D. Salinger. Notice of termination of grant under 17 USC sec. 304; date & manner of service of the notice: 6Jun96, by certified mail, return receipt requested.

For more information on terminations of transfers, see Chapter 9 of *The Copyright Handbook* by attorney Stephen Fishman (Nolo).

4. What If More Than One Person Owns a Copyright?

A common question is whom to ask for permission if several people jointly own a copyright. Co-ownership of copyright can occur in various ways. For example,

- two people jointly create a work
- the author transfers portions of the rights to different people (for example, giving half to each child), or
- the author sells a portion of the copyright to someone and keeps the remainder.

Co-owners of copyright have a legal status known as "tenants in common." When a co-owner dies, his or her share goes to beneficiaries or heirs, not to the other co-owner. Each co-owner has an independent right to use or nonexclusively license the work—provided that he or she accounts to the other co-owners for any profits. What this means for our purposes is that if you obtain the permission of any one co-owner you can use the work. However, there are a few exceptions to this rule, as explained in the next section.

You can determine whether there is co-ownership of a certain work by reviewing Copyright Office documents as described below. For example, a registration for a song might indicate that a composer and lyricist are co-owners of a song.

5. Are There Any Situations Where You Must Get Multiple Permissions?

There are several situations where you must obtain permission from all the co-owners of a work, instead of just one. All co-owners must consent to an assignment of the work or to an exclusive license. An assignment is a transfer of copyright ownership. An exclusive license is an agreement granting rights solely to one person.

EXAMPLE: Two programmers create a software program. Company A wants an exclusive license to distribute the program, which means that Company A is the only company that can distribute the program. Since the desired license is an exclusive one, the consent of both programmers must be obtained.

In addition, all co-owners must consent if:

- the co-owners have an agreement amongst themselves prohibiting any individual owner from granting a license; and you are aware of this agreement
- you want to use the text on a worldwide non-exclusive basis—some countries require consent of all co-owners even for nonexclusive uses
- you want to use the text for a commercial purpose such as to sell a service or product, or
- the desired license is for the first public release of a song.

6. Is There a Difference Between an Author and a Copyright Owner?

The author is the first owner of copyright. The author is either the creator of the work or the person that employs someone to create the work (see work-for-hire rules discussed above). Many authors do not retain their copyright ownership; they sell or transfer it to someone else in return for a lump sum payment or periodic payment known as a royalty. In this way, the author and copyright owner (sometimes referred to as "copyright claimant") may be two different people. Even if you do not know the name of the current copyright owner, knowing the name of the author will help you find it in the Copyright Office records.

7. What If a Work Does Not Contain a Copyright Notice?

It's common to start copyright research by examining the copyright notice. However, in some cases, the notice may be missing from the work. One reason you may not find a notice is because notice is not required on works first published after March 1, 1989. In addition, for works published prior to that date, notice is required only on visually perceptible copies—that is, copies that can be seen directly or with the aid of a device such as a film projector. Printed books, paintings, drawings, films, architecture and computer programs are all visually perceptible. However, some copies of works are not visually perceptible, such as a song on a compact disc. Copyright notice would be required if the song lyrics were printed on the album cover.

Another reason that a work may not include notice is that the owner failed to affix it, which may result in the loss of copyright. For works first published before 1978, for example, the absence of a copyright notice from a published copy generally indicates that the work is not protected by copyright. The absence of notice on works published between January 1, 1978, and March 1, 1989, may or may not result in the loss of copyright, depending on whether the owner corrected the error within five years of the publication and met other copyright law requirements.

8. What If There Is a Copyright Notice for an Entire Magazine but Not for the Specific Article You Want to Use?

If a story or a photograph is used in a magazine, there may be a copyright notice for the magazine but not for the specific story or photo that you want to use. That's because the owners of magazines, anthologies or greatest hits collections in which many different copyrighted works are collected (referred to as "collective works") can use one copyright notice to protect all the works in the collection. This does not necessarily mean that the magazine owns the copyright in all of the works. It may or may not, depending on the contract with the author or photographer. Copyright Office research may not necessarily help in locating these works because often they are not listed separately by title in Copyright Office records. You may be better off contacting the owner of the collective work directly. The principles for contacting copyright owners are explained in the chapters dealing with specific media (text, artwork, photographs, etc.).

B. Starting Your Copyright Research

There are three parts to copyright research. First, you must isolate elements that are necessary to perform your research. For example, you must examine the work for clues such as copyright notice or publication date that will assist in your research. Second, you must define a method of searching copyright records. You may choose to have the Copyright Office perform the research or you may attempt to search copyright records via the Telnet system on the Internet. Finally, you must initiate the search and examine the documents that are retrieved. This section discusses the first step—an examination of the work.

When doing a physical review of the work you want to use, your goal is to find information that will assist in locating copyright documents in the Copyright Office records. Check the work you want to use for the following information:

- **Copyright notice.** The copyright notice is usually on or near the title page of a book; visible at the end of a movie; printed on a compact disc cover or video box; or stamped on the back of a photograph or artwork. For computer programs, it can be located in the Help File under "About this Program." The copyright notice has three parts: the "c" in a circle (©) or the word "copyright," the date of first publication (or, in rare cases, the date of registration) and the name of the copyright owner.

- **Title of the work.** Since Copyright Office records are indexed by title, the title of the work is one of the most important elements in copyright research. Alternative titles may also be helpful (both main and alternative titles are usually listed on the copyright registration).

- **Name(s) of author(s).** The name of the author of most works such as books, photos and paintings is usually easy to locate. Like the title, the name of the author is helpful when searching Copyright Office records because it is usually listed on every copyright document pertaining to that work. Pseudonyms are also traceable in the Copyright Office. Even "Anonymous," as a listing for an author, when cross-referenced with the title, can be helpful in locating a work.

- **The name of the copyright owner.** This may be the author, publisher or producer of a work. The likely name of the owner is listed in the copyright notice. We say "likely" because you can never rely solely on the copyright notice for determining the current copyright owner. If you're dealing with an older work, for example, it's possible that the ownership may have been transferred or reclaimed since publication. However, the name of the owner listed in the copyright notice can be helpful as a starting point for your copyright search.

- **Year of publication or registration.** The work you are examining will probably list the year of its publication. The date of publication is ordinarily contained in the copyright notice. This date usually (though not always) indicates when copyright protection began. We say "usually" because the year may simply be the year that this particular version of the work was first published.

EXAMPLE: Bruce first publishes a book on guitar repair in 1980. He updates it in 1998. The copyright notice on the new version states 1998, so this notice really refers only to the new material in the update. The publication date for the earlier material is still 1980.

What If the Copyright Notice Does Not Include the Date?

Because certain industries successfully lobbied Congress for the right to omit the year on copyright notice, it's possible that the copyright notice may not include the date of first publication. The date can be omitted on greeting cards, stationery, jewelry, toys or useful articles on which a photograph, graphic or sculptural work (and accompanying text) appears—for example a greeting card may include the notice, "© Hallmark Greetings." In cases where no date is provided, you may need to research Copyright Office records to verify the date of first publication.

- **Title, volume or issue of serialized publication.** If the work you want to use was originally published as a part of a periodical or collection, the title of that publication (for example, *Life* magazine) and other information, such as the volume or issue number, may be useful in searching the Copyright Office records.

- **Underlying works and works contained within works.** Many works, referred to as "derivatives," are based upon other works. For example, motion pictures are often based on books or plays. The work upon which another is based is referred to as the "source" or "underlying" work. For instance, the movie *Jurassic Park* is based upon the novel of the same name. Copyright information about a source work such as its title or author can often be found within the derivative. For example, the motion picture *Jurassic Park* indicates in its opening credits, "Based upon the novel, *Jurassic Park,* by Michael Crichton."

- **Identifying numbers.** Identifying numbers, particularly the registration number or any other indexing data, may help in your copyright search. Many media industries have a system of cataloguing works. For example, publishers use ISBNs (International Standard Book Numbers) or ISSNs (International Standard Serial Numbers for serialized publications). The Library of Congress has its own catalog system known as the LCCN (Library of Congress Catalog Number). These numbers, which are usually located on the same page as the copyright notice, may prove helpful in identifying works when performing copyright research.

C. Searching the Copyright Office and Library of Congress Records

Now that you have isolated the information necessary for searching, you can begin examining the records at the Copyright Office (and to a lesser extent, at the Library of Congress). Think of the Copyright Office as the source for copyright records and consider the Library of Congress as a 200-year-old library catalog. Specific information about ownership, publication, transfers and derivative sources for a work is located at the Copyright Office. General cataloging information about a work such as author, date of publication, subject matter and publisher is located in the Library of Congress catalogs.

Using a system known as Telnet it is possible to search both Copyright Office and Library of Congress records. In the sections below, we explain the Telnet search system, which can assist in determining public domain status and ownership. Telnet is a software application that lets you connect to another computer via the Internet. Unlike the World Wide Web, Telnet is not a graphic program. You do not see graphic images, only text. If you are hesitant about using Telnet, consider hiring the Copyright Office to perform the search on your behalf.

1. Define Your Search

Your search of Copyright Office records will vary depending on what your goal is. Most likely, you have one of two goals: you want to find the current owner of copyright, or you want to know whether the work has fallen into the public domain. Depending on which one of these goals is yours, you'll search different Copyright Office records.

a. Ownership Searching

When trying to determine the owner of copyright, review:

- certificates of registration, and
- assignments or other transfer documents.

Both of these documents are issued by and recorded with the Copyright Office. The registration will indicate who initially acquired ownership and the assignment will indicate if the registration has been transferred to another party. The certificate of registration is issued by the Copyright Office and is the basic copyright document establishing date of publication, author, source of underlying material, contact person and initial owner of copyright. The owner's name is listed in the space in Section 4 entitled "Copyright Claimant." If the owner is a different person than the author, the method of acquiring ownership (for example, "by written contract") is indicated in the space in Section 4 entitled "Transfer."

Assignments are transfers of copyright ownership. For example, an author may transfer rights to a publisher by signing an assignment of copyright, often included as part of a publishing agreement. Filing an assignment with the Copyright Office is not mandatory, but many copyright owners do so. When searching online via Telnet at the Copyright Office, the person acquiring rights (the assignee) is usually listed as PARTY2 or PTY2 and the person transferring rights (the assignor) is usually listed as PARTY1 or PTY1.

b. Public Domain Searching

When researching whether a work is in the public domain, review:

- copyright registrations or other records containing the date of first publication, or
- renewal notices.

Both registrations and renewal notices are issued by and recorded with the Copyright Office. The registration is the initial statement of copyright information about a work and indicates the author, date of registration, copyright claimant (at the time of filing the registration) and date of first publication. A renewal is a document required to be filed in order to extend the length of protection for works published or registered before 1964. Although a renewal is no longer required for works published or registered after 1963, many copyright owners still file it.

Works published during the years of 1923 through 1963 receive 95 years of protection if they were renewed during their 28th year. If not, they are in the public domain. Works published during the years of 1963 through 1977 receive 95 years of protection. Works created after 1977 and all unpublished works are protected for life of the author plus 70 years.

You may be able to determine if a work was published before 1923 (and is in the public domain) by examining the date in the work's copyright notice. For example, we determined that James Joyce's *Dubliners* is in the public domain because the Library of Congress database indicated that *Dubliners* was first published before 1923.

Note that copyright notice dates included in a book are not always accurate, because many public domain works are often republished with new dates in their copyright notices. For example, current editions of James Joyce's *Dubliners* have copyright notices with dates after 1980. These "new" dates reflect the fact that the work contains some new material such as a preface, notes or previously unpublished material. Only this new material is protected under the copyright claim. The public domain work remains in the public domain.

EXAMPLE: To determine if the James Joyce short story collection, *Dubliners,* is in the public domain (that is, was published before 1923), we reviewed the Library of Congress records. The Library of Congress record, below, indicates that the work was first published in 1916. Information about researching Library of Congress records is provided in Section C4.

Title Search For: Dubliners /
ITEM 1.CALL NUMBER: Microfilm 76492 PZ
AUTHOR: Joyce, James, 1882-1941
TITLE: Dubliners,
PUBLISHED: New York, B. W. Huebsch, 1916.
DESCRIPTION:2 p.l., 7-278 p. 20 cm.
LCCN NUMBER:17-24698

Works published in the United States after 1922 and before 1964 are also in the public domain if the owner failed to file a renewal during the 28th year after first publication. Unlike copyright registrations or assignments, renewal notices for works published before 1964 had to be filed with the Copyright Office. If a work published after 1922 and before 1964 was not renewed, it fell into the public domain. According to Copyright Office surveys, the great majority of pre-1964 works were never renewed and therefore are in the public domain. Unfortunately, the Copyright Office does not maintain lists of public domain materials. Copyright Office records must be searched to determine whether a renewal was timely filed for a work.

2. Searching Copyright Office Records

Once you have all the available information about your work and know what you're searching for, you need to choose the search method that best suits your purposes. You can either hire a search firm or work directly with the Copyright Office, who will do your search for a fee. Another option, searching the Copyright Office online, is discussed in the next section.

What Else Can You Get From the Copyright Office?

Besides copyright research, the Copyright Office offers the following:

- information circulars
- answers to common questions
- announcements of changes in federal regulations
- compulsory licensing guidelines, and
- information on pending legislation.

These materials can be obtained by writing to the Copyright Office or by visiting the Copyright Office website at lcWeb.loc.gov/copyright/. Circulars and publications can also be ordered by calling the Forms and Publications 24-Hour Hotline. (Copyright Office information is provided in Chapter 16, "Help Beyond This Book.")

Frequently requested Copyright Office circulars and announcements are also available via the Copyright Office's Fax-on-Demand service. The procedure is simple. Call the fax-on-demand number (202-707-9100) and key in the document numbers. If you don't have an index of document numbers, you can have one faxed to you. Once you've entered the document numbers, key in the phone number where the documents should be faxed. Up to three items can be ordered at one time. The fax is usually received within minutes of your phone call to the Copyright Office. Note that copyright application forms are not available by fax.

a. Hire a Private Search Company

For a fee, you can hire a private company to search Copyright Office records. These companies provide additional services such as tracing the copyright history of a fictional character or locating similarly titled works. These companies may be able to determine if a work is in the public domain or whether rights can be obtained to use the work.

The advantage of using these companies is their speed and thoroughness. Search companies compile comprehensive reports using Copyright Office records as well as other databases and can deliver the materials within two to ten days. The disadvantage is the cost, often $300 or more per search. The largest and best known copyright search company is Thomson & Thomson Copyright Research Group, which can be reached at 800-356-8630.

b. Pay the Copyright Office to Perform the Search

Upon request, the Copyright Office staff will search its records at the statutory rate of $65 for each hour or fraction of an hour consumed. You can initiate a search by submitting a Search Request Form (below) or by calling the Copyright Office at 202-707-6850. The Copyright Office will quote you a fee for the job you need done.

Although the cost of a Copyright Office search is much lower than a private search company, the disadvantage is that it may take one or two months to receive a response. The Copyright Office will conduct an expedited search if you pay a higher fee. For more information, see Copyright Circular 22. Also, note that the search fee does not include the cost of additional certificates, photocopies of deposits or copies of other Copyright Office records. For information concerning these services, request Copyright Office Circular 6. (See Chapter 16, Section A1, for information on how to obtain Copyright Office publications.)

Below is an example of the Copyright Office's Search Request Form. You can use this form to have the Copyright Office locate registrations, renewals, assignments and addresses of copyright owners. A tear-out copy of the form is located in the Appendix at the end of this book.

The Search Request Form is on the forms disk in the back of this book under the file name COPSRCH.

Search Request Form

TYPE OF WORK:

☐ Book   ☐ Music   ☐ Motion Picture   ☐ Drama   ☐ Sound Recording
☐ Photography / Artwork   ☐ Map   ☐ Periodical   ☐ Contribution
☐ Computer Program   ☐ Mask Work

SEARCH INFORMATION YOU REQUIRE:

☐ Registration   ☐ Renewal   ☐ Assignment   ☐ Address

SPECIFICS OF WORK TO BE SEARCHED:

TITLE: _____

AUTHOR: _____

COPYRIGHT CLAIMANT (if known): _____ (name in

copyright notice)

APPROXIMATE YEAR DATE OF PUBLICATION/CREATION: _____

REGISTRATION NUMBER (if known) _____

OTHER IDENTIFYING INFORMATION: _____

If you need more space please attach additional pages.

YOUR NAME: _____

DATE: _____

ADDRESS: _____

DAYTIME TELEPHONE NO.: _____

Convey results of estimate/research by telephone?   ☐ Yes   ☐ No

Fee Enclosed?   ☐ Yes. Amount $ ____   ☐ No

If You Only Need a Certificate of Registration

It's possible that all you need is the certificate of registration—the document recorded at the Copyright Office indicating who owns the work. You can use the search form above to obtain a copy or simply furnish a letter to the Copyright Office with the following information:

- title of the work
- type of work involved (novel, lyrics, etc.)
- the registration number, including the preceding letters (for example, TX000-000)
- year of registration or publication
- the author(s), including any pseudonym by which the author may be known, and
- any other information needed to identify the registration.

If you do not have all this information, you can furnish what you have. If the information furnished is insufficient for locating the certificate, you may need to pay for a copyright search as outlined above in Section C2.

There is an $8 fee for the certificate. Your check or money order payable to the Register of Copyrights should accompany the request.

All requests for copies of Copyright Office records should be submitted to the Certifications and Documents Section, LM-402, Copyright Office, Library of Congress, Washington, DC 20559; 202-707-6787. It is also possible to go to the office and request records in person (see the Sidebar "Searching in Person").

Searching in Person

It's possible to inspect Copyright Office records by visiting the Library of Congress in Washington D.C. It's located at 101 Independence Avenue, S.E., on the 4th floor of the James Madison Memorial Building. It is open on weekdays from 8:30 a.m. to 5 p.m. There is a card catalog available to the public in Room 459. You can use the catalog to obtain essential facts about registrations, such as copyright ownership and whether a work was renewed. Alternatively, you may ask the Reference and Bibliography Section in Room 450 to conduct a search for an hourly fee. You can get extensive information on the Copyright Office Card Catalog by visiting the Copyright Office website and downloading Circular 23 or using Fax-on-Demand (explained above).

Another important research tool you can access in person is *The Catalog of Copyright Entries* (CCE). The CCE contains the same information as the card catalog, but is in book form (and is actually more complete than the card catalog). The CCE is available not only at the Copyright Office but in many libraries throughout the country—typically large university research libraries and city libraries such as the New York Pubic Library. Portions of the CCE are available only in microfiche form (a photographic format requiring a special viewer). The CCE contains essential facts about registrations, such as copyright ownership and whether a work was renewed, but does not include verbatim reproductions of the registration record. In addition there is a time lag, and more recent registrations may not be included. Finally, the CCE cannot be used for researching the transfer of rights, since it does not include entries for assignments or other recorded documents.

3. Searching Copyright Office Records Online: Welcome to LOCIS

There is good news and bad news about online searching of the Copyright Office records. The good news is that it is free. All you need to do is to connect to the Library of Congress Information System (LOCIS). The bad news is that you can only connect to LOCIS by use of an Internet system known as Telnet. Telnet is a text-only online system (that is, no graphic images) that can be daunting for first-time users and non-techies.

a. Using Telnet to Access LOCIS

Telnet requires special software, which you can usually obtain for free by contacting your Internet Service Provider (ISP). America Online, like most ISPs, provides a free version of a Telnet program. Telnet software is often included with new computers and is located within the Windows file folder.

Telnet can be used in one of two ways. One way is to have a Telnet account and run the software by itself with your computer connected to the Telnet system via telephone. The other, more common, way is to "piggy-back" the program on your Internet connection. Using this method, you would connect to the Internet and then start your Telnet program.

Once you've got Telnet up and running, enter the Telnet address (locis.loc.gov—the numeric address is 140.147.254.3). These addresses will not work if you type them into your Web browser. You must use a Telnet connection.

b. LOCIS Copyright Directories

LOCIS contains a series of copyright files. It is possible to search multiple files at one time, following the instructions in the Search Guide (see below). All copyright information is located in the following three directories:

- **COHM:** Contains information about works registered since January 1978. Included are published and unpublished text works, maps, motion pictures, music, sound recordings, works of the performing and visual arts, graphic artworks and games. Also included are renewals of previous registrations. You can search by author, claimant, title and registration number. COHM is updated weekly. Note: The renewal information available on LOCIS is available only for works published after 1949.
- **COHS:** contains information about serial publications (magazine or other periodic publications). COHS is updated twice yearly.
- **COHD:** The COHD File is a collection of legal records maintained by the Copyright Office since January 1, 1978. The file includes transfers of copyright, termination notices, statements that an author is still alive or that an author has died, documents identifying anonymous or pseudonymous authors, and statements identifying an erroneous name in a copyright notice. A typical document contains the names of the parties involved, the date of recordation and the date of execution, and the titles of the works involved. COHD is updated weekly.

c. Some Suggestions for LOCIS Searching

We warned you at the beginning of this section that the searching procedure used in LOCIS is not pretty. In fact, if you're not prepared to "tech it out," you should probably avoid this method of research. In order to search properly, here are some suggestions.

- *Can't connect?* Check with your Internet service provider. Don't contact the Copyright Office; it does not offer search assistance to users of LOCIS and does not offer assistance with software, hardware or other computer-related problems.

- *Obtain the "LOCIS Quick Search Guide."* The Library of Congress has prepared a 30-page step-by-step guide for the novice using the LOCIS file. It is essential reading if you want to avoid hassles using LOCIS. Advanced techniques are described, and pointers to help screens are also provided. The "Quick Search Guide" is available in three versions for downloading from ftp.loc.gov/pub/lc.online. (FTP is shorthand for file transfer protocol.) Printed copies of the "Quick Search Guide" are also available from the Library of Congress Cataloging Distribution Service, at 202-707-6100, or fax 202-707-1334.

- *Learn the Commands and Prompts.* LOCIS searching is built around a complex series of commands, prompts and abbreviations. For example, to display a record in full (not in abbreviated form) you must type "d full" along with the number of the record. If you run into problems and are unsure of how to proceed, type in HELP COMMAND for a list of commands or type HELP for general assistance.

The following abbreviations are especially important:

Copyright Registration Terms

AUTH (author)

DREG (date of registration)

CLNA (name of copyright claimant or owner)

DCRE (date of creation)

DPUB (date of publication)

OREG (original date of registration, or in the case of renewals, original registration number)

ODAT (original date of publication)

Copyright Registration Categories

TX (nondramatic text works)

SR (sound recordings)

RE (renewal of copyright)

VA (visual arts such as pictorial, graphic, sculptural)

PA (performing arts such as musical and dramatic works, motion pictures and other audiovisual works)

EXAMPLE: Below is an example of a renewal record for the book, *Franny and Zooey,* from the Copyright Office LOCIS/COHM file. The copyright owner is the author, J.D. Salinger. The date of first publication was August 23, 1961, and the copyright was renewed on October 10, 1989. The original registration number is A591015. Based upon this information we can conclude that this work is not in the public domain because the owner filed a timely renewal of copyright after 28 years. (For more information on renewal requirements, see Chapter 8).

RE-438-737
TITL: Franny and Zooey. By Jerome David Salinger.
CLNA: J. D. Salinger (A)
DREG: 10Oct89
ODAT: 23Aug61;
OREG: A591015.
LINM: NM: author's note.
XREF: acJ. D. Salinger. SEE Jerome David Salinger , 1919-.

4. Searching Library of Congress Records

In addition to Copyright Office records, there is another catalog of helpful information at the Library of Congress in Washington D.C. The Library of Congress is the largest library in the world and has been collecting and cataloging materials for over 200 years. However, contrary to popular belief, the Library of Congress does not contain copies of every work ever published in the United States.

This Library of Congress catalog includes data for books, serials, (magazines and periodicals) music and sound recordings, maps, visual materials such as photos and graphics, computer files from 1975 and an index of names and subjects. It also includes an incomplete, unedited listing of books cataloged between 1898 and 1975. Best of all, the Library of Congress catalog can be searched using a standard Internet browser. In other words, you do not need the Telnet program described above, (although if inclined, you can use Telnet to search LOC records as well). The catalog is located at lcWeb.loc.gov/.

Because of the ease of searching and because of the vast catalog of materials, we recommend using the Library of Congress LOC catalog for basic research such as locating the publisher or owner of a work and for researching public domain information.

Unlike Copyright Office files, the LOC catalog is searchable by subject matter. Or, you can search by the ISBN, ISSN or LCCN (Library of Congress catalog number). You can even limit or define your search by language. For example, you can search for books that are not in English. You may be able to use Library of Congress files to identify an author, title or publisher and then use that information to search the Copyright Office records. There are several methods of searching including the EZ Search Form that allows searching by title and author's name.

■

After Permission

Unfortunately, your problems don't necessarily end once you have tracked down a copyright owner and obtained permission to use his or her work. To avoid disputes that could result in lawsuits, you need to keep careful records and efficiently manage the permissions process. To help you, we have provided a tracking sheet to administer permissions. However, even a diligent publisher can still end up in a dispute with a copyright owner. Common disputes include unauthorized uses or failure to honor the terms of a permission agreement. We'll discuss those types of conflicts and suggest some means of minimizing your liability including the use of business insurance.

A. The Permission Tracking Sheet

The permissions process creates responsibilities. For example, if you fail to make a timely payment or to send a sample for approval, you can lose the right to reproduce the work. That's why if you are managing multiple permissions—for example, reproducing several photographs in a book—you will need to properly track all the details.

A tracking sheet that lists information such as ownership, the rights acquired and payment arrangements enables the user to keep a running total of fees paid and due, and to keep track of who must receive samples or complimentary copies. Since the tracking sheet is a modified spreadsheet, it can be prepared using a computer program such as Excel or Quattro Pro.

Below is a tracking sheet for managing the details of multiple permissions. An explanation for each section of the tracking sheet is also provided. This sheet is geared primarily towards copyright permissions, though it can be modified for use for trademark permissions as well.

A tear-out copy of the Permissions Tracking Sheet is included in the Appendix. A digital copy can be downloaded from the forms disk at the end of this book.

 The Permissions Tracking Sheet is on the forms disk under the file name PERMTRK.

Permissions Tracking Sheet

PTN	Type of Work, Title, Source and ID Numbers	Author	Owner, Contact Person, Address, Phone, Email	Payment	Payment Due Date	Date Paid and Form of Payment	Credit	Sample Approval or Comp Copies

1. PTN (Permission Tracking Number)

Create a number for each permission use, adopting a coding system that reflects the project name. For example, if preparing a text on how to prevent hand injuries, each permission could be consecutively titled as HAND1, HAND2, etc. The tracking numbers do not have to reflect the order in which the works are used or acquired; what's important is that each permission use has its own PTN.

2. Type of Work

Insert the type of work for which permission is acquired—for example, photograph, graphic work, text or trademark.

3. Title

Insert the title of the work—for example, the title of the article, novel, photograph or graphic image for which permission has been acquired. If there is no title or the title is not available, create a title that helps to identify the work—for example, "Boy with dog." If the work is a trademark, insert the name of the mark or a description.

4. Source

If you're using a work originally printed in another work—for example, a photograph within a book—insert the title of the source work. For works from serialized publications such as magazines or journals, insert the title and volume or issue number. If the work is from a website, insert the URL.

5. Identifying Numbers

Many works are identified by code numbers such as the ISBN, ISSN, LCCN or Dewey Decimal number catalog numbers for textual works. Sound record-

ings also have catalog numbers. If the copyright registration number or trademark registration number is available, list it here.

6. Author(s)

Insert the name of the author (the person who created the work). The author may not be the same as the copyright owner. If no author is listed—for example, you're using a newspaper article without a byline, or the author is "anonymous" or uses a pseudonym—include that information.

7. Owner and Contact Information

Insert all contact information for the copyright or trademark owner, including the right person to contact (such as a manager or agent, if the owner has one), address, phone number and email. As indicated in Chapter 15, the author of a copyrighted work is the original owner, but he or she may have transferred rights to a company or another individual.

8. Payments Due

If a payment is required, insert the terms of payment here—for example, "$50 per year"—and list when payment is due.

9. Payments Made

When payment is made, insert the date and the method of payment, such as check or credit card. If paid by check, include the check number.

10. Credit Required

If the copyright owner requires that a credit line be included, insert the type of credit here—for example, "Photograph copyright Prudence O'Neal."

11. Sample Approval/Complimentary Copies

In some cases, the owner has a right to approve samples prior to production or the owner is entitled to complimentary copies. If either samples or complimentary copies are required per your agreement, insert that information and insert the name of theperson who should receive the samples or copies.

12. Rights Acquired

List the rights that were acquired under the permission agreement. In general, your primary concerns are exclusivity, territory, language and term (or length of use). For example, the rights acquired might be stated as: "Non-exclusive English language rights for four years."

13. How the Work Is Used

Indicate where and how the work will be used in the work. For example, if you're creating a book, insert the page number in the book in which the work is used; if the work will be used in a website, insert the page or URL.

Permissions Calendar

If you're performing a lot of permission work, use a calendaring system to keep track of any renewals, payments or dates when samples must be furnished for approval. If possible, use a computer-based system that can provide timely reminders (known as a "tickler" system).

B. Good Permissions Gone Bad

Regardless of the degree of care exercised by the user, not all disputes can be prevented. Two categories of permission disputes often arise: contract disputes and intellectual property infringements. Quite often these types of claims overlap. For example, a use that exceeds the written permission agreement may end up as a contract dispute or a copyright dispute. Each type of claim has different remedies and may be brought in different courts. Below we'll discuss how to approach such disputes.

1. Cease and Desist Letters

The opening salvo in breach of contract or infringement situations is usually a letter from an attorney asking that the user "cease and desist" from any further uses. To minimize any potential damages, you should:

- respond immediately to the owner that you have received the letter and are investigating the claims
- investigate the claims and, if necessary, request further information from the copyright owner such as proof of ownership
- if possible, stop using or distributing the work (for example, remove the photo from a website or stop selling a book) until the claim has been fully investigated, and
- contact an attorney knowledgeable in copyright law. Information about finding and evaluating an attorney is provided in Chapter 16, "Help Beyond This Book."

Not all legal threats are valid. An attorney's opinion will assist in evaluating the claim. As part of the evaluation, seek an estimate of the legal expenses for fighting the dispute.

2. Contract Disputes

A contract dispute can arise if the terms of the permission agreement are broken (also termed "breached"). The two most common disputes that arise under a license agreement is that the use exceeds the permission grant or that a payment was not made.

- **The use exceeds the grant.** One basis for disputes is that the work is used in a manner that exceeds the rights granted under the agreement. A prudent approach to avoiding this type of dispute is to monitor the work in all stages of production and review the final product (that is, the book, website, movie, etc.) to make sure the use of the work is within the rights granted by the permissions agreement.

- **Payment was not made.** If payment is a condition of permission and the payment is not made, the agreement may be terminated by the copyright owner. A prudent approach to avoid this problem is to calendar any dates when payments are due and mark when the payment is made. (Note, many companies demand payment prior to production.)

The permission agreement may provide specific remedies for disputes—for example, arbitration or mediation. In cases of breach, the owner can sue for monetary damages and, if provided under the agreement, attorney fees. Breach of contract claims are usually brought in state courts, although these claims can also be brought in federal court—for instance, as part of a copyright infringement claim.

3. Intellectual Property Infringement

The owner of a work you're using such as a photograph or text can sue in federal court and seek monetary damages (and in some cases attorney fees) if you infringe on his or her copyright, trademark or publicity rights.

Infringement claims are typically brought because of unauthorized uses. If the use is not addressed at all in the license agreement (for example, the grant is for use of a photo in a book and you use it on T-shirts), the copyright owner will usually bring the lawsuit under copyright law (although it's possible to bring the claim under contract law in some cases). If the use simply exceeds the dimensions of the grant (for example, you are permitted to reproduce a photograph in a 5,000-print run of a book and you use it in 7,000 copies), a court will probably consider the claim to be a breach of the license (a contract claim as discussed in the previous section) rather than an infringement of copyright. The determinations in these cases—whether copyright law or contract law controls—varies depending upon the facts of the case and the judicial district in which the case is filed.

Sometimes a copyright infringement suit is filed because permission was obtained from the wrong person and the correct owner is now asserting his or her rights. For example, a magazine may claim to own a photograph but, after publication, the photographer enters the picture, claims ownership and sues for infringement. This type of dispute is difficult to predict and equally difficult to prevent. One approach to minimizing liability in this situation is to require that the person signing the permission agreement promise that he or she has authority to grant the permission, and if possible provide indemnity. Throughout this book, sample indemnity provisions are provided for many of the permission agreements.

Libel, Invasion of Privacy and Other Claims

Unauthorized uses of work may give rise to additional claims such as defamation or invasion of privacy. These claims are discussed in Chapter 12, "Releases." If confronted by a claim of libel or defamation, seek the advice of an attorney knowledgeable in media law.

C. Insurance

Insurance may shield a user from some potential damages. The protection will vary depending upon the insurance. Some general business insurance policies contain a provision entitled "advertising injuries" that protect against trademark, copyright or libel claims. The extent of protection depends upon the wording of the policy and the manner in which insurance policies are interpreted in the state. The model form language used by the insurance industry in defining advertising injuries has changed repeatedly over the past two decades as insurers seek ways to avoid paying for claims.

If you are threatened with a claim, immediately examine your business insurance for coverage. An attorney should be able to advise you as to whether the insurance company must assume coverage. Publishers and media companies sometimes acquire more comprehensive insurance known as "media perils" policies. Check with your insurance agent for more information.

It is quite common for insurance carriers to attempt to deny coverage to copyright owners. That means that if you assert a claim, the company will look for a way out. One of the most common methods an insurance company uses to avoid payment is to argue that the type of claim is not listed explicitly in the policy—for example, the policy does not cover claims from a certain time period or claims involving certain works.

In other situations, the carrier will seek to deny coverage if the insurance company is not promptly informed of the claim. For example, in 1994, the Andy Warhol estate was sued by Time-Life, Inc., and a photographer over Warhol's use of a photograph of Jacqueline Kennedy. The Warhol estate waited until 1996 to notify its insurance company and on the basis of this late reporting, the insurance company refused to provide coverage. The decision was later upheld by a federal court. (*The Andy Warhol Foundation for the Visual Arts Inc. v. Federal Insurance Co.*, 97 Civ. 2716 (TPG), 1998 U.S. Dist. LEXIS 8094, June 2, 1998 (S.D. N.Y., June 2, 1998).) Therefore, if a claim is made against your company, investigate coverage immediately and report the claim promptly to your carrier.

■

Assignments and Works Made for Hire

The rest of this book discusses the rules and process for getting permission from the owner of a work. This chapter, on the other hand, is not about getting permission—it's about acquiring ownership. Once you become the owner of a copyrighted work, you don't need permission from anyone to use it. Instead, others must obtain permission from you.

There are various situations when acquiring ownership may be your best option—for example, when you want an illustration for permanent use at your website. This chapter discusses the two methods of acquiring ownership: by assignment and by commissioning a work for hire.

An assignment is a permanent transfer of ownership, such as acquiring copyright ownership of a photograph from the photographer. A work-for-hire agreement is different because the person paying for the work is considered as the owner and author of the work. For example, the Disney Company employs animators who create a cartoon; the Disney Company is the author and owner of the cartoon. There are advantages and disadvantages to both approaches and we discuss them in this chapter. In addition we provide several model assignments and work-for-hire agreements that can be used with copyright owners, artists and musicians.

A. Copyright Assignments

When someone who owns a copyrighted work sells all rights in it to another party, the transaction is called an assignment. Unlike a license agreement in which the licensee obtains only a temporary, conditional right to use the work which is still owned by the licensor, in an assignment the buyer (assignee) purchases the copyright and the person selling the copyright (the assignor) retains no rights. There are some exceptions, and it is possible to acquire an assignment of a part interest in a copyright, for example, from a co-owner of copyright. In that case, only a part ownership is purchased and the purchaser becomes a co-owner. However, in this chapter we are only concerned with acquiring full ownership of the copyrighted work.

Depending on the terms of the assignment, the assignor may be paid by the assignee with a lump sum or periodic royalty payments. In addition, an assignment may provide a method whereby the rights are assigned back to the assignor in the event of a certain condition—for example, if the assignee stops selling the work.

An assignment is a transfer of ownership, but it may not last for the full term of copyright protection. This is because copyright law permits creators of work transferred after 1977 to recapture all the copyrights that were assigned 35 years from the date of the assignment. (Terminations of transfers for works transferred in or before 1977 are subject to fairly complex rules that are beyond the scope of this book. See *The Copyright Handbook* by attorney Stephen Fishman for more information.) For example, an author that assigned rights to a book publisher in 2000 can reclaim the rights in 2035. This recapture right is usually not important, because few works have a useful economic life of more than 35 years. This recapture right does not apply to the creator of a work made for hire, as discussed below.

An assignment can be used when acquiring a work that already exists or an artist can agree to assign a work that will be created. An assignment must be in writing. Notarization is not required but is recommended, especially if the assignee is concerned about the assignment's validity. Notarization creates a legal presumption that the transfer is valid. If there are multiple owners of a copyright, the signature of all owners must be obtained for the assignment.

Assignments may be recorded (made a pubic record) by being filed with the Copyright Office. There is no legal requirement that an assignment be recorded, but recordation provides public notice of the transfer. For information regarding recording assignments, call the Copyright Office's Public Information Office at 202-679-0700, or the Certification and Documents office at 202-707-6850. The assignment and fee should be mailed to Documents Unit LM-462, Cataloging Office, Library of Congress, Washington, DC 20559.

1. Basic Copyright Assignment

The agreement below is a basic copyright assignment that can be used for any type of work. More specific assignments for musicians and artists are included in Sections A3 and A5.

 The Basic Copyright Assignment is on the forms disk under the file name ASSGNAGR.

Basic Copyright Assignment

I, _____ ("Assignor"), am owner of the work entitled _____ (the "Work") and described as follows: _____

_____ .

In consideration of $ _____ and other valuable consideration, paid by _____ ("Assignee"), I assign to Assignee and Assignee's heirs and assigns, all my right title and interest in the copyright to the Work and all renewals and extensions of the copyright that may be secured under the laws of the United States of America and any other countries, as such may now or later be in effect. I agree to cooperate with Assignee and to execute and deliver all papers as may be necessary to vest all rights to the Work.

Signature of assignor(s)_____

2. Explanation for Basic Copyright Assignment

- In the first two blanks of the first paragraph, insert the assignor's name (usually the author) and the title of the work. In the next blank space, either describe the work or enter "See attached Exhibit A" and attach a copy of the work to the assignment. If you attach a copy, be sure to label it "Exhibit A."

- In the next paragraph, insert the amount of the payment and the name of the assignee.
- The assignor must sign the agreement. To have the agreement notarized, the assignor should wait to sign the agreement until in the presence of a notary, who will fill out the rest of the notary section.

Notarization

We recommend notarization for copyright assignments. The purpose of notarization is to provide verification of the signature and identity of the person executing the agreement. You can usually locate a notary public through your local Yellow Pages. To include notarization, add the following statement at the end of the agreement.

On this___day of_____ , year___ , before me,_____ , the undersigned Notary Public, personally appeared_____ and proved to me based on satisfactory evidence to be the person(s) who executed this instrument.

Witness my hand and official seal.

_____

Notary Public

Sometimes this section does not have to be added, as the notary may have a stamp that includes all such information. Wait to have the assignor sign the agreement until in the presence of the notary.

- If there is more than one assignor, or if the assignor is married in a community property state, signing the agreement may involve a few more issues.

Multiple Assignors: If there are multiple copyright owners you will need the signature of all owners for your assignment. There are many ways that a copyright can have co-owners. For example, the work may have been created by joint authors or it may have been bequeathed under a will to several children who became co-owners. If you are unsure whether there are multiple co-owners, you can research this using the techniques in Chapter 13.

Spousal Consent in Community Property States: A community property state is one in which any property acquired by either spouse during marriage (other than by gift or inheritance), belongs to the husband and wife equally. Copyrights may be co-owned by a spouse in community property states, though the court cases on the subject are conflicting. One court has held that a spouse in a community property state has a co-ownership interest in the other spouse's copyrighted work. (*In Re Marriage of Worth*, 195 Cal.App.3d 768, 241 Cal. Rptr. 185 (1987).) Another court held that a spouse in a community property state did not acquire co-ownership rights. (*Rodrigue v. Rodrigue*, 50 U.S.P.Q.2D 1278 (E.D. La. 1999).) Since the courts aren't in total agreement on the issue, it may be the safest route for an assignor who lives in a community property state to obtain his or her spouse's consent to any assignment. The provision below can be added to the assignment and should be notarized.

Spousal Consent Provision

I am the spouse of Assignor and acknowledge that I have read and understand this Agreement. I am aware that my spouse agrees to assign all interest in the Work, including any community property interest or other equitable property interest that I may have in it. I consent to the assignment, and agree that my interest, if any, in the Work is subject to the provisions of this Agreement. I will take no action to hinder the Agreement or the underlying assignment of rights.

[Spouse signature] _____

3. Musician Assignment Agreement

If you are hiring a musician to record a composition—for instance, you hire a guitarist to record musical phrases for a video game—you may want to use a more detailed assignment agreement. We offer one below. The assignment is for the musician's recorded performance; not for the song. As explained in Chapter 5, there are two separate music copyrights: one in the musical composition or song (musical work) and another in the way in which the song is recorded (sound recording). If the musician has composed the song, you would use the assignment above, in Section 1, to transfer the rights to the composition itself.

 The Musician Assignment Agreement is on the forms disk under the file name MUSCASGN.

Musician Assignment Agreement

This Musician Assignment Agreement (the "Agreement") is made between _____
("Company"), and _____ ("Musician").

Grant

Musician has performed or recorded performance(s) for the Company in conjunction with the
Company recording under the titles:

_____

_____

_____

   In consideration of the payments provided in this Agreement, Musician assigns all rights,
including all rights under copyright law, in the recorded performance to the Company, its assigns,
licensees or successors and grants the right to use the recorded performance for any purposes and in
all forms and media and waives any claim to moral rights.

Payment

Company shall pay Musician as follows: $ _____ .

Warranty & Release

Musician has the authority to grant the rights under this Agreement and Musician releases Company
and Company's assigns, licensees and successors from any claims that may arise regarding the use of
the performance including any claims of infringement of moral rights, rights of publicity or copyright.
Company is permitted, although not obligated, to include musician's name as a credit in connection
with the performance.

   Company is not obligated to utilize any of the rights granted in this Agreement.

   Musician has read and understood this agreement and is over the age of 18. This Agreement
expresses the complete understanding of the parties.

Musician Signature: _____

Musician Name: _____

Musician's Address: _____

Date: _____

4. Explanation for Musician Assignment Agreement

- Since the musician is assigning all rights in the performance, the Grant section is as broad as possible and the musician will not retain any rights to the recorded performance.
- The Warranty and Release section is an assurance that the musician owns the rights being granted. For example, some musicians are signed to exclusive recording agreements and a record company owns all of their performances, or the musician may be prohibited from recording altogether. The warranty also provides a promise not to sue the company for legal claims such as copyright infringement. The warranty section also includes additional statements that "Company is permitted, although not obligated, to include musician's name as a credit in connection with the performance" and "Company is not obligated to utilize any of the rights granted in this Agreement." These provisions give the company the ability to ditch the performance, if necessary, and to avoid liability in the event the musician is not credited.
- It is unusual that the musician would be a minor, but in that event, the musician's parent or guardian should sign a consent similar to the parent/guardian consent in the model release in Chapter 12, "Releases."

Arbitration and Mediation

An arbitration and/or mediation clause provides alternate methods of resolving any disputes that may arise, rather than filing a lawsuit. Although we have not included one in the artist or musician assignments, you may, if you wish, include the following provision in either agreement. (For a more detailed explanation of arbitration and mediation review Chapter 11, dealing with merchandise licenses.)

Mediation; Arbitration. If a dispute arises under this Agreement, the parties agree to first try to resolve the dispute with the help of a mutually agreed upon mediator in the state of _____ . Any costs and fees other than attorney fees shall be shared equally by the parties. If it proves impossible to arrive at a mutually satisfactory solution, the parties agree to submit the dispute to binding arbitration in the same city or region, conducted on a confidential basis pursuant to the Commercial Arbitration Rules of the American Arbitration Association.

5. Artwork Assignment Agreement

The artwork assignment provides for assignment of artwork, but can be modified for photography as well. The assignment includes optional provisions for payment of expenses and for dispute resolution.

 The Artwork Assignment Agreement is on the forms disk under the file name ARTASSGN.

Artwork Assignment Agreement

This Artwork Assignment Agreement (the "Agreement") is made between _____ ("Company"), and _____ ("Artist").

Services

Artist agrees to perform the following services: _____
and create the following artwork (the "Art") entitled: _____.

The Art shall be completed by the following date: _____.

During the process, Artist shall keep the Company informed of work in progress and shall furnish test prints of the Art prior to completion.

Payment

Company agrees to pay Artist as follows:

$ _____ for performance of the art services and acquisition of the rights provided below.

Rights

Artist assigns to the Company all copyright to the Art and agrees to cooperate in the preparation of any documents necessary to demonstrate this assignment of rights. Artist retains the right to display the work as part of artist's portfolio and to reproduce the artwork in connection with the promotion of artist's services.

Expenses

Company agrees to reimburse Artist for all reasonable production expenses including halftones, stats, photography, disks, illustrations or related costs. These expenses shall be itemized on invoices and in no event shall any expense exceed $50 without approval from the Company.

Credit

Credit for Artist shall be included on reproductions of the Art as follows: _____

Artist Warranties

Artist is the owner of all rights to the Art and warrants that the Art does not infringe any intellectual property rights or violate any laws.

Artwork Assignment Agreement (cont.)

Artist Signature: _____

Artist Name: _____

Artist Address: _____

Date: _____

Company Authorized Signature: _____

Name and Title: _____

Address: _____

Date: _____

---

6. Explanation for Artwork Assignment Agreement

- Since the artist is assigning all rights in the performance, the grant section is as broad as possible and the artist will not retain any rights to the artwork.
- The services section should be used if the artist has been hired to perform a specific job. If the artwork has already been completed and this provision is not needed, strike it or enter "NA" for "not applicable."
- The warranty is an assurance that the artist owns the rights being granted and a promise not to sue the company for legal claims such as copyright infringement. If you wish, you may include an arbitration or mediation section (see Sidebar in Section A4).
- It is unusual that the artist would be a minor, but in that event, the artist's parent or guardian should sign a consent similar to the parent/guardian consent in the model release in Chapter 12, "Releases."

B. Works Made for Hire

Sometimes for copyright purposes the author of a work is the person who pays for it, not the person who creates it. The resulting work is called a work made for hire, or often simply a "work for hire." The basis for this principle is that a business that authorizes and pays for a work should own the rights to the work.

There are two distinct types of work that may be classified as "made for hire":

- a work created by an employee within the scope of employment, or
- a commissioned work created by an independent contractor (non-employee) that is the subject of a written work-for-hire agreement and that falls within a special group of categories.

Below, we discuss these work-for-hire rules for employees and independent contractors in more detail. First, we'll explain some general rules regarding copyright ownership and duration for works-for-hire.

1. Significance of Work-for-Hire Status

If a work qualifies as a work made for hire under one of the two methods described above, the person paying for the work (the hiring party) is both the author and copyright owner. As such, the hiring party must be named as the author on an application for copyright registration.

The work-for-hire status of a work also affects the length of copyright protection and termination rights.

a. Copyright Duration

Works made for hire created after 1977 are protected for a period of 95 years from first publication or 120 years from creation, whichever is shorter. Therefore if a website company created a work made for hire in 2000 but did not publish it until 2001, copyright protection would extend to 2096 (95 years from the date of publication).

b. No Termination Rights

As discussed above, someone who assigns their copyright to someone else may be able to recapture their copyright after 35 years. However, a work made for hire cannot be terminated later by the creator. This means that the owner of a work made for hire is assured that he or she will retain ownership for the full copyright term.

2. Works Created by Employees

Every copyrightable work created by an employee within the scope of employment is automatically a work made for hire. There are no other requirements, no review of the special categories (outlined in Section 3b below) and no need for a written agreement. It is for this reason that when sorting out ownership issues courts first analyze whether an employer-employee relationship exists.

 For more information on the law regarding independent contractors, see *Hiring Independent Contractors: The Employer's Legal Guide,* by Stephen Fishman (Nolo).

Whether an employment relationship exists is determined by weighing the following factors:

- **The hiring party's right to control the manner and means by which the work is accomplished.** If the hiring party exercises control, this factor weighs in favor of an employment relationship.
- **The skill required in the particular occupation.** If the work to be performed requires a unique skill—for example, sculpting—this factor weighs against an employment relationship.
- **Whether the employer or the worker supplies the instrumentalities and tools of the trade.** If the worker supplies his own tools, this factor weighs against an employment relationship.
- **Where the work is done.** If the hiring party determines the location of the work, this factor weighs in favor of an employment relationship.
- **The length of time for which the worker is employed.** The longer the period of work, the more this factor weighs in favor of an employment relationship.
- **Whether the hiring party has the right to assign additional work projects to the worker.** If the hiring party can assign additional tasks—including tasks that do not result in copyrightable works—this factor weighs in favor of an employment relationship.
- **The extent of the worker's discretion over when and how long to work.** If the hiring party controls the working times—particularly if it is a regular work week—this factor weighs in favor of an employment relationship.
- **The method of payment.** If the payment is per job—not per day or week—this factor weighs against an employment relationship.

- **The hired party's role in hiring and paying assistants.** If the worker cannot hire and pay assistants, this factor weighs in favor of an employment relationship.
- **Whether the work is part of the regular business of the hiring party.** If the hiring party does not regularly perform this type of work—for example, creating photography—this factor weighs against an employment relationship.
- **Whether the worker is in business.** If the worker has a business, this factor weighs against an employment relationship.
- **The provision of employee benefits.** If vacation or health benefits are granted to the worker, this factor weighs in favor of an employment relationship.
- **The tax treatment of the hired party.** If the hiring party pays payroll and employment taxes, this factor weighs strongly in favor of an employment relationship. *This factor is virtually determinative by itself.*

3. Works Created by Independent Contractors

A work created by an independent contractor (unlike a work created by an employee) is not automatically classified as a work made for hire. For an independent contractor's work to qualify as a work made for hire, three requirements must be met:

- the work must be specially ordered or commissioned—for example, the hiring party must request the work; it cannot already be in existence
- the work must fall within a group of specially enumerated categories (outlined below), and
- a written agreement must be signed by both parties indicating it is a work made for hire.

a. Ordering the Work and Executing an Agreement

A work-for-hire agreement with an independent contractor should be signed before the work commences. However, at least one court has held that the agreement can be executed after the work is completed, provided that at the time the work was created, the parties intended to enter into such an agreement. In that case, a magazine paid an artist by check and on the back of each check was a statement that indicated the drawings were works made for hire. A court of appeals ruled that the artist's continued signature on the checks over a seven-year period demonstrated that he was aware of and accepted the arrangement. (*Playboy Enterprises, Inc. v. Dumas*, 53 F.3d 549 (2d Cir. 1995).)

b. Work-for-Hire Categories

An independent contractor's work will be a work for hire only if it falls within one the following categories:

- a contribution to a collective work—for example, writing a short story for a collection or creating an introduction to an anthology
- a part of a motion picture or other audiovisual work
- a translation
- a supplementary work (that is, a work prepared for publication as a supplement to a work by another author for the purpose of introducing, concluding, illustrating, explaining, revising, commenting upon or assisting in the use of the other work, such as forewords, afterwords, pictorial illustrations, maps, charts, tables, editorial notes, musical arrangements, answer material for tests, bibliographies, appendices and indexes)
- a compilation such as a collection of statistics on stock car racing
- an instructional text (a literary, pictorial or graphic work prepared for use in day-to-day instructional activities—for example, a text-

book would be an instructional text, but a novel used in a literature class would not)

- a test or answer material for a test, or
- an atlas.

Any work created by an independent contractor that does not fall within one of the above categories cannot be a work made for hire. This is so even if the parties have signed a written agreement stating that the work is a work made for hire.

EXAMPLE: A painter is commissioned to create a mural for a school. The painter signs an agreement entitled "Work Made for Hire." The painter (not the school) owns the painting because paintings are not included among the enumerated categories of works by independent contractors that can be works made for hire.

4. Work-for-Hire Agreement

Below is a simple work-for-hire agreement. Remember—it is always necessary to use this agreement with an independent contractor. Strictly speaking, it is not necessary to use this agreement when a work is to be created by an employee. The employer automatically owns an employee's work created within the course of employment regardless of whether there is a written agreement. However, employers often prefer to use written agreements to make it clear to employees that the employer owns copyright.

This agreement can be used for other workers besides artists. Simply revise the appropriate sections to describe the worker and the work made for hire.

 A copy of the Work-for-Hire Agreement is on the forms disk under the file name WFHAGR.

Work-Made-for-Hire Agreement

This Work-Made-for-Hire Agreement (the "Agreement") is made between _____ ("Company"), and _____ ("Artist").

Services

In consideration of the payments provided in this Agreement, Artist agrees to perform the following services: _____

Payment

Company agrees to pay Artist as follows: _____ .

Works Made for Hire—Assignment of Intellectual Property Rights

Artist agrees that, for consideration that is acknowledged, any works of authorship commissioned pursuant to this Agreement (the "Works") shall be considered works made for hire as that term is defined under U.S. copyright law. To the extent that any such Work created for Company by Artist is not a work made for hire belonging to Company, Artist hereby assigns and transfers to Company all rights Artist has or may acquire to all such Works. Artist agrees to sign and deliver to Company, either during or subsequent to the term of this Agreement, such other documents as Company considers desirable to evidence the assignment of copyright.

Artist Warranties

Artist warrants that the Work does not infringe any intellectual property rights or violate any laws and that the work is original to Artist.

Miscellaneous

This Agreement constitutes the entire understanding between the parties and can only be modified by written agreement. The laws of the State of _____ shall govern this Agreement. In the event of any dispute arising under this agreement, the prevailing party shall be entitled to its reasonable attorney fees.

Artist Signature: _____   Company Authorized Signature: _____

Artist Name: _____   Name and Title: _____

Artist Address: _____   Address: _____

Date: _____   Date: _____

5. Explanation for Work-Made-for-Hire Agreement

- In the Services section, insert the work that the artist is supposed to perform, for example: "Create a series of photographs for a KeepClean toothbrush advertisement." Insert the amount to be paid to artist in the payment section.

- The section titled "Works Made for Hire— Assignment of Intellectual Property Rights" establishes that the work is made for hire. However, if the work does not meet the requirements of copyright law, a back-up provision is added that converts the arrangement to an assignment. This type of provision is commonly used by businesses seeking to make sure that ownership rights have been acquired.

- The Warranty provision provides an assurance that the artist owns the work and that the work is not an infringement. This is necessary to provide an assurance that the work is not taken from another source.

- This agreement includes some miscellaneous provisions. One provision provides that this is the entire agreement and therefore negates any previous oral or written agreements. In addition, any changes to the agreement must be in writing. Insert the home state of the hiring party in the blank space. This simply means that state's law will govern the interpretation of the agreement in the event of a dispute. The attorney provision provides that the winning party in any lawsuit will get attorney fees paid by the loser. For a more detailed explanation of these provisions, read Chapter 11, "Art & Merchandise Agreements."

■

Help Beyond This Book

Using the information in this book, you should be able to handle most permission situations yourself. However, it's possible that you could find yourself needing additional legal information or professional advice from an attorney. For example, if you used material based upon a fair use determination and later the copyright owner enters the picture claiming otherwise, you might well want to consult an attorney for advice.

The resources provided in this chapter focus primarily on the three areas of law discussed in this book: copyright, trademarks and the right of publicity. We have included many websites that provide current news on these changing areas of law as well as links to statutes, cases and articles.

By educating yourself with this book and the other resources listed in this chapter, you'll be able to work with attorneys more efficiently, keep your costs down, and be in a better position to evaluate the attorney's services.

Updates and Contacting the Author

Because some of the information in this book may change—website addresses, for example—I have established a site for current update information at members.aol.com/rwstim/permissions/update.htm. Also, you can contact me at rich@nolo.com.

A. Resources for More Detailed Permissions Research

The primary areas of law discussed in this book (copyrights, trademarks and the right of publicity) are part of a body of law known as intellectual property. Most of the resources in this section deal with researching intellectual property law.

1. Copyright Information

- The Copyright Office can provide a broad range of information including circulars, kits and other publications related to permission issues. Contact the Copyright Office at the Library of Congress, Washington, DC 20559-6000, or visit its website at lcWeb.loc.gov/copyright. In addition, the following phone numbers will connect you with various information services the Copyright Office offers.

   Forms Hotline: 202-707-9100 (24 hours), 202-707-3000 (9 a.m. to 5 p.m.).

   Fax on Demand: 202-707-2600.

   Publications Sections: LM-455, Copyright Office, Library of Congress, Washington DC 20559.

   Licensing Division Section, LM-458, Copyright Office, Library of Congress, Washington, DC 20559; 202-707-8150.

- The Cornell University law school site (www.law.cornell.edu/topics/copyright.html) provides text of copyright statutes and related cases and also provides trademark and right of publicity statutes and cases.
- Stanford University has an excellent resource site devoted to fair use issues at fairuse.stanford.edu.

2. Trademark Information

- The U.S. Trademark Office is a division of the Patent and Trademark Office. Its Web address is www.uspto.gov. The PTO site includes relevant applications and trademark office forms. You can write to the Assistant Commissioner for Trademarks, 2900 Crystal Drive, Arlington VA 22202-3515.

- The Trade Secrets Home Page at www.execpc.com/~mhallign/ explores trade secret statutes and related information.
- Other helpful trademark Web sites are: ARI Trademark Research Information (www.warrior.com/tmsearch), Master McNeil's Trademark Links (www.naming.com/trademark2.html), and the largest trademark searching company, Thomson & Thomson (www.thomson-thomson.com).

3. General Intellectual Property Resources

- Yahoo! provides a thorough directory of intellectual property resources on the Internet at www.yahoo.com/Government/Law/Intellectual_Property/.
- The Intellectual Property Center (www.ipcenter.com) provides current intellectual property news and cases.
- The Intellectual Property Mall (www.ipmall.fplc.edu) provides helpful copyright and trademark links.
- If you would like to better understand the principles of intellectual property, Nolo.com (www.nolo.com), the publisher of this book, also publishes several titles on intellectual property, including:

  The Copyright Handbook, by attorney Stephen Fishman.

  Copyright Your Software, by attorney Stephen Fishman.

  Patent, Copyright and Trademark: A Desk Reference to Intellectual Property Law, by attorney Stephen Elias.

  Software Development, A Legal Guide, by attorney Stephen Fishman.

Trademark: Legal Care for Your Business & Product Name, by attorneys Kate McGrath and Stephen Elias.

4. Online Issues

- The American Association of Domain Name Holders maintains a site at www.domains.org with current issues about domain name and related website disputes.
- Website issues are also covered at the Cyberights site at www.cyberights.com.

B. Conducting Legal Research

Throughout this book we have referenced legal cases and laws. You may want to read these cases and laws or pursue more detailed research on your own. For example, you may want to learn more about defamation law within your state. Finding out more on a specific legal question generally involves reading legal books and finding applicable law and cases.

Conducting legal research is not as difficult as it may seem. Nolo.com publishes a basic legal research guide, *Legal Research: How to Find and Understand the Law,* written by attorneys Stephen Elias and Susan Levinkind. It walks you through the various sources of law, explains how they fit together and shows you how to use them to answer your legal question.

While there are good online sources for legal research (see "Nolo's Legal Encyclopedia" below), for detailed legal research you may have to visit a local law library. If there's a public law school in your area, it probably has a law library that's open to the public. Other public law libraries are often run by local bar associations or as an adjunct to the local courts. Law libraries associated with private law schools often allow only limited public access. Call to speak with the law librarian to determine your right to access. You can always call your local bar association to find out what public law libraries are in your area.

Nolo's Legal Encyclopedia

Nolo.com's website at www.nolo.com also offers an extensive Legal Encyclopedia which includes a section on intellectual property. This is a good place to start for online legal research. You'll find answers to frequently asked questions about patents, copyrights, trademarks and other related topics, as well as sample chapters of Nolo books and a wide range of articles. Simply click on "Legal Encyclopedia" and then on "Patents, Copyright & Trademark."

C. Working With an Attorney

A number of permission situations may lead you to seek an attorney's advice. Attorneys have various specialties, and you will need to select a lawyer who is qualified to provide the advice you need.

Generally, an attorney knowledgeable in intellectual property law can answer most permission questions. Intellectual property attorneys are familiar with copyrights, trademarks, right of publicity and to some extent with media disputes based on defamation and the right of privacy. Don't make the mistake of hiring a lawyer whom you trust but who works in a different field—such as the lawyer who masterfully handled your friend's house purchase.

It's also a good idea to try to find an attorney that has expertise in the particular type of intellectual property that applies to your permission situation. Some intellectual property attorneys specialize in one type of intellectual property, either copyrights, trademarks or patents. If, for example, you are concerned about a potential trademark dispute, you should seek an intellectual property attorney who specializes in trademarks.

In addition to all these specialties, some intellectual property lawyers focus on litigation. Not all intellectual property attorneys are litigators. If you have a license dispute and want to sue someone (or someone has threatened to sue you) you will need an intellectual property attorney who is an experienced litigator. Litigators usually bill on an hourly basis, though sometimes for plaintiffs they may take a case on contingency. Under this arrangement, if you win, the attorney receives a percentage, usually one-third to one-half, of any money recovered in the lawsuit. If you lose, the attorney receives nothing—except for out-of-pocket expenses, which can easily run into the thousands even for relatively simple cases. Read the below information on fees carefully.

The American Intellectual Property Law Association (AIPLA) may be able to assist you in locating attorneys in your area. Contact it at 2001 Jefferson Davis Highway, Suite 203, Arlington VA 22202, 703-415-0780. The Intellectual Property Law Association of the American Bar Association also has a listing of intellectual property attorneys. You can reach it at 312-988-5000.

Defamation and Invasion of Privacy

If your dispute is based on defamation or invasion of privacy, you may need a media law specialist. In this case, the attorney may not be an intellectual property expert but is knowledgeable in disputes regarding libel, slander and other personal claims known as torts, especially as they relate to media industries such as publishing and music. If you are locating an attorney through a bar association referral service, ask for a media law attorney.

1. Finding an Attorney

The best way to locate an attorney is by referrals through friends or others in your field. It is also possible to locate an attorney through a state, county or city bar association. Check your local Yellow Pages and ask the bar association if they have a lawyer referral service. When interviewing an attorney, ask questions about clientele, work performed, rates and experience. If you speak with one of the attorney's clients (for example, another website owner), ask questions about the attorney's response time, billing practices and temperament.

2. How to Keep Your Fees Down

Most attorneys bill on an hourly basis ($150 to $300 an hour) and send a bill at the end of each month. Some attorneys bill on a fixed fee basis where you pay a set fee for certain services—for example, $5,000 for a license negotiation.

Here are some tips to reduce the size of your bills.

a. Get a Fee Agreement

It's crucial that you get a written fee agreement when dealing with an attorney. The fee agreement is a negotiated arrangement establishing fixed fees for certain work rather than hourly billings. Read it and understand your rights as a client. Make sure that your fee agreement includes provisions that require an itemized statement along with the bill detailing the work done and time spent, and that allow you to drop the attorney at any time. If you can't get fixed billings, ask your attorney to estimate fees for work and ask for an explanation if the bill exceeds the estimates.

b. Keep It Short

If your attorney is being paid on an hourly basis, then keep your conversations short (the meter is always running) and avoid making several calls a day. Consolidate your questions so that you can ask them all in one conversation.

Mad at Your Lawyer?

In many states, such as California, a client always has the right to terminate the attorney—although this does not terminate the obligation to pay the attorney. If you don't respect and trust your attorney's professional abilities you should switch and find a new attorney. Beware, though, switching attorneys is a nuisance and you may lose time and money. For more information on how to handle a dispute with your lawyer, see Nolo's book *Mad at Your Lawyer*, by attorney Tanya Starnes.

c. Review Billings Carefully

Your legal bill should be prompt and clear. Do not accept summary billings such as the single phrase "litigation work" used to explain a block of time for which you are billed a great deal of money. Every item should be explained with the rate and hours billed. Late billings are not acceptable, especially in litigation. When you get bills you don't understand, ask the attorney for an explanation—and ask the attorney not to bill you for the explanation.

d. Be Careful If You Engage a Law Firm

If you sign a fee agreement with a law firm (rather than a single attorney), be careful to avoid a particular billing problem sometimes referred to as multiple or "bounced" billings. This occurs when several attorneys perform the same work. For example, two attorneys at the firm have a 15-minute discussion about your case. Both attorneys bill you. To avoid this, make sure that your fee agreement does not bind you to this type of arrangement. If you are billed for these conferences, send a letter to your attorney at the firm explaining that you only want that attorney to work on your case and that you should be contacted before work is assigned to another attorney at the firm.

e. Watch Out for Hidden Expenses

Find out what expenses you must cover. This is especially important if you're hiring a lawyer on contingency, since you must often pay the lawyer's costs even if you lose the case, which can come as a nasty surprise. Watch out if your attorney wants to bill for services such as word processing or administrative services. This means you will be paying the secretary's salary. Also beware of fax and copying charges. Some firms charge clients per page for incoming and outgoing faxes. Other firms charge a per page copy fee which surpasses any commercial copy center. Look out for these hidden expenses in your fee agreement.

What Is a Retainer?

A retainer is an advance payment to an attorney. The attorney places the retainer in a bank account (in some states, this must be an interest-bearing account) and the attorney deducts money from the retainer at the end of each month to pay your bill. When the retainer is depleted, the attorney may ask for a new retainer. If the retainer is not used up at the end of the services, the attorney must return what's left. The amount of the retainer usually depends on the project. Retainers for litigation, for instance, are often between $2,000 and $5,000.

---

f. Don't Take Litigation Lightly

As a general rule, beware of litigation! If you are involved in a lawsuit, it may take months or years to resolve. Some go on for decades. It often costs $10,000 or more and the only ones who profit are usually the lawyers. If you're in a dispute, ask your attorney about dispute resolution methods such as arbitration and mediation. Often these procedures can save money and they're faster than litigation.

If those methods don't work or aren't available, ask your attorney for an assessment of your odds and the potential costs before filing a lawsuit. The assessment and underlying reasoning should be in plain English. If a lawyer can't explain your situation clearly to you, he probably won't be able to explain it clearly to a judge or jury.

■

How to Use the Forms Disk

Most of the sample forms in this appendix are included on a 3½" floppy disk in the back of the book.

This forms disk is formatted for the PC (MS-DOS), and can be used by any PC running Windows or DOS. If you use a Mac, you must have a Super Disk drive and PC Exchange, or a similar utility, to use this disk. These files can be opened, filled in and printed out with your word processing program or text editor.

⚠ **The disk does not contain software and you do not need to install any files.** The forms disk contains only files that can be opened and edited using a word processor. This is not a software program. See below and the README.TXT file included on the disk for additional instructions on how to use these files.

How to View the README File

If you do not know how to view the file README.TXT, insert the forms disk into your computer's floppy disk drive and follow these instructions:

- Windows 95: (1) On your PC's desktop, double-click the My Computer icon; (2) double-click the icon for the floppy disk drive into which the forms disk was inserted; (3) double-click the file README.TXT.
- Windows 3.1: (1) Open File Manager; (2) double-click the icon for the floppy disk drive into which the forms disk was inserted; (3) double-click the file README.TXT.
- Macintosh: (1) On your Mac desktop, double-click the icon for the floppy disk that you inserted; (2) double-click on the file README.TXT.
- DOS: At the DOS prompt, type EDIT A:README.TXT and press the Enter key.

While the README file is open, print it out by using the Print command in the File menu.

A. Copying the Disk Files Onto Your Computer

Before you do anything else, copy the files from the forms disk onto your hard disk. Then work on these copies only. This way the original files and instructions will be untouched and can be used again. Instructions on how to copy files are provided below. In accordance with U.S. copyright laws, remember that copies of the disk and its files are for your personal use only.

Insert the forms disk and follow one of the following sets of instructions, depending on which system you are using.

1. Windows 95 Users

(These instructions assume that the A: drive is the source you want to copy from and that the C: drive is the location you want to copy the files to.)

Step 1. Double-click the My Computer icon to open the My Computer window.

Step 2. Double-click the A: drive icon in the My Computer window to open the drive window.

Step 3. First, choose Select All from the Edit menu (Ctrl+A). Then choose Copy from the Edit menu (Ctrl+C). Then close the drive window.

Step 4. Double-click the My Computer icon to open the My Computer window.

Step 5. Double-click the C: drive icon in the My Computer window to open the drive window.

Step 6. Choose New... from the File menu, then choose Folder to create a new, untitled folder on the C drive.

Step 7. Type "Licensing Forms" to rename the untitled folder.

Step 8. Double-click on the "Licensing Forms" folder icon to open that folder.

Step 9. Choose Paste from the Edit menu (Ctrl+V).

2. Windows 3.1 Users

(These instructions assume that the A: drive is the source you want to copy from and that the C: drive is the location you want to copy the files to.)

Step 1. Open File Manager.

Step 2. Double-click the A: drive icon at the top of the File Manager window.

Step 3. Choose Select Files... from the File menu to open the Select Files dialog box.

Step 4. First, click the Select button to select all the files on the floppy disk. Then click the Close button to close the Select Files dialog box.

Step 5. Choose Copy... from the File menu to open the Copy dialog box.

Step 6. In the TO box, type C:\LICENSE and click OK. Click OK again when you're asked if you want to copy the selected files to the C:\LICENSE directory.

3. Macintosh Users

Step 1. If the LICENSE folder is open, close it.

Step 2. Click on the LICENSE disk icon and drag it onto the icon of your hard disk.

Step 3. Read the message to make sure you want to go ahead, then click OK.

4. DOS Users

(These instructions assume that the A: drive is the source you want to copy from and that the C: drive is the location you want to copy the files to.)

Step 1. To create a directory named "LICENSE" on your C: hard disk drive, type the following at the DOS prompt:

C: <ENTER>
CD\ <ENTER>
MD LICENSE <ENTER>

Step 2. To change to the LICENSE directory you just created, type:

CD LICENSE <ENTER>

Step 3. To copy all the files from the floppy disk (in your A: drive) to the current directory, at the C:\LICENSE> prompt, type:

XCOPY A:*.* /s <ENTER>

All of the files in all directories on the floppy disk will be copied to the LICENSE directory on your C: drive.

B. Creating Your Documents With the Forms Disk Files

This disk contains all forms in two file types (or formats):

- the standard ASCII text format (TXT), and
- rich text format (RTF).

For example, the form for the Artwork Permission Agreement discussed in Chapter 4 is on the files ARTPERM.RTF and ARTPERM.TXT.

ASCII text files can be read by every word processor or text editor including DOS Edit, all flavors of MS Word and WordPerfect (including Macintosh), Windows Notepad, Write and WordPad, and Macintosh SimpleText and TeachText.

RTF files have the same text as the ASCII files, but have additional formatting. They can be read by most recent word processing programs including all versions of MS Word for Windows and Macintosh, WordPad for Windows 95, and recent versions of WordPerfect for Windows and Macintosh.

To use a form on the disk to create your documents you must: (1) open a file in your word processor or text editor; (2) edit the form by filling in the required information; (3) print it out; (4) save your revised file.

The following are general instructions on how to do this. However, each word processor uses different commands to open, format, save and print documents. Please read your word processor's manual for specific instructions on performing these tasks.

DO NOT CALL NOLO'S TECHNICAL SUPPORT IF YOU HAVE QUESTIONS ON HOW TO USE YOUR WORD PROCESSOR.

Step 1: Opening a File

To open a file in your word processor, you need to start your word processing program and open the file from within the program. This process usually entails going to the File menu and choosing the Open command. This opens a dialog box where you will tell the program (1) the type of file you want to open (either *.TXT or *.RTF) and (2) the location and name of the file (you will need to navigate through the directory tree to get to the folder/directory on your hard disk that you created and copied the disk's files to). If these directions are unclear you will need to look through the manual for your word processing program—Nolo's technical support department will NOT be able to help you with the use of your word processing program.

Which File Format Should You Use?

If you are not sure which file format to use with your word processor, try opening the RTF files first. Rich text files (RTF) contain most of the formatting included in the sample forms found in this book and in Appendix B. Most current Windows and Macintosh word processing programs, such as Microsoft Word or WordPerfect, can read RTF files.

If you are unable to open the RTF file in your word processor, or a bunch of "garbage" characters appear on screen when you do, then use the TXT files instead. All word processors and text editors can read TXT files, which contain only text, tabs and carriage returns; all other formatting and special characters have been stripped.

Windows and Mac users can also open a file more directly by double-clicking on it. Use File Manager (Windows 3.1), My Computer or Windows Explorer (Windows 95) or the Finder (Macintosh) to go to the folder/directory you created and copied the disk's files to. Then, double-click on the specific file you want to open. If you click on an RTF file

and you have a program installed that "understands" RTF, your word processor should launch and load the file that you double-clicked on. If the file isn't loaded, or if it contains a bunch of garbage characters, use your word processor's Open command, as described above, to open the TXT file instead. If you directly double-click on a TXT file, it will load into a basic text editor like Notepad or SimpleText rather than your word processor.

Step 2: Editing Your Document

Fill in the appropriate information according to the instructions and sample agreements in the book. Underlines are used to indicate where you need to enter your information, frequently followed by instructions in brackets. Be sure to delete the underlines and instructions from your edited document. If you do not know how to use your word processor to edit a document, you will need to look through the manual for your word processing program—Nolo's technical support department will NOT be able to help you with the use of your word processing program.

Editing Forms That Have Check Boxes

Some of the forms have check boxes before text. The check boxes indicate:

- optional text, which you choose whether to include or exclude
- alternative text, where you select one alternative to include and exclude the other alternatives.

If you are using the tear-out forms in the Appendix, you simply mark the appropriate box to make your choice.

If you are using the forms disk, however, we recommend that instead of marking the check boxes, you do the following:

Optional text

If you **don't want** to include optional text, just delete it from your document.

If you **do want** to include optional text, just leave it in your document.

In either case, delete the check box itself as well as the italicized instructions that the text is optional.

Alternative text

First delete all the alternatives that you do not want to include.

Then delete the remaining check box, as well as the italicized instructions that you need to select one of the alternatives provided.

Step 3: Printing Out the Document

Use your word processor's or text editor's Print command to print out your document. If you do not know how to use your word processor to print a document, you will need to look through the manual for your word processing program—Nolo's technical support department will NOT be able to help you with the use of your word processing program.

Step 4: Saving Your Document

After filling in the form, do a "save as" and give the file a new name. IF YOU DO NOT RENAME THE FILE, THE UNDERLINES THAT INDICATE WHERE YOU NEED TO ENTER YOUR INFORMATION WILL BE LOST AND YOU WILL NOT BE ABLE TO CREATE A NEW DOCUMENT WITH THIS FILE WITHOUT RECOPYING THE ORIGINAL FILE FROM THE FLOPPY DISK. MAKE SURE NEVER TO EDIT THE ORIGINAL FILE ON YOUR FLOPPY.

If you do not know how to use your word processor to save a document, you will need to look through the manual for your word processing program—Nolo's technical support department will NOT be able to help you with the use of your word processing program.

■

APPENDIX

B

Forms

All of the following forms are on the disk which accompanies this book except where noted. All of the forms are provided as tear-out forms in this Appendix.

Chapter	Section	Form	File Name
2	G1	Text Permission Worksheet	TXTWKSHT
2	G4	Text Permission Letter Agreement	TXTPRMLT
2	G4	Text Permission Agreement	TXTPRM
3	E1	Photo Permission Worksheet	PICWKSHT
3	F3	Photo Permission Agreement	PICPERM
4	G1	Artwork Permission Agreement	ARTPERM
4	G3	Agreement to Use Artwork in Motion Picture	ARTFILM
5	C3	Lyric Permission Letter Agreement	LYRPRMLT
5	E1	Notice of Intention to Obtain Compulsory License for Making and Distributing Sound Recordings	COMPLCNS
5	G1	Music Synchronization and Videogram License Agreement	SYNCVID
5	G2	Master Use and Videogram License	MSTVIDLC
6	C2	Linking Agreement	LINKAGR
7	A3	APS/CCC Coursepack Agreement	CCCPERM
7	A4	Coursepack Permission Request Form	CRSRQST
7	A4	Coursepack Permission Agreement	CRSPERM
10	B9	Basic Permission to Use a Trademark in a Book or Magazine	TMBKMAG
10	B9	Basic Permission to Use a Trademark in a Movie	TMFILMAG
10	B9	Basic Permission to Use a Trademark in a Photograph or Artwork	TMPHTART

Chapter	Section	Form	File Name
10	D3	Trademark License Agreement	TMLICNS
11	B	Merchandise License Agreement	MRCHLIC
11	D	Merchandise License Worksheet	MRCHWK
11	E	Short-Form Merchandise License Agreement	SHMRCHLC
12	C2	Unlimited Personal Release Agreement	PRSRLSUL
12	C3	Limited Personal Release Agreement	PRSRELLT
12	D1	Interview Release Agreement	INTVRLS
12	D2	Property Release Agreement	PROPRLS
13	C2	Search Request Form	COPSRCH
14	A	Permissions Tracking Sheet	PERMTRK (not included)
15	A1	Basic Copyright Assignment Agreement	ASSGNAGR
15	A3	Musician Assignment Agreement	MUSCASGN
15	A5	Artwork Assignment Agreement	ARTASSGN
15	B4	Work-Made-for-Hire Agreement	WFHAGR

Text Permission Worksheet

MATERIAL YOU ARE USING: THE SELECTION	
Title of text you want to use:	
Name of author:	
The source publication or product from which it came:	
If from a periodical, indicate the ISSN, volume, issue and date:	
If from a book, indicate the ISBN:	
If from the Internet, the entire URL address (the website address that starts with "http") as it appears when viewing the document:	
Number of pages or segments to be used (actual page numbers are helpful). If you can, provide a word count, since some permission fees are based upon word use:	
INTENDED USE: YOUR WORK	
Title of your publication, program, product or website:	
Name of publisher or sponsor:	
Type of publication in which the selection will appear (book, periodical, handout, diskette, electronic program, website):	
If it is a website use, the average number of visitors to the site per month:	
Estimated number of copies to be printed or produced. If a book, include the estimated first print run:	
If copies are to be sold, indicate the price. If copies are free to attendees of an event, indicate cost of event:	
The date the material will be distributed (for example, the estimated publication date of your book):	
Rights needed (for example, right to translate or modify the agreement) :	

Text Permission Letter Agreement

To _____("Licensor"):

I am writing to you to request permission to use the following material.

Licensor Information

Title of Text (the "Selection"): _____

Author: _____

Source publication (or product from which it came): _____

If from a periodical, the ISSN, volume, issue and date. If from a book, the ISBN: _____

If from the Internet, the entire URL: _____

Number of pages (or actual page numbers) to be used: _____

If you are not the copyright holder or if worldwide rights must be obtained elsewhere, please indicate that information: _____

Licensee Publication Information

The Selection will appear in the following publication(s) (the "Work"): _____

Title: _____

Name of publisher or sponsor ("Licensee"): _____

Author(s): _____

Type of publication: _____

If print publication, estimated print run: _____

If print publication, projected publishing date: _____

If print publication, expected price: $ _____

If website, the URL: _____

If website, estimated monthly hits: _____

If website, the posting date: _____

Rights needed: _____

Fee

Licensee shall pay a fee of $ _____ to Licensor at the following address:

_____ upon publication of

the Work or within 6 months of executing this agreement, whichever is earlier.

Credit

A standard credit line including your company name will appear where the Selection is used. If you have a special credit line you would prefer, indicate it below:

_____

Samples

Upon publication, Licensee shall furnish _____ copies of the Work to Licensor.

Signed by Licensee: _____

Name: _____

Title: _____

Address: _____

Date: _____

Licensor's Approval of Request

I warrant that I am the owner of rights for the Selection and have the right to grant the permission to republish the materials as specified above. I grant to Licensee and Licensee's successors, licensees and assigns, the nonexclusive worldwide right to republish the Selection in all editions of the Work.

Permission Granted By: _____

Signed by Licensor: _____

Name: _____

Title: _____

Address: _____

Date: _____

Text Permission Agreement

_____ ("Licensor") is the owner of rights for certain textual material defined below (the "Selection"). _____ ("Licensee") wants to acquire the right to use the Selection as specified in this agreement (the "Agreement").

Licensor Information

Title of Text (the "Selection"): _____

Author: _____

Source publication (or product from which it came): _____

If from a periodical, the ISSN, volume, issue and date. If from a book, the ISBN: _____

If from the Internet, the entire URL: _____

Number of pages or actual page numbers to be used: _____

Licensee Publication Information

The Selection will appear in the following publication(s) (the "Work"): _____

(check if applicable and fill in blanks)

☐   book—title: _____

☐   periodical—title: _____

☐   event handout—title of event: _____

☐   website—URL: _____

☐   diskette—title: _____

Name of publisher or sponsor: _____

Author(s): _____

Estimated date(s) of publication or posting: _____

Estimated number of copies to be printed or produced (if a book, the estimated first print run): _____

If for sale, the price: $ _____

If copies are free to attendees of a program, cost of program: _____

If a Website, indicate the average number of visitors per month: _____

Grant of Rights

Licensor grants to Licensee and Licensee's successors and assigns, the:

(select one)

☐ nonexclusive

☐ exclusive

right to reproduce and distribute the Selection in:

(select all that apply)

☐ the current edition of the Work.

☐ all editions of the Work.

☐ all foreign language versions of the Work.

☐ all derivative versions of the Work.

☐ in all media now known or later devised.

☐ in promotional materials published and distributed in conjunction with the Work.

☐ other rights _____

Territory

The rights granted under this Agreement shall be for _____ (the "Territory").

Fees

Licensee shall pay Licensor as follows:

(select one and fill in appropriate blanks)

☐ **Flat Fee.** Licensee shall pay Licensor a flat fee of $ _____ as full payment for all rights granted. Payment shall be made:

   ☐ upon execution of this Agreement

   ☐ upon publication

☐ **Royalties and Advance.** Licensee agrees to pay Licensor a royalty of _____ % of Net Sales. Net Sales are defined as gross sales (the gross invoice amount billed customers) less quantity discounts and returns actually credited. Licensee agrees to pay Licensor an advance against royalties of $ _____ upon execution of this Agreement. Licensee shall pay Licensor within 30 days after the end of each quarter. Licensee shall furnish an accurate statement of sales during that quarter. Licensor shall have the right to inspect Licensee's books upon reasonable notice.

Credit & Samples

(check if applicable and fill in blanks)

☐ **Credit.** All versions of the Work that include the Selection shall contain the following statement: _____

☐ **Samples.** Upon publication, Licensee shall furnish _____ copies of the Work to Licensor.

Warranty

Licensor warrants that it has the right to grant permission for the uses of the Selection as specified above and that the Selection does not infringe the rights of any third parties.

Miscellaneous

This Agreement may not be amended except in a written document signed by both parties. If a court finds any provision of this Agreement invalid or unenforceable, the remainder of this Agreement shall be interpreted so as best to effect the intent of the parties. This Agreement shall be governed by and interpreted in accordance with the laws of the State of _____.This Agreement expresses the complete understanding of the parties with respect to the subject matter and supersedes all prior representations and understandings.

Licensor	Licensee
By: _____	By: _____
Name: _____	Name: _____
Title: _____	Title: _____
Address: _____	Address: _____
Date: _____	Date: _____
	Tax ID # _____

Photo Permission Worksheet

PHOTOGRAPHIC USE		
Title of Publication, program, product, or website in which the photograph will appear:		
Name of publisher or sponsor:		
Type of publication (book, periodical, annual report, handout, diskette, electronic program):		
Estimated number of copies to be printed or produced. If a book, include the estimated first print run:		
If copies are to be sold, indicate the price. If copies are free to attendees of an event, indicate cost of event:		
The date the material will be distributed (for example, the estimated publication date of a book, or the posting date of a website):		
Will the publication be in any language other than English?	no	yes
If yes, identify which language:		
Website uses:		
Does the site include advertising?	no	yes
Is the site commercial or editorial?	commercial	editorial
Will the photo be used on a home or on an internal page?	home page	internal page
The number of visitors or hits per day:		
Will the photograph be used in both a print publication and a related website (for example, in a magazine, and in the magazine's website)?		
If using in a presentation, the sponsor of the presentation, the number of attendees, and the cost of attendance:		
Rights needed:		
(1) reproduction of the photograph		
(2) display of the photograph		
(3) modification of the photograph		

PHOTOGRAPHIC USE (cont.)	
Territory (for example, North American or world rights):	
The format in which you will need the photograph: scan, print, transparency, digital (if digital, what DPI and file format):	
The date you need the photo:	
If for a film or TV show, the context of the use (supply a synopsis of the plot):	

Photo Permission Agreement

_____ ("Licensor") is the owner of rights for the photograph described below (the "Selection"). _____ ("Licensee") wants to acquire the right to use the Selection as specified in this agreement (the "Agreement").

Licensor Information

Title of work (the "Selection"): _____

Catalog number (if applicable): _____

Photographer: _____

Licensee Publication Information

The Selection will appear in the following publication(s) (the "Work"):

(check if applicable and fill in blanks)

☐ book—title: _____

☐ periodical—title: _____

☐ event handout—title of event: _____

☐ diskette–title: _____

☐ website—URL: _____

If to be used on a website, the Selection will appear on:

(check if applicable)

☐ home page

☐ internal page

Name of publisher or sponsor (if different from Licensee): _____

Estimated date(s) of publication or posting: _____

If applicable, the estimated number of copies to be printed or produced (if a book, the estimated first print run): _____

If for sale, the price: $ _____

If copies are free to attendees of a program, cost of program: _____

If a website, indicate the average number of visitors per month: _____

Grant of Rights

Licensor grants to Licensee and Licensee's successors and assigns, the:

(select one)

☐   nonexclusive

☐   exclusive

right to reproduce and distribute the Selection in:

(select all that apply)

☐   the current edition of the Work.

☐   all editions of the Work.

☐   all foreign language versions of the Work.

☐   all derivative versions of the Work.

☐   in all media now known or later devised.

☐   in promotional materials published and distributed in conjunction with the Work.

☐   other rights _____

Territory

The rights granted under this Agreement shall be for _____ (the "Territory").

Fees

Licensee shall pay Licensor as follows:

(select payment option and fill in blanks)

☐   **Flat Fee.** As full payment for all rights granted, Licensee shall pay Licensor a flat fee of:

     $ _____ . Payment shall be made:

     ☐ upon execution of this Agreement.

     ☐ upon publication.

☐   **Royalties and Advance.** Licensee agrees to pay Licensor a royalty of____% of Net Sales. Net Sales are defined as gross sales (the gross invoice amount billed customers) less quantity discounts and returns actually credited. Licensee agrees to pay Licensor an advance against royalties of $_____ upon execution of this Agreement. Licensee shall pay Licensor within thirty

(30) days of the end of each quarter. Licensee shall furnish an accurate statement of sales during that quarter. Licensor shall have the right to inspect Licensee's books upon reasonable notice.

Credit & Samples

(check if applicable and fill in blanks)

☐ **Credit.** All versions of the Work that include the Selection shall contain the following statement: _____

☐ **Samples.** Upon publication, Licensee shall furnish _____ copies of the Work to Licensor.

Warranty

Licensor warrants that it has the right to grant permission for the uses of the Selection as specified above and that the Selection does not infringe the rights of any third parties.

(check if applicable)

☐ Licensor warrants that a model release is on file for the Selection.

Miscellaneous

This Agreement may not be amended except in a written document signed by both parties. If a court finds any provision of this Agreement invalid or unenforceable, the remainder of this Agreement shall be interpreted so as best to effect the intent of the parties. This Agreement shall be governed by and interpreted in accordance with the laws of the State of _____. This Agreement expresses the complete understanding of the parties with respect to the subject matter and supersedes all prior representations and understandings.

Licensor	Licensee
By: _____	By: _____
Name: _____	Name: _____
Title: _____	Title: _____
Address: _____	Address: _____
Date: _____	Date: _____
	Tax ID # _____

Artwork Permission Agreement

_____ ("Licensor") is the owner of rights for the artwork described below (the "Selection"). _____ ("Licensee") wants to acquire the right to use the Selection as specified in this agreement (the "Agreement").

Licensor Information

Title of work (the "Selection"): _____

Catalog number (if applicable): _____

Artist: _____

Licensee Publication Information

The Selection will appear in the following publication(s) (the "Work"):

(check if applicable and fill in blanks)

☐ book—title: _____

☐ periodical—title: _____

☐ event handout—title of event: _____

☐ diskette–title: _____

☐ website—URL: _____

If to be used on a website, the Selection will appear on:

(check if applicable)

☐ home page

☐ internal page

Name of publisher or sponsor (if different from Licensee): _____

Estimated date(s) of publication: _____

If applicable, the estimated number of copies to be printed or produced (if a book, the estimated first print run): _____

If for sale, the price: $ _____

If copies are free to attendees of a program, cost of program: _____

If a website, indicate the average number of visitors per month: _____

Grant of Rights

Licensor grants to Licensee and Licensee's successors and assigns, the:

(select one)

☐ nonexclusive

☐ exclusive

right to reproduce and distribute the Selection in:

(select all that apply)

☐ the current edition of the Work.

☐ all editions of the Work.

☐ all foreign language versions of the Work.

☐ all derivative versions of the Work.

☐ in all media now known or later devised.

☐ in promotional materials published and distributed in conjunction with the Work.

☐ other rights _____

Territory

The rights granted under this Agreement shall be for _____ (the "Territory").

Fees

Licensee shall pay Licensor as follows:

(select payment option and fill in blanks)

☐ **Flat Fee.** As full payment for all rights granted, Licensee shall pay Licensor a flat fee of:

$ _____ . Payment shall be made:

☐ upon execution of this Agreement.

☐ upon publication.

☐ **Royalties and Advance.** Licensee agrees to pay Licensor a royalty of____% of Net Sales. Net Sales are defined as gross sales (the gross invoice amount billed customers) less quantity discounts and returns actually credited. Licensee agrees to pay Licensor an advance against royalties of $_____ upon execution of this Agreement. Licensee shall pay Licensor within thirty

(30) days of the end of each quarter. Licensee shall furnish an accurate statement of sales during that quarter. Licensor shall have the right to inspect Licensee's books upon reasonable notice.

Credit & Samples

(check if applicable and fill in blanks)

[ ]   **Credit.** All versions of the Work that include the Selection shall contain the following statement: _____

[ ]   **Samples.** Upon publication, Licensee shall furnish _____ copies of the Work to Licensor.

Warranty

Licensor warrants that it has the right to grant permission for the uses of the Selection as specified above and that the Selection does not infringe the rights of any third parties.

(check if applicable)

[ ]   Licensor warrants that a model release is on file for the Selection.

Miscellaneous

This Agreement may not be amended except in a written document signed by both parties. If a court finds any provision of this Agreement invalid or unenforceable, the remainder of this Agreement shall be interpreted so as best to effect the intent of the parties. This Agreement shall be governed by and interpreted in accordance with the laws of the State of _____. This Agreement expresses the complete understanding of the parties with respect to the subject matter and supersedes all prior representations and understandings.

Licensor	Licensee
By: _____	By: _____
Name: _____	Name: _____
Title: _____	Title: _____
Address: _____	Address: _____
Date: _____	Date: _____
	Tax ID # _____

Agreement to Use Artwork in Motion Picture

_____ ("Licensor") is the owner of rights for the artwork described below (the "Selection"). _____ ("Licensee") wants to acquire the right to use the Artwork as specified in this agreement (the "Agreement").

Use of the Artwork

The Artwork will appear in:

(choose one)

☐ motion picture

☐ television program

☐ music video

☐ other:

☐ entitled _____ (the "Picture").

Grant of Rights

Licensor grants to Licensee and Licensee's successors and assigns, the nonexclusive worldwide right (but not the obligation) to include the Artwork in the Picture for the unlimited distribution, advertising and promotion of the Picture in all languages and in all forms or devices now known or later devised. This use includes, but is not limited to, use of the Artwork in foreign language versions of the Picture, advertising, publicity or trailers of the Picture and music videos derived from the Picture.

Limitations on Use

Licensee will use the Artwork in a manner that is consistent with the general practices of the television and motion picture industry. Licensee will not materially alter the Artwork or depict it in any manner that conflicts with the restrictions below, without the consent of Licensor.

Restrictions: _____

Fees

As full payment for all rights granted, Licensee shall pay Licensor a flat fee of $_____. Payment shall be made upon execution of this agreement.

Credit

The Picture shall include the following credit for the Artwork: _____

Warranty & Release

Licensor warrants that it has the right to grant permission for use of the Artwork as specified above and that the Artwork does not infringe upon the rights of any third parties. Licensor waives any claims, known or unknown, arising out of Licensee's use of the Artwork. In the event that Licensee breaches this agreement, Licensor's relief shall be limited to damages and Licensor shall not be entitled to injunctive or equitable relief.

Miscellaneous

This Agreement may not be amended except in a written document signed by both parties. If a court finds any provision of this Agreement invalid or unenforceable, the remainder of this Agreement shall be interpreted so as best to effect the intent of the parties. This Agreement shall be governed by and interpreted in accordance with the laws of the State of _____ . This Agreement expresses the complete understanding of the parties with respect to the subject matter and supersedes all prior representations and understandings.

Licensor	Licensee
By:_____	By: _____
Name:_____	Name: _____
Title:_____	Title: _____
Address:_____	Address: _____
Date:_____	Date: _____
	Tax ID # _____

Lyric Permission Letter Agreement

To _____ ("Music Publisher"):

I am writing to you to obtain permission to reprint portions of the lyrics (the "Lyrics") from the song

_____ , written by _____ on behalf of _____ ("Licensee").

The lyrics will appear in the following publication(s) (the "Work"):

(check if applicable and fill in blanks)

☐ Book Use

Book title: _____

Name of publisher or sponsor: _____

Author(s): _____

ISBN: _____

Estimated date(s) of publication: _____

Estimated number of copies to be printed or produced (if a book, the estimated first print run): _____

Language editions: _____

Territory of publication: _____

Estimated price: $ _____

☐ Magazine

Magazine title: _____

Volume, issue, ISSN: _____

Estimated date of publication: _____

Circulation: _____

☐ Website

URL: _____

Name of publisher or sponsor: _____

Estimated dates of use: _____

Estimated visitors per day: _____

☐ Other (describe): _____

_____

Fee

Licensee shall pay a fee of $ _____ to Music Publisher at the following address: _____ upon publication of the Work or within 6 months of executing this Agreement, whichever is earlier.

Samples

Upon publication, Licensee shall furnish _____ copies of the Work to Music Publisher.

Credit

The following credit shall be included with the Work: _____

Signed by Licensee _____

Name: _____

Title: _____

Address: _____

Date: _____

Music Publisher's Approval of Request

Music Publisher warrants that it is the owner of rights for the lyrics and has the right to grant the permission to republish the lyrics as specified above. This license is for the nonexclusive worldwide right to republish the lyrics in all editions of the Work.

Signed by Music Publisher _____

Name: _____

Title: _____

Address: _____

Date: _____

Notice of Intention to Obtain Compulsory License for Making and Distributing Sound Recordings

To _____ , the copyright owner of _____ , written by _____ :

Pursuant to the compulsory license provisions of the U.S. Copyright Act (17 U.S.C.§ 1115), we apply for a license to make and distribute phonorecords of _____ and provide the following information:

Legal name or entity seeking the compulsory license:	
Fictitious or assumed names used for making and distributing phonorecords:	
Address:	
Business organization:	☐ corporation ☐ LLC ☐ partnership ☐ sole proprietor
Name of individuals who own a beneficial interest of 25% or more in the entity:	
If a corporation, names of the officers and directors:	
Configurations(s) to be made under the compulsory license (check all that apply):	☐ 7- or 12-inch vinyl single ☐ 12-inch long playing vinyl record ☐ cassette ☐ compact disc ☐ minidisc ☐ digital cassette recording
Catalog number(s):	
Label name(s):	
Principal recording artists:	
Anticipated date of initial release:	
We agree to pay the copyright owner royalties at the statutory rate provided by the Copyright Act. Date:_____ By:_____ Name/Title:_____	

Music Synchronization and Videogram License Agreement

Music Synchronization and Videogram License Agreement (the "Agreement") is made between:

_____ ("Publisher") and _____ ("Producer").

Publisher is the owner of rights for the compositions listed below:

_____

_____

(the "Compositions").

Producer is the owner of rights for the Motion Picture tentatively entitled _____

(the "Motion Picture"). Producer desires to license the Compositions for use in the Motion Picture and in audiovisual devices for home use such as videotapes and laser discs ("Videograms"). The parties agree as follows:

Grant

(select one or more Grant provisions)

☐ **Grant of Audiovisual License.** Publisher grants to Producer and Producer's successors and assigns, the nonexclusive right to record the Compositions solely in synchronization with the Motion Picture (in any medium, now known or later created) within the Territory. Publisher grants to Producer the right to publicly perform the Compositions solely in synchronization to the Motion Picture within the Territory. These public performance rights include public exhibitions of the Motion Picture in theaters and other public places where motion pictures are customarily exhibited, provided that performances outside the United States are cleared by performing rights societies in accordance with customary practice and customary fees. The public performance rights also include television exhibition of the Motion Picture within the Territory, including all methods of television reproduction and transmissions, provided that the entities broadcasting those performances have licenses from the appropriate performing rights societies. Any television performance not licensed by performing rights societies must be cleared directly by the Publisher.

☐ **Grant of Videogram License.** Publisher grants to Producer and his successors and assigns, the nonexclusive right to record, copy and synchronize the Composition, solely as part of the Motion Picture, on audiovisual devices including, but not limited to video cassettes, video discs and similar compact audiovisual devices that reproduce the entire motion picture in substantially its original form ("Videogram"). This Videogram license is solely for the distribution of Videograms intended primarily for home use in the Territory.

☐ **Use in Trailers.** Publisher grants to Producer and his successors and assigns, the nonexclusive right to record, copy, synchronize and perform the Composition in connection with trailers used for the advertising and exploitation of the Motion Picture.

Reservation of Rights

Publisher reserves all rights not granted in this Agreement.

Modifications to Composition

Producer shall not make any change in the original lyrics, if any, or in the fundamental character of the music of the Composition or use the title or any portion of the lyrics of the Composition as the title or subtitle of the Motion Picture without written prior authorization from Publisher.

Territory

The rights granted in this Agreement are for the following: _____
(the "Territory").

Audiovisual License Payments

As payment for the rights granted for the Audiovisual License, Producer shall pay Publisher as follows:

(select payment option and fill in blanks)

☐ **One-Time Payment.** Producer shall pay Publisher one-time payment of $_____ upon first public performance of the Motion Picture or within nine (9) months of signing this agreement, whichever is earlier.

☐ **Advance and Royalties.** Producer shall pay Publisher nonrefundable advance ("Motion Picture Advance") in the sum of $_____ recoupable against royalties derived from the Audiovisual License ("Audiovisual Royalties"). Producer shall pay Publisher Audiovisual Royalties of ___% of net profits from the public exhibition and public performance of the Motion Picture.

☐ **Royalties.** Producer shall pay Publisher _____% of the net profits from the public exhibition and public performance of the Motion Picture.

Videogram License Payments

As payment for the rights granted for the Videogram License, Producer shall pay Publisher as follows: (select payment option and fill in blanks)

☐ **One-Time Payment.** Producer shall pay Publisher one-time payment of $_____ within nine (9) months of signing this agreement.

☐ **Advance and Royalties.** Producer shall pay Publisher a nonrefundable advance ("Videogram Advance") in the sum of $_____ recoupable against royalties derived from the Videogram License ("Videogram Royalties"). Videogram Royalties for Videogram copies of the Motion Picture shall be paid as follows:

    ☐ **Net Profits.** Producer shall pay Publisher_____% of the Producer's net profits for all Videograms revenues including all sales, licenses, or other sources of revenue for Videogram distribution (not including shipping charges or taxes).

    ☐ **Pro Rata Option.** Producer shall pay Publisher_____% ("Publisher's Pro-Rata Portion") of_____% of the net revenue for all Videogram income including all sales, licenses, or other sources of revenue for Videogram distribution. Publisher's Pro-Rata Portion represents the proportion the Composition bears to the total number of Royalty-bearing compositions contained in the Motion Picture.

Payments; Statements

Within forty-five (45) days after the end of each calendar quarter (the "Royalty Period"), Producer shall furnish accurate statement of net revenues derived from the licenses granted in this agreement along with any royalty payments. Producer may withhold a reasonable reserve for anticipated returns, refunds, and exchanges of Videograms, and this reserve shall be liquidated no later than twelve (12) months after the respective accounting statement.

Favorable Rates

If a higher royalty rate than set forth in this Agreement becomes payable by operation of law with respect to Videograms sold in a particular country within the Territory, Producer shall either pay the higher royalty to Publisher with respect to that country, or delete the Compositions from the Motion Picture with respect to this country. In the event a musical composition is licensed for a substantially similar use in connection with the Videogram exploitation of the Motion Picture on a more favorable rate, Producer agrees that such favorable rate shall also be granted to Publisher for the licensing of the Composition.

Audit

Producer shall keep accurate books of account and records covering all transactions relating to the licenses granted in this Agreement, and Publisher or its duly authorized representatives shall have the right upon five (5) days prior written notice, and during normal business hours, to inspect and audit these accounts and records.

Warranty

Publisher warrants that it has the power and authority to grant the rights in this Agreement and that the Compositions do not infringe any third-party rights. In no event shall Publisher's liability for a breach of this Warranty exceed the amount of payments received under this Agreement.

Credits

Publisher shall receive credit in the following form: _____

This credit shall be provided as follows:

(select all that apply)

- [ ] credit similar to all other musical compositions used in the Motion Picture.
- [ ] a single card in the main titles on all prints of the Motion Picture and Videograms.
- [ ] in all paid advertising similar to all other musical compositions used in the Motion Picture.

Samples

Producer shall promptly furnish Publisher with _____ copies of each format of Videogram release.

Cue Sheets

Producer agrees to furnish Publisher a cue sheet of the Motion Picture within thirty (30) days after the first public exhibition of the Motion Picture.

Term

The term of this Agreement is for the term of United States copyright in the Composition including renewal terms, if any.

Termination and Breach

In the event that Producer (or Producer's assigns or licensees) breach this Agreement and fails to cure such breach within thirty (30) days after notice by Publisher to Producer, this license will automatically terminate and all rights granted under this Agreement shall revert to Publisher. Failure to make timely payments or to provide credit as provided in this Agreement shall be considered a material breach of this Agreement.

Miscellaneous

This Agreement may not be amended except in a writing signed by both parties. If a court finds any provision of this Agreement invalid or unenforceable, the remainder of this Agreement shall be interpreted so as best to effect the intent of the parties. This Agreement shall be governed by and interpreted in accordance with the laws of the State of _____. This Agreement expresses the complete understanding of the parties with respect to the subject matter and supersedes all prior representations and understandings. Any controversy or claim arising out of or relating to this Agreement shall be settled by binding arbitration in accordance with the rules of the American Arbitration Association and judgment upon the award rendered by the arbitrator(s) may be entered in any court having jurisdiction. All notices provided for under this Agreement must be in writing and mailed to the addresses provided in the signature portion of this Agreement.

_____

PUBLISHER

_____

PRODUCER

Master Use and Videogram License

This Master Use and Videogram License Agreement (the "Agreement") is made between:

_____ ("Owner") and _____ ("Producer").

Owner is the owner of rights for the master recordings: _____

_____

_____

(the "Masters").

Producer is the owner of rights for the Motion Picture tentatively entitled _____

 (the "Motion Picture").

Producer desires to license the Masters for use in the Motion Picture and in audiovisual devices for home use such as videotapes and laser discs ("Videograms"). The parties agree as follows:

Grant

(select one or more Grant provisions if applicable)

☐ **Grant of Audiovisual License.** Owner grants to Producer and Producer's successors and assigns, the nonexclusive right to use and reproduce the Masters solely in synchronization with the Motion Picture in any medium, now known or later created within the Territory. Owner grants to Producer the right to publicly perform the Masters solely in synchronization to the Motion Picture within the Territory. These public performance rights include the public exhibitions of the Motion Picture in theaters and other public places where motion pictures are customarily exhibited and for television exhibition of the Motion Picture including all methods of television reproduction and transmissions within the Territory.

☐ **Grant of Videogram License.** Owner grants to Producer and Producer's successors and assigns, the nonexclusive right to record, copy and synchronize the Masters, solely as part of the Motion Picture, on audiovisual devices including, but not limited to video cassettes, video discs and similar compact audiovisual devices that reproduce the entire motion picture in substantially its original form ("Videogram"). This Videogram license is solely for the distribution of Videograms intended primarily for home use in the Territory.

☐ **Use in Trailers.** Owner grants to Producer and Producer's successors and assigns, the nonexclusive right to record, copy, synchronize and perform the Masters in connection with trailers used for the advertising and exploitation of the Motion Picture.

Reservation of Rights

Owner reserves all rights not granted in this Agreement.

Modifications to Masters

Producer shall not make any change in the Masters without written prior authorization from Owner.

Territory

The rights granted in this Agreement are for the following: _____
(the "Territory").

Union Re-use Fees

Owner agrees to provide Producer with all information regarding any re-use fees required by unions or guilds as a result of this license. Producer agrees to pay all such re-use payments including related pension or welfare payments and to indemnify Owner from claims arising from such payments.

Musical Works Synchronization Rights

Producer agrees to obtain all appropriate synchronization, performance and reproduction rights for the musical compositions embodied on the Masters and to indemnify Owner for any claims arising from such rights.

Audiovisual License Payments

As payment for the rights granted for the Audiovisual License, Producer shall pay Owner as follows: (select payment option and fill in blanks)

☐ **One-Time Payment.** Producer shall pay Owner one-time payment of $_____ upon first public performance of the Motion Picture or within nine (9) months of signing this agreement, whichever is earlier.

☐ **Advance and Royalties.** Producer shall pay Owner nonrefundable advance ("Motion Picture Advance") in the sum of $_____ recoupable against royalties derived from the Audiovisual License ("Audiovisual Royalties"). Producer shall pay Owner Audiovisual Royalties of __% of net profits from the public exhibition and public performance of the Motion Picture.

☐ **Royalties.** Producer shall pay Owner _____ % of the net profits from the public exhibition and public performance of the Motion Picture.

Videogram License Payments

As payment for the rights granted for the Videogram License, Producer shall pay Owner as follows: (select payment option and fill in blanks)

☐ **One-Time Payment.** Producer shall pay Owner one-time payment of $ _____ within nine (9) months of signing this agreement.

☐ **Advance and Royalties.** Producer shall pay Owner a nonrefundable advance ("Videogram Advance") in the sum of $ _____ recoupable against royalties derived from the Videogram License ("Videogram Royalties"). Videogram Royalties for Videogram copies of the Motion Picture shall be paid as follows:

☐ **Net Profits.** Producer shall pay Owner _____ % of the Producer's net profits for all Videograms revenues including all sales, licenses, or other sources of revenue for Videogram distribution (not including shipping charges or taxes).

☐ **Pro Rata Option.** Producer shall pay Owner _____ % ("Owner's Pro-Rata Portion") of _____ % of the net revenue for all Videogram income including all sales, licenses, or other sources of revenue for Videogram distribution. Owner's Pro-Rata Portion represents the proportion the Composition bears to the total number of Royalty-bearing compositions contained in the Motion Picture.

Payments; Statements

Within forty-five (45) days after the end of each calendar quarter (the "Royalty Period"), Producer shall furnish accurate statement of net revenues derived from the licenses granted in this agreement along with any royalty payments. Producer may withhold a reasonable reserve for anticipated returns, refunds, and exchanges of Videograms, and this reserve shall be liquidated no later than twelve (12) months after the respective accounting statement.

Audit

Producer shall keep accurate books of account and records covering all transactions relating to the licenses granted in this Agreement, and Owner or its duly authorized representatives shall have the right upon five (5) days prior written notice, and during normal business hours, to inspect and audit these accounts and records.

Warranty

Owner warrants that it has the power and authority to grant the rights in this Agreement and that the Masters do not infringe any third-party rights. In no event shall Owner's liability for a breach of this warranty exceed the amount of payments received under this Agreement.

Credits

Owner shall receive credit in the following form: _____

This credit shall be provided as follows:

(select one or more if appropriate)

☐ credit similar to all other Masters used in the Motion Picture.

☐ in all paid advertising similar to all other musical Masters used in the Motion Picture.

Samples

Producer shall promptly furnish Owner with ___ copies of each format of Videogram release.

Cue Sheets

Producer agrees to furnish Owner a cue sheet of the Motion Picture within thirty (30) days after the first public exhibition of the Motion Picture.

Term

The term of this Agreement is for the term of United States copyright in the Masters including renewal terms, if any.

Termination and Breach

In the event that Producer (or Producer's assigns or licensees) breach this Agreement and fails to cure such breach within thirty (30) days after notice by Owner to Producer, then this license will automatically terminate and all rights granted under this Agreement shall revert to Owner. Failure to make timely payments or to provide credit as provided in this Agreement shall be considered a material breach of this Agreement.

Miscellaneous

This Agreement may not be amended except in a writing signed by both parties. If a court finds any provision of this Agreement invalid or unenforceable, the remainder of this Agreement shall be interpreted so as best to effect the intent of the parties. This Agreement shall be governed by and interpreted in accordance with the laws of the State of _____ . This Agreement expresses the complete understanding of the parties with respect to the subject matter and supersedes all prior representations and understandings. Any controversy or claim arising out of or relating to this Agreement shall be settled by binding arbitration in accordance with the rules of the American Arbitration Association and judgment upon the award rendered by the arbitrator(s) may be entered in any court having jurisdiction. All notices provided for under this Agreement must be in writing and mailed to the addresses provided in the signature portion of this Agreement.

_____

OWNER

_____

PRODUCER

Linking Agreement

This Agreement (the "Agreement") is made between _____ ("Source Site")
with its homepage URL of _____ and _____ ("Destination
Site") with its homepage URL of _____ .
The parties agree as follows:

The Link

The Source Site will provide a link to the Destination Site as follows: _____
_____ (the "Link")

The Link includes Destination Site's URL and:

(select if appropriate)

☐   Hypertext link—the words: _____ .

☐   Image link: _____ .

☐   Framed link: _____ .

Grant

Destination Site grants the right to display the Link at the Source Site and the nonexclusive right to
display publicly the trademarks or images in the Link. Source Site obtains no trademark rights under
this Agreement other than the right to display the marks. Any goodwill associated with the Source
Site's trademarks automatically vests in the Destination Site.

Standards and Notifications

(select if appropriate)

☐   Source Site shall maintain its site in accordance with industry standards and upon notice from
Destination Site shall promptly remove the Link if required. Source Site shall promptly notify
Destination Site of any change to the Link or changes to the Source Site affecting the Link.

By: _____   By: _____
Date: _____   Date: _____
Source Site Title: _____   Destination Site Title: _____
Source Site Mailing Address: _____   Destination Site Mailing Address: _____

_____   _____
email: _____   email: _____

APS/CCC Coursepack Agreement
(courtesy Copyright Clearance Center)

PERMISSIONS AGREEMENT made this _____ day of _____ , _____ , between the Copyright Clearance Center, Inc. ("CCC") and _____ ("User").

1. Nature and Form of Program. This Agreement provides for participation by User in CCC's Academic Permissions Service ("APS"). The APS grants authorizations to photocopy and to create photocopy anthologies for sale and/or distribution to students and other academic customers. The copies and anthologies may be made and assembled by faculty members individually or at their request by on-campus bookstores or copy centers, or by off-campus copy shops and other similar entities. It does not permit "publishing ventures" where any particular anthology would be systematically marketed at multiple institutions. User acknowledges that the holders of copyright rights have complete discretion under the United States Copyright Act, 17 United States Code, whether to grant any permission, and whether to place any limitations on any grant, and that CCC has no right to supersede or to modify any such discretionary act by a rightsholder.

2. Grant of Permissions. In order to receive a permission to photocopy a portion of a printed publication, User must first submit to CCC a form as prescribed in CCC's published APS Guidelines. CCC shall not accept any form that is not complete. Within CCC's published response time (measured from CCC's receipt of a completed form), CCC shall notify User whether or not a permission has been granted and the royalty fee due, if any. CCC shall notify User of any limitations imposed by a rightsholder on that permission and, unless User notifies CCC of its intention to decline any particular permission, User shall pay the amount due as set forth in the notification and shall be bound by any such limitation. Any act by User that involves copying beyond that set forth in the notification shall be deemed in its entirety to be an unpermitted act of copying. Separate portions of a work, even if they are to be included in the same anthology, shall require a separate permission under the APS.

3. Payment for Permissions. User shall pay to CCC the amount set forth in the permissions notification in full payment for any permission set forth therein (which will include both the amount due to the rightsholder and the service fee payable to CCC), within the time set forth therein. In the event of a failure by User to pay any such amount by the due date, the applicable permission shall be null and void. In the event that User sells fewer copies than the number for which permissions were granted, User shall pay CCC only for the total number of copies sold, and permissions for the unsold copies shall be null and void.

4. General Terms and Conditions of the Program. Subject to any further limitations determined by any particular rightsholder, the copying permitted under the APS is limited as follows:

(i)   no more than 25% of the text of a book or of the items in a published collection of essays, poems or articles may be copied;

(ii)   no more than the greater of (A) 25% of the text of an issue or of a journal or other periodical, or (B) two articles from such an issue, may be copied;

(iii)   no User may sell or distribute any particular anthology at more than one institution of learning;

(iv)   each copy sold by User must contain a proper copyright notice, identifying the copyright rightsholder in whose name CCC has granted permission and a statement to the effect that such copy was made pursuant to permission; and

(v)   no materials may be entered into electronic memory by User except in order to produce an identical copy of a work before or during the academic term (or analogous period) as to which any particular permission is granted.

In the event that User shall choose to retain the materials in electronic memory for purposes of producing identical copies more than one day after such retention (but still within the scope of any permission granted), User must notify CCC of such fact in the applicable permission request form and such retention shall constitute one copy actually sold for purposes of calculating permissions fees. No permission granted under the APS shall in any way include any right by User to create a non-identical copy of the work or to edit or in any other way modify the work (except by means of deleting material immediately preceding or following the entire portion of the work copied).

5. Term and Termination. This Agreement shall be in force beginning as of the date hereof and shall continue for an initial period of one year. This Agreement is automatically renewable for subsequent one year periods in the absence of timely notice of termination. Either party may terminate this Agreement for any reason by giving 90 days' prior written notice thereof to the other party. In the event of termination of this Agreement for any reason, any permissions the periods of which have not yet ended shall remain in effect until their respective terminations. Termination of this Agreement shall have no effect on any party's obligation to pay money to the other party.

6. Warranty. Each copyright rightsholder which has granted CCC the right to grant permission under the APS to use any particular Work has warranted that it has all rights necessary to authorize CCC to act on its behalf.

7. Books and Records; Right to Audit. As to each permission granted under the APS, User shall maintain for at least four full calendar years books and records sufficient for CCC to determine the numbers of copies made by user under such permission. CCC and any representatives it may designate shall have the right to audit such books and records at any time during User's ordinary business hours, upon two days' prior notice. If any such audit shall determine that User shall have underpaid for, or underreported, any copies sold by three percent (3%) or more, then User shall bear all the costs of any such audit; otherwise, CCC shall bear the costs of any such audit. Any amount determined by such audit to have been underpaid by User shall immediately be paid to CCC by User, together with interest thereon at the rate of 10% per annum from the date such amount was originally due. The provisions of this paragraph shall survive the termination of this Agreement for any reason.

8. Notices. All notices and communications under this Agreement shall be in writing addressed, in the case of User, to the person designated below, and in the case of CCC, its President, and shall be deemed to have been given on the day of delivery or transmission if delivered by hand or if sent by electronic mail or facsimile transmission (with receipt confirmed), or on the fifth business day following the day of mailing if mailed, postage prepaid:

Person and/or title: _____

Address: _____

(if different from that set forth at end of Agreement)

Telephone Number: _____

Facsimile Number: _____

Email Address: _____

9. No Assignment; Integrated Agreement; Governing Law. Neither party to this Agreement shall have the right to assign or sublicense any of its rights or obligations hereunder without the prior written consent of the other party. This agreement constitutes the entire agreement between the parties with respect to the subject matter hereof and may not be modified or amended except in a writing signed by the parties hereto. This Agreement shall be interpreted, construed, governed and enforced in accordance with and under the laws of the State of New York, without giving effect to the principles thereof of conflicts of law.

User's Name: _____

Address: _____

Signature: _____

Printed Name: _____

Title: _____

Copyright Clearance Center, Inc.

222 Rosewood Drive

Danvers, Massachusetts 01923 USA

Signature: _____

Coursepack Permission Request Form (Association of Academic Publishers)

To:

Publisher Contact: _____

Publisher: _____

Fax Number: _____

Date of Request: _____

From:

Your Name: _____

Department: _____

School name: _____

Address: _____

City: _____

State: _____

Zip code: _____

Phone #: _____

Fax #: _____

Course name and number: _____

Number of copies needed: _____

Instructor: _____

Semester and year: _____

ISBN/ISSN number: _____

Book or journal title: _____

Author: _____

Translator: _____

Editor: _____

Edition: _____

Volume: _____

Copyright year: _____

Publication year: _____

Chapter/article title: _____

Chapter/article author: _____

Page numbers: _____

Total pages: _____

Is it an out-of-print work? _____

Have you included a copy of the material with this request? _____

Are you the author? _____

Permission is requested for use during one term only. _____

Coursepack Permission Agreement

_____ ("Licensor")

_____ ("User")

Department: _____

School Name: _____

Course name and number: _____ ("the Course").

Date when Course starts: _____ (the "Course date").

Authorization

Licensor authorizes User to photocopy the Selection, as defined below, for purposes of creating a photocopy anthology (the "Coursepack") for sale or distribution to students and academic customers in the Course.

Number of Copies & Assembly

_____ copies of the Coursepack shall be assembled and distributed for the Course:

☐   by User

☐   by on-campus bookstores or copy centers, or

☐   by off-campus copy shops.

Number of pages (or actual page numbers) to be used _____ .

The permission granted in this Agreement is limited to the Course and institution listed above and to be used for one semester only. Any further rights must be negotiated separately.

Material for Which Permission Is Sought

Title of text or artwork: _____ (the "Selection").

Author: _____

Source publication (or product from which it came): _____ .

If from a periodical, the ISSN, volume, issue and date. If from a book, the ISBN: _____ .

If from the Internet, the entire URL address: _____ .

Credit

A standard credit line including User's name will appear where the Selection is used. If you have a special credit line you would prefer, indicate it here: _____ .

Fee

User shall pay a fee of $ _____ to Licensor at the following address: _____

_____ within 30 days of commencement date, listed above.

Warranty

Licensor warrants that it is the owner of rights for the Selection and has the right to grant the permission to republish the materials as specified above.

_____ (User signature)

Name: _____

Title: _____

Address: _____

Date: _____

Permission Granted By:

_____ (Licensor signature)

Name: _____

Title: _____

Address: _____

Date: _____

Basic Permission to Use a Trademark in a Book or Magazine

_____ ("Owner") is the owner of rights in the trademark_____ (the "Trademark"). Owner grants permission for the Trademark's reproduction in the format indicated below in the publication, _____ , and in any subsequent editions or derivative versions in any media. Any goodwill associated with the Trademark vests in Owner.

Owner Name _____

Signature _____

Date _____

Insert Sample of Trademark

Basic Permission to Use a Trademark in a Movie

_____ ("Owner") is the owner of rights in the trademark, _____ (the "Trademark"). Owner grants permission for the Trademark's reproduction in the format indicated below in all versions of the film, _____ (the "Film"), and any derivative versions in any media. Any goodwill associated with the Trademark vests in Owner.

Owner Name _____

Signature _____

Date _____

Insert Sample of Trademark

Basic Permission to Use a Trademark in a Photograph or Artwork

_____ ("Owner") is the owner of rights in trademark _____ (the "Trademark"). Owner grants permission for the Trademark's reproduction in the format indicated below in all versions of the artwork, _____ , (the "Artwork"), and any derivative versions in any media. Any goodwill associated with the Trademark vests in Owner.

Owner Name _____

Signature _____

Date _____

Insert Sample of Trademark

Trademark License Agreement

Introduction

This Trademark License Agreement (the "Agreement") is made between _____ (referred to as "Licensor") and _____ (referred to as "Licensee").

The parties agree as follows:

The Trademarks

The "Trademarks" refer to any trademark, service mark, trade name, logo, or other device and its associated good will used to identify and distinguish Licensor's products and services as included in Exhibit A. Licensor is the owner of all rights to the Trademarks and Licensee shall not claim any right to use the Trademarks except under the terms of this Agreement.

Licensed Products

Licensed Products are defined as the licensee's products incorporating the Trademarks specifically described in Exhibit A (the "Licensed Products").

Grant of Rights

Licensor grants to Licensee:

(select one)

☐　　an exclusive license

☐　　a nonexclusive license

to reproduce and distribute the Trademarks on the Licensed Products.

Sublicense

(select one)

☐　　**Consent required.** Licensee may sublicense the rights granted pursuant to this Agreement provided: Licensee obtains Licensor's prior written consent to such sublicense; and Licensor receives such revenue or royalty payment as provided in the Payment section below. Any sublicense granted in violation of this provision shall be void.

☐ **No sublicensing permitted.** Licensee may not sublicense the rights granted under this Agreement.

Reservation of Rights: Assignment of Good Will

Licensor reserves all rights other than those being conveyed or granted in this Agreement. Licensee assigns to Licensor any good will from the Trademarks that may accrue under this Agreement or from the distribution of the Licensed Products and agrees that all uses of the Trademarks shall inure to Licensor. Licensee's rights to the Trademarks are only in connection with the Licensed Products and Licensee shall not assert any other association with Licensor or the Trademarks. Licensee acknowledges the validity of the Trademarks and agrees not to challenge Licensor's ownership of the Trademarks or their validity.

Territory

The rights granted to Licensee are limited to _____ (the "Territory").

Term

The "Effective Date" of this Agreement is defined as the date when the agreement commences and is established by the latest signature date.

(select one)

☐ **Specified term with renewal rights.** This Agreement shall commence upon the Effective Date and shall extend for a period of _____ years (the "Initial Term"). Following the Initial Term, Licensee may renew this Agreement under the same terms and conditions for___ consecutive _____ periods (the "Renewal Terms") provided that Licensee provides written notice of its intention to renew this Agreement within thirty (30) days before the expiration of the current term.

☐ **Term with renewal based upon sales.** This Agreement shall commence upon the Effective Date and shall extend for a period of _____ years (the "Initial Term") and may be renewed by Licensee under the same terms and conditions for consecutive _____ year periods (the "Renewal Terms"), provided that:

(a) Licensee provides written notice of its intention to renew this Agreement within thirty days before the expiration of the current term; and

(b) Licensee has met the sales requirements as established in Exhibit A.

☐ **Indefinite term.** This Agreement shall commence upon the Effective Date and shall continue until terminated pursuant to a provision of this Agreement.

☐ **Fixed term.** This Agreement shall commence upon the Effective Date and shall continue for _____ unless sooner terminated pursuant to a provision of this Agreement.

☐ **Term for as long as Licensee sells Licensed Products.** This Agreement shall commence upon the Effective Date as specified in Exhibit A and shall continue for as long as Licensee continues to offer the Licensed Products in commercially reasonable quantities or unless sooner terminated pursuant to a provision of this Agreement.

Approval of Samples & Quality Control

Pre-Production. Licensee shall submit to Licensor a reasonable number of pre-production designs and prototypes at no cost prior to production as well as production samples of every Licensed Product to assure that the product meets Licensor's quality standards. Licensee agrees not to distribute any Licensed Product until receipt of Licensor's written approval of such Licensed Product.

Production and Promotion. At least once every six (6) months, Licensee shall submit to Licensor two (2) production samples of each Licensed Product for review. Licensee shall pay all costs for delivery of these materials. In the event that any production sample does not meet Licensor's quality standards, licensee agrees to immediately correct such deficiencies. Licensor shall have the right to inspect Licensee's premises upon reasonable notice for purposes of observing the manufacturing process. Licensee shall submit all advertising and promotional materials to Licensor and shall not distribute such materials until receipt of written approval from Licensor.

Royalties

All royalties ("Royalties") provided for under this Agreement shall accrue when the respective Licensed Products are sold, shipped, distributed, billed or paid for, whichever occurs first.

Net Sales

"Net Sales" are defined as Licensee's gross sales (i.e., the gross invoice amount billed customers) less quantity discounts or rebates and returns actually credited. A quantity discount or rebate is a discount made at the time of shipment. No deductions shall be made for cash or other discounts, commissions, manufacturing costs, uncollectible accounts, or for fees or expenses of any kind which the Licensee may incur in connection with the Royalty payments.

Fees

(select one or more provisions)

☐ **Advance Against Royalties.** As a nonrefundable advance against royalties (the "Advance"), Licensee agrees to pay to Licensor upon execution of this Agreement the sum of $ _____ .

☐ **Licensed Product Royalty.** Licensee agrees to pay a Royalty of ___ % percent of all Net Sales revenue of the Licensed Products ("Licensed Product Royalty").

Per Unit Royalty. Licensee agrees to pay a Royalty of $ ___ for each unit of the Licensed Product that is ☐ manufactured ☐ sold [select one].

☐ **Guaranteed Minimum Annual Royalty Payment.** In addition to any other advances or fees, Licensee shall pay an annual guaranteed royalty (the "GMAR") as follows: $ _____ . The GMAR shall be paid to Licensor annually on _____ . The GMAR is an advance against royalties for the twelve-month (12-month) period commencing upon payment. Royalty payments based on Net Sales made during any year of this Agreement shall be credited against the GMAR due for the year in which such Net Sales were made. In the event that annual royalties exceed the GMAR, Licensee shall pay the difference to Licensor. Any annual royalty payments in excess of the GMAR shall not be carried forward from previous years or applied against the GMAR.

☐ **License Fee.** As a nonrefundable, nonrecoupable fee for executing this license, Licensee agrees to pay to Licensor upon execution of this Agreement the sum of $ _____ .

☐ **Sublicensing Revenues.** In the event of any sublicense of the rights granted pursuant to this Agreement, Licensee shall pay to Licensor _____ % percent of all sublicensing revenues.

Payments and Statements to Licensor

Within thirty (30) days after the end of each calendar quarter (the "Royalty Period"), an accurate statement of Net Sales of Licensed Products along with any royalty payments or sublicensing revenues due to Licensor shall be provided to Licensor, regardless of whether any Licensed Products were sold during the Royalty Period. All payments shall be paid in United States currency drawn on a United States bank. The acceptance by Licensor of any of the statements furnished or royalties paid shall not preclude Licensor questioning the correctness at any time of any payments or statements.

Audit

Licensee shall keep accurate books of account and records covering all transactions relating to the license granted in this Agreement, and Licensor or its duly authorized representatives shall have the right upon five days prior written notice, and during normal business hours, to inspect and audit Licensee's records relating to the Licensed Products under this Agreement. Licensor shall bear the cost of such inspection and audit, unless the results indicate an underpayment greater than $ _____ for any six-month (6-month) period. In that case, Licensee shall promptly reimburse Licensor for all costs of the audit along with the amount due with interest on such sums. Interest shall accrue from the date the payment was originally due and the interest rate shall be 1.5% per month, or the maximum rate permitted by law, whichever is less. All books of account and records shall be made available in the United States and kept available for at least two years after the termination of this Agreement.

Late Payment

Time is of the essence with respect to all payments to be made by Licensee under this Agreement. If Licensee is late in any payment provided for in this Agreement, Licensee shall pay interest on the payment from the date due until paid at a rate of 1.5% per month, or the maximum rate permitted by law, whichever is less.

Licensor Warranties

Licensor warrants that it has the power and authority to enter into this Agreement and has no knowledge as to any third-party claims regarding the proprietary rights in the Trademarks that would interfere with the rights granted under this Agreement.

Indemnification by Licensor

(select one if appropriate)

☐ **Licensor indemnification without limitations.** Licensor shall indemnify Licensee and hold Licensee harmless from any damages and liabilities (including reasonable attorney fees and costs), arising from any breach of Licensor's warranties as defined in Licensor's Warranties, above.

☐ **Licensor indemnification limited to amounts paid.** Licensor shall indemnify Licensee and hold Licensee harmless from any damages and liabilities (including reasonable attorney fees and costs), arising from any breach of Licensor's warranties as defined in Licensor's Warranties, above. Licensor's maximum liability under this provision shall in no event exceed the total amount earned by Licensor under this Agreement.

Licensee Warranties

Licensee warrants that it will use its best commercial efforts to market the Licensed Products and that their sale and marketing shall be in conformance with all applicable laws and regulations, including but not limited to all intellectual property laws.

Indemnification by Licensee

Licensee shall indemnify Licensor and hold Licensor harmless from any damages and liabilities (including reasonable attorney fees and costs), arising from any breach of Licensee's warranties and representation as defined in the Licensee Warranties above, or arising out of any alleged defects of the Licensed Products, any product liability claims or any claims arising out of advertising, distribution or marketing of the Licensed Products.

Intellectual Property Rights

The license granted in this Agreement is conditioned on Licensee's compliance with the provisions of the intellectual property laws of the United States and any foreign country in the Territory.

Proprietary Notices

Licensee shall identify Licensor as the owner of rights to the Trademarks and shall include the notices provided in Exhibit A on all copies of the Licensed Products.

Infringement Against Third Parties

In the event that either party learns of imitations or infringements of the Trademarks or Licensed Products, that party shall notify the other in writing of the infringements or imitations. Licensor shall have the right to commence lawsuits against third persons arising from infringement of the Trademarks or Licensed Products. In the event that Licensor does not commence a lawsuit against an alleged infringer within sixty (60) days of notification by Licensee, Licensee may commence a lawsuit against the third party. Before filing suit, Licensee shall obtain the written consent of Licensor to do so and such consent shall not be unreasonably withheld. Licensor will cooperate fully and in good faith with Licensee for the purpose of securing and preserving Licensee's rights to the Trademarks.

Any recovery (including, but not limited to a judgment, settlement or licensing agreement included as resolution of an infringement dispute) shall be divided equally between the parties after deduction and payment of reasonable attorney fees to the party bringing the lawsuit.

Exploitation Date

Licensee agrees to manufacture, distribute and sell the Licensed Products in commercially reasonable quantities during the term of this Agreement and to commence such manufacture, distribution and sale by _____ . This is a material provision of this Agreement.

Advertising Budget

(select if appropriate)

☐ Licensee agrees to spend at least _____% of estimated annual gross sales for promotional efforts and advertising of the Licensed Products.

Licensor Copies and Right to Purchase

Licensee shall provide Licensor with _____ copies of each Licensed Product. Licensor has the right to purchase from Licensee, at Licensee's manufacturing cost, at least _____ copies of any Licensed Product and such payments shall be deducted from royalties due to Licensor.

Confidentiality

The parties acknowledge that each may have access to confidential information that relates to each other's business (the "Information"). The parties agree to protect the confidentiality of the Information and maintain it with the strictest confidence, and no party shall disclose such information to third parties without the prior written consent of the other.

Insurance

(select if appropriate)

☐ Licensee shall, throughout the Term, obtain and maintain, at its own expense, standard product liability insurance coverage, naming Licensor as an additional named insured. Such policy shall provide protection against any claims, demands and causes of action arising out of any alleged defects or failure to perform of the Licensed Products or any use of the Licensed Products. The amount of coverage shall be a minimum of $ _____ with no deductible amount for each single occurrence for bodily injury or property damage. The policy shall provide for notice to the Licensor from the insurer by Registered or Certified Mail in the event of any modification or termination of insurance. The provisions of this section shall survive termination for three (3) years.

Licensor's Right to Terminate

Licensor shall have the right to terminate this Agreement in the following situations:

(select one or more provisions)

☐ **Failure to Make Timely Payment.** Licensee fails to pay Royalties when due or fails to accurately report Net Sales, as defined in the Payment Section of this Agreement, and such failure is not cured within thirty days after written notice from the Licensor.

☐ **Failure to Introduce Product.** Licensee fails to introduce the product to market by the date set in the Exploitation section of this Agreement or to offer the Licensed Products in commercially reasonable quantities during any subsequent year.

☐ **Assignment or Sublicensing.** Licensee assigns or sublicenses in violation of the Agreement.

☐ **Failure to Maintain Insurance.** Licensee fails to maintain or obtain product liability insurance as required by the provisions of this Agreement.

☐ **Failure to Meet Quality Standards for Submit Samples.** Licensee fails to provide Licensor with samples for approval or fails to meet the quality standards established by Licensor.

Licensor shall have the right to terminate the grant of license under this Agreement with respect to any country or region included in the Territory in which Licensee fails to offer the Licensed Products for sale or distributions or to secure a sublicensing agreement for the marketing, distribution and sale of the product within two years of the Effective Date.

Effect of Termination

Upon termination of this Agreement, all Royalty obligations as established in the Payments Section shall immediately become due. After the termination of this license, all rights granted to Licensee under this Agreement shall terminate and revert to Licensor, and Licensee will refrain from further manufacturing, copying, marketing, distribution, or use of any Licensed Product or other product which incorporates the Trademarks. Within thirty (30) days after termination, Licensee shall deliver to Licensor a statement indicating the number and description of the Licensed Products that it had on hand or is in the process of manufacturing as of the termination date.

Sell-Off Period

Licensee may dispose of the Licensed Products covered by this Agreement for a period of ninety (90) days after termination or expiration, except that Licensee shall have no such right in the event this agreement is terminated according to the Licensor's Right to Terminate, above. At the end of the post-termination sale period, Licensee shall furnish a royalty payment and statement as required under the Payment Section. Upon termination, Licensee shall deliver to Licensor all original designs or reproductions of Trademarks used in the manufacture of the Licensed Products. Licensor shall bear the costs of shipping for these materials.

Attorney Fees and Expenses

The prevailing party shall have the right to collect from the other party its reasonable costs and necessary disbursements and attorney fees incurred in enforcing this Agreement.

Dispute Resolution

(select one if appropriate)

☐ **Mediation & Arbitration.** The Parties agree that every dispute or difference between them, arising under this Agreement, shall be settled first by a meeting of the Parties attempting to confer and resolve the dispute in a good faith manner. If the Parties cannot resolve their dispute after conferring, any Party may require the other Parties to submit the matter to nonbinding mediation, utilizing the services of an impartial professional mediator approved by all Parties. If the Parties cannot come to an agreement following mediation, the Parties agree to submit the matter to binding arbitration at a location mutually agreeable to the parties. The arbitration shall be conducted on a confidential basis pursuant to the Commercial Arbitration Rules of the American Arbitration Association. Any decision or award as a result of any such arbitration proceeding shall be in writing and shall provide an explanation for all conclusions of law and fact and shall include the assessment of costs, expenses and reasonable attorney fees. An arbitrator experienced in trademark and merchandising law shall conduct any such arbitration. An award of arbitration may be confirmed in a court of competent jurisdiction.

☐ **Arbitration.** If a dispute arises under or relating to this Agreement, the parties agree to submit such dispute to binding arbitration in the state of _____ or another location mutually agreeable to the parties. The arbitration shall be conducted on a confidential basis pursuant to the Commercial Arbitration Rules of the American Arbitration Association. Any decision or award as a result of any such arbitration proceeding shall be in writing and shall provide an explanation for all conclusions of law and fact and shall include the assessment of costs, expenses and reasonable attorney fees. An arbitrator experienced in trademark and merchandising law shall conduct any such arbitration. An award of arbitration may be confirmed in a court of competent jurisdiction.

Governing Law

This Agreement shall be governed in accordance with the laws of the State of _____ .

Jurisdiction

The parties consent to the exclusive jurisdiction and venue of the federal and state courts located in _____ in any action arising out of or relating to this Agreement. The parties waive any other venue to which either party might be entitled by domicile or otherwise.

Waiver

The failure to exercise any right provided in this Agreement shall not be a waiver of prior or subsequent rights.

Invalidity

If any provision of this Agreement is invalid under applicable statute or rule of law, it is to be considered omitted and the remaining provisions of this Agreement shall in no way be affected.

Entire Understanding

This Agreement expresses the complete understanding of the parties and supersedes all prior representations, agreements and understandings, whether written or oral. This Agreement may not be altered except by a written document signed by both parties.

Attachments & Exhibits

The parties agree and acknowledge that all attachments, exhibits and schedules referred to in this Agreement are incorporated in this Agreement by reference.

No Special Damages

Licensor shall not be liable to Licensee for any incidental, consequential, punitive or special damages.

Notices

Any notice or communication required or permitted to be given under this Agreement shall be sufficiently given when received by certified mail, or sent by facsimile transmission or overnight courier.

No Joint Venture

Nothing contained in this Agreement shall be construed to place the parties in the relationship of agent, employee, franchisee, officer, partners or joint ventures. Neither party may create or assume any obligation on behalf of the other.

Assignability

(select one)

☐ **Assignment Requires Licensor Consent.** Licensee may not assign or transfer its rights or obligations pursuant to this Agreement without the prior written consent of Licensor. Any assignment or transfer in violation of this section shall be void.

☐ **Licensor Consent Not Required for Assignment to Parent or Acquiring Company.** Licensee may not assign or transfer its rights or obligations pursuant to this Agreement without the prior written consent of Licensor. However, no consent is required for an assignment or transfer that occurs: (a) to an entity in which Licensee owns more than fifty percent of the assets; or (b) as part of a transfer of all or substantially all of the assets of Licensee to any party. Any assignment or transfer in violation of this Section shall be void.

Each party has signed this Agreement through its authorized representative. The parties, having read this Agreement, indicate their consent to the terms and conditions by their signature below.

By: _____ By: _____

Date: _____ Date: _____

Licensor Name: _____ Licensee Name/Title: _____

Exhibit A

The Property _____

_____

Licensed Products _____

_____

Sales Requirements

$ _____ in Gross Sales per year.

Proprietary Notices

All licensed products shall bear the following proprietary notice: _____

_____

Merchandise License Agreement

Introduction

This License Agreement (the "Agreement") is made between _____ (referred to as "Licensor") and_____ (referred to as "Licensee").

The parties agree as follows:

The Work

The Work refers to the work described in Exhibit A. Licensor is the owner of all rights to the Work and Licensee shall not claim any right to use the Work except under the terms of this Agreement.

Licensed Products

Licensed Products are defined as the licensee's products incorporating the Work specifically _____ described in Exhibit A (the "Licensed Products").

Grant of Rights

Licensor grants to Licensee:

(select one)

☐   an exclusive license

☐   a nonexclusive license

to reproduce and distribute the Work in or on the Licensed Products.

Licensor grants to Licensee:

(select if appropriate)

☐   the right to modify the Work to incorporate it in or on the Licensed Products provided that Licensee agrees to assign to Licensor its rights, if any, in any derivative works resulting from Licensee's modification of the Work. Licensee agrees to execute any documents required to evidence this assignment of copyright and to waive any moral rights and rights of attribution provided in 17 USC § 106A of the Copyright Act.

☐   the right to publicly display the Work as incorporated in or on the Licensed Products.

☐   the right to publicly perform the Work as incorporated in or on the Licensed Products.

Sublicense

(select one)

☐ **Consent required.** Licensee may sublicense the rights granted pursuant to this agreement provided: Licensee obtains Licensor's prior written consent to such sublicense; and Licensor receives such revenue or royalty payment as provided in the Payment section below. Any sublicense granted in violation of this provision shall be void.

☐ **Consent to sublicense not unreasonably withheld.** Licensee may sublicense the rights granted pursuant to this agreement provided: Licensee obtains Licensor's prior written consent to such sublicense. Licensor's consent to any sublicense shall not be unreasonably withheld, and Licensor receives such revenue or royalty payment as provided in the Payment section below. Any sublicense granted in violation of this provision shall be void.

☐ **No sublicensing permitted.** Licensee may not sublicense the rights granted under this agreement.

Reservation of Rights: Assignment of Good Will

Licensor reserves all rights other than those being conveyed or granted in this Agreement.

Territory

The rights granted to Licensee are limited to _____ (the "Territory").

Term

The "Effective Date" of this Agreement is defined as the date when the agreement commences and is established by the latest signature date.

(select one)

☐ **Specified term with renewal rights.** This Agreement shall commence upon the Effective Date and shall extend for a period of __ years (the "Initial Term"). Following the Initial Term, _____ Licensee may renew this agreement under the same terms and conditions for __ consecutive _____ periods (the "Renewal Terms") provided that Licensee provides written notice of its intention to renew this agreement within thirty (30) days before the expiration of the current term. In no event shall the Term extend beyond the period of United States copyright protection for the Work.

☐ **Term with renewal based upon sales.** This Agreement shall commence upon the Effective Date and shall extend for a period of ___ years (the "Initial Term") and may be renewed by Licensee under the same terms and conditions for consecutive _____year periods (the "Renewal Terms"), provided that:

(a) Licensee provides written notice of its intention to renew this agreement within thirty days before the expiration of the current term; and

(b) Licensee has met the sales requirements as established in Exhibit A.

☐ **Indefinite term.** This Agreement shall commence upon the Effective Date and shall continue until terminated pursuant to a provision of this Agreement.

☐ **Fixed term.** This Agreement shall commence upon the Effective Date and shall continue for _____ unless sooner terminated pursuant to a provision of this Agreement.

☐ **Term for as long as Licensee sells Licensed Products.** This Agreement shall commence upon the Effective Date as specified in Exhibit A and shall continue for as long as Licensee continues to offer the Licensed Products in commercially reasonable quantities or unless sooner terminated pursuant to a provision of this Agreement. In no event shall the Term extend beyond the period of U.S. copyright protection for the Work.

Payments

All royalties ("Royalties") provided for under this Agreement shall accrue when the respective Licensed Products are sold, shipped, distributed, billed or paid for, whichever occurs first.

Net Sales

Net Sales are defined as Licensee's gross sales (i.e., the gross invoice amount billed customers) less quantity discounts or rebates and returns actually credited. A quantity discount or rebate is a discount made at the time of shipment. No deductions shall be made for cash or other discounts, commissions, manufacturing costs, uncollectible accounts, or for fees or expenses of any kind which the Licensee may incur in connection with the Royalty payments.

Fees

(select one or more provisions)

☐ **Advance Against Royalties.** As a nonrefundable advance against royalties (the "Advance"), Licensee agrees to pay to Licensor upon execution of this Agreement the sum of $ _____ .

☐ **Licensed Product Royalty.** Licensee agrees to pay a Royalty of ___% percent of all Net Sales revenue of the Licensed Products ("Licensed Product Royalty").

☐ **Per Unit Royalty.** Licensee agrees to pay a Royalty of $___for each unit of the Licensed Product that is: (select one)

   ☐ manufactured.

   ☐ sold.

☐ **Guaranteed Minimum Annual Royalty Payment.** In addition to any other advances or fees, Licensee shall pay an annual guaranteed royalty (the "GMAR") as follows: $ _____. The GMAR shall be paid to Licensor annually on _____ . The GMAR is an advance against royalties for the twelve-month period commencing upon payment. Royalty payments based on Net Sales made during any year of this Agreement shall be credited against the GMAR due for the year in which such Net Sales were made. In the event that annual royalties exceed the GMAR, Licensee shall pay the difference to Licensor. Any annual royalty payments in excess of the GMAR shall not be carried forward from previous years or applied against the GMAR.

☐ **License Fee.** As a nonrefundable, nonrecoupable fee for executing this license, Licensee agrees to pay to Licensor upon execution of this Agreement the sum of $_____ .

☐ **Sublicensing Revenues.** In the event of any sublicense of the rights granted pursuant to this Agreement, Licensee shall pay to Licensor_____% percent of all sublicensing revenues.

Payments and Statements to Licensor

Within thirty (30) days after the end of each calendar quarter (the "Royalty Period"), an accurate statement of Net Sales of Licensed Products along with any royalty payments or sublicensing revenues due to Licensor shall be provided to Licensor, regardless of whether any Licensed Products were sold during the Royalty Period. All payments shall be paid in United States currency drawn on a United States bank. The acceptance by Licensor of any of the statements furnished or royalties paid shall not preclude Licensor questioning the correctness at any time of any payments or statements.

Audit

Licensee shall keep accurate books of account and records covering all transactions relating to the license granted in this Agreement, and Licensor or its duly authorized representatives shall have the right upon five days prior written notice, and during normal business hours, to inspect and audit

Licensee's records relating to the Work licensed under this Agreement. Licensor shall bear the cost of such inspection and audit, unless the results indicate an underpayment greater than $ _____ for any six-month (6-month) period. In that case, Licensee shall promptly reimburse Licensor for all costs of the audit along with the amount due with interest on such sums. Interest shall accrue from the date the payment was originally due and the interest rate shall be 1.5% per month, or the maximum rate permitted by law, whichever is less. All books of account and records shall be made available in the United States and kept available for at least two years after the termination of this Agreement.

Late Payment

Time is of the essence with respect to all payments to be made by Licensee under this Agreement. If Licensee is late in any payment provided for in this Agreement, Licensee shall pay interest on the payment from the date due until paid at a rate of 1.5% per month, or the maximum rate permitted by law, whichever is less.

Licensor Warranties

Licensor warrants that it has the power and authority to enter into this Agreement and has no knowledge as to any third-party claims regarding the proprietary rights in the Work that would interfere with the rights granted under this Agreement.

Indemnification by Licensor

(select one if appropriate)

☐ **Licensor indemnification without limitations.** Licensor shall indemnify Licensee and hold Licensee harmless from any damages and liabilities (including reasonable attorney fees and costs), arising from any breach of Licensor's warranties as defined in Licensor's Warranties, above.

☐ **Licensor indemnification limited to amounts paid.** Licensor shall indemnify Licensee and hold Licensee harmless from any damages and liabilities (including reasonable attorney fees and costs), arising from any breach of Licensor's warranties as defined in Licensor's Warranties, above. Licensor's maximum liability under this provision shall in no event exceed the total amount earned by Licensor under this Agreement.

☐ **Licensor indemnification with limitations.** Licensor shall indemnify Licensee and hold Licensee harmless from any damages and liabilities (including reasonable attorney fees and costs), arising from any breach of Licensor's warranties as defined in Licensor's Warranties, above, provided:

(a) such claim, if sustained, would prevent Licensee from marketing the Licensed Products or the Work;

(b) such claim arises solely out of the Work as disclosed to the Licensee, and not out of any change in the Work made by Licensee or a vendor;

(c) Licensee gives Licensor prompt written notice of any such claim;

(d) such indemnity shall only be applicable in the event of a final decision by a court of competent jurisdiction from which no right to appeal exists; and

(e) that the maximum amount due from Licensor to Licensee under this paragraph shall not exceed the amounts due to Licensor under the Payment Section from the date that Licensor notifies Licensee of the existence of such a claim.

Licensee Warranties

Licensee warrants that it will use its best commercial efforts to market the Licensed Products and that their sale and marketing shall be in conformance with all applicable laws and regulations, including but not limited to all intellectual property laws.

Indemnification by Licensee

Licensee shall indemnify Licensor and hold Licensor harmless from any damages and liabilities (including reasonable attorney fees and costs),

(a) arising from any breach of Licensee's warranties and representation as defined in the Licensee Warranties, above;

(b) arising out of any alleged defects or failures to perform of the Licensed Products or any product liability claims or use of the Licensed Products; and

(c) any claims arising out of advertising, distribution or marketing of the Licensed Products.

Intellectual Property Registration

Licensor may, but is not obligated to, seek in its own name and at its own expense, appropriate copyright registrations for the Work. Licensor makes no warranty with respect to the validity of any copyright that may be granted. Licensor grants to Licensee the right to apply for registration of the Work or Licensed Products provided that such registrations shall be applied for in the name of

Licensor and licensed to Licensee during the Term and according to the conditions of this Agreement. Licensee shall have the right to deduct its reasonable out-of-pocket expenses for the preparation and filing of any such registrations from future royalties due to Licensor under this Agreement. Licensee shall obtain Licensor's prior written consent before incurring expenses for any foreign copyright applications.

Compliance With Intellectual Property Laws

The license granted in this Agreement is conditioned on Licensee's compliance with the provisions of the intellectual property laws of the United States and any foreign country in the Territory. All copies of the Licensed Product as well as all promotional material shall bear appropriate proprietary notices.

Licensor Credits

Licensee shall identify Licensor as the owner of rights to the Work and shall include the following notice on all copies of the Licensed Products: "_____. All rights reserved."

Licensee may, with Licensor's consent, use Licensor's name, image or trademark in advertising or promotional materials associated with the sale of the Licensed Products.

Infringement Against Third Parties

In the event that either party learns of imitations or infringements of the Work or Licensed Products, that party shall notify the other in writing of the infringements or imitations. Licensor shall have the right to commence lawsuits against third persons arising from infringement of the Work or Licensed Products. In the event that Licensor does not commence a lawsuit against an alleged infringer within sixty days of notification by Licensee, Licensee may commence a lawsuit against the third party. Before filing suit, Licensee shall obtain the written consent of Licensor to do so and such consent shall not be unreasonably withheld. Licensor will cooperate fully and in good faith with Licensee for the purpose of securing and preserving Licensee's rights to the Work. Any recovery (including, but not limited to a judgment, settlement or licensing agreement included as resolution of an infringement dispute) shall be divided equally between the parties after deduction and payment of reasonable attorney fees to the party bringing the lawsuit.

Exploitation Date

Licensee agrees to manufacture, distribute and sell the Licensed Products in commercially reasonable quantities during the term of this Agreement and to commence such manufacture, distribution and sale by _____ . This is a material provision of this Agreement.

Advertising Budget

(select if appropriate)

☐   Licensee agrees to spend at least _____ % of estimated annual gross sales for promotional efforts and advertising of the Licensed Products.

Approval of Samples & Quality Control

Licensee shall submit a reasonable number of pre-production designs, prototypes, and camera-ready artwork prior to production as well as pre-production samples of the Licensed Product to Licensor to assure that the product meets Licensor's quality standards. In the event that Licensor fails to object in writing within ten (10) business days after the date of receipt of any such materials, such materials shall be deemed to be acceptable. At least once during each calendar year, Licensee shall submit two (2) production samples of each Licensed Product for review. Licensee shall pay all costs for delivery of these approval materials. The quality standards applied by Licensor shall be no more rigorous than the quality standards applied by Licensor to similar products.

Licensor Copies and Right to Purchase

Licensee shall provide Licensor with ____ copies of each Licensed Product. Licensor has the right to purchase from Licensee, at Licensee's manufacturing cost, at least _____ copies of any Licensed Product and such payments shall be deducted from royalties due to Licensor.

Confidentiality

The parties acknowledge that each may have access to confidential information that relates to each other's business (the "Information"). The parties agree to protect the confidentiality of the Information and maintain it with the strictest confidence, and no party shall disclose such information to third parties without the prior written consent of the other.

Insurance

Licensee shall, throughout the Term, obtain and maintain, at its own expense, standard product liability insurance coverage, naming Licensor as an additional named insured. Such policy shall provide protection against any claims, demands and causes of action arising out of any alleged defects or failure to perform of the Licensed Products or any use of the Licensed Products. The amount of coverage shall be a minimum of $ _____ with no deductible amount for each single occurrence for bodily injury or property damage. The policy shall provide for notice to the Licensor from the insurer by Registered or Certified Mail in the event of any modification or termination of insurance. The provisions of this section shall survive termination for three years.

Licensor's Right to Terminate

Licensor shall have the right to terminate this Agreement for the following reasons:

(select one or more provisions)

- [ ] **Failure to Make Timely Payment.** Licensee fails to pay Royalties when due or fails to accurately report Net Sales, as defined in the Payment Section of this Agreement, and such failure is not cured within thirty (30) days after written notice from the Licensor.

- [ ] **Failure to Introduce Product.** Licensee fails to introduce the product to market by the date set in the Exploitation section of this Agreement or to offer the Licensed Products in commercially reasonable quantities during any subsequent year.

- [ ] **Assignment or Sublicensing.** Licensee assigns or sublicenses in violation of this Agreement.

- [ ] **Failure to Maintain Insurance.** Licensee fails to maintain or obtain product liability insurance as required by the provisions of this Agreement.

- [ ] **Failure to Submit Samples.** Licensee fails to provide Licensor with pre-production samples for approval.

- [ ] **Termination As to Unexploited Portion of Territory.** Licensor shall have the right to terminate the grant of license under this Agreement with respect to any country or region included in the Territory in which Licensee fails to offer the Licensed Products for sale or distribution or to secure a sublicensing agreement for the marketing, distribution and sale of the product within two (2) years of the Effective Date.

Effect of Termination

Upon termination of this Agreement ("Termination"), all Royalty obligations as established in the Payments Section shall immediately become due. After the Termination of this license, all rights granted to Licensee under this Agreement shall terminate and revert to Licensor, and Licensee will refrain from further manufacturing, copying, marketing, distribution, or use of any Licensed Product or other product which incorporates the Work. Within thirty (30) days after Termination, Licensee shall deliver to Licensor a statement indicating the number and description of the Licensed Products that it had on hand or is in the process of manufacturing as of the Termination date.

Sell-Off Period

Licensee may dispose of the Licensed Products covered by this Agreement for a period of 90 days after Termination or expiration except that Licensee shall have no such right in the event this agreement is terminated according to the Licensor's Right to Terminate, above. At the end of the post-Termination sale period, Licensee shall furnish a royalty payment and statement as required under the Payment Section. Upon termination, Licensee shall deliver to Licensor all original artwork and camera-ready reproductions used in the manufacture of the Licensed Products. Licensor shall bear the costs of shipping for the artwork and reproductions.

Attorney Fees and Expenses

The prevailing party shall have the right to collect from the other party its reasonable costs and necessary disbursements and attorney fees incurred in enforcing this Agreement.

Dispute Resolution

(select one if appropriate)

☐ **Mediation & Arbitration.** The Parties agree that every dispute or difference between them, arising under this Agreement, shall be settled first by a meeting of the Parties attempting to confer and resolve the dispute in a good faith manner. If the Parties cannot resolve their dispute after conferring, any Party may require the other Parties to submit the matter to nonbinding mediation, utilizing the services of an impartial professional mediator approved by all Parties. If the Parties cannot come to an agreement following mediation, the Parties agree to submit the matter to binding arbitration at a location mutually agreeable to the Parties. The arbitration shall be conducted on a confidential basis pursuant to the

Commercial Arbitration Rules of the American Arbitration Association. Any decision or award as a result of any such arbitration proceeding shall include the assessment of costs, expenses and reasonable attorney's fees and shall include a written record of the proceedings and a written determination of the arbitrators. An arbitrator experienced in copyright and merchandising law shall conduct any such arbitration. An award of arbitration shall be final and binding on the Parties and may be confirmed in a court of competent jurisdiction.

☐ **Arbitration.** If a dispute arises under or relating to this Agreement, the parties agree to submit such dispute to binding arbitration in the state of_____or another location mutually agreeable to the parties. The arbitration shall be conducted on a confidential basis pursuant to the Commercial Arbitration Rules of the American Arbitration Association. Any decision or award as a result of any such arbitration proceeding shall be in writing and shall provide an explanation for all conclusions of law and fact and shall include the assessment of costs, expenses and reasonable attorney fees. An arbitrator experienced in copyright and merchandising law shall conduct any such arbitration. An award of arbitration may be confirmed in a court of competent jurisdiction.

Governing Law

This Agreement shall be governed in accordance with the laws of the State of _____.

Jurisdiction

The parties consent to the exclusive jurisdiction and venue of the federal and state courts located in _____ in any action arising out of or relating to this Agreement. The parties waive any other venue to which either party might be entitled by domicile or otherwise.

Waiver

The failure to exercise any right provided in this Agreement shall not be a waiver of prior or subsequent rights.

Invalidity

If any provision of this Agreement is invalid under applicable statute or rule of law, it is to be considered omitted and the remaining provisions of this Agreement shall in no way be affected.

Entire Understanding

This Agreement expresses the complete understanding of the parties and supersedes all prior representations, agreements and understandings, whether written or oral. This Agreement may not be altered except by a written document signed by both parties.

Attachments & Exhibits

The parties agree and acknowledge that all attachments, exhibits and schedules referred to in this Agreement are incorporated in this Agreement by reference.

No Special Damages

Licensor shall not be liable to Licensee for any incidental, consequential, punitive or special damages.

Notices

Any notice or communication required or permitted to be given under this Agreement shall be sufficiently given when received by certified mail, or sent by facsimile transmission or overnight courier.

No Joint Venture

Nothing contained in this Agreement shall be construed to place the parties in the relationship of agent, employee, franchisee, officer, partners or joint ventures. Neither party may create or assume any obligation on behalf of the other.

Assignability

(select one)

☐ **Assignment Requires Licensor Consent.** Licensee may not assign or transfer its rights or obligations pursuant to this Agreement without the prior written consent of Licensor. Any assignment or transfer in violation of this section shall be void.

☐ **Licensor Consent Not Unreasonably Withheld.** Licensee may not assign or transfer its rights or obligations pursuant to this Agreement without the prior written consent of Licensor. Such consent shall not be unreasonably withheld. Any assignment or transfer in violation of this section shall be void.

☐ **Licensor Consent Not Required for Assignment to Parent or Acquiring Company.** Licensee may not assign or transfer its rights or obligations pursuant to this Agreement without the prior written consent of Licensor. However, no consent is required for an assignment or transfer that occurs: (a) to an entity in which Licensee owns more than fifty percent of the assets; or (b) as part of a transfer of all or substantially all of the assets of Licensee to any party. Any assignment or transfer in violation of this Section shall be void.

Each party has signed this Agreement through its authorized representative. The parties, having read this Agreement, indicate their consent to the terms and conditions by their signature below.

By: _____   By: _____

Date: _____   Date: _____

Licensor Name: _____   Licensee Name/Title: _____

Exhibit A

The Property _____
_____

Licensed Products _____
_____

Sales Requirements

$ _____ in Gross Sales per year.

Merchandise License Worksheet

Licensor	Name of licensor business: _____ Licensor address: _____ Licensor business form: ☐ sole proprietorship ☐ general partnership ☐ limited partnership ☐ corporation ☐ state of incorporation _____ ☐ limited liability company ☐ state of organization _____ Name and position of person signing for licensor: _____
The Work(s)	Source: _____ Description: _____ Page Number: _____ Relevant data (e.g., ISBN, copyright notice):_____
Licensed Product(s)	Tentative title: _____ Format: _____
Grant of Rights (check those rights needed)	☐ reproduce ☐ distribute ☐ modify, adapt ☐ display ☐ perform
Market and Format Limitations	☐ specific market _____ ☐ specific format _____
Territory	☐ worldwide ☐ countries or states (name which): _____
Exclusivity	☐ exclusive ☐ nonexclusive

Merchandise License Worksheet (cont.)

Term	☐ no time limits ☐ fixed term (how long: _____) ☐ unlimited term until one party terminates ☐ an initial term with renewals (see below) ☐ other _____
Renewals	If the parties have agreed upon an initial term with renewals: _____ How many renewal periods? _____ How long is each renewal period? _____ What triggers renewal? _____

Fee	☐ one time fee $ _____
	date due: _____
	☐ recurring fee $ _____
	date due/trigger: _____
	☐ advance against royalties $ _____
	date due: _____
	☐ royalty rate(s): _____% of
	   ☐ net sales
	   ☐ gross sales
	☐ If royalty payments, are there any
	   ☐ deductions: _____
	   ☐ audits. How many per year: _____

Warranties	☐ licensor warranty conditions _____ ☐ licensee warranty conditions _____
Indemnity	☐ licensor indemnity conditions _____ ☐ licensee indemnity conditions _____
Credit	☐ licensor credit _____
Furnished Samples	☐ licensor samples required. How many: _____ When _____
Miscellaneous	☐ jurisdiction state _____ ☐ governing law state _____ ☐ arbitration
Termination	☐ conditions _____

Short-Form Merchandise License Agreement

Introduction

This License Agreement (the "Agreement") is made between _____ (referred to as "Licensor") and _____ (referred to as "Licensee").

The parties agree as follows:

Grant of Rights

The "Work" is defined as follows: _____ .

Licensed Products are Licensee products incorporating the Work, specifically

("Licensed Products").

Licensor is the owner of all rights to the Work and Licensee shall not claim any right to use the Works except under the terms of this Agreement. Licensor grants to Licensee:

(select one)

☐   an exclusive license

☐   a nonexclusive license

to reproduce and distribute the Work in or on the Licensed Products.

Sublicense

Licensee may sublicense the rights granted pursuant to this agreement provided: Licensee obtains Licensor's prior written consent to such sublicense, and Licensor receives such revenue or royalty payment as provided in the Payment section below. Licensor's consent to any sublicense shall not be unreasonably withheld. Any sublicense granted in violation of this provision shall be void. Licensor reserves all rights other than those being conveyed or granted in this Agreement.

Territory

The rights granted to Licensee are limited to _____ (the "Territory").

Term

This Agreement shall commence upon the "Effective Date," established by the latest signature date, and shall extend for a period of ____ years (the "Initial Term"). Following the Initial Term, Licensee may renew this agreement under the same terms and conditions for _____ consecutive _____ periods (the "Renewal Terms") provided that Licensee provides written notice of its intention to renew this agreement within thirty (30) days before the expiration of the current term.

Royalties

All royalties ("Royalties") provided for under this Agreement shall accrue when the respective Licensed Products are sold, shipped, distributed, billed or paid for, whichever occurs first.

Net Sales

Net Sales are defined as Licensee's gross sales (i.e., the gross invoice amount billed customers) less quantity discounts or rebates and returns actually credited. A quantity discount or rebate is a discount made at the time of shipment. No deductions shall be made for cash or other discounts, commissions, manufacturing costs, uncollectible accounts, or for fees or expenses of any kind which the Licensee may incur in connection with the Royalty payments.

Advance Against Royalties

As a nonrefundable advance against royalties (the "Advance"), Licensee agrees to pay to Licensor upon execution of this Agreement the sum of $ _____ .

Licensed Product Royalty

Licensee agrees to pay a Royalty of _____% percent of all Net Sales revenue of the Licensed Products ("Licensed Product Royalty").

Sublicensing Revenues

In the event of any sublicense of the rights granted pursuant to this Agreement, Licensee shall pay to Licensor _____% percent of all sublicensing revenues.

Payments and Statements

Within thirty (30) days after the end of each calendar quarter (the "Royalty Period"), an accurate statement of Net Sales of Licensed Products along with any royalty payments or sublicensing revenues shall be due to Licensor. The acceptance by Licensor of any of the statements furnished or royalties paid shall not preclude Licensor questioning the correctness at any time of any payments or statements.

Audit

Licensee shall keep accurate books of account and records covering all transactions relating to the license granted in this Agreement, and Licensor or its duly authorized representatives shall have the right upon five (5) days prior written notice, and during normal business hours, to inspect Licensee's records relating to the Work licensed under this Agreement.

Late Payment

If Licensee is late in any payment provided for in this Agreement, Licensee shall pay interest on the payment from the date due until paid at a rate of 1.5% per month, or the maximum rate permitted by law, whichever is less.

Warranties

Licensor warrants that it has the power and authority to enter into this Agreement and has no knowledge as to any third-party claims regarding the proprietary rights in the Work that would interfere with the rights granted under this Agreement.

Licensee warrants that it will use its best commercial efforts to market the Licensed Products and that their sale and marketing shall be in conformance with all applicable laws and regulations, including but not limited to all intellectual property laws.

Licensor Credits

Licensee shall identify Licensor as the owner of rights to the Work and shall include the following notice on all copies of the Licensed Products:

"_____ . All rights reserved."

Licensee may, with Licensor's consent, use Licensor's name, image or trademark in advertising or promotional materials associated with the sale of the Licensed Products.

Exploitation

Licensee agrees to manufacture, distribute and sell the Licensed Products in commercially reasonable quantities during the term of this Agreement and to commence such manufacture, distribution and sale by _____ . This is a material provision of this Agreement.

Approval of Samples & Quality Control

Licensee shall submit a reasonable number of pre-production samples of the Licensed Product to Licensor to assure that the product meets Licensor's quality standards. In the event that Licensor fails to object in writing within ten (10) business days after the date of receipt of any such materials, such materials shall be deemed to be acceptable.

Licensor Copies and Right to Purchase

Licensee shall provide Licensor with copies of each Licensed Product. Licensor has the right to purchase from Licensee, at Licensee's manufacturing cost, at least _____ copies of any Licensed Product and such payments shall be deducted from royalties due to Licensor.

Licensor's Right to Terminate

Licensor shall have the right to terminate this Agreement for the following reasons:

(select one or more provisions)

☐ **Failure to Make Timely Payment.** Licensee fails to pay Royalties when due or fails to accurately report Net Sales, as defined in the Payments and Statements section of this Agreement, and such failure is not cured within thirty (30) days after written notice from the Licensor.

☐ **Failure to Introduce Product.** Licensee fails to introduce the product to market by the date set in the Exploitation section of this Agreement or to offer the Licensed Products in commercially reasonable quantities during any subsequent year.

Effect of Termination

After the termination of this license, all rights granted to Licensee under this Agreement shall terminate and revert to Licensor, and Licensee will refrain from further manufacturing, copying, marketing, distribution, or use of any Licensed Product or other product which incorporates the Work. Licensee may dispose of the Licensed Products covered by this Agreement for a period of 90 days after termination or expiration except that Licensee shall have no such right in the event this agreement is terminated according to the Licensor's Right to Terminate, above.

Miscellaneous

The prevailing party shall have the right to collect from the other party its reasonable costs and attorney fees incurred in enforcing this Agreement. This Agreement expresses the full, complete and exclusive understanding of the parties with respect to the subject matter and supersedes all prior proposals, representations and understandings. If a dispute arises between the parties arising under or relating to this Agreement, the parties agree to submit such dispute to arbitration conducted under the rules of the American Arbitration Association. An arbitration award may be confirmed in a court of competent jurisdiction. The waiver or failure of any party to exercise in any respect any right provided for in this Agreement shall not be deemed a waiver of any further right under this Agreement. No party shall represent themselves to be the employee, franchisee, franchiser, joint venturer, officer or partner of the other party and nothing in this Agreement shall be construed to place the parties in the relationship of partners or joint venturers. If any provision of this Agreement is invalid under any applicable statute or rule of law, it is to that extent to be deemed omitted and the remaining provisions of this Agreement shall in no way be affected or impaired. Licensee may not assign or sublicense the rights granted under this Agreement without the written consent of Licensor. Such consent shall not be unreasonably withheld. Each party has signed this Agreement through its authorized representative. The parties, having read this Agreement, indicate their consent to the terms and conditions by their signature below.

By: _____   By: _____

Date: _____   Date: _____

Licensor Name: _____   Licensee Name/Title: _____

Unlimited Personal Release Agreement

Grant

For consideration which I acknowledge, I irrevocably grant to _____ ("Company") and Company's assigns, licensees and successors the right to use my image and name in all forms and media including composite or modified representations for all purposes, including advertising, trade or any commercial purpose throughout the world and in perpetuity. I waive the right to inspect or approve versions of my image used for publication or the written copy that may used in connection with the images.

Release

I release Company and Company's assigns, licensees and successors from any claims that may arise regarding the use of my image including any claims of defamation, invasion of privacy, or infringement of moral rights, rights of publicity or copyright. Company is permitted, although not obligated, to include my name as a credit in connection with the image.

Company is not obligated to utilize any of the rights granted in this Agreement.

I have read and understood this agreement and I am over the age of 18. This Agreement expresses the complete understanding of the parties.

Name: _____ Date: _____

Signature: _____

Address: _____

Witness Signature: _____

Parent/Guardian Consent [include if the person is under 18]

I am the parent or guardian of the minor named above. I have the legal right to consent to and do consent to the terms and conditions of this model release.

Parent/Guardian Name: _____ Date: _____

Parent/Guardian Signature: _____

Parent/Guardian Address: _____

Witness Signature: _____

Limited Personal Release Agreement

Grant

For consideration which I acknowledge, I grant to _____ ("Company") and Company's assigns, licensees and successors, the right to use my image for the following purposes:

_____

_____ in the following territory

_____ for a period of _____ year(s) (the "Term").

I grant the right to use my name and image for the purposes listed above in all forms and media including composite or modified representations and waive the right to inspect or approve versions of my image used for publication or the written copy that may be used in connection with the images.

Payment

(select if appropriate)

☐   For the rights granted during the Term, Company shall pay $_____upon execution of this release.

Renewal

(select if appropriate)

☐   Company may renew this agreement under the same terms and conditions for _____ year(s) provided that Licensee makes payment of $ _____ at the time of renewal.

Release

I release Company and Company's assigns, licensees and successors from any claims that may arise regarding the use of my image including any claims of defamation, invasion of privacy, or infringement of moral rights, rights of publicity or copyright. Company is permitted, although not obligated, to include my name as a credit in connection with the image.

Name: _____   Date: _____

Signature: _____

Address: _____

Witness Signature: _____

Parent/Guardian Consent [include if the person is under 18]

I am the parent or guardian of the minor named above. I have the legal right to consent to and do consent to the terms and conditions of this model release.

Parent/Guardian Name: _____ Date: _____

Parent/Guardian Signature: _____

Parent/Guardian Address: _____

Witness Signature: _____

Interview Release

Grant

For consideration which I acknowledge, I consent to the recording of my statements and grant to
_____ ("Company") and Company's assigns, licensees and successors the right to
copy, reproduce, and use all or a portion of the statements (the "Interview") for incorporation in the
following work _____ (the "Work").

I permit the use of all or a portion of the Interview in the Work in all forms and media including
advertising and related promotion throughout the world and in perpetuity. I grant the right to use my
image and name in connection with all uses of the Interview and waive the right to inspect or
approve use of my Interview as incorporated in the Work.

Release

I release Company and Company's assigns, licensees and successors from any claims that may arise
regarding the use of the Interview including any claims of defamation, invasion of privacy, or
infringement of moral rights, rights of publicity or copyright. I acknowledge that I have no ownership
rights in the Work.

Company is not obligated to utilize the rights granted in this Agreement.

I have read and understood this agreement and I am over the age of 18. This Agreement expresses
the complete understanding of the parties.

Name: _____ Date: _____

Signature: _____

Address: _____

Witness Signature: _____

Parent/Guardian Consent [include if the person is under 18]

I am the parent or guardian of the minor named above. I have the legal right to consent to and do
consent to the terms and conditions of this model release.

Parent/Guardian Name: _____ Date: _____

Parent/Guardian Signature: _____

Parent/Guardian Address: _____

Property Release Agreement

The Property: _____

Grant

For consideration which I acknowledge, I irrevocably grant to _____
("Company") and Company's assigns, licensees and successors the right to enter onto the property
listed above and to photograph, copy, publish, display and use images of the property in all forms
and media including composite or modified representations throughout the world and in perpetuity
for the following purposes: _____

I waive the right to inspect or approve the manner in which the images of the property are used
and waive the right to inspect any text that is used in connection with the images of the property.

Dates of Use

Company shall enter onto the property on the following dates and times: _____

In consideration for the rights granted under this Agreement, Company shall pay me $ _____
upon execution of this Agreement.

Company is not obligated to utilize any of the rights granted in this Agreement.

Warranty, Indemnity & Release

I warrant that I am the owner of the property and have the authority to grant the rights under this
agreement and agree to indemnify Company from any claims regarding my ownership of the
property. I release Company and Company's assigns, licensees and successors from any claims that
may arise regarding the use of the images of the property.

I have read and understood this agreement. This Agreement expresses the complete understanding
of the parties.

Owner's Signature: _____

Owner's Name: _____

Owner's Address: _____

Date: _____

Search Request Form

TYPE OF WORK:

☐ Book ☐ Music ☐ Motion Picture ☐ Drama ☐ Sound Recording
☐ Photography / Artwork ☐ Map ☐ Periodical ☐ Contribution
☐ Computer Program ☐ Mask Work

SEARCH INFORMATION YOU REQUIRE:

☐ Registration ☐ Renewal ☐ Assignment ☐ Address

SPECIFICS OF WORK TO BE SEARCHED:

TITLE: ——————————————————————————————

AUTHOR: ——————————————————————————————

COPYRIGHT CLAIMANT (if known): —————————————————— (name in

copyright notice)

APPROXIMATE YEAR DATE OF PUBLICATION/CREATION: ————————————

REGISTRATION NUMBER (if known) ——————————————————

OTHER IDENTIFYING INFORMATION: —————————————————

If you need more space please attach additional pages.

YOUR NAME: ——————————————————————————————

DATE: ——————————————————————————————

ADDRESS: ——————————————————————————————

DAYTIME TELEPHONE NO.: —————————————————————

Convey results of estimate/research by telephone? ☐ Yes ☐ No

Fee Enclosed? ☐ Yes. Amount $ ——— ☐ No

Permissions Tracking Sheet

PTN	Type of Work, Title, Source and ID Numbers	Author	Owner, Contact Person, Address, Phone, Email	Payment	Payment Due Date	Date Paid and Form of Payment	Credit	Sample Approval or Comp Copies

Basic Copyright Assignment Agreement

I, _____ ("Assignor"), am owner of the work entitled

(the "Work") and described as follows: _____

_____ .

In consideration of $ _____ and other valuable consideration, paid by _____

("Assignee"), I assign to Assignee and Assignee's heirs and assigns, all my right title and interest in

the copyright to the Work and all renewals and extensions of the copyright that may be secured

under the laws of the United States of America and any other countries, as such may now or later be

in effect. I agree to cooperate with Assignee and to execute and deliver all papers as may be

necessary to vest all rights to the Work.

Signature of assignor(s) _____

Musician Assignment Agreement

This Musician Assignment Agreement (the "Agreement") is made between _____ ("Company"), and _____ ("Musician").

Grant

Musician has performed or recorded performance(s) for the Company in conjunction with the Company recording under the titles:

_____

_____

_____

    In consideration of the payments provided in this Agreement, Musician assigns all rights, including all rights under copyright law, in the recorded performance to the Company, its assigns, licensees or successors and grants the right to use the recorded performance for any purposes and in all forms and media and waives any claim to moral rights.

Payment

Company shall pay Musician as follows: $ _____ .

Warranty & Release

Musician has the authority to grant the rights under this Agreement and Musician releases Company and Company's assigns, licensees and successors from any claims that may arise regarding the use of the performance including any claims of infringement of moral rights, rights of publicity or copyright. Company is permitted, although not obligated, to include musician's name as a credit in connection with the performance.

    Company is not obligated to utilize any of the rights granted in this Agreement.

    Musician has read and understood this agreement and is over the age of 18. This Agreement expresses the complete understanding of the parties.

Musician Signature: _____

Musician Name: _____

Musician's Address: _____

Date: _____

Artwork Assignment Agreement

This Artwork Assignment Agreement (the "Agreement") is made between _____
("Company"), and _____ ("Artist").

Services

Artist agrees to perform the following services: _____
and create the following artwork (the "Art") entitled: _____.

The Art shall be completed by the following date: _____ .

During the process, Artist shall keep the Company informed of work in progress and shall furnish test prints of the Art prior to completion.

Payment

Company agrees to pay Artist as follows:

$ _____ for performance of the art services and acquisition of the rights provided below.

Rights

Artist assigns to the Company all copyright to the Art and agrees to cooperate in the preparation of any documents necessary to demonstrate this assignment of rights. Artist retains the right to display the work as part of artist's portfolio and to reproduce the artwork in connection with the promotion of artist's services.

Expenses

Company agrees to reimburse Artist for all reasonable production expenses including halftones, stats, photography, disks, illustrations or related costs. These expenses shall be itemized on invoices and in no event shall any expense exceed $50 without approval from the Company.

Credit

Credit for Artist shall be included on reproductions of the Art as follows: _____

Artist Warranties

Artist is the owner of all rights to the Art and warrants that the Art does not infringe any intellectual property rights or violate any laws.

Artist Signature: _____

Artist Name: _____

Artist Address: _____

Date: _____

Company Authorized Signature: _____

Name and Title: _____

Address: _____

Date: _____

Work-Made-for-Hire Agreement

This Work-Made-for-Hire Agreement (the "Agreement") is made between _____ ("Company"), and _____ ("Artist").

Services

In consideration of the payments provided in this Agreement, Artist agrees to perform the following services: _____

Payment

Company agrees to pay Artist as follows: _____

Works Made for Hire—Assignment of Intellectual Property Rights

Artist agrees that, for consideration that is acknowledged, any works of authorship commissioned pursuant to this Agreement (the "Works") shall be considered works made for hire as that term is defined under U.S. copyright law. To the extent that any such Work created for Company by Artist is not a work made for hire belonging to Company, Artist hereby assigns and transfers to Company all rights Artist has or may acquire to all such Works. Artist agrees to sign and deliver to Company, either during or subsequent to the term of this Agreement, such other documents as Company considers desirable to evidence the assignment of copyright.

Artist Warranties

Artist warrants that the Work does not infringe any intellectual property rights or violate any laws and that the work is original to Artist.

Miscellaneous

This Agreement constitutes the entire understanding between the parties and can only be modified by written agreement. The laws of the State of _____ shall govern this Agreement. In the event of any dispute arising under this agreement, the prevailing party shall be entitled to its reasonable attorney fees.

Artist Signature:_____   Company Authorized Signature: _____

Artist Name: _____   Name and Title: _____

Artist Address: _____   Address: _____

Date: _____   Date: _____

Index

CATALOG

...more from Nolo.com

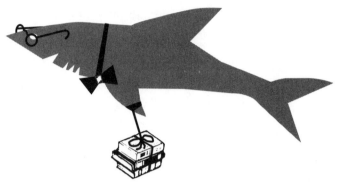

CONSUMER

ESTATE PLANNING & PROBATE

⊟ Book with disk
⊙ Book with CD-ROM

	PRICE	CODE

FAMILY MATTERS

	PRICE	CODE
Child Custody: Building Parenting Agreements That Work	$29.95	CUST
Child Support in California: Go to Court to Get More or Pay Less (Quick & Legal Series)	$24.95	CHLD
The Complete IEP Guide	$24.95	IEP
Divorce & Money: How to Make the Best Financial Decisions During Divorce	$34.95	DIMO
Do Your Own Divorce in Oregon	$19.95	ODIV
Get a Life: You Don't Need a Million to Retire Well	$19.95	LIFE
The Guardianship Book for California	$34.95	GB
◉ How to Adopt Your Stepchild in California (Book w/CD-ROM)	$34.95	ADOP
A Legal Guide for Lesbian and Gay Couples	$25.95	LG
▣ The Living Together Kit (Book w/Disk—PC)	$34.95	LTK
Nolo's Pocket Guide to Family Law	$14.95	FLD
Using Divorce Mediation: Save Your Money & Your Sanity	$21.95	UDMD

GOING TO COURT

	PRICE	CODE
Beat Your Ticket: Go To Court and Win! (National Edition)	$19.95	BEYT
The Criminal Law Handbook: Know Your Rights, Survive the System	$29.95	KYR
Everybody's Guide to Small Claims Court (National Edition)	$18.95	NSCC
Everybody's Guide to Small Claims Court in California	$24.95	CSCC
Fight Your Ticket ... and Win! (California Edition)	$24.95	FYT
How to Change Your Name in California	$34.95	NAME
How to Collect When You Win a Lawsuit (California Edition)	$29.95	JUDG
How to Mediate Your Dispute	$18.95	MEDI
How to Seal Your Juvenile & Criminal Records (California Edition)	$29.95	CRIM
How to Sue for Up to $25,000...and Win! (California Edition)	$29.95	MUNI
Mad at Your Lawyer	$21.95	MAD
Nolo's Deposition Handbook	$29.95	DEP
Represent Yourself in Court: How to Prepare & Try a Winning Case	$29.95	RYC

▣ Book with disk
◉ Book with CD-ROM

ORDER 24 HOURS A DAY
Call 800-992-6656 • www.nolo.com • Mail or fax the order form in this book

▣ Book with disk

◉ Book with CD-ROM

	PRICE	CODE
▣ Credit Repair (Quick & Legal Series, Book w/disk—PC)	$18.95	CREP
▣ The Financial Power of Attorney Workbook (Book w/disk—PC)	$29.95	FINPOA
How to File for Chapter 7 Bankruptcy	$29.95	HFB
IRAs, 401(k)s & Other Retirement Plans: Taking Your Money Out	$24.95	RET
Money Troubles: Legal Strategies to Cope With Your Debts	$24.95	MT
Nolo's Law Form Kit: Personal Bankruptcy	$16.95	KBNK
Stand Up to the IRS	$29.95	SIRS
Surviving an IRS Tax Audit (Quick & Legal Series)	$24.95	SAUD
Take Control of Your Student Loan Debt	$24.95	SLOAN

PATENTS AND COPYRIGHTS

	PRICE	CODE
◉ The Copyright Handbook: How to Protect and Use Written Works (Book w/CD-ROM)	$34.95	COHA
Copyright Your Software	$24.95	CYS
▣ Getting Permission: How to License and Clear Copyrighted Materials Online and Off (Book w/disk—PC)	$34.95	RIPER
How to Make Patent Drawings Yourself	$29.95	DRAW
The Inventor's Notebook	$19.95	INOT
▣ License Your Invention (Book w/Disk—PC)	$39.95	LICE
Patent, Copyright & Trademark	$29.95	PCTM
Patent It Yourself	$46.95	PAT
Patent Searching Made Easy	$29.95	PATSE
◉ Software Development: A Legal Guide (Book with CD-ROM)	$44.95	SFT
Trademark: Legal Care for Your Business and Product Name	$39.95	TRD
The Trademark Registration Kit (Quick & Legal Series)	$19.95	TREG

RESEARCH & REFERENCE

	PRICE	CODE
◉ Government on the Net (Book w/CD-ROM)	$39.95	GONE
Legal Research: How to Find & Understand the Law	$29.95	LRES

▣ Book with disk
◉ Book with CD-ROM

SENIORS

Beat the Nursing Home Trap: A Consumer's Guide to Assisted Living and Long-Term Care .... $21.95   ELD

The Conservatorship Book for California .... $44.95   CNSV

Social Security, Medicare & Pensions .... $24.95   SOA

SOFTWARE

**Call or check our website at www.nolo.com
for special discounts on Software!**

⊙ LeaseWriter CD—Windows/Macintosh $129.95   LWD1

⊙ Living Trust Maker CD—Windows/Macintosh $89.95   LTD3

⊙ Patent It Yourself CD—Windows $229.95   PPC12

⊙ Personal RecordKeeper 5.0 CD—Windows/Macintosh $59.95   RKD5

⊙ Small Business Pro 4 CD—Windows/Macintosh $89.95   SBCD4

⊙ WillMaker 7.0 CD—Windows/Macintosh $69.95   WMD7

Special Upgrade Offer

Save 35% on the latest edition of your Nolo book

Because laws and legal procedures change often, we update our books regularly. To help keep you up-to-date, we are extending this special upgrade offer. Cut out and mail the title portion of the cover of your old Nolo book and we'll give you **35% off** the retail price of the NEW EDITION of that book when you purchase directly from Nolo.com. This offer is to individuals only.

Call us today at 1-800-992-6656

Prices subject to change without notice.

Order Form

Name

Address

City

State, Zip

Daytime Phone

E-mail

Item Code	Quantity	Item	Unit Price	Total Price

Method of payment

☐ Check ☐ VISA ☐ MasterCard
☐ Discover Card ☐ American Express

Subtotal	
Add your local sales tax (California only)	
Shipping: RUSH $8, Basic $3.95 (See below)	
"I bought 3, Ship it to me FREE!"(Ground shipping only)	
TOTAL	

Account Number

Expiration Date

Signature

Shipping and Handling

Rush Delivery-Only $8

We'll ship any order to any street address in the U.S. by UPS 2nd Day Air* for only $8!

* Order by noon Pacific Time and get your order in 2 business days. Orders placed after noon Pacific Time will arrive in 3 business days. P.O. boxes and S.F. Bay Area use basic shipping. Alaska and Hawaii use 2nd Day Air or Priority Mail.

Basic Shipping—$3.95

Use for P.O. Boxes, Northern California and Ground Service.

Allow 1-2 weeks for delivery. U.S. addresses only.

For faster service, use your credit card and our toll-free numbers

Order 24 hours a day

Online	www.nolo.com
Phone	1-800-992-6656
Fax	1-800-645-0895
Mail	Nolo.com
	950 Parker St.
	Berkeley, CA 94710

Visit us online at
www.nolo.com

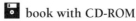

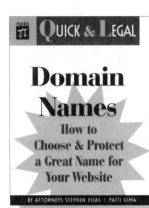

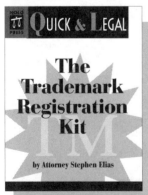

Take 2 Minutes
& Give Us Your 2 cents

Your comments make a big difference in the development and revision of Nolo books and software. Please take a few minutes and register your Nolo product—and your comments—with us. Not only will your input make a difference, you'll receive special offers available only to registered owners of Nolo products on our newest books and software. Register now by:

PHONE
1-800-992-6656

FAX
1-800-645-0895

EMAIL
cs@nolo.com

or **MAIL** us
this registration card

REMEMBER:
Little publishers have big ears. We really listen to you.

fold here

- -

nolo

REGISTRATION CARD

NAME _____ DATE _____

ADDRESS _____

_____

CITY _____ STATE _____ ZIP _____

PHONE _____ E-MAIL _____

WHERE DID YOU HEAR ABOUT THIS PRODUCT? _____

WHERE DID YOU PURCHASE THIS PRODUCT? _____

DID YOU CONSULT A LAWYER? (PLEASE CIRCLE ONE)   YES   NO   NOT APPLICABLE

DID YOU FIND THIS BOOK HELPFUL?   (VERY)   5   4   3   2   1   (NOT AT ALL)

COMMENTS _____

_____

_____

WAS IT EASY TO USE?   (VERY EASY)   5   4   3   2   1   (VERY DIFFICULT)

DO YOU OWN A COMPUTER? IF SO, WHICH FORMAT? (PLEASE CIRCLE ONE)   WINDOWS   DOS   MAC

❏ If you do not wish to receive mailings from these companies, please check this box.
❏ You can quote me in future Nolo.com promotional materials. Daytime phone number _____.

RIPER 1.0

NOLO IN THE NEWS

"Nolo helps lay people perform legal tasks without the aid—or fees—of lawyers."
—USA TODAY

Nolo books are ..."written in plain language, free of legal mumbo jumbo, and spiced with witty personal observations."
—ASSOCIATED PRESS

"...Nolo publications...guide people simply through the how, when, where and why of law."
—WASHINGTON POST

"Increasingly, people who are not lawyers are performing tasks usually regarded as legal work... And consumers, using books like Nolo's, do routine legal work themselves."
—NEW YORK TIMES

"...All of [Nolo's] books are easy-to-understand, are updated regularly, provide pull-out forms...and are often quite moving in their sense of compassion for the struggles of the lay reader."
—SAN FRANCISCO CHRONICLE

fold here

- -

> Place
> stamp here

nolo.com
950 Parker Street
Berkeley, CA 94710-9867

Attn: RIPER 1.0